FRAMES of mind

FRAMES of mind
a rhetorical reader
with occasions for writing

Robert DiYanni
The College Board

Pat C. Hoy II
New York University

Chapter 2, An Introduction to Visual Understanding
by James Dubinsky, *Virginia Polytechnic Institute and State University*

THOMSON
WADSWORTH

Australia • Canada • Mexico • Singapore • Spain • United Kingdom • United States

THOMSON
★
™
WADSWORTH

Frames of Mind
A Rhetorical Reader with Occasions for Writing
Robert DiYanni/Pat C. Hoy II

Publisher: *Michael Rosenberg*
Acquisitions Editor: *Dickson Musslewhite*
Senior Editor: *Aron Keesbury*
Assistant Editor: *Marita Sermolins*
Production Editor: *Eunice Yeates-Fogle/*
Samantha Ross
Marketing Manager: *Katrina Byrd*
Associate Marketing Manager: *Joe Piazza*
Senior Print Buyer: *Mary Beth Hennebury*

Compositor/Project Manager: *Graphic World, Inc*
Photography Manager: *Sheri Blaney*
Text and Photo Researcher: *Marcy Lunetta,*
Page to Page
Cover/Text Designer: *Lisa Buchanan*
Text Printer: *Quebecor World Taunton*
Cover Printer: *Lehigh Press*
Cover Image: *©Hot Ideas/Index Stock Imagery*

For permission to use material from this text or
product, submit a request online at
http://www.thomsonrights.com.
Any additional questions about permissions can
be submitted by email to
thomsonrights@thomson.com

ISBN: 0-8384-6089-5
(Student Edition)
ISBN: 1-4130-0670-1
(Instructor's Edition)

Library of Congress Control Number: 2004103702

Printed in the United States of America.
1 2 3 4 5 6 7 8 9 10 08 07 06 05 04

PREFACE

Frames of Mind: A Rhetorical Reader with Occasions for Writing is an inviting book that will help students learn to think rigorously and write compellingly. Although good writing follows close on the heels of reading and analysis, the act of writing itself also enhances learning—the act of writing changes *what* we think and *how* we think about a given subject. The process that moves us from information to idea to evidence to essay is almost never clean and linear. Writing itself leads to detours, zigzags, and recursive loops. But that exciting, investigative movement leads repeatedly to new discoveries—new evidence, new connections and relationships, and ever-changing ideas.

The investigation of various kinds of information (visual images, written texts, documentaries, movies) gives all researchers and writers, both young and old, interesting things to think about. As we analyze information and learn to ask meaningful questions about that information, we find ourselves almost inadvertently developing our own ideas about it—ideas worth sharing with others—both in and out of the classroom. A rich body of information serves as its own generative source of ideas and good writing.

The analytical work that prepares us to write does not end when the writing begins. Sitting down to write about our new ideas, we quickly learn that some of the information that had set those ideas in motion must be selected as the evidence we use to clarify and substantiate the ideas themselves. And even as we write and consider the various pieces of evidence that seem important to us, a fascinating thing can happen—the way we read, reflect on, and connect the different pieces of evidence continues to make us change our minds about the meaning of our ideas and what we will eventually make of them. Our ideas and our writing become more substantive as we work with and reconsider the rich evidence.

THE PATTERNS OF INQUIRY

This book is designed to help students learn to analyze and think about the information they consider while researching, as well about the evidence they eventually select to give substance to their ideas. It is designed as well to help them write more clearly about their discoveries. The interesting work laid out in *Frames of Mind* is grounded in fundamental patterns of inquiry that shape thought and writing; these patterns encourage writers to think and express themselves in a variety of ways. Throughout the book, we emphasize the necessary interplay among those shaping patterns.

Other rhetorical readers refer to such patterns as modes of discourse, and they tend to ask students to apply the modes rigidly and in isolation from one another. Their presumption seems to be that writers sit down only to write in one mode and that the so-called modes themselves—Narration, Analysis, Description, Classification, Definition, Comparison and Contrast, Process Analysis, Illustration, Cause and

Effect, Argument—are used only to shape the writing. But, in fact, real writers use these patterns of inquiry not only to facilitate and enhance their writing, they also use them in combination to facilitate and enhance thinking as well. Such combinations inform *Frames of Mind.*

Students learn simply that the name of each pattern conceals a verb, an infinitive, if you will: to narrate, to analyze, to describe, to classify, to define, to compare and contrast, to illustrate, to investigate causes and effects, and to argue. Student writers learn to perform these tasks as the need arises, as the evidence and the ideas dictate. They learn, too, the power of synthesis, of bringing together rich patterns of inquiry and complicating pieces of evidence so that the ideas they create and the writing they do can more adequately reflect what they have learned. Students learn quickly that the good storyteller must not only narrate but also analyze; that the act of comparing and contrasting depends on the act of describing and defining; that to classify is to distinguish and to define; that arguing is an act of empathy that depends on the use of multiple patterns of inquiry, so that the reader can come to know clearly and precisely what the writer knows.

HOW *FRAMES OF MIND* WORKS

Each chapter in *Frames of Mind* emphasizes the inextricable connection between reading and thinking and between thinking and writing, while also showing student writers just how the patterns of inquiry reinforce and enhance one another to improve reading, thinking, and writing. Each chapter begins with instruction—a section called **About the Pattern**—outlining its fundamental properties and its normal uses. The "**Pattern in Pure Form**" annotated paragraphs in each chapter—two or more paragraphs, annotated in color on two-page spreads with a brief discussion and accompanying exercises—show writers making use of a pattern of inquiry to think about and reveal a given subject.

Then in each chapter, we present a second set of full-page spreads called "**The Pattern in Its Natural Habitat.**" A single annotated essay illustrates the realistic interaction of different patterns of inquiry (the pattern under discussion in the chapter in one color and the other patterns in a second color).

The three **Readings** (or models) that exemplify the particular pattern under consideration in each chapter are in and of themselves engaging essays on interesting topics treated with traditional, provocative questions on form and function. The readings in each chapter offer a progression from familiar essays to more academic, or formal, writing. Classic essays by writers such as E. B. White and Joan Didion are set alongside less commonly reprinted, but no less compelling, essays by E. O. Wilson, for example, and Loren Eiseley.

"OCCASIONS FOR WRITING" AFTER EVERY ESSAY

Following every reading, "**Occasions for Writing**" offer unique opportunities for students to engage with the essay towards an essay of their own. Each of the Occasions consists of one or more images (a painting, a group of photographs, an advertisement, a sculpture, a chart) and, sometimes, a written text (a poem, a paragraph of information, or an excerpt from an essay). These visual and written texts play off the model essay and extend the reach of its meaning, but these additional texts are also rich and complicated enough in their own right that students need to learn to "read" and better understand them too. The Occasions associated with each of the model essays actually help students learn to read visual and written texts, to generate thinking and writing under the influence of the patterns, and to bring layers of evidence together as a way of clarifying and extending their own thought. The sets of questions associated with each Occasion prepare students to think and write about the objects under consideration (the model essay, the visual image(s), the written text). And even though the pattern being considered in the chapter shapes much of the inquiry, students are encouraged, nevertheless, to develop essays that combine patterns of inquiry as they complete the more advanced writing assignments.

Finally, there are additional exercises at the end of each Occasion that lead students beyond the specific information provided in the chapter to other opportunities for research, thinking, and writing. All of the Occasions in the chapter provide realistic, challenging opportunities for students to learn how to move from the consideration of information, to the development of ideas, to the selection and use of evidence, and to the creation of compelling essays that bring evidence to the service of idea.

FRAMEWORKS FOR ANALYSIS, RESEARCH, AND WRITING

Frames of Mind has four other distinguishing features that make the students' work easier and more interesting. The **Introduction to Visual Understanding,** by James Dubinsky, provides basic instruction in reading and understanding different kinds of visual information; this chapter establishes the foundation for the exercises that students will encounter as they respond to the Occasions in each chapter. In addition to supplying a clear method for analyzing visuals, Professor Dubinsky's informative chapter offers students a vocabulary for writing about them.

The **Brief Introduction to the Essay** establishes in clear language how essays are shaped by a three-part structure and how the presentation of ideas depends on the students' ability to make clear to the reader the relationship between evidence and idea. That relationship must be clearly established by reflective work that explains and unites the various pieces of evidence as well as the various parts of the essay.

The additional essays in the chapter titled **Patterns in Their Natural Habitat** give students yet another opportunity to see how patterns work together within essays. Students see how those patterns have shaped the thinking and the presentation of evidence within each of the essays. Questions and exercises facilitate this learning, just as they do throughout *Frames of Mind*.

Finally, the Appendix, **Finding Evidence and Documenting Sources,** addresses the various kinds of evidence students can work with and how to find, evaluate, and effectively integrate that evidence into a strong, coherent paper. The Appendix features MLA style documentation. Visual annotations point out differences in over 40 sample works cited entries, giving students a quick reference tool for correct documentation using MLA.

FRAMES OF MIND'S INTEGRATION WITH THE *COMP21: COMPOSITION IN THE 21ST CENTURY* CD-ROM

Throughout the book, you will encounter green *Comp21* icons in the margins. These icons mark places where the instruction or exercises in *Frames of Mind* can be extended, reviewed, or otherwise enhanced by the CD-ROM that accompanies the book, *Comp21: Composition in the 21st Century* for *Frames of Mind*.

- **Interactive Instruction in the Patterns of Inquiry.** Every pattern is treated with a special section on *Comp21* with a brief "brush-up" summary, interactive annotated paragraphs, and extra essays for students to read and annotate.
- **Interactive Instruction and Exercises in the Elements of Visual Rhetoric.** As in the book, all the elements of visual rhetoric are covered on *Comp21* and are treated with interactive exercises. Students are encouraged to isolate elements of visual "texts" using the annotation tools of the "explicator" and then to write about these elements.
- **Interactive Annotation with Textual, Visual, and Video "Explicators."** Designed to be used with text, visuals, and video, the "Explicators" are interactive annotation tools that encourage students to interact with verbal and visual texts, as well as with video clips, by highlighting certain elements of the text and writing annotations. When a student has finished annotating any text, visual, or video clip, their annotations appear with the work as an interactive project and can also be collated and printed as notes for a paper.
- **A Full Rhetorical Reader of Extra Essays.** *Comp21* for *Frames of Mind* includes 20 extra readings, arranged both rhetorically—by pattern of inquiry—and thematically. Every reading is loaded automatically into the "Explicator" and can be annotated as students read.
- **Interactive Occasions for Writing in *Comp21*.** As in the book, every reading on *Comp21* is followed by an Occasion for Writing. Unlike in the book, however, students can analyze the text and the items in the Occasion using the interactive annotation tools of the "Explicators." In addition, students have the opportunity to construct their own Occasions by selecting the text and the visual or video items they would like to consider.
- **CNN®Video Extensions of the Occasions in *Frames of Mind*.** At least one Occasion per chapter in *Frames of Mind* is treated with a CNN Video Extension on *Comp21*. Students are encouraged to continue their work with the Occasion in the book by considering a thematically linked CNN video clip from *Comp21*. A clip of the difficulties faced by women artists for example, accompanies the occasion titled "Animating Descriptions: An Occasion for Description" which follows Joan Didion's essay entitled "Georgia O'Keeffe."
- **A Visual Library of Over 200 Visual Texts.** *Comp21* provides students with over 200 visual texts in its multimedia library. Students are encouraged to engage with the visuals with the "visual explicator," to choose from the library for their own Occasions for writing, or to simply browse.
- **Desktop Access to InfoTrac® College Edition.** Every copy of *Comp21* is accompanied by a passcode, which allows students access to InfoTrac College Edition, the online library, right from their desktops. In addition to the wealth of essays, visuals, and video clips included on *Comp21,* InfoTrac College Edition provides full-length articles from thousands of newspapers, magazines, and scholarly journals.

OTHER ANCILLARY MATERIALS

Instructors using *Frames of Mind* for their composition classes will find considerable support through these ancillary materials:

- **Instructor's Manual.** Containing useful synopses of every essay and suggested class activities and discussion topics, the Instructor's Manual also includes in-depth treatment of "Occasions for Writing," highlighting visual elements to explore, and an entire section is devoted to integrating *Comp21* into the classroom.
- **Companion Web Site: http://english.wadsworth.com/diyanni_hoy.** Containing links to specific readings within InfoTrac College Edition, this site also provides students with interactive exercises on the fundamentals of writing, including grammar, mechanics, and punctuation. A student paper library provides sample papers with accompanying editing and revising activities.

ACKNOWLEDGMENTS

Many pleasant and dedicated people have helped develop this unusual new book. We especially want to thank Dickson Musslewhite and Aron Keesbury who sought us out, listened to our ideas, and then helped us develop *Frames of Mind*. Dickson's enthusiasm, cogent ideas, and savvy leadership set all of us in motion, and Aron, who is a genius of forms, gave us a crucible within which the alchemy could occur. He was with us every step of the way, providing ideas, images, and limits, but he never stopped asking for more, never stopped giving. Aron made the day-to-day work a distinct pleasure and a never-ending challenge.

At a greater distance from us, but deep at the heart of the developmental process, were a group of talented folks who compensated for some of our lapses and gave this book its distinctive design. Without them, we would still be somewhere in the midst of chaos. Marita Sermolins, Assistant Editor, kept everything nice and neat, from the manuscript itself, to the process that produced it. Eunice Yeates-Fogle, Production Editor, acted as the book's steward through design and production in its earlier stages. Samantha Ross, Production Editor, took up the helm, and steered an exceptionally complicated project from manuscript to the book you hold in your hands.

James Dubinsky of Virginia Polytechnic Institute provided the exceptionally clear and useful chapter, "An Introduction to Visual Understanding"; and without Bill Coyle at Salem State College, *Comp21* for *Frames of Mind* could never have existed. Jessie Swigger's help with the Instructor's Manual and the appendix was extraordinary. Our thanks also to Marcy Lunetta at Page to Page who cleared both the textual and the complicated visual permissions for the book.

Like any project, *Frames of Mind* benefited from a collaboration with our colleagues. Our thanks to the following professors from across the country who generously offered their input:

Gwen Argersinger, Mesa Community College
Donnelly Barclay, Valenica Community College
Larry Bohlender, Glendale Community College
Barbara Bonallo, Miami Dade College
Karen Courtney-Leyba, Rock Valley College
Gary Davis, Miami Dade College
Suellynn Duffey, Georgia Southern University
David Fabish, Cerritos College
Tom Flynn, St. Louis Community College
Judy Harris, Tomball College
Thomas Hayes, John Carroll University
Michael Hennessy, Texas State University, San Marcos
Jaime Herrera, Mesa Community College

Stephanie Hopkins, New York University
Kay Grosso, Glendale Community College
Eric Gould, University of Denver
Margaret Johnson, Idaho State University
Bette Kirschstein, Pace University
Dennis Lynch, Elgin Community College
Deborah Martinson, Occidental College
Patricia Medeiros, Scottsdale Community College
Susan Miller, Mesa Community College
Kate Mohler, Mesa Community College
Stephanie Mood, Grossmont College
Carol Papper, Ball State University
Katrina Powell, Louisiana State University
Kathleen Shaw, Montgomery County Community College
William Smith, Western Washington University
Joe Trimmer, Ball State University
Victor Uszerowicz, Miami Dade College
Jeremy Venema, Mesa Community College
Lynda Walsh, New Mexico Tech
Darla Wilshire, Pennsylvania State University, Altoona
David Zimmerman, Montgomery County Community College

Finally, Bob and I thank our wives, Mary DiYanni and Ann Hoy, who have stood behind this process, encouraging us just as they have done for so many, many years. Our grown sons (Michael DiYanni and Patrick and Timothy Hoy) and daughter (Karen DiYanni), long gone from the nest, continue to watch these collaborations, amazed perhaps that the work still goes on. So are we—amazed, and, this time especially, pleased that we were fortunate enough to make this book, which we firmly believe can make a lasting difference in the lives of those who use it to enrich their thinking and their writing. There is much here to ponder, and we hope that our own enthusiasm leads to an infectious epidemic.

ABOUT THE AUTHORS

Robert DiYanni

Robert DiYanni is the best-selling author of over 30 textbooks, including *The Scribner Handbook for Writers,* Fourth Edition (with Pat Hoy), *Modern American Prose: A Reader for Writers,* and the best-selling *Literature: Reading, Fiction, Poetry, Drama, and the Essay.* He received his B.A. from Rutgers University and his Ph.D. from the City University of New York, and he currently works for The College Board as the Director of International Services for K-12 programs. Professor DiYanni is also adjunct professor of Humanities at New York University.

Pat C. Hoy II

Pat C. Hoy II, director of the Expository Writing Program and professor of English at New York University, has also held appointments at the U.S. Military Academy and Harvard. He received his Ph.D. from the University of Pennsylvania. Professor Hoy regularly teaches freshman composition.

Professor Hoy is the author of numerous textbooks and articles, including *The Scribner Handbook for Writers,* Fourth Edition (with Robert DiYanni). His essays have appeared in *Sewanee Review, Virginia Quarterly Review, Agni, Twentieth Century Literature, South Atlantic Review,* and *The Wall Street Journal.* Eight of his essays have been selected as "Notables" in *Best American Essays. Instinct for Survival: Essays by Pat C. Hoy II* was selected as a "Notable" collection in *Best American Essays of the Century,* Edited by Joyce Carol Oates and Robert Atwan. He was awarded the 2003 Cecil Woods, Jr. Prize for Nonfiction from the Fellowship of Southern Writers.

CONTENTS

CHAPTER THIRTEEN

THE PATTERNS IN
THEIR NATURAL HABITAT   483

FRAMES of mind

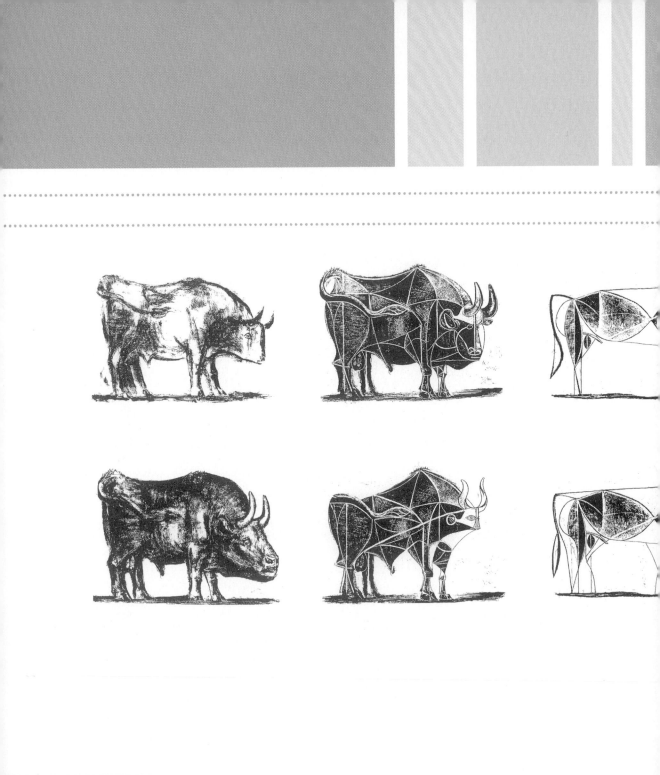

A BRIEF INTRODUCTION to the ESSAY

These images by Pablo Picasso are part of a larger progression of images. In these, notice how the idea of the bull carries through, despite the style.

Frames of Mind is a new type of reader, a book that provides approaches to analyzing and interpreting many kinds of texts, both visual and verbal, and to considering ways of thinking as well as ways of writing. It is also a book filled with ideas, opportunities, and suggestions for explorations and essays. In this chapter we lay out some key terms and essential aspects of essay writing—clear-headed definitions that will prepare you for the work that follows.

Our aim is to give you a clear sense of the fundamental underlying concepts of writing essays. What we have in mind is illustrated by these six images created by Pablo Picasso. These images, from a series of Picasso's sketches, represent the movement of his mind as he developed his own pictorial concept of a bull. The first two renditions, which are detailed and realistic, become archetypal and representative in the final sketches. In the briefest of strokes, Picasso captures the *essence* of the bull in the final images. In many ways the process represented in these sketches is the reverse of the thinking and writing process this book aims to teach. Whereas Picasso finished with an essential sketch, you will begin to form essential ideas—and then you will add into them all the detail necessary to create an effective piece of writing. The book works in much the same way, beginning with a chapter that presents the essentials of each type of thinking and writing (called "patterns of inquiry," or just "patterns," throughout), and building those patterns upon each other to create a fuller understanding.

· · · · · · · · · ·

1

EVIDENCE, IDEA, ESSAY

The key terms *evidence, idea,* and *essay* suggest how the mind moves as it considers a body of evidence, then turns to the creation of an idea, and finally develops an essay to express and substantiate that idea, or *thesis.*

EVIDENCE

Evidence comes from the information you gather as you investigate a topic. As the information begins to make sense to you, as it begins to suggest things to you, you will begin to converse with it, to let it play around in your head. The evidence will eventually lead you to an idea for your own essay.

You can find evidence for your essays from your reading (including written texts of all kinds—books, essays, journal articles, newspapers, magazines), your observation (in the class room or in the outside world), and your own experiences and the stories you construct from them. Your aim is to use that evidence to develop an interesting idea that you have drawn from it.

Frames of Mind provides bodies of evidence, called "Occasions for Writing," after every reading. These Occasions have been carefully selected for the ways in which each item relates to the others and are surrounded by questions that will help you consider these interrelationships, but you will find much of the evidence on your own. Sometimes evidence finds you, as when you see a picture that makes you feel something you wish to express or makes you mad enough that you want to clarify an idea for an audience. This is evidence in the first sense—evidence that drives you to write. You will have to find other types of evidence, often to support (or sometimes even to refute) a growing idea or thesis. For more on the uses of evidence, see the appendix, "Finding Evidence and Documenting Sources," in the back of this book.

IDEA: GETTING TO THE HEART OF THE MATTER

An idea provides a theory about evidence. An idea is your sense of what the evidence means, your explanation or interpretation of the facts that you have gathered from various sources during your research. As an interpreter, you will help your readers understand what the evidence means. This meaning is rarely intuitively obvious to others; they will not have studied it the way you have. Your readers depend on you to interpret the evidence and explain its relationship to your idea. This explanation will be given to them in the form of an essay.

As you search for ideas in the evidence, seek out disagreement, controversy, or areas where a consensus is needed. Within these tensions, typically, is the core of an important matter—that which is really at stake in the debate, or discussion, of your chosen topic. There you will find many different perspectives to investigate. Somewhere at the center of the controversy beats the heart of an idea that you can make your own through analysis and reflection. This idea will be your own reasoned perspective on the controversy—a perspective that has been developed through a careful analysis of the gathered evidence.

You have at your disposal an array of writing and thinking strategies, called *patterns of inquiry* in this book. Because these patterns represent the fundamental ways that people think, they represent effective ways not only of approaching subjects you intend to write about, but also of organizing your thoughts in writing so that your readers will understand.

- **Analysis.** An act of taking something apart and putting it back together as a way of deepening our understanding of it.
- **Description.** An act of translation, an attempt to take an object or an experience from the visible, so-called real world into the mind, where it is translated into words.
- **Narration.** An act of recording and ordering events, most often chronologically— but not necessarily so.
- **Illustration.** An act of clarification and substantiation, an attempt to clarify a concept or idea through examples.
- **Classification.** An act of organization by means of categorizing.
- **Comparison and Contrast.** An act of relating two or more things as a way of understanding them.
- **Cause and Effect.** An act of analyzing the reasons for events and their consequences.
- **Process Analysis.** An act of explanation that relies on analysis with narration to convey a continuous sequence in discrete steps.
- **Definition.** An act of clarification, an attempt to account for a concept.
- **Argument.** An act of empathy, an attempt to allow others to see how evidence and idea are related in a particular way.

These patterns of inquiry are available to you as a writer as you examine a topic and begin to write about it. They will lead you to the discovery of new, exciting ideas.

You know that you have a good idea when it attempts to resolve such a controversy, when your readers say in response to the idea, "Tell me more. I never thought of it that way until now. That's really interesting." You must bring the evidence to life by providing an explanation of its meaning. This explanation constitutes your idea; without the idea, there can be no essay.

ESSAY

The word *essay* comes from the French verb *essayer,* which means "to attempt" or "to try." An essay, then, is a trial or an attempt to develop an idea, work out its implications, and share it with others. The form of the essay itself consists of three parts: a beginning (or introduction), a middle (or body), and an end (or conclusion). Within that three-part structure, an essayist makes an appeal to the readers' interests, develops and supports an interesting idea, and provides a closing perspective on both the subject and the work that has been done within the essay. Essayists seek consensus; they aim to get their readers to see as they see, to think as they think.

Essayists work along a spectrum of essays, ranging from the familiar to the academic, from the less formal to the more formal. *Familiar essays* depend primarily on stories of experience; those stories constitute the essay's primary evidence. In these essays, the writer's stories of experience reveal and substantiate the idea. The writer often appears in these stories as a character named "I." But there is another "I" who is actually assembling these stories and using them as evidence: the discerning, writing "I" who offers his or her perspective on the meaning of the stories. In familiar essays, the development of the idea tends to be digressive as that discerning writer works out the idea under the reader's direct gaze.

More formal and traditional *academic essays* avoid use of the personal pronoun, omit experiential evidence, and offer a more detached perspective. The primary evidence in these essays tends to be more straightforward, somewhat more formal. The writer is, of course, also present in these essays, but that presence manifests itself primarily through the selection and ordering of evidence—both of which reflect the writer's mind at work—and through the quality of the idea.

As different as these forms of the essay can be, they are, essentially, very similar: each calls for the development of an interesting idea, the use of substantial evidence to support that idea, and a rigorous analysis and explanation of that evidence. Each form of the essay requires the presentation of evidence, its analysis, and a body of reflection that makes clear to the reader just what the idea means. In each form of the essay, the work of the writer's mind always takes place within that restricting but enabling three-part structure–beginning, middle, and end.

In the essays you write for your academic courses, you will usually be expected to make your idea explicit and to provide a clear and logical organization that is evident to your readers. On occasion, however, your instructors may invite you to write other kinds of essays that are more exploratory, essays whose internal order mirrors the shape of your thinking, the movement of your mind at play with an idea. The goal in writing such an essay, as with the more traditional academic essay, is to present, explore, explain, and substantiate an idea. The idea should give both writer and reader something interesting to think about, and sometimes even new ways of thinking about it.

. . . .

Framework

ANALYSIS,
INTERPRETATION, REFLECTION

Because analysis is so crucial to understanding, writers learn to depend on it, seeking over time to perfect and hone their analytical skills. The clarity that results from good analytical work leads to considerations about meaning and value. So the writer always faces a series of interpretive tasks whether the focus is on a written text, a historical event, an art object, or a moment of experience. The interpretive work, accompanied by thoughtful and rigorous reflection, leads to a deeper understanding of what has been analyzed, to ideas, and then to the exciting task of writing about the discoveries.

As discussed in more detail in chapter 3, "Analysis," a writer *analyzes* as a way of understanding.

Analysis is primarily an effort on the part of a writer to study an *object*—a book, a poem, a painting, a theory, a personality, a historical event, a performance, or a way of life—so that he or she can understand something significant about that object and then develop an idea about it.

Writers use analysis first to understand and then to record and demonstrate to readers what they have learned. The writing that accompanies analysis, especially in the early stages, is a form of exploration, a joint effort of the mind and the pen (or the keyboard) to learn something about the thing being studied. Later, writing preserves that analytical spirit, revealing to the reader significant parts of the writer's learning process, and shows the reader how the writer's thinking led to the idea being presented about the object.

Analysis is the working companion of every form of persuasive writing. Each of the patterns of inquiry—description, narration, comparison and contrast, classification, definition—depends on analysis to complete its work. In concern with a particular pattern, analysis turns the mind of the reader toward purpose, toward meaning. These patterns and analysis conspire to reveal that a story has meaning, that an act of comparing and contrasting is not done for its own sake, that definition serves a larger idea.

We investigate analysis in isolation only to learn how to do it. But after learning how to study an object, a subject, or even a descriptive passage, the writer's primary task turns to using the information gleaned from that analysis to the development of an idea or an essay. Analysis, combined with other patterns, leads to sense-making, to the formulation and development of those newfound ideas.

INTERPRETATION

Because every individual will analyze—or break down—any one subject differently, the analytical act is also one of interpretation. Each way that a subject is broken down highlights different aspects of the subject and therefore points to different meanings. Analyzing an apple, for example, by looking at its stem, its color, and the texture of its skin—all external characteristics—tells nothing about what's on the inside, how the apple tastes, or what you can do with it. The important work of analysis is not only to break a subject down, but to tell something about it—to interpret it—in the process.

The job of the analytical writer is to convey the results of the analysis and the interpretation so that others not only understand what the object under consideration means to the interpreter, but also how the interpreter explains and accounts for the interpretation. The discerning voice of the writer is the voice of reflection. It is a kind of metavoice—meditative and thoughtful—that makes sense of both analysis and interpretation, reminding us that *to reflect* is to bend back, to create a new image of an object. That reconstituted object amounts to an explanation and a revelation of something the analyst has discovered. The new conception of the object, resulting from the interpretive analysis, constitutes the idea that leads to the essay.

. . . .

AN INTRODUCTION to VISUAL UNDERSTANDING

The poet William Carlos Williams often told a story about a woman who was preparing to buy a painting. As Williams tells it, the woman, an important customer, pointed to the lower part of the picture and asked the salesman, Alanson Hartpence, "What is all this down here in the corner?"

According to Williams, Hartpence inspected the area carefully and said to her, "That, Madam, I should say, is paint."

In telling this story, Williams was making a point about the painting as an object. When confronted with something visual, we can, like the woman, get bogged down in the details and lose sight of the whole. We can forget that we're looking at an object that calls for us to experience it in its entirety.

Take, for example, the picture at the right.

A quick glance, and you might not know exactly what you're looking at. Though you might recognize the rough bark of a tree, you might not see the moth that is resting on it. By choosing a tree with coloring and texture similar to its own, the moth blends in and camouflages itself. To see the moth, you must look carefully, noting its shadow and seeing the white spots behind its head and antennae.

This picture by Thomas Roma is titled "Find the Dog." It first appeared in Doubletake *magazine. Did the composition of the picture make it difficult to see the dog before you knew the title?*

© Thomas Roma, Brooklyn, NY. From "Show and Tell."

© Ralph A. Clevenger/CORBIS.

KEEPING YOUR EYES
OPEN AND LEARNING TO SEE

In her essay "Seeing" (p. 491), Annie Dillard discusses this dilemma of looking but not seeing. She describes a moment when she was walking in late summer and came upon an Osage orange tree. Almost immediately, a hundred birds flew away, and then, when she walked closer, another hundred ascended, and then another. At first, these birds were "invisible." She wonders "how could so many hide in the tree" (para. 4) without her seeing them. Throughout the rest of her essay, she contemplates that question, concluding that there are different kinds of seeing. One can see like a lover, a seeing that involves a "letting go" (para. 33), and one can see like a specialist, a seeing that requires detailed knowledge. Both require keeping your eyes open.

Rudolf Arnheim, a famous art historian and professor of the psychology of art at Harvard University, explains that children develop the habit of using their eyes to learn early in their life. We learn to recognize our parents' faces early, and we learn quickly to sort out those items and people that matter to us. One of the key methods of learning involves categorizing, a process that led some German psychologists to develop a set of principles they called *gestalt*.

The German word *gestalt* is often translated as "whole" or "form," and the main idea is that in order to understand what we see, we find ways to categorize the parts or elements. In other words, "the whole is more than the sum of its parts." Simply put, the mind will try to find the simplest solution to a problem, looking for cues that help organize items into groups with characteristics in common. This method of looking at things helps to explain how people perceive and organize visual data to help them cope with the complex visual world.

. . . .

Framework

A STRATEGY FOR
VISUAL UNDERSTANDING

We will borrow from these theories to help you learn to make sense of what you see and then explain it to others. Communicating what you see and feel isn't always easy. For example, how often have you seen a sunset or a photo of a tragedy and felt something deeply but not been able to articulate exactly what you felt or why? The goal of this chapter, therefore, is twofold: to outline a process that will help you categorize and therefore understand what you see, and to provide a vocabulary that you can use to explain what you see and feel to others. In so doing, you will also begin to understand the rhetorical purposes and functions of visual images (or visual "texts" as they are sometimes called), recognizing that the artist or composer may be suggesting ideas through the design, often "spoken visually" through layout, form, shape, or color.

When you look at things, you most often have reactions first and the need to understand those reactions second. After understanding your reaction, you may explain or share what you have seen and felt with others. Thus, this process involves three activities: looking and responding, analyzing, and communicating.

In essence, these three activities are the essential elements of a strategy for visual understanding.

. . . .

LOOKING
AND RESPONDING

Although we begin in infancy to recognize, categorize, and make sense of what we see, learning to see is a lifelong process, and it involves different kinds of responses, both emotional and intellectual. Seeing is a physical and psychological process; you have a response to what you see, and the response is caused, in part, by the characteristics of the image. In "Seeing," Dillard describes the responses of blind patients who, after operations, are newly sighted: "to one patient, a human hand, unrecognized, is 'something bright and then holes.' Shown a bunch of grapes, a boy calls out, 'It is dark, blue, and shiny'" (para. 28). These newly sighted people respond fully to the objects they see, articulating physical characteristics while experiencing emotions. They

© KEVIN CARTER/CORBIS SYGMA.

don't have a complete set of categories to use yet, but they try to verbalize what they experience using those categories they have begun to acquire (color and value, for instance).

Because we want you to see and respond to the thing itself, our strategy begins by asking you to look at images and respond to them holistically, focusing on the emotions you experience. Does the image convey peacefulness, abject misery, fear, solitude, or joy? Does it reflect a fleeting moment or one that was representative and lasting?

Look at two examples.

Kevin Carter's Pulitzer Prize-winning photograph above of a starving Sudanese child and a vulture in a drought-ridden field usually evokes an immediate emotional response in viewers. Photographs such as this one often are easy to talk about because the subject matter is so clear; people usually sense a story associated with the elements in the picture.

Other kinds of images require more effort. Take, for instance, the photograph of trees in Yosemite shown to the right. Here, there are no human actors, and thus no drama. But there is a composition that evokes a response. The question, however, is why? What about the image evokes those feelings?

To answer this question, you need to consider a language of sensory descriptions. What did you notice about the picture of the trees? Their leaves or branches? The shape and size of their trunks? The angles at which they grow? How are they different from other trees? What about the season and the weather? What other elements are present in the picture?

Once you have a general impression of the image and what it means, the second step is to move beyond the sensory and emotional and talk about the composition and the visual cues present, many of which may have been intended by the artist or photographer. In the following sections you will find some ideas for analyzing and talking about images.

. . . .

Photo © www.danheller.com.

CHAPTER 2: AN INTRODUCTION TO VISUAL UNDERSTANDING

ANALYZING IMAGES
CATEGORIZING TO MAKE SENSE OF WHAT YOU SEE

Analyzing images is similar to reading a verbal text. Like written or spoken language, images have a structure, sometimes even a narrative quality. Whenever we attempt to make sense of what we see, we usually observe similarities and differences and establish relationships with other things that we know. In other words, we try to understand the language of visual texts—sometimes without even knowing it.

Talking about images requires that we be more observant, be willing to experience what we see, and then take time to analyze using a method and a language designed specifically for visual learning. The vocabulary of this language is based upon perception and includes terms such as *focal point, figure-ground contrast, similarity, proximity, orientation, texture, color,* and *shape*. These terms will give us a common language to use to talk, and ultimately to write, about images.

FOCAL POINT AND EMPHASIS

People tend to categorize the elements or figures in a composition depending on their visual properties. Usually there is at least one central figure, and that is often called the *focal point*. Officially defined as the point at which a concentrated light beam demonstrates its smallest diameter, a focal point is the spot where your eyes immediately go when viewing an image—the point on which your eyes focus. When an image has been composed by someone such as a photographer or designer, your attention is drawn to this point for a reason. Determining what you perceive to be the focal point will help guide your understanding of the image.

Look at the group of dots below. Your eye probably moves directly to the red dot near the center, almost as if drawn by a magnet. It does so because the red dot is the object of emphasis, the focal point. Look at the image again briefly and then turn away. How many red dots do you remember? How many black? You will likely remember that there is one red dot, but not that there are 48 black ones. The reason is that human beings tend to remember what is different, unusual, or unexpected.

© Bruno Barbey, Magnum Photos.

Now look at the photograph of a scene that appears to be in a public square. In this picture, there are close to twenty people gathered, although they all do not seem to be together. Our eye is drawn to the white, circular object in the center, around which people seem to be congregating. Its position, which is very close to the center of the photograph as well as almost in the center of the octagon, makes it the focal point. So does the contrast created between the object and the darker, tiled floor beneath it.

Why would the artist focus on this white object so explicitly, and why from an angle above it? Perhaps he wants the viewer to see a natural symmetry between the octagon and the white object, which appears to be a fountain or some kind of washing station. Perhaps he wants us to feel the tension of being both drawn in and propelled outward—while it is clear that people are gathering around the white object, they also seem to radiate from it, almost in an octagonal pattern. In essence, the people in the photograph seem to be extensions of the points of the octagon. Perhaps the photographer is trying to say that shapes, like the octagon, the square, and the circle, have a powerful effect on us. Or perhaps the reason is even simpler: to show off the beauty of this intricately patterned floor that almost has the appearance of a flower surrounded by a number of buzzing bees. Usually a reader of a visual text cannot come to a conclusive analysis of an image based solely on the focal point. However, unless the reader takes the focal point into consideration, there will be no conclusive analysis.

 Learn more about Focal Point and Emphasis using the Explicator visual analysis tool by clicking on "An Introduction to Visual Rhetoric" from the main menu of *Comp21.*

Framework

FIGURE-GROUND CONTRAST

One of the most important elements of analysis is known as *figure-ground contrast,* which is the design principle that emphasizes the difference between what's in front (the *figure*) and what's in back (called the *ground,* as in *background*). The figure is usually the most important thing in the picture, and the composer often deliberately frames the image to display the most important thing in front. Often the figure is also the focal point.

Because people tend to organize what they see into figure and ground, considering the different relationships can help you understand the context. An easy way to imagine this principle is to think of a blank sheet of white writing paper on a smooth, highly polished mahogany desktop. The paper would be the figure, and the desk would be the ground.

There can be several levels in a discussion of figure-ground. For example, the desk is positioned on a cream-colored carpet, and as such, it is the figure and the carpet the ground. In the photograph to the left, the figure is the circular, white object, and the ground is the intricately tiled floor. You might argue, however, that the octagon (and everything contained within it) is also a figure, and the shapes surrounding it (the square formed by the tiles and the rectangle of the actual photograph) are the ground.

Figure-ground contrast plays an important role in all of our reading activities because contrast helps to establish importance. Take, for instance, a paragraph from a memo that was written very early on in the Space Shuttle *Challenger*'s performance testing, seven years before it blew up just 73 seconds after launch.

> The visit on February 1, 1979, to Precision Rubber Products Corporation by Mr. Eudy and Mr. Ray was very well received. Company officials, Mr. Howard Gillette, Vice President for Technical Direction, Mr. John Hoover, Vice President for Engineering, and Mr. Gene Hale, Design Engineer attended the meeting and were presented with the SRM clevis joint seal test data by Mr. Eudy and Mr. Ray. After considerable discussion, company representatives declined to make immediate recommendations because of the need for more time to study the data. They did, however, voice concern for the design, stating that the SRM O-ring extrusion gap was larger than that covered by their experience. They also stated that more tests should be performed with the present design. Mr. Hoover promised to contact MSFC for further discussions within a few days. Mr. Gillette provided Mr. Eudy and Mr. Ray with the names of two consultants who may be able to help. We are indebted to the Precision Rubber Products Corporation for the time and effort being expended by their people in support of this problem, especially since they have no connection with the project.

The central idea of this paragraph, the fact that the "O-ring extrusion gap was larger than that covered by their experience," is buried in the center of the paragraph, and, as a result, had very little impact on the readers. If you were a busy NASA executive and were skimming this document, you might have disregarded it because the paragraph (and the memo itself) seems to be part of a trip report about the visit to Precision Rubber Company rather than a memo outlining potential problems with an essential component of the rocket motor booster.

Framework

The picture of the camouflaged moth we saw earlier and the figure to the left are, in essence, quite analogous to the paragraph on page 15. All are examples of what happens when the distinction between figure and ground is blurred.

Adding contrast can help the reader focus and separate the essential from the inessential. If the author of the paragraph had used italics or boldfaced text or had placed the sentence about the O-ring gap at the normal focal point of written text (first or last), he could have created the necessary figure-ground contrast that might have had more impact.

When there is no immediately recognizable contrast, as in the pictures of the moth and the dog, our eyes will keep searching, trying to find recognizable shapes or things we can use to create contrast and therefore meaning and understanding. If you look long enough at the picture of the dog, you'll see that the dog's head seems to be at a crossroads of two darker patches, which direct the eye toward the center of the picture. Once we "see" the dog, however, it is nearly impossible not to do so.

Learn more about Figure-Ground Contrast using the Explicator visual analysis tool by clicking on "An Introduction to Visual Rhetoric" from the main menu of *Comp21*.

GROUPING: PROXIMITY & SIMILARITY

As psychologists have noted, we make sense of things by categorizing or grouping them together. We talk about "those books" on the shelf and use collective nouns like "a gaggle of geese" or "a parliament of owls," indicating that we are more comfortable representing items in groups rather than individually. Psychological studies in memory also show that we can remember more things in groups than we can individually.

Different relationships tend to give us further information we can use to analyze or read images. We tend to group things in two basic ways: by their relationship in space (*proximity*) or their relationship in size, color, shape, and so on (*similarity*). In the line of dots below, the dots all look alike because they are the same size and are evenly spaced. There is no easy way to differentiate among them.

● ●

However, by changing their physical location (below), we automatically group them by proximity. Now we have six groups of three and one group of six. Close objects, therefore, are perceived as grouped together. Grouping objects together shows a connection, a relationship. The nature of the relationship usually depends on other features of the image.

● ● ●   ● ● ●   ● ● ●   ● ● ●   ● ● ●   ● ● ●   ● ● ● ● ● ●

Framework

If, instead of changing their location, we change some of the black dots to red ones, we will begin to group by similarity—black dots and red dots. Elements that share similar features are often perceived as belonging together. Therefore, even though the dots are the same size and distance from one another, the fact that there are similar groupings (red and black) helps us to analyze the intent.

● ●

Similarity is a very effective grouping concept that often is used to create a sense of unity. In the photograph of the white object and the tiled floor, the figures are grouped by virtue of either their location or their color. The three figures in the lower right all wear some white clothing, and of the three figures in the lower left, two are very close to one another, and all three are wearing black. Overall, there are several pockets of interest caused by proximity and similarity. Some of the figures are moving toward the white object, and some seem to be moving away. The figures wearing very dark clothing seem to be turned away from the white object, while those wearing white seem drawn to it, almost like a magnet. Also, at the points of the octagon, there are what appear to be white, circular shapes, but within the octagon are black lines that tie or link these white shapes together.

　　We tend to order things by size, shape, and texture as well. Shapes work for different purposes: to convey meaning, to provide balance, or to represent the fundamental form of an object.

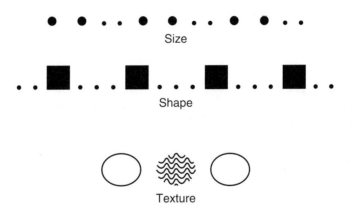

Size

Shape

Texture

Learn more about Grouping: Proximity & Similarity using the Explicator visual analysis tool by clicking on "An Introduction to Visual Rhetoric" from the main menu of *Comp21*.

COLOR

As shown by the responses of the recently sighted patients in Dillard's essay "Seeing," most people respond immediately to color, often in an emotional way. Usually, the brighter the color, the more powerful its effects. These effects are often culturally based. In our culture, for instance, white is the color of purity and is worn by brides, but in China and Japan, it is the color of mourning. Within cultures and subcultures, the meaning of a color can change; for doctors, blue often is associated with death, but for corporate executives, it has a connotation of strength.

ANALYZING IMAGES: CATEGORIZING TO MAKE SENSE OF WHAT YOU SEE

Color can focus our attention (as in the group of dots with the red one in the center), create contrast, appeal to emotions, and help to communicate nuances of meaning. According to Jan White, an award-winning designer and expert on color, it can "increase the velocity of comprehension [and] help to establish identity and character." Some colors remind us of warm things like fire and sun. Some colors remind us of cool things like water and forests. A red face might indicate embarrassment; a green face, envy; a blue face, cold or sickness; a purple face, rage; and a pink one, good health.

 Learn more about Color using the Explicator visual analysis tool by clicking on "An Introduction to Visual Rhetoric" from the main menu of *Comp21*.

CONTINUATION

The principle of "good continuation" focuses on the belief that elements that suggest a continued visual line will be grouped together. This is a primary principle behind how we "see" images in the night sky, such as the zodiac signs and the Big Dipper. The example below helps illustrate how viewers will follow movement through an image and create connections.

In the figure on the left, instead of two dotted lines or four curves, we see a curvy letter X. In the figure on the right, we follow the smiley faces down and across the page and see what appears to be a backward check mark or a letter *L* leaning back.

 Learn more about Continuation using the Explicator visual analysis tool by clicking on "An Introduction to Visual Rhetoric" from the main menu of *Comp21*.

LINE

Lines also help to provide a sense of motion or movement. Artists use lines to create edges and outline objects. The direction of a line can also convey mood. Consider the images at the top of page 19. Horizontal lines, such as those in the picture to the left, create a sense of calm and equilibrium, while vertical lines suggest movement, and diagonal lines can create stress. Finally, wavy lines (as on the right) often imply softness, grace, flow, or change.

Framework

Reprinted by permission of Stephen Loy.

Learn more about Line using the Explicator visual analysis tool by clicking on "An Introduction to Visual Rhetoric" from the main menu of *Comp21*.

CLOSURE

Human beings seem to have an innate need to complete pictures; according to psychologists, it may be part of our survival instinct. Thus, when we see incomplete figures such as the "F" in the word "Frames" below, our minds create familiar patterns by filling in the missing information. In the group of images on the right, for instance, we continue to see a circle, even when only looking at the far right image. Nancy Brown, a commercial photographer, explains that artists will use closure to "encourage the viewer's eyes to move . . . in predictable and desirable ways" to complete forms. Leaving information out creates interest, generates a tension that contributes to the narrative quality of the image, and promotes viewer participation.

FRAMES ○○◌◌◌

Learn more about Closure using the Explicator visual analysis tool by clicking on "An Introduction to Visual Rhetoric" from the main menu of *Comp21*.

NARRATION OR STORY

Once we have a clear method that will help us visually distinguish objects, we can look at the image as a whole and consider whether the image tells a story. In a verbal story, the narrator's voice mediates between the reader and action. The story is

Framework

shaped by the narrator's use of language to present a particular point of view. The themes that emerge can be implicit, as the author's beliefs affect the presentation of the characters, or explicit, as the author selects social concerns and conventions to which she wishes to draw the reader's attention. In an image, the elements are arranged so that the main focal point first attracts the viewer's attention. Each subsequent element, or minor point, creates relationships.

Learn more about Narration or Story using the Explicator visual analysis tool by clicking on "An Introduction to Visual Rhetoric" from the main menu of *Comp21*.

CONTEXT

Responding to images, noting what you see, and classifying and grouping elements will help you decode, explain, and understand the images you see. That said, keeping your eyes open isn't sufficient. Annie Dillard explains that sometimes one needs to be knowledgeable, claiming that "specialists can find the most incredibly well-hidden things" (para. 5). In order to explain your reaction, sometimes you have to think about the context of the image. Aldous Huxley once said, "the more you know, the more you see." Learning more about the world and applying what you learn will enable you, like the knowledgeable herpetologist in Dillard's essay, to find the three bags of snakes even when others claim there are none present (para. 8). Like an experienced observer, it will enable you to understand that the little piles of cut stems you stumble across while walking in the field are the result of mice cutting down grass to reach the seeds at the head (para. 5).

"The God Abandons Anthony," a poem by the Greek poet Cavafy, illustrates how contextual knowledge can assist in understanding. The poem begins with the lines, "When suddenly, at midnight, you hear / an invisible procession going by / with exquisite music, voices, / don't mourn your luck that's failing now." Most readers will see immediately that something is amiss; the narrator has as much said that Anthony's luck is "failing." What many readers won't know, unless they know more about Anthony and his beliefs, is that Anthony believed he had the divine protection of the god Dionysos, but that protection is withdrawn, which leads to his demise. Edward Hirsch, an American poet and teacher who has written about this poem, offers this kind of background information and explains to his readers that unless they know more about Greek and Roman customs, they won't know that midnight is known as the "epiphanic hour of revelation," and this procession is indeed foreshadowing Anthony's downfall.

A similar principle works with our understanding of visual images. If you knew that the photograph of the white object on page 14 was actually taken of a fountain in a courtyard outside of the tomb of Moulay Idriss II, a Moroccan ruler from the ninth century, you might reasonably conclude that the photographer wanted to make a point about the appeal of the white fountain and its water, or perhaps even about the intricate relationship of religion and daily life in Morocco. You might also guess that the people in the photograph have just come from or are going to a religious service. Even if we didn't have the background or contextual information, the postures of the

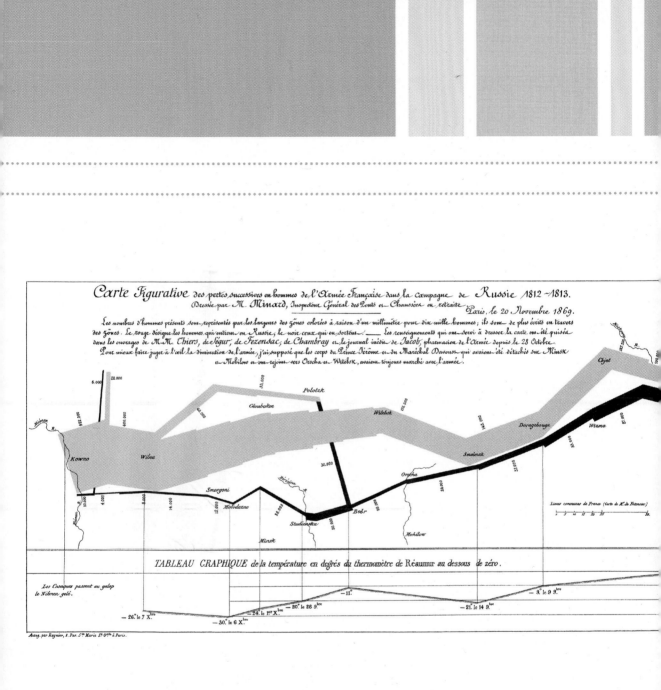

ANALYSIS

chapter THREE

MOSCOU

Tarantino

Malo-jarosewli

Zéro le 18 8.bre
.5
.10
.15
.20
.25
.30 degrés

sth. Regnier et Dourdet.

Edward R. Tufte, *The Visual Display of Quantitative Information,* Graphics Press, 1983.

This chart by Charles Minard illustrates Napoleon's army's march into and out of Russia. Notice how the chart simultaneously illustrates various aspects of the march, including time, number of troops, temperature, and geography.

A writer analyzes as a way of understanding.

To analyze something is to break it down into its parts to make sense of it more easily. But analysis doesn't just stop at the breakdown. The breakdown is the beginning of understanding. Analysis provides a method for putting the whole back together again in a more meaningful way. Analysis is primarily an act of mind, an effort on the part of a writer to study an *object*—a book, a poem, a painting, a theory, a personality, a historical event, a performance, a way of life—so that he or she can understand something significant about that object and then develop an idea about it.

Writers use analysis first to understand and then to record and demonstrate to readers what they have learned. The writing that accompanies analysis, especially in the early stages, is a form of exploration, a joint effort of the mind and the pen (or the keyboard) to learn something about the thing being studied. Subsequent writing preserves that analytical spirit, revealing to readers significant parts of the writer's learning process, and shows the reader how the writer's thinking led to the idea being presented about the object so that, finally, the reader will have an experience similar to that of the writer.

. . . .

THE NATURE OF
ANALYSIS

To read more about Analysis with interactive examples and opportunities to work with interactive texts, click on "The Rhetorical Patterns of Inquiry" from the main menu of *Comp21*.

The analytical act tends to separate a whole into its constituent parts, an object into its elements. During analysis we take things apart so that we can examine them, come to some understanding about the parts and their relationships, and, finally, develop awareness of the chemistry or the logic that holds the parts together. Eventually, the analyst wants to put the parts back together with a deeper understanding of the whole—the object itself and the idea it inspires.

DETERMINING A BASIS
FOR BREAKDOWN

No matter what the object under analysis is, your effort to understand and interpret that object will be determined by what you plan to do with your analysis. The purpose actually has a great deal to do with how you break the object down, how you choose to see it. Consider the difference between two analysts (or buyers) who are trying to select a new sound system. Patrick is as concerned with the looks of the system as he is with the sound because he has just redecorated his bedroom, painting the walls gray and the baseboards and doorframes black. He has created a color scheme that he wants his new sound equipment to complement. His power requirements are moderate given the small size of his room, but he wants high-quality sound, nevertheless.

Patrick's friend, Bob, also in the market for a sound system, has no interest whatsoever in color. His parents have given him the whole third floor of their house, so he is looking for a system that will provide loud, distinctive sound in a very large space. The attic-like rafters of the room are open, with only insulation between the roof and the open space. He needs power and good speakers.

Clearly Patrick and Bob would go about their analyses of sound systems in very different ways, based on their respective needs—the purpose for which they will use the equipment. Even when looking at the same sound systems, they would break the equipment down differently. Their basis for breakdown differs depending on their purpose. The same is true for all kinds of analysis.

When the object under consideration is a written text of some kind—an essay, a book, or the lyrics of a song—the analyst's way of deciphering the object, breaking it down into its component parts for understanding, will also be determined by his or her purpose. One analyst might be a musician who is interested in playing a particular song with her band. When analyzing a song, she would consider the structure, the range of the lead singer's voice, and the musical arrangements available for her band's use. Another analyst might be an essayist who cares about the song's lyrics; he wants to use selected words from the song to reinforce an idea that he is developing in an essay. His analysis would concern itself with interpreting the language of the song and with making sure that his use of selected words fairly represents the song, while also reinforcing the ideas he is developing in the essay.

When you determine a basis for analysis, you predetermine how you will be breaking a thing down, what you will be looking for. There is no single right way to do this. As we have seen, different analysts will look at the same object in different ways depending on their purposes. But when they look, they look piercingly in order to understand more thoroughly.

. . . .

OBJECTIVITY
AND CLAIMS

Most often the analyst (the writer) seeks to be as objective (free of bias, open to various ways of seeing) as possible while trying to understand a particular object, but we know from modern science and linguistics, and from experience, that objectivity is elusive for even the most brilliant scientist. Conclusions always carry with them traces of the analyst—her background, ways of looking at the world, educational strengths and limitations (or biases), quirks, and even desires. The observer is a human being, a person with preconceived notions, with a learned way of thinking, with idiosyncratic likes and dislikes. She may be a scientist with a deep interest in global warming or a writer with a commitment to ecology; her peculiar and passionate interests will color her thinking.

It stands to reason that no one can produce purely objective analysis. Keep in mind that your claims about the object should always be tempered by the knowledge that you are trying to be as objective as possible, but that you are also trying to give your readers a sense of the object as *you* understand it. That understanding will necessarily be, at best, objectively personal. Analysis is at its strongest when the writer recognizes that no understanding is purely objective and uses that knowledge to create a basis for breakdown with the purpose (and audience) squarely in mind.

. . . .

INTERPRETATION

The analytical act is almost always accompanied by an interpretive act. An interpreter is a translator, a person who explains. An interpretive act is, therefore, an explanatory act. Analysis, the careful study of an object by breaking it into its constituent parts, leads to interpretation—the analyst's effort to make sense of the whole, whether it be a book, an essay, a painting, or a historical theory. The analyst-turned-interpreter moves from a consideration of the nature of the object to an explanation of the meanings uncovered through analysis.

Stephen Jay Gould, one of the most eminent scientists of the last century, reminds us that *facts* considered alone offer very little in the way of knowing. The scientist's (and the writer's) primary work is to interpret the facts, to translate them, to tell us what they mean. The writer collects the facts of the written text, the characteristics of a particular painting, or the details of a particular story as a part of the preliminary analysis. The second stage of the analysis calls for the act of interpretation, the creation of meaning. The third stage calls for writing down the results of the analysis and the interpretation so that others not only understand what the object under consideration means to the interpreter, but also how the interpreter explains and accounts for the interpretation.

During the third stage, the writer must bring together evidence (the facts and information collected during analysis), the interpretation and the reasoning behind the interpretation, and, finally, his reflective thoughts about both evidence and interpretation.

ANALYSIS
AND THE OTHER PATTERNS OF INQUIRY

In all good writing, we detect a voice of reflection continually linking evidence and idea so that readers know why they are reading and know always why the piece has been written.

Analysis accompanies every form of persuasive writing. The analytical or sense-making act turns description, narration, comparison and contrast, and even analysis itself toward a specific purpose. Analysis is the most ubiquitous form of academic discourse. Attaching itself to every other pattern, it turns the mind of the writer and the mind of the reader toward a common goal: the understanding of an object, and, finally, the understanding of an idea. Storytelling, or description, or comparison and contrast, when linked with analysis, conspires to persuade, to convince the reader that the story has meaning, that the description points toward something beyond itself, that the comparison actually suggests and substantiates an idea.

We study analysis separately, in isolation, only to learn how to do it. Its usefulness depends finally on the work it does with other patterns, just as the real work the other patterns do depends on analysis. The relationship between analysis and the other patterns is the key to sense-making, which is to say, to the development of ideas.

An experienced writer, for example, moves into description when he needs to have his readers see an object, such as a painting or a particular room. But such a description is part of his larger scheme, an essay perhaps. The painting or the room comes into play because one or the other has something to do with an idea the writer is developing. So the description itself will be accompanied by analysis, which then leads to interpretation and reflection. The analytical reflections that accompany the description allow the reader to better understand just why the painting or the room is being described. Analysis and description work hand in hand. The same is true of analysis and the other patterns, as you will see throughout this book.

· · · · · · · · · ·

ANALYSIS
WITH A PURPOSE

Remember that when you choose an object for analysis, you do so to better understand it yourself so that you can, in turn, help others to understand it as you do. The analytical act always involves interpretation—what you make of the object. Your goal as an analyst should always be to provide the most comprehensive, reasonable analysis that you can provide but not to claim that what you have come up with is definitive. Every good idea, by virtue of its being an idea, is subject to further analysis. The truth about an object is most likely to be found (if it can be found at all) through consensus, through the consideration of many perspectives, through continual—and changing—analysis.

· · · · · · · · · ·

ANALYSIS
IN PURE FORM: AN ANNOTATED PARAGRAPH

Jill Ker Conway was born in New South Wales, Australia. She graduated from the University of Sydney and Harvard and became the vice president for internal affairs at the University of Toronto. She was the first woman president of Smith College, where she served for ten years before becoming a professor at the Massachusetts Institute of Technology. Her books include *The Road from Coorain, Points North, Written by Herself,* and *When Memory Speaks.* The following paragraph comes from a short essay in which she analyzes her reasons for writing *The Road from Coorain,* the first volume of her memoirs. Earlier in the essay, she has given two specific reasons for writing the memoir: to correct the male-myth of Australia depicted in movies such as *Crocodile Dundee* and *Breaker Morant* by writing a story about the Australian outback that had a woman (her mother) as a heroine; and to write free of the academic language ("wretched bureaucratic prose") that had been keeping her from creating a "spontaneous narrative." She continues her analysis:

break down
"life plot" into
its elements:
male and
female

The other motivations were much larger and ongoing in my life. I was interested in seeing if I could come up with a life plot that wasn't a romance, because the archetypal life plot for women in Western society is the bourgeois romance. It's about family and erotic life, and it doesn't concern itself at all with motivations that I think are very important for women, like work and intellectual life and political commitments. But I didn't want to write an odyssey—to just take over the archetypal male plot and create a conquering heroine. I was looking for a way to narrate a life story of a woman that would pay due respect to her attachments to men and to family but would be about something else entirely. I wanted to convey my sense of my education, of my liberation through access to education, and of the variety of steps by which I arrived at taking charge of my own life. Philosophically, you only have to perform one free act to be a free person. Granting all the ways in which we're shaped by society, nevertheless one free choice changes the outcome.

male vs.
female

explain
connection:
freedom
shaped change

Conway ends this first memoir with her departure from Australia to go to Harvard. The choice to leave her homeland was a choice that changed everything for her. In this paragraph Conway is analyzing both her motivation for writing the memoir and the meaning of a "life plot" that would be neither "male" nor "romantic."

Her aim in writing the memoir, Conway tells us, was to allow her readers to see that her life plot was not primarily about "family and erotic life" but was instead about "work and intellectual life and political commitments." Education was central to her liberation. It allowed her to take charge of her own life.

Exercises

1. Highlight the words in Conway's paragraph that suggest her ideas about the qualitative difference between male and female myth. What do you think she means by "life plot"?

2. How would you characterize Conway's reflective voice in this passage? Balanced, biased, scholarly, passionate? Explain by marking the language in the passage that signals Conway's attitude and commitment.

3. Write a short paragraph that expresses your analysis of Conway's reflections.

ANALYSIS
IN PURE FORM: ANNOTATED PARAGRAPHS

Pure Form

The biologist Bernd Heinrich, who spends much of his life in the field doing research and who teaches at the University of Vermont, often writes for both scholarly journals and the general public. Like Jill Ker Conway, Heinrich expresses dissatisfaction with certain restrictions associated with scholarly publishing: "All of the excitement of the process has been squeezed out so that the results will conform to certain expected standards necessary for clear and objective scientific communication." Heinrich understands and respects those standards, but tries in his writing to convey the excitement of the research process and to include readers in the analytical process that leads to the published results.

Heinrich's books include *Ravens in Winter, Bumblebee Economics, The Trees in My Forest, Thermal Warriors: Strategies of Insect Survival,* and *Why We Run: A Natural History.* The following selection is from "Whirligigs," taken from *In a Patch of Fireweed.* In these two paragraphs, Heinrich investigates how whirligig beetles *(Gyrinidae)* congregate on the surface of lakes, clustering into large groups, which he calls aggregations.

hypothesis →
fact →
research in Europe →

3 breakdowns:
1. secretions

The beetles were attracted to each other in spite of (or maybe because of) their bodily secretions. Water beetles exude noxious odiferous substances especially when they are touched or otherwise disturbed. Several German researchers became curious about these secretions because it was noted that some people in the Alps were able to elicit certain responses from their domestic cows and horses that had been fed some of these beetles, which suggested to them that the beetles possessed aphrodisiac substances. Working with water beetles closely related to the ones we examined in Minnesota, the European researchers found cortisone and the male sex hormone testosterone, as well as three other steroid chemicals, in the beetle's defensive secretions. The testosterone had the effect of narcotizing goldfish, making them float belly up. In addition, unsuspecting toads and frogs that gulped down these beetles violently regurgitated them in bloody mucus.

2. findings

another fact →
U.S. research →

The beetles contain still other noxious chemicals in their secretions. In this country researchers have isolated another class of organic compounds—chemically identified as norsesquiterpenoid aldehydes, appropriately shortened to "gyrinidal," because they have been identified only from gyrinids. These substances are highly distasteful to a large range of potential predators. It seems, therefore, that the beetles have gone to some lengths, evolutionarily speaking, to make themselves noxious, at least to fishes, frogs, and toads. No wonder fish seldom seem to eat them, and perhaps their noxiousness may provide a key to their flocking behavior. There is only one thing that is more noxious than a beetle, and that is many.

3. conclusion

Heinrich and another researcher observed the beetles from a boat during a twenty-four-hour period. Their method of observation, and Heinrich's resulting analysis, are highly scientific. As you read, note how many sentences Heinrich devotes to the behavior of the beetles on the lake (as he observes them) and how many sentences are devoted to the analysis of the chemical makeup of the beetles' hormones and secretions. The analysis of the chemicals has clearly been performed before or after Heinrich and his colleague observed the beetles. Nonetheless, that analysis only serves as the basis for his analysis of the beetles' observed behavior. Heinrich, in analyzing behavior, has used the chemical breakdown of the beetles' hormones as his basis for breakdown.

Notice, too, how in these brief paragraphs, Heinrich's interpretation and reflection ring clearly throughout his analysis. Despite the fact that his method and analysis are scientific and thorough, he is able to remain playful and curious—allowing him to engage nonscientific readers in scientific content. Later, Heinrich expresses his curiosity: "I had expected the beetles to be as dispersed as possible, for this should be the most efficient behavior of gathering their scattered food. . . . But instead they were just idling. This meant that something was going on, and somewhere in their behavior lay a challenging puzzle."

Pure Form

Exercises

1. The first of these paragraphs is largely descriptive, focusing on the work of other researchers. Heinrich is laying the groundwork for extended analysis in the second paragraph. What is his focus? What are the signs of his excitement, or his sense of humor, in the language of the paragraph? Explain.

2. How does the second paragraph build on and differ from the first paragraph?

3. In reading only these two paragraphs, you miss Heinrich's account of his observation time in the boat, his paddling around watching the various aggregations of beetles and their individual comings and goings. Why might those narrative paragraphs be important to you as a reader? How might they change your reaction to the "results" as they are presented in these two paragraphs?

ANALYSIS
IN ITS NATURAL HABITAT:
AN ANNOTATED READING

The following op–ed piece is from the *New York Times,* Friday, August 8, 2003. This unsigned piece makes some interesting points about the importance of vultures and the problems they pose for humans, who find them more bothersome than essential.

Although the *New York Times* is known for its coverage of serious news—its motto is "All the news that's fit to print"—this editorial offers a humorous diversion. It is nonetheless

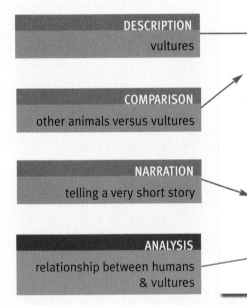

DESCRIPTION
vultures

COMPARISON
other animals versus vultures

NARRATION
telling a very short story

ANALYSIS
relationship between humans & vultures

Neighborly Vultures

There is really nothing adorable about vultures, adorable in human terms, that is. Most of the other animals that have learned to cohabit with humans—to cause trouble in the suburbs, that is—look comparatively warm and fuzzy, endearing enough if they are not eating your roses or your garbage. But a vulture has only the beauty of adaptation, of pure function, and its function—feeding on animal remains—is not a glamorous one. Even the chicks look like skinheads with switchblade beaks.

Some places, especially in the South, have gotten way more exposure to vultures than they want in recent years. Sooner or later, nearly every wild animal that tolerates the presence of humans reaches the limits of human tolerance. It just takes a little longer for the cute

Exercises

1. Identify those sections of this short piece that seem analytical and those that seem narrative (more like storytelling). Notice how the writer moves fluidly from one pattern to the other.

2. If the vulture and its habits are the focus of this editorial piece, what is its implied purpose? How does the analysis serve that purpose? Explain.

analytical. As you read the essay, notice the different bases for breakdown the authors use in the first two paragraphs. What, exactly, is being analyzed? Notice how the different analyses add together to make a larger point. Notice, too, how the interpretation and reflection rely on the breakdown and vice versa.

ones. Most Americans like nature, but they like it to stay in its place, especially if it means a roosting colony of vultures that smell like what they eat. Yet vultures who choose to live near humans do so because that is where the food is. They create the ultimate not-in-my-backyard problem. Because they scavenge animal remains, including roadkill, they play a critical role in the regenerative cycle of nature.

PROCESS ANALYSIS
unexpected outcome

But no one wants to wake up and find a colony of roosting vultures doing their regenerating just over the fence.

Reducing the attractions, like the improper disposal of dead animals, is the critical first step to controlling the problem. Pablo Neruda once called the vulture "God's spy." That wouldn't make one any more welcome as a neighbor, would it?

DESCRIPTION
metaphor

3. Connect the quotation in the last paragraph with the rest of the piece. What do the quotation and the title tell us about the writer's attitude to his material and to the problem he raises for our consideration?

4. Is the writer arguing for a better relationship between humans and the necessary vultures, or for a deeper understanding about the important role that vultures play in our lives? Or is this a "clean-up-the-neighborhood" argument? Explain how you know by examining the author's analytical reflections throughout the piece.

SASKIA VERLAAN

Saskia Verlaan was born in New York City, but has spent the majority of her life in the town of Bovina, located in the Catskill Mountains of New York state. She is a member of the class of 2006 at New York University and is an English and art history major. Her other interests include medical history, Renaissance studies, music, theater, and the natural world. Verlaan wrote "Perspectives on Fear" in an advanced class on the essay during her first year at NYU, and it was selected to be published in *Mercer Street,* the university's journal of student writing.

Perspectives on Fear

In "Perspectives on Fear," Verlaan analyzes her own fears, trying to come to terms with fear itself; she is concerned ultimately with the beneficial effects that fear can have on the development of self. She tells a number of stories about her own fear, cites from a study on fear, analyzes Picasso and cubism as a way of gaining new perspectives on fear and self-development, and concludes that fear exposes her to her own contradictory nature. Understanding her contradictions leads to a deeper understanding of who she is.

"At the University of California at Irvine, experiments in rats indicate that the brain's hormonal reaction to fear can be inhibited, softening the formation of memories and the emotions they evoke" (Baard).

1 Sometimes I have trouble sleeping. I lie in bed for hours while my mind churns through endless streams of fragmented thoughts and memories, bits of brain matter that I do not have time for in my waking life. I have tried the homeopathic remedies. I drink "calming" teas, take showers, and inhale scents advertised to promote sleep and relaxation. I even have a lavender neck pillow. Nevertheless, when I am inflicted with a bout of sleeplessness, there is usually very little I can do but wait it out. I stay away from sleep drugs.

The streetlamp outside paints shapes across the wall next to my bed. I can see them in the darkness, dull orange lines that have become familiar in my many restless nights. At the heart of their canvas, they intersect to form a rectangle. A rectangle? For months I believed in this reality of form with the inborn certainty that accompanies that which is obvious. I didn't have

to think about it. Nightly, I would study the shape in a sleep haze, unconsciously harboring knowledge of its regularity. Except that it is not a rectangle.

Two forty-seven. Nearly three hours after my first attempt at sleep, I stared up at the wall and realized for the first time the distortion within the orange light. Where the lines connected to form the shape, the rectangle, were angles. Obtuse and acute, they had none of the symmetrical regularity that geometry dictates of a true rectangle. The outline on the wall was crooked, skewed, an imperfect representation of the form.

I tend to think of my memories as shoeboxes, precise, neatly uniform components that stack tidily in the mind. Somehow I have trained myself to believe that in regularity and order I will uncover the diagram of my true self, a clear-cut explanation for all that I think, say, and do. But in sleepless nights I realize that even old recurring thoughts can be strangely misshapen, and I am thrown into a tailspin. My memories of experiencing fear seem contorted. Among the most vivid of my recollections, they stand out with their potent doses of color, emotion, and experience. They have been with me so long that I rarely question the nature of their composition. I trust in their regularity, so often failing to notice their glaring deviations from box form, a wayward corner or a fifth side. Yet, there are times that they do seem strange to me, cartoon like and yet luridly real, carefully preserved though strangely altered. They carry with them the nagging ache of contradiction.

I was eight when I got lost at the Grand Canyon.

Momentarily forgetting the spectacular vistas of the place, I had chased after fat squirrels, reverse pied pipers that scampered beneath the boulders and scrappy brush that lined the canyon's edge. Soon, however, they left me, and I realized with childhood's sudden, ambiguous sensation of horror the absence of my mother, sister, and grandmother.

Panic set in. Wild thoughts of abandonment took hold while I quickly retraced my steps along a rocky path. My surroundings, sparse cliffs with deeply incised furrows, became sinister, abstract forms in an alien landscape. As I strained my eyes ahead, trying to discern a recognizable form in a throng of distant onlookers, the intense heat of the day blurred everything ahead of me with the hallucinogenic appearance of a mirage. I felt infinitely small compared to the massive pit torn into the ground beside me. Staring over the edge, I could see myself tumbling over, a pebble plummeting down through the miles and miles of emptiness that stretched far below me.

Fear is a powerful presence in the mind. Long after the incident is past, it remains vivid in the memory. I can remember the feel of the hot air against my skin, the gravelly texture of the ground beneath my feet as I ran, the tight, sickly spasm of my stomach as it twisted in upon itself.

But I was never truly lost. When my mother, sister, and grandmother "found" me, I was reassured that they had known where I was the entire time. The fear that I felt, the ideas that I had formed in my panic of abandonment and death were unnecessary in the face of a danger that had never existed. The whole thing was funny really, my intense, panicked reaction comical. Nevertheless, I could not, still cannot shake the terror of being lost. How could I when it is the fear of that experience that I recall with every wrong turn I take,

every path down an unfamiliar street? Whether legitimate or not, it is this fear that has seared itself into my mind to become inseparable from the lighter reality of the moment. What results is a memory that is a composite of contradictions where terror and death stick out at odd angles from what I know to be true, like the noses, eyes, and limbs of a Picasso.

I saw one of his paintings from the nineteen thirties recently. It was titled the *Weeping Woman*. His subject is portrayed in the particular style of cubism that is among the most recognizable forms of Picasso's work. Her face exists as a caricature, seeming almost to have been cleaved in two and then pasted back together in some grotesque fashion. This maceration provides a fractured view of both frontal and profile perspectives that miraculously seem to have been forced to exist simultaneously on the two-dimensional plane.

The painting's color is vividly bright, lending an air of absurdity to the unhappy subject. Thick stripes of yellow and ochre stream down the wall in the background, while atop the woman's head is perched a broad-brimmed hat, colored in bold chunks of orange, purple, and electric blue. Over the contorted, angular mouth is a jagged area, like broken bits of pottery, made artificially gray through the clever use of indigo, lavender, and violet pigments. The remainder of the woman's skin reflects the yellow of the wall, contrasted with shadows formed in robust shades of green and occasional splotches of dark sugary pink.

I leaned in, scrutinizing the details of the deformed figure, my eyes lingering momentarily upon the brilliant blue of the flower in the woman's hat that blazed along sharp lines and rugged contours. My memories of fear burn themselves into my mind with a similar richness of pigment, saturating the cerebral tissues with bright, indelible inks. In thinking about my experiences I am aware of a similar sensation of looking at a picture from many angles all at once, an amalgamation of perspectives.

Recently I read an article in *The Village Voice* entitled "The Guilt-Free Soldier" which discussed the development of new drugs and therapies by scientists in several different institutions that could numb the effects of fear in the mind. It provided a description of the way in which fear is remembered: "The web of your

Reading

worst nightmares, your hauntings and panics . . . radiate from a dense knot of neurons called the amygdala. With each new frightening . . . experience, or even the reliving of an old one, this fear center releases a flood of hormones that sear horrifying impressions into your brain. That which is unbearable becomes unforgettable too."

Fear inevitably distorts. In a moment of panic the world appears changed, is changed within the mind.

A sudden jolt of adrenaline from the brain and neurons and synapses launches the imagination and senses into action. The mind wildly grasps at ideas as they occur, sweeping the self into mounting waves of panic. These notions, though by nature temporal, are nonetheless included among the images branded into the folds of the psyche and become inherent to the experience. They stay embedded, remaining even as old opinions are regained or new ones are adopted. The original comforting ideas born in safe, familiar conditions continue on, but are augmented by the rough, jagged angles of anxiety. Ultimately the memory becomes fractured, combining two perspectives on a single plane, a cubist masterpiece of thought.

I stared at the painting. Searching the outline of the misshapen head, the angular nose, the skewed eyes, I could remember fright's twinge in my stomach.

Rats, at least those of the upstate New York variety, don't look as mean as you would expect. Little more than overgrown mice, there is something in their tawny color and lithe frame that is reminiscent of the sun-bleached grasses of autumn fields, a casual reminder of their place in nature. Even their faces bear none of the typical features, the gleaming red eyes, gnashing fang-like teeth, and pointy elongated snouts that are usually associated with their species. Instead, their muzzles are blunt and boxy and their eyes are not red but rather a deep glossy black, hinting at an innocence that is no more or less profound than that of their cousins, the chipmunk and the deer mouse.

Nevertheless, I hate them.

As I moved from room to room in the chicken coop I was haunted by my fear of their naked scaly tails, their gorged yet astonishingly limber bodies, their rapid sinuous movements. They had invaded nearly a year earlier, a persistent plague that gnawed through wood and

wire, and evaded traps of glue, glass, and metal. The mere thought of seeing a rat caused a tingle to race up my spine and stay ringing in my ears, and in my mind I conjured up sudden, terrifying images of one darting out ahead of me. Already I could feel the yelp of fright that it would elicit, a lump in my stomach.

The final section of the coop was home to small bantam chicken breeds, an assortment of roosters, and a few select hens that lived in cages lining the walls. Stepping just inside, I hit the wall next to me with an old, battered broom, attempting to frighten away any lurking rodents with the noise. My eyes scanned the ground and the tops of cages for signs of the quick, fluid movements that were characteristic of the rats I had seen there before, but the room remained still, and I set about my work with a tentative feeling of relief.

Nothing struck me as unusual when I opened the door to one of the taller cages. However, as I reached my hand in past its single, obliviously good-natured occupant, an old tawny hen, I became suddenly and horrifyingly aware of the startled figures of four enormous rats. Piled on top of each other, they had wedged themselves into a small gap between the outside of the cage and the wall. Their eyes wide, they stared fixedly at me through the layer of chicken wire to which they desperately clung, frozen in a moment of terrified surprise. My expression mirrored theirs for a moment before I began to scream. Stumbling back, I dropped the bucket I was holding, spilling corn over the ground. The rats too, sprang to action, writhing in their confinement, desperately clawing over one another.

Even as I screamed, a new thought cut jaggedly through to my mind. I wanted to hit them, to beat them and mash them with my broom as they struggled, to step on them and hear their bones break, to feel the delicious pop as their skulls cracked. My grip tightened around the broom's handle, and I could feel its chipped paint pressed hard into my sweating palm as I made ready for action. But I hesitated. Looking up at the rats I saw their shiny black eyes, their wheat-colored fur, and their tails. It was too much. Terror and pity made me drop my weapon. I was running before it even hit the ground, stumbling past the door. Running far away from the coop.

How am I to interpret the memories that fear produces? Tossing in my bed at night I am plagued by their nagging contradictions, their obscurities, and their abstractions. Trying to sort through the meaning of my experiences I have attempted to explain my actions in the chicken coop to myself. I wanted to kill the rats out of fear, I ran from them out of fear, I pitied them, loved them for their natural innocence out of fear. But such conclusions provide little more than additional confusion. I find myself wondering how all these contradictory reactions could have occurred within the mind of a single person in reaction to a single event. I desperately want to apply a rational order to an emotion and an experience in which there is none to be found. I want my memory of the rats to conform to my ideal shoebox logic, but my reaction in that situation, a reaction bred by fear, was not logical. Instead, it was the product of confusion. Ultimately, it has been its source as well.

Sometimes at night I hate looking at the shape on the wall. I clench my eyes closed so tightly that they water through the fringe of my lashes. I bury my head beneath the covers where I cannot breathe. I try to hide from it, to block out its pale light of deformity. But inevitably the lids spring open, and the covers fly off to reveal the hard points of the non-rectangle's lopsided corners where they stand out crisply against the wall's shadows, monuments to disorder.

25   I hate confusion. I become tired of the endless struggle with its snares and tangles, the way it warps the metal of my mind, the way it muddles my thoughts, the way it keeps me awake at night. I toss repeatedly in my bed, hoping for the chance of escape.

"Researchers are mastering the means of short-circuiting the very wiring of primal fear" (Baard). Drugs for fear, drugs for sleep. The temptation to medicate my way into unconsciousness is often strong. Now I wonder if I might not someday do the same with fear. Pop pills to ease the brain, ebb the tide of thoughts, but at what cost? Beyond my confusion I want to believe that there is some purpose to the multiple perspectives that fear creates. Something that exists whether or not I am able to understand it.

Someone asked me recently if I understand cubism. I paused for a moment while I inwardly struggled with the reality of the question. Then, "No, not really." I considered my answer for a moment. I have a basic knowledge of certain of its aspects picked up in reading and conversation. Very loosely I could tell you that cubism involves an attempt to see every side of a figure at once, but I don't understand the way in which it is created, the manner in which the artists decide how to portray their subjects. I replied again, more certain this time. "No."

I didn't understand cubism, and I didn't understand the *Weeping Woman*. The mechanics, the technical questions, the how's and why's of the painting's creation all evaded me, and yet I realized that I still loved and appreciated it. It was not something that I had to make sense of except to see exactly what was in front of me. Within his painting, Picasso invites us to see parts of his subject rather than the whole. This inevitably leads to distortion of the figure, but through this abstract form it also implies the depth and realism of the character.

The woman on the canvas looks bizarrely deformed, but in that deformity we are given a sense of a truth that is not easily represented in any media. Within her jagged contours and brisk lines, we see the multiple facets that are inherent to her identity; the splintering of her portrait reveals the complex dimensions of her entirety. It is only physically that the painting is distorted, for within its fractures Picasso has rendered a portrayal of the woman's character that is more pure. There is a suggestion of form and dimension that transcends the distortion it requires. Perhaps it is the same with my memories. Perhaps it is not they that are deformed but my understanding of them that is.

Do the multiple perspectives that I have gained   30 through fear provide a more precise representation of reality? I have tried so often to understand myself through the disregard of the fractures and irregularities within my memories, but perhaps it is precisely their idiosyncrasies that are essential to my ability to comprehend them.

I am reminded of the early history of art, in which human beings were often portrayed through composite views showing the head and legs in profile, while the torso was represented as it would have appeared from the front. The laws that govern human physiology prevent this position from being replicated in real life;

nevertheless, it served a purpose for the ancients who used it. Composite perspective gave the most obvious depiction of a person by combining distinct traits that were "very descriptive of what a human body is—as opposed to what it looks like from any one viewpoint" (Kleiner, 14). Through distortion ancient artists achieved a portrait that was faithful to the characteristics of a human being. Thousands of years later this method of functional distortion is still being used: in the painting of Picasso and in my mind.

For so long I have desired to assign order to myself in an attempt to comprehend something that I am now beginning to believe must, by its very nature, be understood through its confusion and distortion. Rather than being obscured by them, my experiences of fear reveal themselves through their facets, their fractures, and even their contradictions. This is most clearly demonstrated in my reaction to the rats in the chicken coop. Once the paradigm of my confusion, I now wonder if my conflicting emotional responses of hate, love, and pity in that situation are the key to understanding the role of fear in my memories. Each feeling represented a different aspect of myself at that time, a self that was capable of interpreting a situation in a variety of ways. More and more I am convinced that the episodes of fear that I have experienced and stored within my memory are not in opposition to my quest for self-understanding, but have in fact provided me with the multiple perspectives that are essential to furthering this aim. I can see now that these aspects of my memory are windows into the multiple aspects of a single personality, attesting to the complexity that exists within the self.

Works Cited

Baard, Erik. "The Guilt-Free Soldier." *The Village Voice*. 22–28. February, 2003: 33.

Kleiner, Fred S., et al. *Gardner's Art Through the Ages—The Western Perspective*. Volume I. 11th ed. Belmont, CA: Wadsworth, 2003.

Reading and Thinking

1. Verlaan's essay is an analysis of fear. The analytical work allows her to understand something significant about fear in general. Begin by breaking down Verlaan's analysis. In each section of the essay, she examines some aspect of fear and its effects. She breaks fear into parts so that she can better understand it. Complete this chart to see how she links each section with a new understanding of some aspect of fear.

Sections of the essay	Her (and your) understanding
Lying in bed (paras. 1–3)	The nature of misshaped thoughts. There is something challenging about the difference, something to figure out about form and fear.
Grand Canyon (paras. 5–9)	
Cubism (the *Weeping Woman*) (paras. 10–12)	
The Village Voice (para. 13)	
Rats (paras. 17–22)	
Cubism (again) (paras. 27–29)	

2. The image of shoeboxes appears in the fourth paragraph and then again later in Verlaan's essay. What do you think she came to understand about her "ideal shoebox logic"? Why is a shoebox an apt metaphor in this case?

3. Verlaan examines the relationship between fear and cubism. What did she figure out about fear and self-development by examining Picasso's painting, *Weeping Woman?*

Picasso, Pablo (1881–1973) © ARS, NY.

Thinking and Writing

1. Turn to the "rats" section of Verlaan's essay (paras. 17–22). Note how Verlaan breaks down that section. Remember that her purpose is to learn something about fear and self-development. Make marginal notes in the text, naming just what she does in each of the six paragraphs. Explain in writing how she interprets the encounter.

2. Write a paragraph explaining what you think Verlaan tells us in her essay about the relationship among fear, jagged perspectives, and self-development.

3. Think about the rats encounter in terms of your own experiences. Select a moment from memory, an experience that startled you enough to stay with you (it need not have anything to do with fear). First, recreate that experience, and then analyze it, figuring out what it means to you. Then, reveal your interpretation in a reflective, convincing voice.

FORMS OF MIND
AN OCCASION FOR ANALYSIS

You will now have additional opportunities to practice analysis. Saskia Verlaan uses stories of experience, studies on fear, paintings, and analysis to help her reveal her own idea about the way fear can prompt a better understanding of the self. In her essay Verlaan learns something about particular aspects of fear; each broken down and interpreted. This Occasion for Analysis asks you to look at and analyze paintings by René Magritte and Sandro Botticelli.

RENÉ MAGRITTE

René Magritte (1898–1967) remains one of the most popular figures in modern art. He was born and grew up in Belgium. Although Magritte was influenced by cubism, his most arresting images are decidedly realistic, and yet have an uncanny way of becoming surreal, strangely haunting and evocative.

PREPARING TO WRITE: THE IMPORTANCE OF MARVELS, 1927

1. How many separate parts, or elements, can you see in *The Importance of Marvels*? Name them.
2. How do the different shapes complement or complicate one another? How do you characterize the background of the painting? What is its relationship to the woman?
3. Characterize the colors of the painting. What do they suggest?
4. The title refers to "marvels" and their importance. What important marvels do you see in the painting?

Occasion

Magritte, The Importance of Marvels, 1927

Occasion

Magritte, The Treachery of Images, 1929

PREPARING TO WRITE: THE TREACHERY OF IMAGES, 1929

1. Count the parts in the painting. Name them. Did you count the background of the painting?

2. In the title, Magritte refers to "images." What are the images? Name them. Did you consider the words as images? What might be treacherous about these images?

MOVING TOWARD ESSAY: ANALYSIS AND REFLECTION

The Importance of Marvels

1. What is the effect of the three body parts that seem sculptural (made by hand or by machine) and the other body parts that seem to be real (human and animate)? How do the two different types of representations play off one another in your mind? Explain.

2. Focus on the figure. You could begin at the bottom and sense that she evolves from something crafted (or mechanically reproduced) to something more human. Or you could begin at the head and move in the opposite evolutionary direction. Which seems the more appropriate direction and why?

3. What is the woman's relationship to the sea? In your explanation, consider her size, her position on the beach, and her nature. Is she a marvel? Explain.

4. What do you make of the woman's hair? What does it suggest?

5. What do you think Magritte is trying to get us to see and understand?

The Treachery of Images

1. This image of an ordinary pipe includes cursive writing declaring that what we see is not a pipe. (The text reads "Ceci n'est pas une pipe," or "This is not a pipe.") What is the effect of that declaration? If it is not a pipe, what is it? How do the image and the message work together? Toward what meaning?

2. Is Magritte simply trying to focus on the physical qualities (color, texture, composition, flatness) of the painting? What do those words try to elicit philosophically that an image by itself could not elicit? Explain.

Occasion

WRITING THOUGHTFULLY: IDEA AND ESSAY

1. David Sylvester, a biographer of Magritte and an art critic, has suggested that *The Importance of Marvels* owes a debt to Botticelli's *Birth of Venus,* shown on this page. What do you think? Consider the shape of Botticelli's seashell and the elliptical body parts of Magritte's woman. Consider too the act of birth. Are the two women being born from the sea? What does the myth of Venus suggest about such a birth that might help you better understand both paintings?

© Arte & Immagini srl/CORBIS.

2. Consider what Saskia Verlaan tells us about cubism. When viewing Picasso's *Weeping Woman,* she has a sensation that she is "looking at a picture from many angles all at once, an amalgamation of perspectives." Does Magritte create a similar sensation for you with the woman's body parts in *The Importance of Marvels?* Explain your reaction. What does Magritte's surreal perspective suggest to you about women in general and about the culture in which women are now born and shaped?

3. You have seen in *The Treachery of Images* that Magritte likes to play with images and words. What kind of playfulness do you find in *The Importance of Marvels*?

4. Magritte has offered these comments about words and images:

   - "We see images and words differently in a picture."
   - "In a picture words are of the same substance as images."
   - "An image can take the place of a word in a Proposition."
   - "Everything tends to suggest that there is little connection between an object and what it represents."

   On the evidence of all that you have been considering about these two Magritte paintings, provide an interpretation of one or the other—or of the two together. Offer this interpretation in the form of a short essay.

5. Develop a short essay about any idea that your analysis of Magritte's work has uncovered. It could have to do with perspective, with language, with playfulness, with gender, or with interpretation itself. Make use, as you deem appropriate, of the paintings and the analytical work that you have done for this Occasion.

CREATING OCCASIONS

1. Visit an art museum or find artwork on the Internet. Select a painting that interests you, one that turns your head, grabs you. Create a word-picture of that painting so that your classmates who were not with you will be able to visualize the painting.

2. Analyze the selected painting. Identify its elements; consider the images within the larger picture; and think about color, background, and foreground. Pay attention to the title. Write a reflective interpretation of the painting.

3. Consider your individual relationship to the painting. Analyze that relationship. What is there about the painting that grabbed you? Why do you care about it? What have you learned about it? About yourself? If Verlaan learned about fear from analyzing Picasso's painting, what have you learned from your selected painting and your analysis of it? Write a short essay developing this idea.

4. Create your own interactive Occasion on *Comp21* using the textual, visual, and video libraries, as well as the Explicator analysis tools. From the main menu, choose "Build Your Own Occasion for Writing."

I missed my chance. I should have gone for the throat. I should have lunged for that streak of white under the weasel's chin and held on, held on through mud and into the wild rose, held on for a dearer life. We could live under the wild rose wild as weasels, mute and uncomprehending. I could very calmly go wild. I could live two days in the den, curled, leaning on mouse fur, sniffing bird bones, blinking, licking, breathing musk, my hair tangled in the roots of grasses. Down is a good place to go, where the mind is single. Down is out, out of your ever-loving mind and back to your careless senses. I remember muteness as a prolonged and giddy fast, where every moment is a feast of utterance received. Time and events are merely poured, unremarked, and ingested directly, like blood pulsed into my gut through a jugular vein. Could two live that way? Could two live under the wild rose, and explore by the pond, so that the smooth mind of each is as everywhere present to the other, and as received and as unchallenged, as falling snow?

We could, you know. We can live any way we want. People take vows of poverty, chastity, and obedience—even of silence—by choice. The thing is to stalk your calling in a certain skilled and supple way, to locate the most tender and live spot and plug into that pulse. This is yielding, not fighting. A weasel doesn't "attack" anything; a weasel lives as he's meant to, yielding at every moment to the perfect freedom of single necessity.

I think it would be well, and proper, and obedient, and pure, to grasp your one necessity and not let it go, to dangle from it limp wherever it takes you. Then even death, where you're going no matter how you live, cannot you part. Seize it and let it seize you up aloft even, till your eyes burn out and drop; let your musky flesh fall off in shreds, and let your very bones unhinge and scatter, loosened over fields, over fields and woods, lightly, thoughtless, from any height at all, from as high as eagles.

Reading and Thinking

1. Go through Dillard's essay and note the white space—the breaks between sections of the essay—throughout. Make notes in the margin that indicate what Dillard is doing in each of these sections. Think about two things: her purpose in each section and what she actually reveals in each section.

2. Consider the first section after the introduction that deals with the physical location of her weasel sighting. As you read through the five paragraphs, highlight the images that have to do with nature and civilization. What do you think Dillard is suggesting? Why does she begin her analysis of the weasel encounter with this section?

3. Focus on the section that begins, "Weasel!" Go through that section using two different colored pens. Mark what you consider *verifiable facts* with one color and *the analysis or interpretation* of those facts with another color.

4. The following section ("I would like to learn . . .") represents a shift in thinking, a movement past the moment of encounter. How would you characterize that shift in thinking? What is Dillard aiming at in this section? Is she effective?

Thinking and Writing

1. Consider the next-to-last section of the essay. Is Dillard backing away from what she suggested about "mindlessness" in the previous section as she attempts to accommodate the ways of weasel to the ways of man and woman? How can mindlessness and commitment go together? Explain.

2. Has Dillard left anything significant out of her analysis of the weasel encounter? What do you think it means to live "without bias or motive"? What might be the consequences if all of us chose to live without either bias or motive? What might the conflicts be between individual decisions and communal decisions? Write Dillard a short letter addressing your concerns. Let her see the results of your own analysis of her analysis.

3. The weasel itself has no written or spoken language. What part does language play in the development of one's "single necessity"?

THE NATURE OF CONSCIOUSNESS
AN OCCASION FOR ANALYSIS

The four photographs in this Occasion will give you an opportunity to think and write about some of the ideas Annie Dillard has raised regarding human nature, wilderness, and the relationship between our individual needs and our need to live in community.

BRUCE DAVIDSON

Bruce Davidson (b. 1933) was born in Oak Park, Illinois. He studied photography at Rochester Institute of Technology and also attended Yale University. After military service, he worked for a year as a freelance photographer for *Life* magazine. In 1958 he became a member of the international photography agency Magnum Photos. His widely acclaimed work can be seen in the permanent collections of the Metropolitan Museum and Museum of Modern Art in New York, and in Museum Ludwig in Köln, Germany. His printed collections include *Bruce Davidson: East 100th Street; Time of Change: Civil Rights Photographs, 1961–1965; Central Park; Bruce Davidson Photographs;* and *Portraits.* He has received two awards from the National Endowment for the Arts, a Guggenheim Fellowship, and the Eastman Kodak Reedy Award.

   Three of the images included here appeared in *Central Park,* a series of photographs Davidson worked on for four years in the early 1990s. His photographs are known for their depth of feeling and poetic mood. Davidson has a fascination for people not in the limelight—celebrities are not his subjects.

Davidson, Young Interracial Couple

PREPARING TO WRITE: YOUNG INTERRACIAL COUPLE

1. Divide the photograph into two parts, one on each side of the couple. List what you see to the right and then list what you see to the left. What do the lists suggest about what might be Davidson's concerns and values? Explain.

2. Start at the intersection of the two faces. Follow the line along the curve of the girl's face and extend the line up toward the top of the photograph. What do you notice with this extension? Look for other lines and movement. How do those lines break up the photograph? What do you see in the various sections created by these lines?

3. Focus on the expression of each face. How would you describe each expression?

Davidson, Central Park with Boys in Trees

PREPARING TO WRITE: CENTRAL PARK WITH BOYS IN TREES

1. Divide the photograph into two parts. List what you see to the right and then list what you see to the left. Attend to details, making the lists as complete as you can. What do the lists suggest about what might be Davidson's concerns and values? Explain.

2. How does the photograph divide itself into parts? Are the divisions predominantly vertical or horizontal? Identify and describe them.

3. What dominates this image? Is it one thing, or might there be tension between two forces? Explain.

4. Characterize the play between light and shadow throughout the entire photograph. Does it suggest meaning, or is it simply aesthetic?

MOVING TOWARD ESSAY: ANALYSIS AND REFLECTION

© Bruce Davidson/Magnum Photos.

Young Interracial Couple

1. What does the photograph suggest about the couple's relationship? Anna Norris, when she was studying photography at the Tisch School of the Arts in New York, wrote that "pictures are fashioned to serve a particular purpose." Do you imagine Davidson's purpose was to give us the couple or to give us something more? Explain.

2. Return to paragraphs 3–8 of "Living Like Weasels." What does this photograph have in common with that section of Dillard's essay? What does Dillard make you see that you might have missed? Dillard suggests that the weasel "lives as he's meant to, yielding at every moment to the perfect freedom of single necessity." She implies that we too can live that way. Do you think this couple is in such a state, or do you believe that there are forces at work in the photograph, or elsewhere, that are at odds with such living? Explain.

3. Anna Norris tells us that, in photographs, "truth is complicated by the reality that produces them." What do you imagine is the reality that produced this photograph? The truth as Davidson sees it? Consider the two photographs as a pair. Do you get a clearer sense of those relationships between the reality we sense and the truth being expressed?

Central Park with Boys in Trees

1. The boys dominate the foreground of this photograph and tall buildings dominate the background. Between them, we see the reflective serenity of nature. What does Davidson's photograph suggest about the movement from foreground to background, or from background to foreground? More specifically, what do you think happens to the boys when they move back into the background, back into the city?

2. Laura Wilson, a photographer from Texas, once said that she edits her photographs to rip our hearts out. Do you imagine that Davidson has something like that in mind when he prints out his own images? Explain, on the basis of these two photographs.

WRITING THOUGHTFULLY: IDEA AND ESSAY

1. The two photographs on these pages are both by Bruce Davidson. Analyze them both for yourself, just as you did in the earlier exercises. Render a brief written account about how your own sense of Davidson's vision was changed or confirmed by analyzing these two photographs. What changed? What remained the same?

2. People are central in all four of Davidson's photographs, even in the panorama of Central Park. Use Davidson's photographs as a starting point and develop your own essay about the relationship between nature and civilization. Consider what the

Davidson, Central Park

© Bruce Davidson/Magnum Photos.

Occasion

E. O. Wilson
Harvard Un
Academy of
Pulitzer priz
The New Sy

Wilson
the wo
artists,
nitely v
adise. I
Wilson
that is

Wha
cerning
the poe
look ba
bird's b
answer

1 The role of
mate image
already und
patterns tha
truth. Biolo
the course c
out of the in

Picture t
the size and
projecting f
land. When
Harvard an
places with
courage I ha
rectly across
a sample of
up from the
tains. To the
gist to take

weasel in Dillard's essay led her to imagine. Think too about this comment by the noted naturalist, Terry Tempest Williams:

> Everything feels upside-down these days, created for our entertainment.... The natural world is becoming invisible, appearing only as a backdrop for our own human dramas and catastrophes: hurricanes, tornadoes, earthquakes, and floods. Perhaps if we bring art to the discussion of the wild we can create a sensation where people will pay attention to the shock of what has always been here.
>
> *Away from the Flock* (1994)

Develop your essay as a general response to Davidson, Dillard, and Williams. Use those three artists to help you analyze the ever-changing relationship between nature and civilization and to formulate your own interpretation of this complex issue.

© Bruce Davidson/Magnum Photos.

Davidson, Youth Holding Kitten

was the cloud forest, a labyrinth of interlocking trunks and branches blanketed by a thick layer of moss, orchids, and other epiphytes that ran unbroken off the tree trunks and across the ground. To follow game trails across this high country was like crawling through a dimly illuminated cave lined with a spongy green carpet.

A thousand feet below, the vegetation opened up a bit and assumed the appearance of typical lowland rain forest, except that the trees were denser and smaller and only a few flared out into a circle of blade-thin buttresses at the base. This is the zone botanists call the mid-mountain forest. It is an enchanted world of thousands of species of birds, frogs, insects, flowering plants, and other organisms, many found nowhere else. Together they form one of the richest and most nearly pure segments of the Papuan flora and fauna. To visit the mid-mountain forest is to see life as it existed before the coming of man thousands of years ago.

5   The jewel of the setting is the male Emperor of Germany bird of paradise *(Paradisaea guilielmi),* arguably the most beautiful bird in the world, certainly one of the twenty or so most striking in appearance. By moving quietly along secondary trails you might glimpse one on a lichen-encrusted branch near the treetops. Its head is shaped like that of a crow—no surprise, since the birds of paradise and crows have a close common lineage—but there the outward resemblance to any ordinary bird ends. The crown and upper breast of the bird are metallic oil-green and shine in the sunlight. The back is glossy yellow, the wings and tail deep maroon. Tufts of ivory-white plumes sprout from the flanks and sides of the breast, turning lacy in texture toward the tips. The plume rectrices continue on as wirelike appendages past the breast and tail for a distance equal to the full length of the bird. The bill is blue-gray, the eyes clear amber, the claws brown and black.

In the mating season the male joins others in leks, common courtship arenas in the upper tree branches, where they display their dazzling ornaments to the more somberly caparisoned females. The male spreads his wings and vibrates them while lifting the gossamer flank plumes. He calls loudly with bubbling and flutelike notes and turns upside down on the perch, spreading wings and tail and pointing his rectrices skyward. The dance reaches a climax as he fluffs up the green breast feathers and opens out the flank plumes until they form a bril-liant white circle around his body, with only the head, tail, and wings projecting beyond. The male sways gently from side to side, causing the plumes to wave gracefully as if caught in an errant breeze. Seen from a distance, his body now resembles a spinning and slightly out-of-focus white disk.

This improbable spectacle in the Huon forest has been fashioned by thousands of generations of natural selection in which males competed and females made choices, and the accouterments of display were driven to a visual extreme. But this is only one trait, seen in physiological time and thought about at a single level of causation. Beneath its plumed surface, the Emperor of Germany bird of paradise possesses an architecture marking the culmination of an equally ancient history, with details exceeding those that can be imagined from the elaborate visible display of color and dance.

Consider one such bird analytically, as an object of biological research. Encoded within its chromosomes is the developmental program that has led to a male *Paradisaea guilielmi.* Its nervous system is a structure of fiber tracts more complex than that of any existing computer, and as challenging as all the rain forests of New Guinea surveyed on foot. Someday microscopic studies will permit us to trace the events culminating in the electric commands carried by the efferent neurons to the skeletal-muscular system and to reproduce, in part, the dance of the courting male. We will be able to dissect and understand this machinery at the level of the cell through enzymatic catalysis, microfilament configuration, and active sodium transport during electric discharge. Because biology sweeps the full range of space and time, more and more discoveries will renew our sense of wonder at each step of research. Altering the scale of perception to the micrometer and millisecond, the cellular biologist's trek parallels that of the naturalist across the land. He looks out from his own version of the mountain crest. His spirit of adventure, as well as personal history of hardship, misdirection, and triumph, is fundamentally the same.

Described this way, the bird of paradise may seem to have been turned into a metaphor of what humanists dislike most about science: that it reduces nature and is insensitive to art, that scientists are conquistadors who melt down the Inca gold. But science is not just analytic; it is also synthetic. It uses artlike intuition and imagery. True, in the early analytic stages, individual behavior can be mechanically reduced to the level of genes and neurosensory cells. But in the synthetic phase even the most elementary activity of these biological units is seen to create rich and subtle patterns at the levels of organism and society. The outer qualities of *Paradisaea guilielmi,* its plumes, dance, and daily life, are functional traits open to a deeper understanding through the exact description of their constituent parts. They can be redefined as holistic properties that alter our perception and emotion in surprising ways.

There will come a time when the bird of paradise is reconstituted through a synthesis of all the hard-won analytic information. The mind, exercising a new-found power, will journey back to the familiar world of seconds and centimeters, where once again the glittering plumage takes form and is viewed at a distance through a network of leaves and mist. Once again we see the bright eye open, the head swivel, the wings extend. But the familiar motions are now viewed across a far greater range of cause and effect. The species is understood more completely; misleading illusions have given way to more com-prehensive light and wisdom. With the completion of one full cycle of intellect, the scientist's search for the true material nature of the species is partially replaced by the more enduring responses of the hunter and poet.

What are these ancient responses? The full answer is available only through a combined idiom of science and the humanities, whereby the investigation turns back into itself. The human being, like the bird of paradise, awaits our examination in the analytic-synthetic manner. Feeling and myth can be viewed at a distance through physiological time, idiosyncratically, in the manner of traditional art. But they can also be penetrated more deeply than was ever possible in the prescientific age, to their physical basis in the processes of mental development, the brain structure, and indeed the genes themselves. It may even be possible to trace them back beyond the formation of cultures to the evolutionary origins of human nature. As each new phase of synthesis emerges from biological inquiry, the humanities will expand their reach and capability. In symmetric fashion, with each redirection of the humanities, science will add dimensions to human biology.

Reading and Thinking

1. Identify the key terms in Wilson's first sentence. Look them up if you do not understand them. In the first paragraph, what idea does Wilson promise to develop in his essay?

2. Consider the next three paragraphs (2–4). Why do you imagine Wilson has chosen to focus on the Huon Peninsula of New Guinea? Why does he pause during his trek to give us the distant, panoramic view?

3. Now focus on paragraphs 5–6. What is the relationship between those two descriptive paragraphs and the previous three paragraphs about his trek across the peninsula?

4. Finally, consider paragraphs 7–11. How does Wilson create his argument in those paragraphs? Can you detect a further organizational division within these last five paragraphs that points to the changing nature of scientific analysis? Explain.

Thinking and Writing

1. Why do you suppose Wilson singles out the bird of paradise to convey his argument? Is his explanation about going back into the origin of things adequate, or do you suppose there is more to it?

2. Consider paragraphs 5–6 again. Compare them to the paragraphs in Dillard's essay in which she describes the weasel. Compare and contrast those two paragraphs in terms of each writer's descriptive powers and in terms of their own interest in the creature being described. Are those seemingly pure descriptions colored by the writers' relationship to the creature being observed?

3. Look at Wilson's title again. What do the hunter and the poet have to do with one another? Working together, what can hunter and poet (analyst and synthesizer) achieve that they might miss working in only one frame of mind or the other?

4. How do Wilson's and Dillard's concerns differ? Write a short comparison and contrast piece based on your analysis of the two essays.

POETIC MOMENTS:
AN OCCASION FOR ANALYSIS

Turn now to this Occasion for thinking and writing about some of the ideas E. O. Wilson has raised about the analytical process, about how the scientist and the poet must somehow combine their ways of seeing and knowing to arrive at a deeper understanding about nature. Wilson's deep interest in origins pushes him back always to the beginnings. For him, going back is a way of going forward into deeper understanding. This Occasion asks you to respond to the beauty and mystery of a single photograph by Yann Arthus-Bertrand and then to re-examine your reaction through deeper analysis.

YANN ARTHUS-BERTRAND

Yann Arthus-Bertrand (b. 1946) is a French photographer and naturalist who is known the world over for his aerial photographs. He was once a game reserve director in France and he studied lions in Kenya. He founded the Earth from Above project in 1995 and has been awarded the Legion D'Honneur for his environmental work. His photographs have appeared in numerous books, including *Kenya from the Air*, *Turkey from the Air*, and *The Earth from Above*. This photograph was taken above Tsavo East National Park in Kenya.

PREPARING TO WRITE: TSAVO EAST NATIONAL PARK

1. Record your initial impression of the photograph, trying to capture the poetic essence of what you see. Be imaginative. Create a brief word-picture that will allow others to see what you are seeing.

2. Reconsider the photograph. Look carefully at the details. Be aware that you are looking down from above. What is the object with shadow near the very center? What might the bare spot around object and shadow be? What about the web of lines that seems to converge (or diverge) on that bare area? What can you see now that you did not see when you formed your initial impression of the photographic image?

Occasion

MOVING TOWARD ESSAY: ANALYSIS AND REFLECTION

1. Here is the text that accompanies Arthus-Bertrand's photograph in his book *Earth from Above*:

   > The acacia in Tsavo East National park is a symbol of life in vast desolate expanses, where wild animals come to take advantage of its leaves or its shade. Crossed by the Nairobi-Mobasa road and railway axis, the western region of the park is open to the public, whereas two-thirds of its more arid eastern segment is reserved to scientists. Tsavo was already famous for its many elephants when, in the 1970s, more pachyderms fleeing drought or poachers entered the park. Crowded into the limited space of the park, the elephants seriously damaged the vegetation. Controversy surrounded the question of whether selective slaughter was necessary, but poachers put a clear-cut end to the debate by exterminating more than 80 percent of the 36,000 elephants in the park. Today, Tsavo East National Park receives 100,000 visitors a day.

   How does this written text influence your thinking about the photograph? Do you consider this the final word about what you see? Explain.

2. The title of this photograph is "Tree of Life"—a reference as much to the function of the tree in the park as to the biblical Tree of Life in the Garden of Eden, also sometimes called "The Tree of Knowledge." In the biblical story, God has forbidden Adam and Eve to eat the fruit of the tree. However a serpent tempts Eve to eat the fruit, and she, in turn, tempts Adam. By eating the fruit, they have disobeyed God's order, and they are banished from the garden's paradise forever. What does the biblical reference in the title suggest about the tree in the photograph? Would you consider what you see in the photograph a kind of paradise lost (as in the biblical story), or an unspoiled paradise? Explain.

3. Think about E. O. Wilson's discussion of the poet and the hunter, and consider this poem by Aron Keesbury about the biblical story:

   > ### And Eve,
   >
   > she didn't know
   > who to believe
   >
   > so she chose
   >
   > the most reasonable
   > argument.

   How do Wilson's ideas about the poet and the hunter relate to Eve's experience as it is portrayed in this poem? Considering that the Tree of Life is also called the Tree of Knowledge, what choice does Eve face? What is she choosing between? In this poem, which is she, poet or hunter? Explain. In experiencing the photograph, which are you? Make notes toward a short paragraph, providing details from the photograph and elsewhere that you will use to convince your readers to see what you see, to experience what you experience.

WRITING THOUGHTFULLY: IDEA AND ESSAY

1. Revisit the question of whether this is an image of Paradise Lost or an image of beauty. Before you formulate your response, consider Daphne Sheldrick's argument that the "destruction" that elephants do to the landscape is actually crucial to the park and its ecostructure from an article entitled "The Impact of Elephants in Tsavo," found on The Sheldrick Wildlife Trust Web site. Consider her argument before you construct your argument about what the photograph reveals. Make your argument in the form of a short essay, using appropriate evidence from your analysis.

2. Write a brief account of how your seeing the image was affected by your knowing. What part did reason play? How do reason and beauty interact in your experience of the photograph? Consider whether at some point in your analysis, "knowing" began to limit what you could see in the photograph, or whether knowing more was always beneficial to your deeper understanding of the photograph. Think again of Wilson. Did you find yourself shifting between being a poet and being a hunter, being a synthesizer and being an analyst? Explain in your account.

3. *Comp21* **Video Extension.** Extend this Occasion to include CNN® video footage using the Explicator video analysis tool on *Comp21*. From the main menu choose "Frames of Mind: Extending Occasions" and select "Poetic Moments: An Occasion for Analysis" from the list.

Occasion

CREATING OCCASIONS

1. Consider another of Arthus-Bertrand's photographs. Begin this time with both his image and his title. Record your poetic impression of what you see. Does the title restrict what you are able to see? Explain.

Arthus-Bertrand, Thunderstorm

2. Consider the scientific representation of a thunderstorm above. Think carefully about the relationship between the photograph and the illustration. Identify what each leaves out. What is the effect of putting the two images together? Explain.

Occasion

Life Cycle of a Thunderstorm

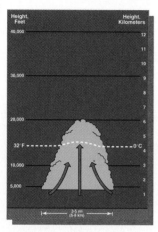

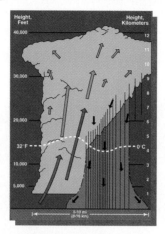

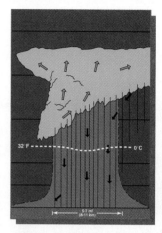

Developing Stage

✓ Towering cumulus cloud indicates rising air.
✓ Usually little if any rain during this stage
✓ Lasts about 10 minutes.
✓ Occasional lightning during this stage.

Mature Stage

✓ Most likely time for hail, heavy rain, frequent lightning, strong winds, and tornadoes.
✓ Storm occasionally has a black or dark green appearance.
✓ Lasts an average of 10 to 20 minutes but may last much longer in some storms.

Dissipating Stage

✓ Rainfall decreases in intensity.
✓ Some thunderstorms produce a burst of strong winds during this stage.
✓ Lightning remains a danger during this stage.

3. Considering the photograph, the illustration, and your experience, use your poetic mind to create for readers your own sense of a thunderstorm.

4. Create your own interactive Occasion on *Comp21* using the textual, visual, and video libraries, as well as the Explicator analysis tools. From the main menu, choose "Build Your Own Occasion for Writing."

chapter FOUR

DESCRIPTION

Description is an act of appropriation. We might playfully call it a writerly heist.

When describing, a writer attempts to take an object or an experience—most often from the visible world—into the mind, where it is translated into words to be made visible to others. Description can also be of abstract things—ideas, theories, thoughts, or dreams. In every case, language becomes the medium of exchange between writer and reader.

The effective translation of the thing into words allows the writer to transfer the selected object or experience to the reader, permitting the reader to see what the writer has seen, to experience what the writer has experienced.

But, of course, the descriptive act is always an imperfect act because language can never entirely capture the appropriated object or experience. Selected words and details always carry the mark, or personal stamp, of the translator. This mark is what makes each description unique and worth our close attention. For the writer, descriptions almost always serve a larger purpose.

. . . .

What makes an accurate description? Imagine trying to describe this photograph to a painter who cannot see the picture but has to reproduce it exactly. Since describing every detail would be impossible, what middle ground might you try to find?

THE NATURE OF
DESCRIPTION

To read more about Description with interactive examples and opportunities to work with interactive texts, click on "The Rhetorical Patterns of Inquiry" from the main menu of *Comp21*.

Writers rarely describe an object or experience for the sake of describing. They describe so that readers can see and experience and understand as they do. The grocer, trying to sell his wares, might say that the shiny red apple in his bin is juicy, delicious, firm in its ripeness, and ready for eating. The woman in the emergency room of the hospital would likely tell the story of an apple that was too green for eating, tart and acidic, too hard and sour to be digested. A chef might have spoken of a golden, delicious apple just picked from the back pasture, ripe but firm, juicy but not too sweet, and just right for baking.

Always, there is a purpose, a point of view, that informs the descriptive work.

Description is, by its very nature, a conflicted act—personal even as it aims to translate the object or the experience into a true-to-life linguistic version of itself. The writer is always deciding what to put in and what to leave out of the description. That dual act of selecting and omitting depends, as we will see again and again, on purpose.

Description is a sensual act, an attempt to capture the very nature of an object or an experience, an attempt to account for its sensory qualities. The descriptive act calls on the writer to pay particular attention to the five senses: touch, taste, smell, sound, and sight. A descriptive text will always contain rich details that carry distinctive sensory qualities to the reader.

. . . .

CREATING A LASTING
IMPRESSION BY SELECTING DETAILS

The world of experience is virtually infinite, so as a writer you have to select significant, representative moments to serve a particular rhetorical purpose. Whereas experience is infinite, language is limited, so the selection of details is crucial. Imagine trying to describe every spot on one side of an apple. The reader would be lost in too much detail. The details the writer selects allow readers to see, savor, and perhaps even experience the selected event. Organizing those details to create a desired effect enhances the translation of the moment into words.

The following paragraph is a student writer's effort to recreate a moment from childhood when her grandfather helped her unlock the secret of a kaleidoscope. As you read, think about the details themselves and the way that Lauren Covello has organized them to achieve a certain effect:

> It finds its way into my hands—the small kaleidoscope—a trinket my grandfather passes along to me after finding it at the bottom of his toolbox one afternoon. "Hold it up to the light, Lauren," he advises me, upon witnessing my attempts to unlock the kaleidoscope's magic by aiming it toward the shadowy pavement. With hands clasped, eyes squinted, and head cocked, I finally spot the colored chips, a glittering lattice of blue, green, yellow, stagnantly arranged and defined. "Turn it now," my grandfather orders, smiling. Suddenly, the composition unravels. It becomes a moving color war, triangles and rectangles interacting, skirting around one another to form patterns that linger only fleetingly before changing again. I gasp, intrigued. "That's the beautiful part," my grandfather observes. "It's beautiful when it's turning."

The selected details provide access to the sensory quality of the experience between a young girl and her grandfather. We can see the blankness in the instrument when it is pointed toward the "shadowy pavement"; we can see a difference when she finds the light and spots the "colored chips," the brighter but "stagnant pattern"; and, finally, we can see the movement as she turns the kaleidoscope, revealing even more of its "magic." There is also the telling detail about herself: "I gasp, intrigued." In this paragraph, Covello gives us three stages of discovery. Each stage is delineated by the details, and each set of details takes us deeper and deeper into her moment of discovery.

· · · · · · · · · ·

ORGANIZING DETAILS

The details you select will have to be arranged carefully in order to share effectively your experience with an audience. There are infinite ways to organize details—by importance, by intensity, or chronologically, to name a few. You will want to organize the details as you selected them, carefully considering what you would like your audience to experience. Covello's description is organized chronologically, as if the discovery were happening to us. Notice the marvelous sentence that reveals the moment when light and rotation unleash the "color war" for Covello and for us. Look carefully at how that sentence is organized within itself to bring the color war to life, extending the moment for us as Covello must have experienced it. We see as she did.

There is, of course, a larger purpose to this paragraph. This is only the beginning of a longer essay in which Covello develops the idea that our personality, our very identity, bears a striking resemblance to the colors and shapes and layers within the kaleidoscope. We are, she argues, a "work-in-progress," and a beautiful work at that, changing and evolving over a lifetime. The sensory details and their organization in this excerpt create a lasting impression of a moment plucked out of childhood and are also significant for their contribution to the greater meaning of the essay.

· · · · · · · · · ·

USING
FIGURATIVE LANGUAGE

The language of description is often highly suggestive, figurative, and metaphorical. The suggestive, comparative nature of such descriptive language suggests a larger rhetorical purpose. Recall how Saskia Verlaan likens the "lithe frame" of the rats to "the sun-bleached grasses of autumn fields, a casual reminder of their place in nature" (p. 44). She also asks us to see that certain features of the rats' anatomy hint at their "innocence." These comparisons and connections allow us to see, finally, that we have been led, by Verlaan, to understand how the rats could be repulsive and terrifying, while simultaneously eliciting Verlaan's compassion. Her descriptive work complicates our sense of the rats and foreshadows her complex response to them.

METAPHOR

A metaphor compares two dissimilar things. We are asked to see one thing as another; one is more concrete, more immediately apparent, than the other. The writer links the things, or objects, so that we may gain a better sense of the thing being described. The metaphor points us into a mystery of sorts.

When we say that identity is a kaleidoscope, the comparison is never intended to define precisely a concept as complicated as identity; it serves merely to help us better understand some aspect of identity. The kaleidoscope does not give us a solid definition, but through it we glimpse Covello's idea—that our identity forms over time, that it is continually changing, that there are layers and layers built up through the years.

SIMILE

Simile too effects a comparison. But the comparison is not as direct as in metaphor. Identity is like a kaleidoscope. The words *like* and *as* mark such a comparison, softening its effect. "My love is like a red, red rose," the poet exclaims. Upon hearing the comparison, we wait to know just how the rose might inform the poet's sense of love. The comparison draws our attention and sets the mind in motion.

The immediate effect of metaphor and simile is to shock us into awareness while simultaneously exciting our curiosity. We want to know just what the comparison will reveal in the hands of a thoughtful and skillful writer.

Beginning writers sometimes have a tendency to overdo descriptive work or to allow a metaphor to extend itself too far. They push the comparison beyond the breaking point, or they load sentences with adjectives and adverbs, giving the recreated moment, the object, or even the comparison more weight than it deserves. Writers become more effective with figurative language as they become more selective and precise in their choice of words and more apt in their comparisons.

Description works best when it does not call undue attention to itself, when it blends into the fabric of whatever else is being done, whether it be analysis, storytelling, illustration, or classification. Description strikes at the subliminal level, arousing us, almost always, with a sensory nudge.

· · · · · · · · · ·

DESCRIPTION
WITH A PURPOSE

A soccer player describing the pain of being kicked to a referee might use the word "splitting." However, the same player describing it to the television cameras might call it "exhilarating." In the first case, the player's purpose was to gain sympathy and, as simple as her one-word description was, she geared it toward doing exactly that. In the second case, her purpose was to impress the fans at home and gain their support. Clearly, her description of the pain as "exhilarating" is meant to convey a certain fortitude of spirit, a winning attitude. Later that afternoon, the same player describing the pain to the team physician may extend the description, selecting and organizing details to provide him with as much information as possible.

> When my left knee hit the ground, I could feel the cleats against my right knee. It felt like my kneecap twisted under the pressure of the other player's foot as she fell sideways. When her foot fell away, I felt a slight pop. Now it feels like there is a bruise underneath my kneecap and whenever I bend my leg, pain shoots through the whole area.

In an attempt to explain exactly what the pain feels like, this injured player selected details according to the *action* of the event. As a way of describing the *feeling* of pain, the player ends up describing the event that caused that pain. She organizes the details chronologically so that the doctor (who has no doubt experienced pain himself) can imagine the experience. Finally, she uses the metaphor "shoots" to allow the doctor to better envision her internal state.

Whether you are describing apples to a baker; rats to your classmates; or the pain of an injury to a referee, television cameras, or a doctor, your description will serve a larger purpose. The details you select, and the order in which you arrange those details, will depend greatly on what you are trying to accomplish with your description. In writing—especially writing a paper for a class—it is important to consider your audience. What do you want *them* to see, feel, smell, touch, hear? Why?

· · · · · · · · ·

DESCRIPTION
AND THE OTHER PATTERNS OF INQUIRY

Description most often sets something else in motion—an analytical act, a story, or an illustration. Not quite as ubiquitous as analysis, description nevertheless bears an especially close relationship to the other patterns of inquiry.

Recall the first reading in the chapter on analysis (p. 42-46). In her essay, Saskia Verlaan makes effective use of this apt description of rats:

> Rats, at least those of the upstate New York variety, don't look as mean as you would expect. Little more than overgrown mice, there is something in their tawny color and lithe frame that is reminiscent of the sun-bleached grasses of autumn fields, a casual reminder of their place in nature. Even their faces bear none of the typical features, the gleaming red eyes, gnashing fang-like teeth, and pointy elongated snouts that are usually associated with their species. Instead, their muzzles are blunt and boxy and their eyes are not red but rather a deep glossy black, hinting at an innocence that is no more or less profound than that of their cousins, the chipmunk and the deer mouse.

Verlaan was not developing an idea about rats; she was developing perspectives on fear, as the essay's title suggests, trying to figure out how the ragged edges of fear somehow suggest something significant about the complexity of the self.

Although not her primary subject, the rats were central to Verlaan's analysis, and her descriptive act set in motion an entire analytical section of her essay. Through a narrative account of her particular encounter with a group of rats, she moves us closer to her idea about fear. We can actually classify that entire section of her essay as a descriptive, narrative analysis of a haunting encounter between her and the rats.

We are most likely to find descriptive acts blended into other patterns. Description, properly done, allows us to see and to experience and allows the writer to give substance to other work he is doing. The primary use of description is to make us see, to make us feel and experience, and to put us in close proximity to an object or experience that we cannot otherwise access and savor.

· · · · · · · · · ·

DESCRIPTION
IN PURE FORM: ANNOTATED PARAGRAPHS

Virginia Woolf (1882–1941) came from a family of prominent Victorians. Woolf, who was self-educated, is often considered one of the finest writers of the twentieth century. Her novels changed the face of fiction, and her essays sparked controversy in her time and continue to do so in ours. She has become the subject of numerous biographies and critical studies, and her work—including stories, sketches, essays, and novels—has created a worldwide critical industry. Her most significant novels—*To The Lighthouse, Mrs. Dalloway, Jacob's Room, The Waves*—stand against time, a class unto themselves. The selected paragraphs come from a collection of Woolf's essays entitled *Moments of Being*. In the first selection, Woolf focuses on one of her favorite places, a house in the coastal village of St. Ives, in England. She recounts one of her earliest recollections, attempting to describe the nursery where she slept as a child.

But to fix my mind on the nursery—it had a balcony; there was a partition, but it joined the balcony of my father's and mother's bedroom. My mother would come out onto her balcony in her white dressing gown. There were passion flowers growing on the wall; there were great starry blossoms, with purple streaks, and large green buds, part empty, part full.

If I were a painter, I would paint these first impressions in pale yellow, silver, and green. There was the pale yellow blind; the green sea; and the silver of the passion flowers. I should make a picture that was globular; semi-transparent. I should make a picture of curved petals; of shells; of things that were semi-transparent; I should make curved shapes, showing the light through, but not giving a clear outline. Everything would be large and dim; and what was seen at the time would at the same time have been heard; sounds would come through this petal or leaf—sounds indistinguishable from sights. Sound and sight seem to make equal parts of these first impressions. When I think of the early morning in bed I also hear the caw of rooks falling from a great height. The sound seems to fall through an elastic, gummy air; which holds it up; which prevents it from being sharp and distinct. The quality of the air above Talland House seemed to suspend sound, to let it sink down slowly, as if it were caught in a blue gummy veil. The rooks cawing is part of the waves breaking—one, two, one, two—and the splash as the wave drew back and then it gathered again, and I lay there half awake, half asleep, drawing in such ecstasy as I cannot describe.

Annotations (margin notes):
- details: spatial
- colors
- painting now: colors, shapes
- sounds and sights
- memory
- air and sound
- outcome

We can imagine that Woolf, starting her description in a traditional way in that first short paragraph, feels she cannot give us as much of the experience as she wants to give us, so in the next paragraph she offers that interesting comparison between herself and a painter. She wants to push our imaginations into something more complex than the average, untrained eye can see. So she heightens the effect of her work by mixing sight and sound as a poet might, linking the two senses (through color and rhythm) in tandem.

Exercises

1. How effective is the opening phrase, "to fix my mind"? What does Woolf achieve by using it? How does it color that first short paragraph?

2. In the second paragraph, Woolf tells us what she would do if she were a painter. Then she paints. What does she permit you to see through her word-painting that you might not otherwise see? Explain.

3. What do you think Woolf's primary aim is in this descriptive work—to give you the room as it was, or to give you something else as well? Explain.

4. Could you draw a sketch of the room based on what Woolf has told you? If not, what have you been left with? What do you suppose has been left out?

DESCRIPTION
IN PURE FORM: AN ANNOTATED PARAGRAPH

In this next example, Woolf writes to recreate an experience instead of an object. Note her concerns as a writer as she goes about her descriptive work.

memory again — sense of touch → spatial — sound — effects →

now robust and sensual — sound, sight, touch, smell — all five senses

The next memory—all these color-and-sound memories hang together at St. Ives—was much more robust; it was highly sensual. It was later. It still makes me feel warm, as if everything were ripe; humming; sunny; smelling so many smells at once; and all making a whole that even now makes me stop—as I stopped then going down to the beach; I stopped at the top to look down at the gardens. They were sunk beneath the road. The apples were on a level with one's head. The gardens gave off a murmur of bees; the apples were red and gold; there were also pink flowers; and grey and silver leaves. The buzz, the croon, the smell, all seemed to press voluptuously against some membrane; not to burst it; but to hum round one such a complete rapture of pleasure that I stopped; smelt; and looked. But again I cannot describe that rapture. It was rapture rather than ecstasy.

For Woolf, years later, those two recollected moments could still be "more real than the present moment." Notice how she once again calls on the senses: sight, sound, smell, and touch. All of this descriptive work is done, according to Woolf, to give us the "whole" of a simple but profound and lasting moment.

Exercises

1. Focus on the sentence that begins, "It still makes me feel warm." What is the effect of Woolf's use of semicolons where there might ordinarily be commas? How does the rhythm thus created affect your understanding of the moment she describes? Explain.

2. Relate the words *buzz, smell,* and *croon* to the word *voluptuous*. How do those four words change your sense of Woolf's purpose? Explain.

3. Mark the alternating pattern, the movement from long to short, of Woolf's sentences. Describe the variety of sentences in this paragraph and then reflect on what those variations might have to do with your understanding of how a simple walk to the beach could be *voluptuous*.

4. Look up the words *ecstasy* and *rapture*. Explain why you think Woolf considered the experience of listening to the waves an ecstasy, and the experience of walking to the beach a rapture. The answer should be in her descriptions.

DESCRIPTION
IN ITS NATURAL HABITAT:
AN ANNOTATED READING

Cynthia Ozick (b. 1928) was born in New York City and earned her B.A. at New York University. After earning an M.A. at Ohio State University, she began writing fiction. She went on to write novels, novellas, short stories, and essays. Her many books include the novels *Trust, The Shawl, The Messiah of Stockholm,* and *The Puttermesser Papers* and two collections of essays, *Art and Ardor* and *Metaphor and Memory*. Her rich, precise language draws its power from a profusion of telling details and striking images.

NARRATION
count & identify the stories

COMPARISON & CONTRAST
Ozick & cousin

DESCRIPTION
trace the flaw

COMPARISON & CONTRAST
Uncle Jake & mother

CYNTHIA OZICK
The Seam of the Snail

In my Depression childhood, whenever I had a new dress, my cousin Sarah would get suspicious. The nicer the dress was, and especially the more expensive it looked, the more suspicious she would get. Finally she would lift the hem and check the seams. This was to see if the dress had been bought or if my mother had sewed it. Sarah could always tell. My mother's sewing had elegant outsides, but there was something catch-as-catch-can about the insides. Sarah's sewing, by contrast, was as impeccably finished inside as out; not one stray thread dangled.

My uncle Jake built meticulous grandfather clocks out of rosewood; he was a perfectionist, and sent to England for the clockworks. My mother built serviceable radiator covers and a serviceable cabinet, with hinged doors, for the pantry. She built a pair of bookcases for the living room. Once, after I was grown and in a house of my own, she fixed the sewer pipe. She painted ceilings, and also landscapes; she reupholstered chairs. One summer she planted a whole yard of tall corn. She thought herself capable of doing anything, and did everything she imagined. But nothing was perfect. There was always some clear flaw, never visible head-on. You had to look underneath where the seams were. The corn thrived, though not in rows. The stalks elbowed one another like gossips in a dense little village.

"The Seam of the Snail" displays Ozick's penchant for simile and metaphor and her ability to bring characters to life through detail and speech patterns. As you read the essay, pay attention to Ozick's various descriptions. What is she actually describing in each case? Note as well the different senses she appeals to.

"Miss Brrrrooooobaker," my mother used to mock, rolling her Russian *r*s, whenever I crossed a *t* she had left uncrossed, or corrected a word she had misspelled, or became impatient with a *v* that had tangled itself up with a *w* in her speech. ("*Vvv*entriloquist," I would say, "*Vvv*entriloquist," she would obediently repeat. And the next time it would come out "wiolinist.") Miss Brubaker was my high school English teacher, and my mother invoked her name as an emblem of raging finical obsession. "Miss Brrrrooooobaker," my mother's voice hoots at me down the years, as I go on casting and recasting sentences in a tiny handwriting on monomaniacally uniform paper. The loops of my mother's handwriting—it was the Palmer Method—were as big as hoops, spilling generous splashy ebullience. She could pull off, at five minutes' notice, a satisfying dinner for 10 concocted out of nothing more than originality and panache. But the napkin would be folded a little off-center, and the spoon might be on the wrong side of the knife. She was an optimist who ignored trifles; for her, God was not in the details but in the intent. And all these culinary and agricultural efflorescences were extracurricular, accomplished in the crevices and niches of a 14-hour business day. When she scribbled out her family memoirs, in heaps of dog-eared notebooks, or on the backs of old bills, or on the margins of last year's calendar, I would resist typing them; in the speed of the chase she often omitted words like "the," "and," "will." The same flashing and

DESCRIPTION
details: handwriting sentences

COMPARISON & CONTRAST
Ozick & mother

COMPARISON & CONTRAST
details vs. intent

DESCRIPTION
simile

DESCRIPTION
details of mother

COMPARISON & CONTRAST
block form: mother vs. Ozick

DESCRIPTION
Ozick herself

bountiful hand fashioned and fired ceramic pots, and painted brilliant autumn views and vases of imaginary flowers and ferns, and decorated ordinary Woolworth platters with lavish enameled gardens. But bits of the painted petals would chip away.

Lavish; my mother was as lavish as nature. She woke early and saturated the hours with work and inventiveness, and read late into the night. She was all profusion, abundance, fabrication. Angry at her children, she would run after us whirling the cord of the electric iron, like a lasso or a whip; but she never caught us. When, in the seventh grade, I was afraid of failing the Music Appreciation final exam because I could not tell the difference between "To a Wild Rose" and "Barcarolle," she got the idea of sending me to school with a gauze sling rigged up on my writing arm, and an explanatory note that was purest fiction. But the sling kept slipping off. My mother gave advice like mad—she boiled over with so much passion for the predicaments of strangers that they turned into permanent cronies. She told intimate stories about people I had never heard of.

Despite the gargantuan Palmer loops (or possibly because of them), I have always known that my mother's was a life of—intricately abashing word!—excellence: insofar as excellence means ripe generosity. She burgeoned, she proliferated; she was endlessly leafy and flowering. She wore red hats, and called herself a gypsy. In her girlhood she marched with the suffragettes and for Margaret Sanger and called herself a Red. She made me laugh, she was so varied: like a tree on which lemons, pomegranates, and prickly pears absurdly all hang together. She had the comedy of prodigality.

My own way is a thousand times more confined. I am a pinched perfectionist, the ultimate fruition of Miss Brubaker; I attend to crabbed minutiae and am self-trammeled through taking pains. I am a kind of human snail, locked in and condemned by my own nature. The ancients believed that the moist track left by the snail as it crept was the snail's own essence, depleting its body little by little; the farther the snail toiled, the smaller it be-

came, until it finally rubbed itself out. That is how per-
fectionists are. Say to us Excellence, and we will show you
how we use up our substance and wear ourselves away,
while making scarcely any progress at all. The fact that I
am an exacting perfectionist in a narrow strait only, and
nowhere else, is hardly to the point, since nothing matters to me so much as a comely and muscular sentence. It
is my narrow strait, this snail's road: the track of the sentence I am writing now; and when I have eked out the
wet substance, ink or blood, that is its mark, I will begin
the next sentence. Only in reading out sentences am I
perfectionist; but then there is nothing else I know how
to do, or take much interest in. I miter every pair of abut-
ting sentences as scrupulously as Uncle Jake fitted one
strip of rosewood against another. My mother's worldly
and bountiful hand has escaped me. The sentence I am
writing is my cabin and my shell, compact, self-sufficient.
It is the burnished horizon—a merciless planet where
flawlessness is the single standard, where even the inmost
seams, however hidden from a laxer eye, must meet perfection. Here "excellence" is not strewn casually from a
tipped cornucopia, here disorder does not account for
charm, here trifles rule like tyrants.

I measure my life in sentences, and my sentences
are superior to my mother's, pressed out, line by line,
like the lustrous ooze on the underside of the snail, the
snail's secret open seam, its wound, leaking attar. My
mother was too mettlesome to feel the force of a
comma. She scorned minutiae. She measured her life
according to what poured from the horn of plenty,
which was her ample, cascading, elastic, susceptible,
inexact heart. My narrower heart rides between the
tiny horns of the snail, dwindling as it goes.

And out of this thinnest thread, this ink-wet line of
words, must rise a visionary fog, a mist, a smoke, forg-
ing cities, histories, sorrows, quagmires, entangle-
ments, lives of sinners, even the life of my furnace-
hearted mother: so much wilderness, waywardness,
plentitude on the head of the precise and impeccable
snail, between the horns.

DESCRIPTION
metaphor extended

DESCRIPTION
writing perfect sentences

COMPARISON & CONTRAST
writer-mother

Natural Habitat

Ozick's brilliant descriptive work rides on the back of the stories she tells about different characters (herself, her cousin Sarah, her uncle Jake, her mother, and Miss Brrrroooobaker) and the comparisons she makes among these characters. The most important of these comparisons is, of course, that between Ozick and her mother. That comparison works itself out beautifully in the extended metaphor that takes up the last three paragraphs of the essay. Ozick wants us to see more clearly the difference between her own pinched perfection and her mother's abundance. We see that comparison manifested in the details: sewing, handwriting, and the two women's basic natures. The metaphor at the end draws on the descriptive work that comes before it.

Exercises

1. Beginning in the first paragraph, Ozick makes a number of cogent comparisons. Identify each comparison in the essay from beginning to end.

2. Highlight the details in the comparison between Ozick and her mother (para. 3). What do these details and their organization suggest to us about where this essay is headed?

3. The vehicle for Ozick's most elaborate and extended comparison appears in the third paragraph: the word *handwriting*. Trace, paragraph by paragraph, the way Ozick extends our sense of that word. In your own descriptive language, account for the importance of those turns and elaborations.

4. In the last three paragraphs, Ozick creates what we might call a qualified metaphor: "I am a kind of human snail." At the end of the essay, write a metaphor to replace those three, as if you were Ozick. Convey what the metaphor suggests without referring to it. Note what happens to your language. What is gained or lost?

READING

RICHARD SELZER

Richard Selzer (b. 1928) was born in Troy, New York, and was educated at Union College, Albany Medical College, and Yale University. He began writing at age forty, while still a surgeon at Yale. His work almost always focuses on some aspect of surgery. We get to see him in the operating room, making rounds, and meditating about his patients long after they have left his immediate care. His powerful descriptive language can make readers queasy as they go inside the human body to witness a bloody surgical procedure—an amputation, an excision, a moment of panic. His many books (including essays, short stories, and memoir) include *Rituals of Surgery; Mortal Lessons: Notes on the Art of Surgery; Confessions of a Knife; Down from Troy: A Doctor Comes of Age; Imagine a Woman and Other Tales; Raising the Dead: A Doctor's Encounter with His Own Mortality;* and *The Doctor Stories.*

Love Sick

"Love Sick" was taken from *Confessions of a Knife.* The essay gives you a vivid sense of Selzer's descriptive powers and his rousing sense of humor. As you will see in the essay, Selzer uses a different kind of language to describe love than you might immediately expect. As you read, pay attention to how Selzer's word choices describe love and how much his descriptions are of something else. Notice also his use of metaphor.

1   Love is an illness, and has its own set of obsessive thoughts. Behold the poor wretch afflicted with love: one moment strewn upon a sofa, scarcely breathing save for an occasional sigh upsucked from the deep well of his despair; the next, pacing *agitato,* his cheek alternately pale and flushed. Is he pricked? What barb, what gnat stings him thus?

At noon he waves away his plate of food. Unloved, he loathes his own body, and refuses it the smallest nourishment. At half-past twelve, he receives a letter. She loves him! And soon he is snout-deep in his dish, voracious as any wolf at entrails. Greeted by a friend, a brother, he makes no discernible reply, but gazes to and fro, unable to recall who it is that salutes him. Distraught, he picks up a magazine, only to stand wondering what it is he is holding. Was he once clever at the guitar? He can no longer play at all. And so it goes.

Ah, Cupid, thou wanton boy. How cruel thy sport!

See how the man of sorrows leans against a wall, one hand shielding his eyes from vertigo, the other gripping his chest to muffle the palpitations there. Let some stray image of his beloved flit across his mind, her toe perhaps, or scarf, and all at once, his chin and brow gleam with idiotic rapture. But wait! Now some trivial slight is recalled, and once again, his face is a mask of anguish, empurpled and carved with deep lines.

Such, such are the joys of love. May Heaven protect us, one and all, from this happiness. One marvels at the single-celled paramecium, who, without the least utterance of distemper, procreates by splitting in two. One can but envy the paramecium his solitary fission.

Love is an illness and, not unlike its sister maladies, hysteria, hypochondriasis, and melancholia, has its own set of obsessive thoughts. In love, the *idée fixe* that harries the patient every waking hour is not remorse, nor the fear of cancer, nor the dread of death, but that single other *person.* Every disease has its domain, its *locus operandi.* If, in madness, it is the brain, in cirrhosis, the liver, and lumbago, the spine, in love it is that web of knobs and filaments known as the autonomic nervous system. How ironic that here, in this all but invisible network, should lie hidden the ultimate carnal mystery. Mischievous Nature, having arranged to incite copulation by assigning opposite hormones to half the human race, and sculpted the curves of the flesh to accommodate the process, now throws over the primitive rite a magic veil, a web of difficulty that is the autonomic nervous system. It is the malfunction, the deficiency of this system that produces the disease of love. Here it fulminates, driving its luckless victims to madness or suicide. How many the lovers that have taken that final tragic step, and were found swinging from the limb of some lonely tree, airing their pathetic rags? The autonomic nervous system! Why not the massive liver? The solid spleen? Or the skin, from which the poison might be drawn with knife or poultice?

Lying upon the front of each of the vertebrae, from the base of the skull to the tip of the coccyx, is a paired chain of tiny nodes, each of which is connected to the spinal cord and to each other. From these nodes, bundles of nerves extend to meet at relay stations scattered in profusion throughout the body. These ganglia are in anatomical touch with their fellows by a system of circuitry complex and various enough to confound into self-destruction a whole race of computers. Here all is chemical rush and wave-to-wave ripple. Here is fear translated for the flesh, and pride and jealousy. Here dwell zeal and ardor. And love is contracted. By microscopic nervelets, the impulses are carried to all the capillaries, hair follicles and sweat glands of the body. The smooth muscle of the intestine, the lachrymal glands, the bladder, and the genitalia are all subject to the bombardment that issues from this vibrating harp of knobs and strings. Innumerable are the orders delivered: Constrict! Dilate! Secrete! Stand erect! It is all very busy, effervescent.

In defense of the autonomic nervous system, it must be said that it is uncrippled by the intellect or the force of the will. Intuition governs here. Here is one's flesh wholly trustworthy, for it speaks with honesty all the attractions and repulsions of our lives. Consciousness here would be an intruder, justly driven away from the realm of the transcendent. One *feels;* therefore one

is. No opinion but spontaneous feeling prevails. Is tomorrow's love expected? Yesterday's recalled? Instantly, the thought is captured by the autonomic nervous system. And alchemy turns wish and dream to ruddy reality. The billion capillaries of the face dilate and fill with blood. You blush. You are prettier. Is love spurned? Again the rippling, the dance of energy, and the bed of capillaries constricts, squeezing the blood from the surface to some more central pool. Now you blanch. The pallor of death is upon you. Icy are your own fingertips. It is the flesh responding to the death of love with its own facsimile.

Imagine that you are in the painful state of unrequited love. You are seated at a restaurant table with your beloved. You reach for the salt; at the same moment, she for the pepper goes. Your fingers accidentally touch cellar-side. There is a sudden instantaneous discharge of the autonomic nervous system, and your hand recoils. It is singed by fire. Now, the capillaries of your cheeks are commanded to dilate. They fill with blood. Its color is visible in your skin. You go from salmon pink to fiery red. "Why, you are blushing," she says, and smiles cruelly. Even as she speaks, your sweat glands have opened their gates, and you are coated with wetness. You sop. She sees, and raises one eyebrow. Now the sounds of your intestine, those gurgles and gaseous pops called borborygmi, come distinctly to your ears. You press your abdomen to still them. But, she hears! The people at the neighboring tables do, too. All at once, she turns her face to the door. She rises. Suddenly, it is time for her to go. Unhappy lover, you are in the grip of your autonomic nervous system, and by its betrayal you are thus undone.

Despite that love is an incurable disease, yet is there reason for hope. Should the victim survive the acute stages, he may then expect that love will lose much of its virulence, that it will burn itself out, like other self-limiting maladies. In fact, this is becoming more and more the natural history of love, and a good thing at that. Lucky is he in whom love dies, and lust lives on. For he who is tormented by the protracted fevers of chronic undying love await but a premature and exhausted death. While lust, which engages not the spirit, serves but to restore the vigor and stimulate the circulation.

10

Still, one dreams of bringing about a cure. For the discoverer of such, a thousand Nobels would be too paltry a reward. Thus I have engaged the initial hypothesis (call it a hunch) that there is somewhere in the body, under the kneecap perhaps, or between the fourth and fifth toes . . . somewhere . . . a single, as yet unnoticed master gland, the removal of which would render the person so operated upon immune to love. Daily, in my surgery, I hunt this *glans amoris,* turning over membranes, reaching into dim tunnels, straining all the warm extrusions of the body for some residue that will point the way.

Perhaps I shall not find it in my lifetime. But never, I vow it, shall I cease from these labors, and shall charge those who come after me to carry on the search. Until then, I would agree with my Uncle Frank, who recommends a cold shower and three laps around the block for the immediate relief of the discomforts of love.

Reading and Thinking

1. Focusing on the afflicted lover, Selzer begins this essay with an extended description of the effects of love. In these early paragraphs, what idea about love does his descriptive work suggest?

2. In the first six paragraphs, Selzer's language is hyperbolic—it exaggerates and plays. Does it work? Why?

3. In paragraph 6, Selzer repeats a part of the essay's first sentence: "Love is an illness." Concurrently, he shifts the focus of his descriptive work from the victim to the nature of the illness itself. How effective is his description of the illness in this paragraph? Explain.

4. What does the *paramecium* in paragraph 5 have to do with the *human race* in paragraph 6?

Thinking and Writing

1. When Selzer begins to account for the "autonomic nervous system," he uses technical language. Besides using humor, how else does Selzer accommodate this technical language to those of us who do not ordinarily speak it?

2. Four paragraphs from the end of the essay, Selzer addresses the reader directly: "Imagine that you are in a state of unrequited love." Does this direct address work? Why or why not?

3. Write Selzer a letter, trying to locate for him the *glans amoris* in some unsuspecting spot, rather than the usual sensual places. Be playful, vivid, and hyperbolic. Seek out odd comparisons.

THE TRUTH OF MIND
AN OCCASION FOR DESCRIPTION

In "Love Sick," Selzer describes the highly abstract notion of love in terms of its physical manifestation. This Occasion will give you a chance to describe an abstraction in much the same way. Here, though, the subject is lying.

Look at the first pair of images, which will give you a sense of the brain's structure. The bottom images show what happens in a person's brain when he or she makes a deliberate decision to lie. The brain scans that appear in these illustrations were done on a subject who was participating in an experiment called a Guilty Knowledge Test.

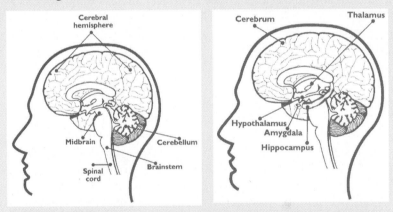

The parts of the brain

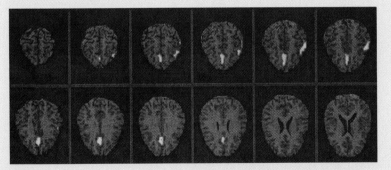

These brain scans were done with a procedure called functional magnetic resonance imaging (fMRI), which takes pictures of the brain in cross-sectional slices. The colored areas show where the brain is active when a person is lying.

Occasion

PREPARING TO WRITE: BRAIN IMAGES

1. Compare the first pair of images. Describe their differences. Note the technical terms that you recognize.

2. Use a dictionary or the Internet to define the terms that accompany the right-hand image. See if you can also find "prefrontal cortex."

3. The final panel of images shows a sequence of brain scans taken during the Guilty Knowledge Test. What do these photographs tell us about what happens? Account for what you think you see.

MOVING TOWARD ESSAY: ANALYSIS AND REFLECTION

1. Britton Chance, a biophysicist, supervises a team of researchers at the University of Pennsylvania. One of the researchers has designed a headband, outfitted with lights and detectors, that allows researchers access to a person's prefrontal cortex, where the brain makes decisions. The device can detect "a milliseconds-long burst of blood flow" such as the brain produces at the moment a person makes the decision to lie. Britton believes that one day the headband will not be needed; researchers or others will simply be able to point a sensing device at the front of the brain and detect the symptoms of lying. What questions does this procedure raise in your mind—about law-enforcement benefits, privacy rights, and medical benefits?

2. Another team of researchers at the University of Pennsylvania, led by assistant professor of psychiatry Daniel Langleben, conducted the Guilty Knowledge Test on a small group of volunteers. Each person chose an envelope that contained a five-of-clubs playing card and a cash incentive; each was told not to divulge what card he or she held.

   While being scrutinized inside an MRI machine, these subjects were sometimes told (by a computer) to utter a string of falsehoods and at other times to utter a string of truthful statements. According to Scientific American, it "turned out that all areas [of the brain] activated during truth telling were also triggered during lying but that a number of areas were active particularly during lying." According to Langleben, "That suggests that the default position is truth, and deception is some sort of process you perform on truth." He told Scientific American that several areas of the brain, including the anterior cingulate cortex and part of the left prefrontal cortex, areas where the brain chooses between conflicting responses, are activated more often during lying.

   What are your tentative conclusions about these two scientific procedures for catching liars? Should this preliminary research be curtailed or continued? Explain.

Occasion

3. Reconsider your response to the last question. MRIs are used to scan the brain for disease. They also detect other diseases, going well beyond genetic tests. Brain imaging can probe into the biology of behavior, and even thoughts. Do these benefits change your mind? Explain.

WRITING THOUGHTFULLY: IDEA AND ESSAY

1. Describe the effects of lying on the liar, leaving out of this initial description what you know about MRIs. Treat lying as Selzer treated love at the beginning of "Love Sick." Bring the malady to life.

2. Recall an occasion from your own life in which you observed firsthand the effects of lying. Render that moment as a scene. Pay particular attention to the importance of descriptive details and the way you order, or organize, the scene.

3. Shift your attention now to the general effects of lying on the body of the liar. Take advantage of the MRIs, the scientific research, and what Selzer has taught you about presenting this kind of information.

4. Write an essay about lying in which you make use of the work that you have done in response to the first three questions. Your task is to develop an idea of your own about lying.

CREATING OCCASIONS

1. Consider the ethical implications of "brain imagining," especially a person's right to privacy and constitutional protection. Consult at least two written sources as a part of your research. Write a short essay expressing your idea about the extent to which brain imagining should be controlled.

2. Consider another malady that would be fun to explore in an essay: stress, fear, or jealousy, for example. Research the subject on the Internet or in the library. See if brain imagining might provide useful information. If not, consider at least one scientific article about the malady. Write a short essay, developing your own humorous response to it.

 3. Create your own interactive Occasion on *Comp21* using the textual, visual, and video libraries, as well as the Explicator analysis tools. From the main menu, choose "Build Your Own Occasion for Writing."

E. M. FORSTER

E. M. Forster (1879–1970) is known to us today through his novels and the movies that have been based on them, especially *A Room with a View* and *Howards End*. But Forster was also a fine essayist with a wry, self-deprecating sense of humor. His style is brisk, clear, and often playful as he sets out with us to explore difficult, far-reaching topics. Always, we sense that we are in the company of someone who cares about decency, meaningful human relationships, and a world free of cant and the misuse of power. People and art matter more to him than conquest, so reading him, we begin to know that we can trust his judgments, whether they be about looking at art, the strong, the sensual pull of Italy and the Mediterranean, or the foibles of the English at home and abroad.

On Not Looking at Pictures

In "On Not Looking at Pictures," Forster takes us into an art gallery with his friends Roger Fry and Charles Mauron. Each friend teaches Forster and the reader (as eavesdropper) something about art that Forster himself claims not to know much about—its structure or form. When Forster tries to look at art, his mind darts off to other places; the images set his imagination to work. Fry and Mauron insist that we look not only at the image itself but at the way it is made. They focus our attention on diagonals, paint, composition, texture, foreground, background, and movement. The reader is asked to see the paintings and to not see the paintings, to learn and to play under Forster's guidance.

1 Pictures are not easy to look at. They generate private fantasies, they furnish material for jokes, they recall scraps of historical knowledge, they show landscapes where one would like to wander and human beings whom one would like to resemble or adore, but looking at them is another matter, yet they must have been painted to be looked at. They were intended to appeal to the eye, but almost as if it were gazing at the sun itself the eye often reacts by closing as soon as it catches sight of them. The mind takes charge instead and goes off on some alien vision. The mind has such a congenial time that it forgets what set it going. Van Gogh and Corot and Michelangelo are three different painters, but if the mind is indisciplined and uncontrolled by the eye, they may all three induce the same mood, we may take just the same course through dreamland or funland from them, each time, and never experience anything new.

I am bad at looking at pictures myself, and the late Roger Fry enjoyed going to a gallery with me now and then, for this very reason. He found it an amusing change to be with someone who scarcely ever saw what the painter had painted. "Tell me, why do you like this, why do you prefer it to that?" he would ask, and listen agape for the ridiculous answer. One day we looked at a fifteenth-century Italian predella, where a St. George was engaged in spearing a dragon of the plesiosaurus type. I laughed. "Now, *what* is there funny in this?" pounced Fry. I readily explained. The fun was to be found in the expression upon the dragon's face. The spear had gone through its hooped-up neck once, and now startled it by arriving at a second thickness. "Oh dear, here it comes again, I hoped that was all" it was thinking. Fry laughed too, but not at the misfortunes of the dragon. He was amazed that anyone could go so completely off the lines. There was no harm in it—but really, really! He was even more amazed when our enthusiasms coincided: "I fancy we are talking about different things," he would say, and we always were; I liked the mountain-back because it reminded me of a peacock, he because it had some structural significance, though not as much as the sack of potatoes in the foreground.

Long years of wandering down miles of galleries have convinced me that there must be something rare in those coloured slabs called "pictures," something which I am incapable of detecting for myself, though glimpses of it are to be had through the eyes of others. How much am I missing? And what? And are other modern sight-seers in the same fix? Ours is an aural rather than a visual age, we do not get so lost in the concert hall, we seem able to hear music for ourselves, and to hear it as music, but in galleries so many of us go off at once into a laugh or a sigh or an amorous daydream. In vain does the picture recall us. "What have your obsessions got to do with me?" it complains. "I am neither a theatre of varieties nor a spring-mattress, but paint. Look at my paint." Back we go—the picture kindly standing still meanwhile, and being to that extent more obliging than music—and resume the looking-business. But something is sure to intervene— a tress of hair, the half-open door of a summer-house, a Crivelli dessert, a Bosch fish-and-fiend salad—and to draw us away.

One of the things that helps us to keep looking is composition. For many years now I have associated composition with a diagonal line, and when I find such a line I imagine I have gutted the picture's secret. Giorgione's Castelfranco Madonna has such a line in the lance of the warrior-saint, and Titian's Entombment at Venice has a very good one indeed. Five figures contribute to make up the diagonal; beginning high on the left with the statue of Moses, it passes through the heads of the Magdalene, Mary, and the dead Christ, and plunges through the body of Joseph of Arimathea into the ground. Making a right angle to it, flits the winged Genius of Burial. And to the right, apart from it, and perpendicular, balancing the Moses, towers the statue of Faith. Titian's Entombment is one of my easiest pictures. I look at photographs of it intelligently, and encourage the diagonal and the pathos to reinforce one another. I see, with more than usual vividness, the grim alcove at the back and the sinister tusked pedestals upon which the two statues stand. Stone shuts in flesh; the whole picture is a tomb. I hear

sounds of lamentation, though not to the extent of shattering the general scheme; that is held together by the emphatic diagonal, which no emotion breaks. Titian was a very old man when he achieved this masterpiece; that too I realise, but not immoderately. Composition here really has been a help, and it is a composition which no one can miss; the diagonal slopes as obviously as the band on a threshing-machine, and vibrates with power.

Unfortunately, having no natural esthetic aptitude, I look for diagonals everywhere, and if I cannot find one think the composition must be at fault. It is a word which I have learnt—a solitary word in a foreign language. For instance, I was completely baffled by Velásquez's Las Meninas. Wherever was the diagonal? Then the friend I was with—Charles Mauron, the friend who, after Roger Fry, has helped me with pictures most—set to work on my behalf, and cautiously underlined the themes. There is a wave. There is a half-wave. The wave starts up on the left, with the head of the painter, and curves down and up through the heads of the three girls. The half-wave starts with the head of Isabel de Velasco, and sinks out of the canvas through the dwarfs. Responding to these great curves, or inverting them, are smaller ones on the women's dresses or elsewhere. All these waves are not merely pattern; they are doing other work too—e.g., helping to bring out the effect of depth in the room, and the effect of air. Important too is the pushing forward of objects in the extreme left and right foregrounds, the easel of the painter in the one case, the paws of a placid dog in the other. From these, the composition curves back to the central figure, the lovely child-princess. I put it more crudely than did Charles Mauron, nor do I suppose that his account would have been Velásquez's, or that Velásquez would have given any account at all. But it is an example of the way in which pictures should be tackled for the benefit of us outsiders: coolly and patiently, as if they were designs, so that we are helped at last to the appreciation of something non-mathematical. Here again, as in the case of the Entombment, the composition and the action reinforced one another. I viewed with increasing joy that adorable party, which had been surprised not only by myself but by the King and Queen of Spain. There they were in the looking-glass! Las Meninas has snap-shot quality. The party might have been taken by Philip IV, if Philip IV had had a Kodak. It is all so casual—and yet it is all so elaborate and sophisticated, and I suppose those curves and the rest of it help to bring this out, and to evoke a vanished civilisation.

Besides composition there is colour. I look for that, too, but with even less success. Colour is visible when thrown in my face—like the two cherries in the great grey Michael Sweertz group in the National Gallery. But as a rule it is only material for dream.

On the whole, I am improving, and after all these years, I am learning to get myself out of the way a little, and to be more receptive, and my appreciation of pictures does increase. If I can make any progress at all, the average outsider should do better still. A combination of courage and modesty is what he wants. It is so unenterprising to annihilate everything that's made to a green thought, even when the thought is an exquisite one. Not looking at art leads to one goal only. Looking at it leads to so many.

Reading and Thinking

1. What do you think of Forster's claim that when looking at pictures, the "mind takes charge . . . and goes off on some alien vision"? Is that true of your own experience?
2. Roger Fry was a distinguished art critic during the last century. Why do you think that Forster puts him in this essay along with Charles Mauron?
3. Besides describing the paintings that he and Fry see in the gallery, Forster describes other things. Select the description that most interests you, and characterize how Forster uses descriptive language and how he organizes his description. Account for his larger purpose.

Thinking and Writing

1. Describe Forster's way of approaching a painting. Describe Roger Fry's way.
2. Look up the word *esthetic* (or *aesthetic*). Forster uses the phrase "esthetic aptitude" and claims that he doesn't have any. Based on what he tells you about his way of seeing and Fry's way of seeing, do you believe Forster's claim about himself? Explain.
3. Write a short essay in response to Forster's final pair of claims: "Not looking at art leads to one goal only. Looking at it leads to so many." Select your own art objects to help you support your idea. Be sure to recreate those objects so that the reader can see them through your words.

Reading

WAYS OF SEEING (AND NOT)
AN OCCASION FOR DESCRIPTION

In this Occasion, you will have an opportunity to describe a painting by Diego Velásquez—*Las Meninas,* 1656. The painting may seem outdated. But as you begin to look closely, you may begin to think less of a particular historical time period than of the playful mind of the painter himself. Velásquez seems to want to teach us something about *seeing* by playing with our minds and our eyes.

DIEGO VELÁSQUEZ

Diego Velásquez (1599–1660) was born in Seville, Spain, the oldest of six children. He was an apprentice to artist Francisco Pacheco, married Pacheco's daughter, and became court painter for King Philip IV. His work is said to have influenced Goya, Corot, Courbet, Manet, and Whistler. His most famous paintings include *The Surrender of Breda, Pope Innocent X, Christ at Emmaus,* and *Las Meninas (Maids of Honor).*

PREPARING TO WRITE: LAS MENINAS

1. Where does your eye settle in this painting? Why does it settle there?

2. Find eleven people in the painting. Describe each of them briefly.

3. Count at least nine frames in the painting. Describe the boundaries of each.

4. The mirror to the painter's left reflects Queen Mariana and King Philip IV. Where are they actually located?

5. Which figure is the young princess (Infanta Margarita) and which are the maids of honor? Describe how you know.

Velásquez, Las Meninas

Diego Velásquez, Las Meninas, 1656, Oil on Canvas. Courtesy of Museo Nacional Del Prado.

1. Consider this painting by Titian entitled *Entombment (Pietà)*.

Tiziano, "La Pietà" c. 1577, Gallerie dell' Academia, Venezia.

Forster, serving as museum guide, invites us to see the diagonal that runs from the top of Moses' head on the left down across all of the figures to Joseph of Arimathea on the right. Describe your reaction to Forster's encouragement that the "diagonal and the pathos reinforce one another" in the painting.

2. Turn your attention to what Forster and his friend Charles Mauron have to say about the composition of *Las Meninas* (para. 5). Describe your reaction to their claim about the waves. Can you see them? Trace the various lines that you see forming within the painting (they need not be wavy or circular).

Occasion

WRITING THOUGHTFULLY: IDEA AND ESSAY

1. Assume that you are King Philip IV, that you and your wife are standing outside the frame looking in on the scene as Velásquez paints *Las Meninas*. Tell Velásquez what you think of his representation of you and the court. Write out your assessment in the form of an official decree.

2. In her essay "Georgia O'Keeffe" (pp. 106-108), Joan Didion reveals that O'Keeffe's paintings tell us something about her character. Didion generalizes, "style is character." What do you think *Las Meninas* tells us about Velásquez's character? Reveal your answer in a letter to a museum curator who is assembling an exhibit focusing on humor in classical art.

3. Assume that after all these years, Velásquez is still standing there looking at his viewers. Today, you are the subject of his painterly eye. You have replaced the king and queen in the mirror. Describe what Velásquez can represent of you physically, but also describe what he can see in your eyes in your reaction to his painting.

CREATING OCCASIONS

1. Go to the Internet or the library and locate one of René Magritte's paintings from the *Human Condition* series. Consider any one of those paintings in terms of *Las Meninas*. Describe one of those paintings so that Velásquez could both see and understand it in terms of *Las Meninas*. Have fun with this description.

2. Create your own interactive Occasion on *Comp21* using the textual, visual, and video libraries, as well as the Explicator analysis tools. From the main menu, choose "Build Your Own Occasion for Writing."

READING

JOAN DIDION

Joan Didion (b. 1934) is a novelist and essayist whose work often focuses on American politics and popular culture. In all of her work, there is a subtle, understated longing for a less complex, more stable world than the one we inhabit, but she looks steadfastly into the whirl of contemporary events, reporting what she sees in a style that probes beneath the surface of things. For Didion, to face the personal, the self, is to face the world. We sense behind her fragile physical appearance a tough, clear-headed woman who knows what we need to know to survive against the odds. Her books include *Slouching toward Bethlehem, The White Album, Salvador, Miami,* and *After Henry* (all nonfiction), as well as the novels *Run River Run, Play It As It Lays,* and *The Book of Common Prayer.*

Georgia O'Keeffe

In her essay "Georgia O'Keeffe," Didion conveys something important about O'Keeffe and her art. For Didion, O'Keeffe's toughness, her independence from the men who wanted her to paint in a certain way, is reflected in her paintings. Didion calls this special quality *hardness,* and she sees it as a virtue. Those paintings—their composition, their subject matter, and their distinctiveness—convince Didion that "style is character," that O'Keeffe's style represents her character. We learn about the men of New York and their criticism and about O'Keeffe's response to them. Our learning takes place through the fine descriptive work in the essay; she makes it possible for us simultaneously to see the selected paintings and to peer into O'Keeffe's character.

1 "Where I was born and where and how I have lived is unimportant," Georgia O'Keeffe told us in the book of paintings and words published in her ninetieth year on earth. She seemed to be advising us to forget the beautiful face in the Stieglitz photographs. She appeared to be dismissing the rather condescending romance that had attached to her by then, the romance of extreme good looks and advanced age and deliberate isolation. "It is what I have done with where I have been that should be of interest." I recall an August afternoon in Chicago in 1973 when I took my daughter, then seven, to see what Georgia O'Keeffe had done with where she had been. One of the vast O'Keeffe "Sky Above Clouds" canvases floated over the back stairs in the Chicago Art Institute that day, dominating what seemed to be several stories of empty light, and my daughter looked at it once, ran to the landing, and kept on looking. "Who drew it," she whispered after a while. I told her. "I need to talk to her," she said finally.

My daughter was making, that day in Chicago, an entirely unconscious but quite basic assumption about people and the work they do. She was assuming that the glory she saw in the work reflected a glory in its maker, that the painting was the painter as the poem is the poet, that every choice one made alone—every word chosen or rejected, every brush stroke laid or not laid down—betrayed one's character. *Style is character.* It seemed to me that afternoon that I had rarely seen so instinctive an application of this familiar principle, and I recall being pleased not only that my daughter responded to style as character but that it was Georgia O'Keeffe's particular style to which she responded: this was a hard woman who had imposed her 192 square feet of clouds on Chicago.

"Hardness" has not been in our century a quality much admired in women, nor in the past twenty years has it even been in official favor for men. When hardness surfaces in the very old we tend to transform it into "crustiness" or eccentricity, some tonic pepperiness to be indulged at a distance. On the evidence of her work and what she has said about it, Georgia O'Keeffe is neither "crusty" nor eccentric. She is simply hard, a straight shooter, a woman clean of received wisdom and open to what she sees. This is a woman who could early on dismiss most of her contemporaries as "dreamy," and would later single out one she liked as "a very poor painter." (And then add, apparently by way of softening the judgment: "I guess he wasn't a painter at all. He had no courage and I believe that to create one's own world in any of the arts takes courage.") This is a woman who in 1939 could advise her admirers that they were missing her point, that their appreciation of her famous flowers was merely sentimental. "When I paint a red hill," she observed coolly in the catalogue for an exhibition that year, "you say it is too bad that I don't always paint flowers. A flower touches almost everyone's heart. A red hill doesn't touch everyone's heart." This is a woman who could describe the genesis of one of her most well-known paintings—the "Cow's Skull: Red, White and Blue" owned by the Metropolitan—as an act of quite deliberate and derisive orneriness. "I thought of the city men I had been seeing in the East," she wrote. "They talked so often of writing the Great American Novel—the Great American Play—the Great American Poetry. . . . So as I was painting my cow's head on blue I thought to myself, 'I'll make it an American painting. They will not think it great with the red stripes down the sides—Red, White and Blue—but they will notice it.'"

The city men. The men. They. The words crop up again and again as this astonishingly aggressive woman tells us what was on her mind when she was making her astonishingly aggressive paintings. It was those city men who stood accused of sentimentalizing her flowers: "I made you take time to look at what I saw and when you took time to really notice my flower you hung all your associations with flowers on my flower and you write about my flower as if I think and see what you think and see—and I don't." *And I don't.* Imagine those words spoken, and the sound you hear is *don't tread on me.* "The men" believed it impossible to paint New York, so Georgia O'Keeffe painted New York. "The men" didn't think much of her bright color, so she made it brighter. The men yearned toward Europe so she went to Texas, and then New Mexico. The men talked about Cézanne, "long involved remarks about the 'plastic quality' of his form and color," and took one another's long involved remarks, in the view of this angelic rattlesnake in their midst, altogether too seriously. "I can paint one of those dismal-colored paintings like the men," the woman who regarded herself always as an outsider remembers thinking one day in 1922, and she did: a painting of a shed "all low-toned and dreary with the tree beside the door." She called this act of rancor "The Shanty" and hung it in her next show. "The men seemed to approve of it," she reported fifty-four years later, her contempt undimmed. "They seemed to think that maybe I was beginning to paint. That was my only low-toned dismal-colored painting."

Some women fight and others do not. Like so many successful guerrillas in the war between the sexes, Georgia O'Keeffe seems to have been equipped early with an immutable sense of who she was and a fairly clear understanding that she would be required to prove it. On the surface her upbringing was conventional. She was a child on the Wisconsin prairie who played with china dolls and painted watercolors with cloudy skies because sunlight was too hard to paint and, with her brother and sisters, listened every night to her mother read stories of the Wild West, of Texas, of Kit Carson and Billy the Kid. She told adults that she wanted to be an artist and was embarrassed when they asked what kind of artist she wanted to be: she had no idea "what kind." She had no idea what artists did. She had never seen a picture that interested her, other than a pen-and-ink Maid of Athens in one of her mother's books, some Mother Goose illustrations printed on cloth, a tablet cover that showed a little girl with pink roses, and the painting of Arabs on horseback that hung in her grandmother's parlor. At thirteen, in a Dominican convent, she was mortified when the sister corrected her drawing. At Chatham Episcopal Institute in Virginia she painted lilacs and sneaked time alone to walk out to where she could see the line of the Blue Ridge Mountains on the horizon. At the Art Institute in Chicago she was shocked by the presence of live models and wanted to abandon anatomy lessons. At the Art Students League in New York one of her fellow students advised her that, since he would be a great painter and she would end up teaching painting in a girls' school, any work of hers was less important than modeling for him. Another painted over her work to show her how the Impressionists did trees. She had not before heard how the Impressionists did trees and she did not much care.

At twenty-four she left all those opinions behind and went for the first time to live in Texas, where there were no trees to paint and no one to tell her how not to paint them. In Texas there was only the horizon she craved. In Texas she had her sister Claudia with her for a while, and in the late afternoons they would walk away from town and toward the horizon and watch the evening star come out. "That evening star fascinated me," she wrote. "It was in some way very exciting to me. My sister had a gun, and as we walked she would throw bottles into the air and shoot as many as she could before they hit the ground. I had nothing but to walk into nowhere and the wide sunset space with the star. Ten watercolors were made from that star." In a way one's interest is compelled as much by the sister Claudia with the gun as by the painter Georgia with the star, but only the painter left us this shining record. Ten watercolors were made from that star.

Reading and Thinking

1. In the first two paragraphs, Didion describes O'Keeffe and the large painting that fascinated her daughter, *Sky Above Clouds*. How do those descriptions differ as she tries to give us a woman on the one hand and a painting on the other?

2. Throughout the essay Didion pays particular attention to three objects: O'Keeffe, her art, and the men. How do Didion's descriptions of these objects contribute to her ideas about "hardness" and the notion that style is character?

3. Turn to Didion's fourth paragraph about *"the city men."* As she describes the battle between an "angelic rattlesnake" and "the men," how does she, through various kinds of descriptions, give substance to her claim that O'Keeffe was actually set in motion by these men?

Thinking and Writing

1. In paragraph 6, Didion accounts for O'Keeffe's life from childhood until the time she moved to Texas. How does her description help her account for such a long period of time in such a short space? Explain in terms of selected detail and organization.

2. In the essay's last paragraph, what do the descriptions of O'Keeffe in Texas tell us about why she was such an effective adversary for the men of New York?

3. Referring to the men, O'Keeffe makes this judgment: "I made you take time to look at what I saw and when you took time to really notice my flower you hung all your associations with flowers on my flower and you write about my flower as if I think and see what you think and see—and I don't." Write a short letter to O'Keeffe telling her whether you think that we are capable of seeing an object (such as one of her paintings) as it really is, free of our own associations.

ANIMATING DESCRIPTIONS
AN OCCASION FOR DESCRIPTION

In this Occasion, you will have an opportunity to use your descriptive powers to capture the essence of two compelling art objects: *Cow's Skull: Red, White, and Blue* and *Train at Night in the Desert*. Didion and O'Keeffe will be your guides as you try to figure out for yourself just what an artist's work can reveal to an interested observer and just what your own descriptive work can contribute to your understanding.

Georgia O'Keeffe

Georgia O'Keeffe (1887–1986) was, as Didion has told us, a woman of great strength. Her paintings appear in museums all over the world and in the Georgia O'Keeffe Museum in Santa Fe, New Mexico. She changed art critics' minds about what a woman could paint, what a woman could do. Her work with particular objects (flowers, buildings, landscapes) tends toward the abstract but almost never abandons the objects themselves. The work is sensuous, but it can also be stark at the same time, especially in the paintings that focus on aspects of the American southwest.

PREPARING TO WRITE: COW'S SKULL: RED, WHITE, AND BLUE

1. Where does the painting draw your eye when you first look at it? Describe the way your eye and mind move into the painting.

2. Concentrate on the colors. Name them. Describe how O'Keeffe's use of color affects you.

3. Consider shapes. How many triangular shapes do you see? Describe them.

4. Finally, think about flatness and depth. Describe how O'Keeffe achieves depth in this painting. Describe how her use of flatness and depth affects your reaction to the painting.

Occasion

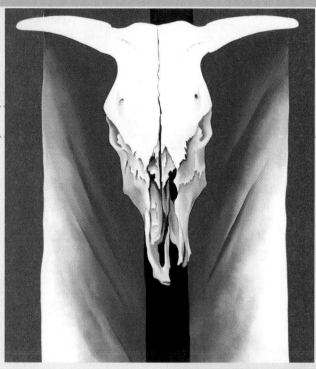

Occasion

ANIMATING DESCRIPTIONS: AN OCCASION FOR DESCRIPTION

PREPARING TO WRITE: TRAIN AT NIGHT IN THE DESERT

1. Describe the various shapes that you see in this watercolor.

2. Name the colors. Select two or three of them and describe how they affect one another. How do they affect you?

3. Do you see this as a static image or a moving image? Explain.

4. What happens to the image when you become aware of its title: *Train at Night in the Desert*? Does the title bring the image to rest or set it in motion? Is the train moving toward us or away from us? Explain.

5. Do you see any signs in this watercolor that O'Keeffe is having fun with her art? Explain.

MOVING TOWARD ESSAY: ANALYSIS AND REFLECTION

1. Create a two-paragraph word-picture of *Cow's Skull*. In the first paragraph, let your reader see the painting as it is. In the second paragraph, let your reader see it as you see it with your mental eye. Repeat this process for *Train at Night in the Desert*.

2. Didion, writing about style as character, chooses *Cow's Skull* to tell us something important about O'Keeffe's character. Considering what Didion says and what you see in the painting, what can you add to Didion's assessment about O'Keeffe's "hardness"?

3. To what extent is Didion's sense of O'Keeffe's "hardness" called into account by *Train at Night in the Desert*? Explain.

WRITING THOUGHTFULLY: IDEA AND ESSAY

1. Go to the Internet or the library and find one of O'Keeffe's flower paintings. Describe how that painting affects your assessment of Didion's claim about "hardness."

2. Describe the various relationships, correspondences, or differences that you see among O'Keeffe's paintings of the skull, the train, and the flower you selected. Then use the descriptions to help you make and establish a claim about what is in those paintings besides the objects themselves.

3. Broaden your consideration of Didion's claim that "style is character." Consider other artists (painters, movie makers, song writers, photographers). As you develop your own independent claim, be sure to make clear what you mean by style and by character.

4. *Comp21* **Video Extension.** Extend this Occasion to include CNN® video footage using the Explicator video analysis tool on *Comp21*. From the main menu choose "Frames of Mind: Extending Occasions" and select "Animating Descriptions: An Occasion for Description" from the list.

CREATING OCCASIONS

1. Select your favorite art object (photograph, painting, sculpture, or building) and create a word-picture of it. Account for your relationship to the selected object. Either describe the relationship, or create a short scene that reveals it. What does the relationship between you and the selected object suggest about human nature in general? Let that suggestion draw you to another moment of experience that seems related to your idea. Recreate that moment. Finally, bring yourself, the object, and the related moment together, and write a short paper that accounts for your findings, citing descriptive evidence.

2. Create your own interactive Occasion on *Comp21* using the textual, visual, and video libraries, as well as the Explicator analysis tools. From the main menu, choose "Build Your Own Occasion for Writing."

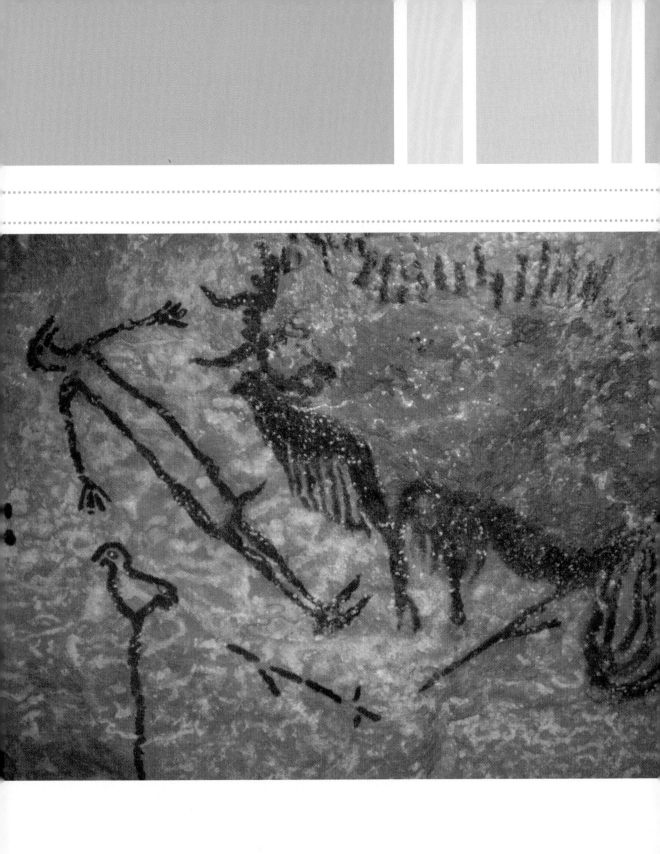

chapter FIVE

NARRATION

This photograph, taken from the caves at Lascaux in France, tells a simple story. As one of the first known "written" records, it illustrates that narration has been a central form of communication since communication began.

© Charles & Josette Lenars/CORBIS.

Narration is a form of storytelling—perhaps our most natural way of accounting for our lives.

- "Let me tell you about what happened at the barbecue last week," Uncle Joe says.
- "You will never believe what happened in chemistry class today," your roommate tells you.
- "Did you hear about John and Mary Hope?" Forest asks.

And so the stories begin. Some of us are better than others at telling these stories, but we all tell them. They are the currency of our daily exchange. We swap our lives through the stories we tell.

When writers tell stories, they always *order* the events of the stories so that listeners can follow the telling. That ordering may simply repeat what happened as the writer remembers it, or the writer may change the order to emphasize certain aspects of the story and create a *desired effect.*

The best storytellers want us to understand the story from their point of view, so they select *telling details* and emphasize relationships among events. One event says something about another event, and these *causal connections* point toward meaning—or the storyteller's intended purpose for the story.

around us because this is a different county. The only time I see the friends I knew is when we go back to our old church. The new school is the former state penitentiary. It is a large stone building, cold and drafty, crammed to overflowing with boisterous, ill-disciplined children. On the third floor there is a huge circular imprint of some partition that has been torn out.

"What used to be here?" I ask a sullen girl next to me on our way past it to lunch.

"The electric chair," says she.

At night I have nightmares about the electric chair, and about all the people reputedly "fried" in it. I am afraid of the school, where all the students seem to be budding criminals.

20   "What's the matter with your eye?" they ask, critically.

When I don't answer (I cannot decide whether it was an "accident" or not), they shove me, insist on a fight.

My brother, the one who created the story about the wire, comes to my rescue. But then brags so much about "protecting" me, I become sick.

After months of torture at school, my parents decide to send me back to our old community, to my old school. I live with my grandparents and the teacher they board. But there is no room for Phoebe, my cat. By the time my grandparents decide there is room, and I ask for my cat, she cannot be found. Miss Yarborough, the boarding teacher, takes me under her wing, and begins to teach me to play the piano. But soon she marries an African—a "prince," she says—and is whisked away to his continent.

At my old school there is at least one teacher who loves me. She is the teacher who "knew me before I was born" and bought my first baby clothes. It is she who makes life bearable. It is her presence that finally helps me turn on the one child at the school who continually calls me "one-eyed bitch." One day I simply grab him by his coat and beat him until I am satisfied. It is my teacher who tells me my mother is ill.

25   My mother is lying in bed in the middle of the day, something I have never seen. She is in too much pain to speak. She has an abscess in her ear. I stand looking down on her, knowing that if she dies, I cannot live.

She is being treated with warm oils and hot bricks held against her cheek. Finally a doctor comes. But I must go back to my grandparents' house. The weeks pass but I am hardly aware of it. All I know is that my mother might die, my father is not so jolly, my brothers still have their guns, and I am the one sent away from home.

"You did not change," they say.

Did I imagine the anguish of never looking up?

I am twelve. When relatives come to visit I hide in my room. My cousin Brenda, just my age, whose father works in the post office and whose mother is a nurse, comes to find me. "Hello," she says. And then she asks, looking at my recent school picture, which I did not want taken, and on which the "glob," as I think of it, is clearly visible, "You still can't see out of that eye?"

"No," I say, and flop back on the bed over my book.

That night, as I do almost every night, I abuse my eye. I rant and rave at it, in front of the mirror. I plead with it to clear up before morning. I tell it I hate and despise it. I do not pray for sight. I pray for beauty.

"You did not change," they say.

I am fourteen and baby-sitting for my brother Bill, who lives in Boston. He is my favorite brother and there is a strong bond between us. Understanding my feelings of shame and ugliness he and his wife take me to a local hospital, where the "glob" is removed by a doctor named O. Henry. There is still a small bluish crater where the scar tissue was, but the ugly white stuff is gone. Almost immediately I become a different person from the girl who does not raise her head. Or so I think. Now that I've raised my head I win the boyfriend of my dreams. Now that I've raised my head I have plenty of friends. Now that I've raised my head classwork comes from my lips as faultlessly as Easter speeches did, and I leave high school as valedictorian, most popular student, and *queen,* hardly believing my luck. Ironically, the girl who was voted most beautiful in our class (and was) was later shot twice through the chest by a male companion, using a "real" gun, while she was pregnant. But that's another story in itself. Or is it?

"You did not change," they say.

It is now thirty years since the "accident." A beautiful journalist comes to visit and to interview me. She is going to write a cover story for her magazine that focuses on my latest book. "Decide how you want to look on the cover," she says. "Glamorous, or whatever."

35 Never mind "glamorous," it is the "whatever" that I hear. Suddenly all I can think of is whether I will get enough sleep the night before the photography session: If I don't, my eye will be tired and wander, as blind eyes will.

At night in bed with my lover I think up reasons why I should not appear on the cover of a magazine. "My meanest critics will say I've sold out," I say. "My family will now realize I write scandalous books."

"But what's the real reason you don't want to do this?" he asks.

"Because in all probability," I say in a rush, "my eye won't be straight."

"It will be straight enough," he says. Then, "Besides, I thought you'd made your peace with that."

40 And I suddenly remember that I have.

I remember:

I am talking to my brother Jimmy, asking if he remembers anything unusual about the day I was shot. He does not know I consider that day the last time my father, with his sweet home remedy of cool lily leaves, chose me, and that I suffered and raged inside because of this. "Well," he says, "all I remember is standing by the side of the highway with Daddy, trying to flag down a car. A white man stopped, but when Daddy said he needed somebody to take his little girl to the doctor, he drove off."

I remember:

I am in the desert for the first time. I fall totally in love with it. I am so overwhelmed by its beauty, I confront for the first time, consciously, the meaning of the doctor's words years ago: "Eyes are sympathetic. If one is blind, the other will likely become blind too." I realize I have dashed about the world madly, looking at this, looking at that, storing up images against the fading of the light. *But I might have missed seeing the desert!* The shock of that possibility—and gratitude for over twenty-five years of sight—sends me literally to my knees. Poem after poem comes—which is perhaps how poets pray.

On Sight 45

I am so thankful I have seen
The Desert
And the creatures in the desert
And the desert Itself.

The desert has its own moon
Which I have seen
With my own eye.
There is no flag on it.

Trees of the desert have arms
All of which are always up
That is because the moon is up
The sun is up
Also the sky
The Stars
Clouds
None with flags.

If there were flags, I doubt
the trees would point.
Would you?

But mostly, I remember this: 50

I am twenty-seven, and my baby daughter is almost three. Since her birth I have worried about her discovery that her mother's eyes are different from other people's. Will she be embarrassed? I think. What will she say? Every day she watches a television program called *Big Blue Marble*. It begins with a picture of the earth as it appears from the moon. It is bluish, a little battered-looking, but full of light, with whitish clouds swirling around it. Every time I see it I weep with love, as if it is a picture of Grandma's house. One day when I am putting Rebecca down for her nap, she suddenly focuses on my eye. Something inside me cringes, gets ready to try to protect myself. All children are cruel about physical differences, I know from experience, and that they don't always mean to be is another matter. I assume Rebecca will be the same.

But no-o-o-o. She studies my face intently as we stand, her inside and me outside her crib. She even holds my face maternally between her dimpled little hands. Then, looking every bit as serious and lawyer-like as her father, she says, as if it may just possibly have slipped my attention: "Mommy, there's a *world* in your eye." (As in, "Don't be alarmed, or do anything crazy.") And then gently, but with great interest: "Mommy, where did you *get* that world in your eye?"

For the most part, the pain left then. (So what, if my brothers grew up to buy even more powerful pellet guns for their sons and to carry real guns themselves. So what, if a young "Morehouse man" once nearly fell off the steps of Trevor Arnett Library because he thought my eyes were blue.) Crying and laughing I ran to the bathroom, while Rebecca mumbled and sang herself to sleep. Yes indeed, I realized, looking into the mirror. There *was* a world in my eye. And I saw that it was possible to love it: that in fact, for all it had taught me of shame and anger and inner vision, I *did* love it. Even to see it drifting out of orbit in boredom, or rolling up out of fatigue, not to mention floating back at attention in excitement (bearing witness, a friend has called it), deeply suitable to my personality, and even characteristic of me.

That night I dream I am dancing to Stevie Wonder's song "Always" (the name of the song is really "As," but I hear it as "Always"). As I dance, whirling and joyous, happier than I've ever been in my life, another bright-faced dancer joins me. We dance and kiss each other and hold each other through the night. The other dancer has obviously come through all right, as I have done. She is beautiful, whole, and free. And she is also me.

Reading and Thinking

1. Walker's essay consists of a series of stories. Account for each of the stories Walker includes in the essay. Consider also why Walker arranges the stories as she does. What is the effect of this arrangement on our understanding of her idea about beauty?

2. Consider how Walker uses an important detail—the image of Walker's eye—in the essay. How does the movement from the literal to the metaphorical eye help Walker develop her sense of beauty?

3. Explain how Walker's concept of family changes from story to story.

Thinking and Writing

1. Select a moment in your life that marked a significant change or turning point. Tell two stories to highlight that change—one that accounts for the way you were before the moment and another that accounts for the way you were after the moment.

2. Re-examine your two stories to see what ideas they suggest to you. Ask others to read or listen to the stories and tell you what ideas come to mind. In an essay of your own, develop the idea that seems most appropriate to you. Use three stories (including the two that you have already written) to develop that idea. Let Walker's example guide you.

SEAMS OF TIME
AN OCCASION FOR NARRATION

You have just seen how Alice Walker tells stories about brief moments in her life and stitches them together to create a coherent essay about beauty. The episodes, or stories, constitute Walker's evidence; the result is a whole greater than the sum of its parts. You will now complete a series of exercises that will lead to your own stories.

This Occasion asks you to look at two different scenes of Washington Square Park in New York City. These scenes will provide opportunities for storytelling and then for your use of those stories to create larger essays.

PREPARING TO WRITE: BLACK LINES, 2002

1. Imagine yourself outside the frame of "Black Lines, 2002," looking in. Think about the various black lines—vertical, horizontal, and crooked—within the frame. How do those lines cause you to react to the scene itself?

2. Consider the various contrasts within the frame of the photograph—those related to color, to human mobility, and to life in general. How do these contexts relate to Gretel Ehrlich's idea (p. 122) that in autumn everything is ripe, and yet, everything is dying?

Black Lines, 2002

Lost Dog, 2003

PREPARING TO WRITE: LOST DOG, 2003

1. "Lost Dog, 2003," on first glance, seems to be a study in black and white contrasts. How many other colors do you see in the photograph, and how do they affect your reaction to the photograph?

2. Look carefully for the lost dog mentioned in the title. Which dog seems lost? Lost to whom?

3. How do the black lines in this photograph compare to those in "Black Lines, 2002," taken in the same park just a few months earlier? How do they seem different in this scene? Explain.

Occasion

MOVING TOWARD ESSAY: ANALYSIS AND REFLECTION

1. Step into the October scene depicted in "Black Lines, 2002." Walk to the pedestal, just beyond the man in the gold jacket. The statue of Alexander Lyman Holley (1832–1882), a famous rail and steel engineer, has been there atop the pedestal since 1890. Identify the changes that might have occurred in the park since Holley's statue arrived over a century ago. Write a short narrative account of what you see going on that might interest Holley were he brought back to life today.

2. Assume that you are talking on a cell phone on the way to class and that you walk into the frame of "Lost Dog, 2003," stopping just between the two large trees. Tell your friend on the phone about the "lost dog" in the scene, keeping her guessing about the meaning of "lost." Walk deeper into the scene and tell her about your changing perspective. Record part of your exchange with the friend, focusing on the most interesting and dramatic shift in perspective.

WRITING THOUGHTFULLY: IDEA AND ESSAY

1. Keeping in mind what you have learned from the photographs, step into your own life. Locate and recreate a moment evoked by the photographs. Recreate the moment as a dramatic, scenic story, just as you have seen Walker do in her essay "Beauty."

2. Discuss the scene you created with one or two friends or classmates. Try to discover what ideas may be embedded in it. Then let the scene act as a kind of magnet that draws in a related memory. Recreate that scene in words, just as you did in the previous exercise.

3. Take the two scenes from the two previous exercises and consider them together. What ideas do they reveal to you? Like Walker, bring the scenes together, telling a larger story about what they reveal to you. You may add additional scenes to help you develop your idea and your essay.

CREATING OCCASIONS

1. Consult your family photo album. Select your favorite photograph and tell a story about what is not depicted in the photograph, something about the scene itself that the camera left out.

2. Mine that scene for ideas, asking others to help you see what might be hidden in the scene. Let the emerging idea draw in a separate but related story about your family.

3. Consider the two scenes together. Look for the idea that connects them. See if you can express that idea in one or two sentences without referring to your own family.

4. Using this tentative idea (it should change as you write and develop it), create an essay that uses a number of stories as evidence.

5. Create your own interactive Occasion on *Comp21* using the textual, visual, and video libraries, as well as the Explicator analysis tools. From the main menu, choose "Build Your Own Occasion for Writing."

TIM O'BRIEN

Tim O'Brien was born in 1946 in Austin, Minnesota. He attended Macalaster College and Harvard and was drafted into the Army during the Vietnam War. After serving in that war and being wounded, he began to create interesting accounts of his experiences. His work often combines elements of fiction, nonfiction, and a form he calls *autofiction* (a blend of fiction and autobiography). His books include *If I Die in a Combat Zone: Box Me Up and Send Me Home*; *The Things They Carried*; and *In the Lake of the Woods*.

How to Tell a True War Story

"How to Tell a True War Story" reads like an essay but works through a series of stories and reversals. The piece questions its own truth telling, inviting us to consider how fact and fiction intersect and diverge, blend and separate from one another. O'Brien is a master storyteller whose voice is both seductive and haunting. He invites us to see a disturbing beauty that accompanies destruction.

1   This is true.

I had a buddy in Vietnam. His name was Bob Kiley, but everybody called him Rat.

A friend of his gets killed, so about a week later Rat sits down and writes a letter to the guy's sister. Rat tells her what a great brother she had, how together the guy was, a number one pal and comrade. A real soldier's soldier, Rat says. Then he tells a few stories to make the point, how her brother would always volunteer for stuff nobody else would volunteer for in a million years, dangerous stuff, like doing recon or going out on these really badass night patrols. Stainless steel balls, Rat tells her. The guy was a little crazy, for sure, but crazy in a good way, a real daredevil, because he liked the challenge of it, he liked testing himself, just man against gook. A great, great guy, Rat says.

Anyway, it's a terrific letter, very personal and touching. Rat almost bawls writing it. He gets all teary telling about the good times they had together, how her brother made the war seem almost fun, always raising hell and lighting up villes and bringing smoke to bear every which way. A great sense of humor, too. Like the time at this river when he went fishing with a whole damn crate of hand grenades. Probably the funniest thing in world history, Rat says, all that gore, about twenty zillion dead gook fish. Her brother, he had the right attitude. He knew how to have a good time. On Halloween, this real hot spooky night, the dude paints up his body all different colors and puts on this weird mask and hikes over to a ville and goes trick-or-treating almost stark naked, just boots and balls and an M-16. A tremendous human being, Rat says. Pretty nutso sometimes, but you could trust him with your life.

And then the letter gets very sad and serious. Rat pours his heart out. He says he loved the guy. He says the guy was his best friend in the world. They were like soul mates, he says, like twins or something, they had a whole lot in common. He tells the guy's sister he'll look her up when the war's over.

So what happens?

Rat mails the letter. He waits two months. The dumb cooze never writes back.

A true war story is never moral. It does not instruct, nor encourage virtue, nor suggest models of proper human behavior, nor restrain men from doing the things men have always done. If a story seems moral, do not believe it. If at the end of a war story, you feel uplifted, or if you feel that some small bit of rectitude has been salvaged from the larger waste, then you have been made the victim of a very old and terrible lie. There is no rectitude whatsoever. There is no virtue. As a first rule of thumb, therefore, you can tell a true war story by its absolute and uncompromising allegiance to obscenity and evil. Listen to Rat Kiley. Cooze, he says. He does not say bitch. He certainly does not say woman, or girl. He says cooze. Then he spits and stares. He's nineteen years old—it's too much for him—so he looks at you with those big sad gentle killer eyes and says *cooze,* because his friend is dead, and because it's so incredibly sad and true: she never wrote back.

You can tell a true war story if it embarrasses you. If you don't care for obscenity, you don't care for the truth; if you don't care for the truth, watch how you vote. Send guys to war, they come home talking dirty.

10   Listen to Rat: "Jesus Christ, man, I write this beautiful fuckin' letter, I slave over it, and what happens? The dumb cooze never writes back."

The dead guy's name was Curt Lemon. What happened was, we crossed a muddy river and marched west into the mountains, and on the third day we took a break along a trail junction in deep jungle. Right away, Lemon and Rat Kiley started goofing. They didn't understand about the spookiness. They were kids; they just didn't know. A nature hike, they thought, not even a war, so they went off into the shade of some giant trees—quadruple canopy, no sunlight at all—and they were giggling and calling each other yellow mother and playing a silly game they'd invented. The game involved smoke grenades, which were harmless unless you did stupid things, and what they did was pull out the pin and stand a few feet apart and play catch under the shade of those huge trees. Whoever chickened out was a yellow mother. And if nobody chickened out, the grenade would make a light popping sound and they'd be covered with smoke and they'd laugh and dance around and then do it again.

It's all exactly true.

It happened to *me,* nearly twenty years ago, and I still remember that trail junction and those giant trees and a soft dripping sound somewhere beyond the trees. I remember the smell of moss. Up in the canopy there were tiny white blossoms, but no sunlight at all, and I remember the shadows spreading out under the trees where Curt Lemon and Rat Kiley were playing catch with smoke grenades. Mitchell Sanders sat flipping his yo-yo. Norman Bowker and Kiowa and Dave Jensen were dozing, or half dozing, and all around us were those ragged green mountains.

Except for the laughter things were quiet.

15   At one point, I remember, Mitchell Sanders turned and looked at me, not quite nodding, as if to warn me about something, as if he already *knew,* then after a while he rolled up his yo-yo and moved away.

It's hard to tell you what happened next.

They were just goofing. There was a noise, I suppose, which must've been the detonator, so I glanced behind me and watched Lemon step from the shade into bright sunlight. His face was suddenly brown and shining. A handsome kid, really. Sharp gray eyes, lean and narrow-wasted, and when he died it was almost beautiful, the way the sunlight came around him and lifted him up and sucked him high into a tree full of moss and vines and white blossoms.

In any war story, but especially a true one, it's difficult to separate what happened from what seemed to happen. What seems to happen becomes its own happening and has to be told that way. The angles of vision are skewed. When a booby trap explodes, you close your eyes and duck and float outside yourself. When a guy dies, like Curt Lemon, you look away and then look back for a moment and then look away again. The pictures get jumbled; you tend to miss a lot. And then afterward, when you go to tell about it, there is always that surreal seemingness, which makes the story seem untrue, but which in fact represents the hard and exact truth as it *seemed.*

• • •

In many cases a true war story cannot be believed. If you believe it, be skeptical. It's a question of credibility. Often the crazy stuff is true and the normal stuff isn't, because the normal stuff is necessary to make you believe the truly incredible craziness.

20   In other cases you can't even tell a true war story. Sometimes it's just beyond telling.

I heard this one, for example, from Mitchell Sanders. It was near dusk and we were sitting at my foxhole along a wide muddy river north of Quang Ngai. I remember how peaceful the twilight was. A deep pinkish red spilled out on the river, which moved without sound, and in the morning we would cross the river and march west into the mountains. The occasion was right for a good story.

"God's truth," Mitchell Sanders said. "A six-man patrol goes up into the mountains on a basic listening-post operation. The idea's to spend a week up there, just lie low and listen for enemy movement. They've got a radio along, so if they hear anything suspicious—anything—they're supposed to call in artillery or gunships, whatever it takes. Otherwise they keep strict field discipline. Absolute silence. They just listen."

Sanders glanced at me to make sure I had the scenario. He was playing with his yo-yo, dancing it with short, tight little strokes of the wrist.

His face was blank in the dusk.

25 "We're talking regulation, by-the-book LP. These six guys, they don't say boo for a solid week. They don't got tongues. *All* ears."

"Right," I said.

"Understand me?"

"Invisible."

Sanders nodded.

30 "Affirm," he said. "Invisible. So what happens is, these guys get themselves deep in the bush, all camouflaged up, and they lie down and wait and that's all they do, nothing else, they lie there for seven straight days and just listen. And man, I'll tell you—it's spooky. This is mountains. You don't *know* spooky till you been there. Jungle, sort of, except it's way up in the clouds and there's always this fog—like rain, except its not raining—everything's all wet and swirly and tangled up and you can't see jack, you can't find your own pecker to piss with. Like you don't even have a body. Serious spooky. You just go with the vapors—the fog sort of takes you in . . . And the sounds, man. The sounds carry forever. You hear stuff nobody should *ever* hear."

Sanders was quiet for a second, just working the yo-yo, then he smiled at me.

"So after a couple days the guys start hearing this real soft, kind of wacked-out music. Weird echoes and stuff. Like a radio or something, but it's not a radio, it's this strange gook music that comes right out of the rocks. Faraway, sort of, but right up close, too. They try to ignore it. But it's a listening post, right? So they listen. And every night they keep hearing that crazyass gook concert. All kinds of chimes and xylophones. I mean, this is wilderness—no way, it can't be real—but there it is, like the mountains are tuned in to Radio fucking Hanoi. Naturally they get nervous. One guy sticks Juicy Fruit in his ears. Another guy almost flips. Thing is, though, they can't report music. They can't get on the horn and call back to base and say, 'Hey, listen, we need some firepower, we got to blow away this weirdo gook rock band.' They can't do that. It wouldn't go down. So they lie there in the fog and keep their mouths shut. And what makes it extra bad, see, is the poor dudes can't horse around like normal. Can't joke it away. Can't even talk to each other except maybe in whispers, all hush-hush, and that just revs up the willies. All they do is listen."

Again there was some silence as Mitchell Sanders looked out on the river. The dark was coming on hard now, and off to the west I could see the mountains rising in silhouette, all the mysteries and unknowns.

"This next part," Sanders said quietly, "you won't believe."

"Probably not," I said.

"You won't. And you know why?" He gave me a long, tired smile. "Because it happened. Because every word is absolutely dead-on true."

Sanders made a sound in his throat, like a sigh, as if to say he didn't care if I believed him or not. But he did care. He wanted me to feel the truth, to believe by the raw force of feeling. He seemed sad, in a way.

"These six guys," he said, "they're pretty fried out by now, and one night they start hearing voices. Like at a cocktail party. That's what it sounds like, this big swank gook cocktail party somewhere out there in the fog. Music and chitchat and stuff. It's crazy, I know, but they hear the champagne corks. They hear the actual martini glasses. Real hoity-toity, all very civilized, except this isn't civilization. This is Nam.

"Anyway, the guys try to be cool. They just lie there and groove, but after a while they start hearing—you won't believe this—they hear chamber music. They hear violins and cellos. They hear this terrific mama-san soprano. Then after a while they hear gook opera and a glee club and the Haiphong Boys Choir and a barbershop quartet and all kinds of weird chanting and Buddha-Buddha stuff. And the whole time, in the background, there's still that cocktail party going on. All these different voices. Not human voices, though. Because it's the mountains. Follow me? The rock—it's *talking*. And the fog, too, and the grass and the goddamn mongooses. Everything talks. The trees talk politics, the monkeys talk religion. The whole country. Vietnam. The place talks. It talks. Understand Nam—it truly *talks*.

"The guys can't cope. They lose it. They get on the radio and report enemy movement—a whole army, they say—and they order up the firepower. They get arty and gunships. They call in air strikes. And I'll tell you, they fuckin' crash that cocktail party. All night long, they just smoke those mountains. They make jungle juice. They blow away trees and glee clubs and whatever else there is to blow away. Scorch time. They walk napalm up and down the ridges. They bring in the Cobras and F-4s, they use Willie Peter and HE and incendiaries. It's all fire. They make those mountains burn.

"Around dawn things finally get quiet. Like you never even *heard* quiet before. One of those real thick, real misty days—just clouds and fog, they're off in this special zone—and the mountains are absolutely dead-flat silent. Like Brigadoon—pure vapor, you know? Everything's all sucked up inside the fog. Not a single sound, except they still *hear* it.

"So they pack up and start humping. They head down the mountain, back to base camp, and when they get there they don't say diddly. They don't talk. Not a word, like they're deaf and dumb. Later on this fat bird colonel comes up and asks what the hell happened out there. What'd they hear? Why all the ordnance? The man's ragged out, he gets down tight on their case. I mean, they spent six trillion dollars on firepower, and this fatass colonel wants answers, he wants to know what the fuckin' story is.

"But the guys don't say zip. They just look at him for a while, sort of funny like, sort of amazed, and the whole war is right there in that stare. It says everything you can't ever say. It says, man, you got *wax* in your ears. It says, poor bastard, you'll never know—wrong frequency—you don't *even* want to hear this. Then they salute the fucker and walk away, because certain stories you don't ever tell."

You can tell a true war story by the way it never seems to end. Not then, not ever. Not when Mitchell Sanders stood up and moved off into the dark.

It all happened.

Even now, at this instant, I remember that yo-yo. In a way, I suppose, you had to be there, you had to hear it, but I could tell how desperately Sanders wanted me to believe him, his frustration at not quite getting the details right, not quite pinning down the final and definitive truth.

And I remember sitting at my foxhole that night, watching the shadows of Quang Ngai, thinking about the coming day and how we would cross the river and march west into the mountains, all the ways I might die, all the things I did not understand.

Late in the night Mitchell Sanders touched my shoulder.

"Just came to me," he whispered. "The moral, I mean. Nobody listens. Nobody hears nothin'. Like that fatass colonel. The politicians, all the civilian types. Your girlfriend. My girlfriend. Everybody's sweet little virgin girlfriend. What they need is to go out on LP. The vapors, man. Trees and rocks—you got to *listen* to your enemy."

And then again, in the morning, Sanders came up to me. The platoon was preparing to move out, checking weapons, going through all the little rituals that preceded a day's march. Already the lead squad had crossed the river and was filing off toward the west.

"I got a confession to make," Sanders said. "last night, man, I had to make up a few things."

"I know that."

"The glee club. There wasn't any glee club."

"Right."

"No opera."

"Forget it, I understand."

"Yeah, but listen, it's still true. Those six guys, they heard wicked sounds out there. They heard sound you just plain won't believe."

40

Sanders pulled on his rucksack, closed his eyes for a moment, then almost smiled at me. I knew what was coming.

"All right," I said, "what's the moral?"

60 "Forget it."

"No, go ahead."

For a long while he was quiet, looking away; and the silence kept stretching out until it was almost embarrassing. Then he shrugged and gave me a stare that lasted all day.

"Hear that quiet, man?" he said. "That quiet—just listen. There's your moral."

. . .

In a true war story, if there's a moral at all, it's like the thread that makes the cloth. You can't tease it out. You can't extract the meaning without unraveling the deeper meaning. And in the end, really, there's nothing much to say about a true war story, except maybe "Oh."

65 True war stories do not generalize. They do not indulge in abstraction or analysis.

For example: War is hell. As a moral declaration the old truism seems perfectly true, and yet because it abstracts, because it generalizes, I can't believe it with my stomach. Nothing turns inside.

It comes down to gut instinct. A true war story, if truly told, makes the stomach believe.

• • •

This one does it for me. I've told it before—many times, many versions—but here's what actually happened.

We crossed that river and marched west into the mountains. On the third day, Curt Lemon stepped on a booby-trapped 105 round. He was playing catch with Rat Kiley, laughing, and then he was dead. The trees were thick; it took nearly an hour to cut an LZ for the dustoff.

70 Later, higher in the mountains, we came across a baby VC water buffalo. What it was doing there I don't know—no farms or paddies—but we chased it down and got a rope around it and led it along to a deserted village where we set up for the night. After supper Rat Kiley went over and stroked its nose.

He opened up a can of C rations, pork and beans,

but the baby buffalo wasn't interested.

Rat shrugged.

He stepped back and shot it through the right front knee. The animal did not make a sound. It went down hard, then got up again, and Rat took careful aim and shot off an ear. He shot it in the hindquarters and in the little hump at its back. He shot it twice in the flanks. It wasn't to kill; it was to hurt. He put the rifle muzzle up against the mouth and shot the mouth away. Nobody said much. The whole platoon stood there watching, feeling all kinds of things, but there wasn't a great deal of pity for the baby water buffalo. Curt Lemon was dead. Rat Kiley had lost his best friend in the world. Later in the week he would write a long personal letter to the guy's sister, who would not write back, but for now it was a question of pain. He shot off the tail. He shot away chunks of meat below the ribs. All around us there was the smell of smoke and filth and deep greenery, and the evening was humid and very hot. Rat went to automatic. He shot randomly, almost casually, quick little spurts in the belly and butt. Then he reloaded; squatted down, and shot it in the left front knee. Again the animal fell hard and tried to get up, but this time it couldn't quite make it. It wobbled and went down sideways. Rat shot it in the nose. He bent forward and whispered something, as if talking to a pet, then he shot it in the throat. All the while the baby buffalo was silent, or almost silent, just a light bubbling sound where the nose had been. It lay very still. Nothing moved except the eyes, which were enormous, the pupils shiny black and dumb.

Rat Kiley was crying. He tried to say something, but then cradled his rifle and went off by himself.

The rest of us stood in a ragged circle around the baby buffalo. For a time no one spoke. We had witnessed something essential, something brand-new and profound, a piece of the world so startling there was not yet a name for it.

Somebody kicked the baby buffalo.

It was still alive, though just barely, just in the eyes.

"Amazing," Dave Jensen said. "My whole life, I never seen anything like it."

"Never?"

"Not hardly. Not once."

Kiowa and Mitchell Sanders picked up the baby

buffalo. They hauled it across the open square, hoisted it up, and dumped it in the village well.

Afterward, we sat waiting for Rat to get himself together.

"Amazing," Dave Jensen kept saying. "A new wrinkle. I never seen it before."

Mitchell Sanders took out his yo-yo. "Well, that's Nam," he said. "Garden of Evil. Over here, man, every sin's real fresh and original."

85   How do you generalize?

War is hell, but that's not the half of it, because war is also mystery and terror and adventure and courage and discovery and holiness and pity and despair and longing and love. War is nasty; war is fun. War is thrilling; war is drudgery. War makes you a man; war makes you dead.

The truths are contradictory. It can be argued, for instance, that war is grotesque. But in truth war is also beauty. For all its horror, you can't help but gape at the awful majesty of combat. You stare out at tracer rounds unwinding through the dark like brilliant red ribbons. You crouch in ambush as a cool, impassive moon rises over the nighttime paddies. You admire the fluid symmetries of troops on the move, the harmonies of sound and shape and proportion, the great sheets of metal-fire streaming down from a gunship, the illumination rounds, the white phosphorus, the purply orange glow of napalm, the rocket's red glare. It's not pretty, exactly. It's astonishing. It fills the eye. It commands you. You hate it, yes, but your eyes do not. Like a killer forest fire, like cancer under a microscope, any battle or bombing raid or artillery barrage has the aesthetic purity of absolute moral indifference—a powerful, implacable beauty—and a true war story will tell the truth about this, though the truth is ugly.

To generalize about war is like generalizing about peace. Almost everything is true. Almost nothing is true. At its core, perhaps, war is just another name for death, and yet any soldier will tell you, if he tells the truth, that proximity to death brings with it a corresponding proximity to life. After a firefight, there is always the immense pleasure of aliveness. The trees are alive. The grass, the soil—everything. All around you things are purely living, and you among them, and the

aliveness makes you tremble. You feel an intense, out-of-the-skin awareness of your living self—your truest self, the human being you want to be and then become by the force of wanting it. In the midst of evil you want to be a good man. You want decency. You want justice and courtesy and human concord, things you never knew you wanted. There is a kind of largeness to it, a kind of godliness. Though it's odd, you're never more alive than when you're almost dead. You recognize what's valuable. Freshly, as if for the first time, you love what's best in yourself and in the world, all that might be lost. At the hour of dusk you sit at your foxhole and look out on a wide river turning pinkish red, and at the mountains beyond, and although in the morning you must cross the river and go into the mountains and do terrible things and maybe die, even so, you find yourself studying the fine colors on the river, you feel wonder and awe at the setting of the sun, and you are filled with a hard, aching love for how the world could be and always should be, but now is not.

Mitchell Sanders was right. For the common soldier, at least, war has the feel—the spiritual texture—of a great ghostly fog, thick and permanent. There is no clarity. Everything swirls. The old rules are no longer binding, the old truths no longer true. Right spills over into wrong. Order blends into chaos, love into hate, ugliness into beauty, law into anarchy, civility into savagery. The vapors suck you in. You can't tell where you are, or why you're there, and the only certainty is overwhelming ambiguity.

In war you lose your sense of the definite, hence your sense of truth itself, and therefore it's safe to say that in a true war story nothing is ever absolute true.

90

Often in a true war story there is not even a point, or else the point doesn't hit you until twenty years later, in your sleep, and you wake up and shake your wife and start telling the story to her, except when you get to the end you've forgotten the point again. And then for a long time you lie there watching the story happen in your head. You listen to your wife's breathing. The war's over. You close your eyes. You smile and think, Christ, what's the *point?*

This one wakes me up.

Reading

In the mountains that day, I watched Lemon turn sideways. He laughed and said something to Rat Kiley. Then he took a peculiar half step, moving from shade into bright sunlight, and the booby-trapped 105 round blew him into a tree. The parts were just hanging there, so Dave Jensen and I were ordered to shinny up and peel him off. I remember the white bone of an arm. I remember pieces of skin and something wet and yellow that must've been the intestines. The gore was horrible, and stays with me. But what wakes me up twenty years later is Dave Jensen singing "Lemon Tree" as we threw down the parts.

You can tell a true war story by the questions you ask. Somebody tells a story, let's say, and afterward you ask, "Is it true?" and if the answer matters, you've got your answer.

95   For example, we've all heard this one. Four guys go down a trail. A grenade sails out. One guy jumps on it and takes the blast and saves his three buddies.

Is it true?

The answer matters.

You'd feel cheated if it never happened. Without the grounding reality, it's just a trite bit of puffery, pure Hollywood, untrue in the way all such stories are untrue. Yet even if it did happen—and maybe it did, anything's possible—even then you know it can't be true, because a true war story does not depend upon that kind of truth. Absolute occurrence is irrelevant. A thing may happen and be a total lie; another thing may not happen and be truer than the truth. For example: Four guys go down a trail. A grenade sails out. One guy jumps on it and takes the blast, but it's a killer grenade and everybody dies anyway. Before they die, though, one of the dead guys says, "The fuck you do *that* for?" and the jumper says, "Story of my life, man," and the other guy starts to smile but he's dead.

That's a true story that never happened.

100   Twenty years later, I can still see the sunlight on Lemon's face. I can see him turning, looking back at Rat Kiley, then he laughed and took that curious half step from shade into sunlight, his face suddenly brown and shining, and when his foot touched down, in that instant, he must've thought it was the sunlight that was

killing him. It was not the sunlight. It was a rigged 105 round. But if I could ever get the story right, how the sun seemed to gather around him and pick him up and lift him high into a tree, if I could somehow re-create the fatal whiteness of that light, the quick glare, the obvious cause and effect, then you would believe the last thing Curt Lemon believed, which for him must've been the final truth.

Now and then, when I tell this story, someone will come up to me afterward and say she liked it. It's always a woman. Usually it's an older woman of kindly temperament and humane politics. She'll explain that as a rule she hates war stories; she can't understand why people want to wallow in all the blood and gore. But this one she liked. The poor baby buffalo, it made her sad. Sometimes, even, there are little tears. What I should do, she'll say, is put it all behind me. Find new stories to tell.

I won't say it but I'll think it.

I'll picture Rat Kiley's face, his grief, and I'll think, *You dumb cooze.*

Because she wasn't listening.

It *wasn't* a war story. It was a *love* story.   10

But you can't say that. All you can do is tell it one more time. Patiently, adding and subtracting, making up a few things to get at the real truth. No Mitchell Sanders, you tell her. No Lemon, no Rat Kiley. No trail junction. No baby buffalo. No vines or moss or white blossoms. Beginning to end, you tell her, it's all made up. Every goddamn detail—the mountains and the river and especially that poor dumb baby buffalo. None of it happened. *None* of it. And even if it did happen, it didn't happen in the mountains, it happened in this little village on the Batangan Peninsula, and it was raining like crazy, and one night a guy named Stink Harris woke up screaming with a leech on his tongue. You can tell a true war story if you just keep on telling it.

And in the end, of course, a true war story is never about war. It's about sunlight. It's about the special way that dawn spreads out on a river when you know you must cross the river and march into the mountains and do things you are afraid to do. It's about love and memory. It's about sorrow. It's about sisters who never write back and people who never listen.

Reading and Thinking

1. O'Brien begins his essay with a simple assertion: "This is true." Then he tells a story about Rat Kiley to illustrate or justify his assertion. As soon as he finishes that story, he begins to instruct us on the nature of true war stories. What is the effect of O'Brien's movement back and forth from pure story to commentary about stories in general? Explain.

2. Mark each time O'Brien follows this pattern of story followed by commentary. Note in the margin how he varies that pattern to achieve different effects. Consider the variations and their effects.

3. What is the effect of the shift in point of view that O'Brien uses—from, for example, first-person "I" to omniscient and back again? Explain.

Thinking and Writing

1. O'Brien transforms the horror of war into something of beauty. Find the paragraph or section of the essay in which O'Brien does the most convincing job. Think about how he does it. With details and images? With the way he places one kind of paragraph among others? With a combination of storytelling and commentary? Explain.

2. After O'Brien tells Lemon's story, he returns to it three more times. Explain what that repetition has to do with telling and understanding a true war story. Explain in a paragraph how O'Brien's technique enhances his idea.

Reading

U.S. Soldiers in the Vietnam War

Occasion

THE LEGACY OF MEMORY
AN OCCASION FOR NARRATION

These images from war will give you an opportunity to practice narration using some of the techniques that O'Brien uses. You will also see how other perspectives can color your own perspective and change the way you tell your story.

PREPARING TO WRITE: U.S. SOLDIERS

1. Consider the upper left image in the panel of photographs. The soldier has written on the cover of his helmet (steel pot). What is he keeping track of? What can you tell about him by the look on his face and the writing on the steel pot? Explain.

2. Turn your attention to the soldier in the top right photograph. Make a list of the equipment and other physical objects this soldier is carrying. Does his face suggest that he is carrying something else that cannot be counted? Explain.

3. Focus now on the two bottom images. The soldier on the left is holding a 3.5″ rocket launcher in one hand and a live round in the other hand. If the soldiers in the right image were not Americans, this infantryman would use the anti-tank round that he is carrying to destroy them and their tank. What do you suppose that Tim O'Brien would notice in the aftermath of that destruction? What would trouble him? Write a paragraph imagining that action from O'Brien's point of view, in the style of his story.

MOVING TOWARD ESSAY: ANALYSIS AND REFLECTION

1. General Douglas MacArthur, a hero from World War II and the Korean War, once said, "Upon the fields of friendly strife are sown the seeds that on other fields, on other days, will bear the fruits of victory." That message was emblazoned on the wall of the cadet gymnasium at the United States Military Academy at West Point. Write a paragraph or two reflecting on the meaning of this quote.

2. Call on your own personal experience with "friendly strife," and select a memory that responds in some way to General MacArthur's claim. Recreate that memory in such a way that it suggests your response to him. Create a three to five page essay expressing your ideas about conflicts both violent and non-violent. How might these soldiers respond based on O'Brien's story? What in the story makes you think so?

WRITING THOUGHTFULLY: IDEA AND ESSAY

1. Reflect on September 11, 2001. Try to capture that day in a story of self-contained dramatic moments. Keep the story dramatic and free of commentary. Allow people and dialogue into the story. Let the story represent how 9/11 affected you.

2. Focus on the word *legacy*. What is your war legacy? How far back does war come into play in your own history, or that of your immediate family? War legacy might very well be antiwar legacy, or it might be a legacy of no war at all. Locate a significant moment, for you, in that legacy. Recreate the moment. Again, avoid commentary.

3. Bring together your two stories: the one about 9/11, and the one about war legacy. Consider them as a group to see what they reveal regarding your own ideas about war. Include your thoughts about conflict and strife, both violent and non-violent. How does your own war legacy relate to your own experience? How does strife, friendly or otherwise, relate to war? To you personally?

4. Weave your stories together along with your notes about strife, combining story and commentary as O'Brien does, alternating narrative point of view if it serves your purpose. Your essay should contain three or four stories, each of which must be compressed in your final draft to make room for commentary and reflection. The final essay should be four to six pages.

5. ***Comp21* Video Extension.** Extend this Occasion to include CNN® video footage using the Explicator video analysis tool on *Comp21*. From the main menu choose "Frames of Mind: Extending Occasions" and select "The Legacy of Memory: An Occasion for Narration" from the list.

CREATING OCCASIONS

1. With a partner in the class, think about how to tell *any* good story. Let Walker and O'Brien help you think about storytelling techniques but rely as well on what you have learned in telling and writing your own stories. You might want to read one or two of the essays at the end of the chapter to find other ways to tell good stories.

2. On your own, create a short essay entitled "How to Tell a Compelling Story." Be playful and imaginative, working under the influence of your favorite writers while making good use of your own experience. Be sure to include stories within this essay about stories.

3. Create your own interactive Occasion on *Comp21* using the textual, visual, and video libraries, as well as the Explicator analysis tools. From the main menu, choose "Build Your Own Occasion for Writing."

Occasion

LOREN EISELEY

Loren Eiseley (1907–1977) was an anthropologist by profession (professor and provost, University of Pennsylvania), but he considered himself a writer. What he wrote most and liked best were the pieces he called "concealed" essays in which "personal anecdote [is] allowed gently to bring under observation thoughts of a more purely scientific nature." His works included *The Immense Journey, Darwin's Century, The Firmament of Time, The Unexpected Universe, The Invisible Pyramid, The Night Country, All the Strange Hours, The Star Thrower,* three volumes of poetry, and *The Lost Notebooks of Loren Eiseley.* His many awards include the Joseph Wood Krutch Medal (1976) for significant contribution toward the improvement of life and the environment.

The Illusion of the Two Cultures

"The Illusion of the Two Cultures" is a more demanding and academic essay than the others you will read in this book. Eiseley argues against the perceived split between the sciences and the humanities and looks back in time to see how such a misperception developed about this important relationship. He also looks into the future to speculate about its consequences. Eiseley uses an interesting combination of historical texts and anecdotes (or stories) to substantiate his claims. Like O'Brien, he combines commentary with story in this essay.

1   Not long ago an English scientist, Sir Eric Ashby, remarked that "to train young people in the dialectic between orthodoxy and dissent is the unique contribution which universities make to society." I am sure that Sir Eric meant by this remark that nowhere but in universities are the young given the opportunity to absorb past tradition and at the same time to experience the impact of new ideas—in the sense of a constant dialogue between past and present—lived in every hour of the student's existence. This dialogue, ideally, should lead to a great winnowing and sifting of experience and to a heightened consciousness of self which, in turn, should lead on to greater sensitivity and perception on the part of the individual.

Our lives are the creation of memory and the accompanying power to extend ourselves outward into ideas and relive them. The finest intellect is that which employs an invisible web of gossamer running into the past as well as across the minds of living men and which constantly responds to the vibrations transmitted through these tenuous lines of sympathy. It would be contrary to fact, however, to assume that our universities always perform this unique function of which Sir Eric speaks, with either grace or perfection; in fact our investment in man, it has been justly remarked, is deteriorating even as the financial investment in science grows.

More than thirty years ago, George Santayana had already sensed this trend. He commented, in a now-forgotten essay, that one of the strangest consequences of modern science was that as the visible wealth of nature was more and more transferred and abstracted, the mind seemed to lose courage and to become ashamed of its own fertility. "The hard-pressed natural man will not indulge his imagination," continued Santayana, "unless it poses for truth; and being half-aware of this imposition, he is more troubled at the thought of being deceived than at the fact of being mechanized or being bored; and he would wish to escape imagination altogether."

"Man would wish to escape imagination altogether." I repeat that last phrase, for it defines a peculiar aberration of the human mind found on both sides of that bipolar division between the humanities and the sciences, which C. P. Snow has popularized under the title of *The Two Cultures*. The idea is not solely a product of this age. It was already emerging with the science of the seventeenth century; one finds it in Bacon. One finds the fear of it faintly foreshadowed in Thoreau. Thomas Huxley lent it weight when he referred contemptuously to the "caterwauling of poets."

5   Ironically, professional scientists berated the early evolutionists such as Lamarck and Chambers for overindulgence in the imagination. Almost eighty years ago John Burroughs observed that some of the animus once directed by science toward dogmatic theology seemed in his day increasingly to be vented upon the literary naturalist. In the early 1900s a quarrel over "nature faking" raised a confused din in America and aroused W. H. Hudson to some dry and pungent comment upon the failure to distinguish the purposes of science from those of literature. I know of at least one scholar who, venturing to develop some personal ideas in an essay for the layman, was characterized by a reviewer in a leading professional journal as a worthless writer, although, as it chanced, the work under discussion had received several awards in literature, one of them international in scope. More recently, some scholars not indifferent to humanistic values have exhorted poets to leave their personal songs in order to portray the beauty and symmetry of molecular structures.

Now some very fine verse has been written on scientific subjects, but, I fear, very little under the dictate of scientists as such. Rather there is evident here precisely that restriction of imagination against which Santayana inveighed; namely, an attempt to constrain literature itself to the delineation of objective or empiric truth, and to dismiss the whole domain of value, which after all constitutes the very nature of man, as without significance and beneath contempt.

Unconsciously, the human realm is denied in favor of the world of pure technics. Man, the tool user, grows convinced that he is himself only useful as a tool, that fertility except in the use of the scientific imagination is wasteful and without purpose, even, in some indefinable way, sinful. I was reading J. R. R. Tolkien's great symbolic trilogy, *The Fellowship of the Ring,* a few months ago, when a young scientist of my acquaintance paused and looked over my shoulder. After a little casual interchange the man departed leaving an accusing remark hovering in the air between us. "I wouldn't waste my time with a man who writes fairy stories." He might as well have added, "or with a man who reads them."

As I went back to my book I wondered vaguely in what leafless landscape one grew up without Hans Christian Andersen, or Dunsany, or even Jules Verne. There lingered about the young man's words a puritanism which seemed the more remarkable because, as nearly as I could discover, it was unmotivated by any sectarian religiosity unless a total dedication to science brings to some minds a similar authoritarian desire to shackle the human imagination. After all, it is this impossible, fertile world of our imagination which gave birth to liberty in the midst of oppression, and which persists in seeking until what is sought is seen. Against such invisible and fearful powers, there can be found in all ages and in all institutions—even the institutions of professional learning—the humorless man with the sneer, or if the sneer does not suffice, then the torch, for the bright unperishing letters of the human dream.

One can contrast this recalcitrant attitude with an 1890 reminiscence from that great Egyptologist Sir Flinders Petrie, which steals over into the realm of pure literature. It was written, in unconscious symbolism, from a tomb:

"I here live, and do not scramble to fit myself to the requirements of others. In a narrow tomb, with the figure of Néfermaat standing on each side of me—as he has stood through all that we know as human history—I have just room for my bed, and a row of good reading in which I can take pleasure after dinner. Behind me is that Great Peace, the Desert. It is an entity—a power—just as much as the sea is. No wonder men fled to it from the turmoil of the ancient world."

10   It may now reasonably be asked why one who has similarly, if less dramatically, spent his life among the stones and broken shards of the remote past should be writing here about matters involving literature and science. While I was considering this with humility and trepidation, my eye fell upon a stone in my office. I am

sure that professional journalists must recall times when an approaching deadline has keyed all their senses and led them to glance wildly around in the hope that something might leap out at them from the most prosaic surroundings. At all events my eyes fell upon this stone.

Now the stone antedated anything that the historians would call art; it had been shaped many hundreds of thousands of years ago by men whose faces would frighten us if they sat among us today. Out of old habit, since I like the feel of worked flint, I picked it up and hefted it as I groped for words over this difficult matter of the growing rift between science and art. Certainly the stone was of no help to me; it was a utilitarian thing which had cracked marrow bones, if not heads, in the remote dim morning of the human species. It was nothing if not practical. It was, in fact, an extremely early example of the empirical tradition which has led on to modern science.

The mind which had shaped this artifact knew its precise purpose. It had found out by experimental observation that the stone was tougher, sharper, more enduring than the hand which wielded it. The creature's mind had solved the question of the best form of the implement and how it could be manipulated most effectively. In its day and time this hand ax was as grand an intellectual achievement as a rocket.

As a scientist my admiration went out to that unidentified workman. How he must have labored to understand the forces involved in the fracturing of flint, and all that involved practical survival in his world. My uncalloused twentieth-century hand caressed the yellow stone lovingly. It was then that I made a remarkable discovery.

In the mind of this gross-featured early exponent of the practical approach to nature—the technician, the no-nonsense practitioner of survival—two forces had met and merged. There had not been room in his short and desperate life for the delicate and supercilious separation of the arts from the sciences. There did not exist then the refined distinctions set up between the scholarly percipience of reality and what has sometimes been called the vaporings of the artistic imagination.

As I clasped and unclasped the stone, running my fingers down its edges, I began to perceive the ghostly emanations from a long-vanished mind, the kind of mind which, once having shaped an object of any sort, leaves an individual trace behind it which speaks to others across the barriers of time and language. It was not the practical experimental aspect of this mind that startled me, but rather that the fellow had wasted time.

In an incalculably brutish and dangerous world he had both shaped an instrument of practical application and then, with a virtuoso's elegance, proceeded to embellish his product. He had not been content to produce a plain, utilitarian implement. In some wistful, inarticulate way, in the grip of the dim aesthetic feelings which are one of the marks of man—or perhaps I should say, some men—this archaic creature had lingered over his handiwork.

One could still feel him crouching among the stones on a long-vanished river bar, turning the thing over in his hands, feeling its polished surface, striking, here and there, just one more flow that no longer had usefulness as its criterion. He had, like myself, enjoyed the texture of the stone. With skills lost to me, he had gone on flaking the implement with an eye to beauty until it had become a kind of rough jewel, equivalent in its day to the carved and gold-inlaid pommel of the iron dagger placed in Tutankhamen's tomb.

All the later history of man contains these impractical exertions expended upon a great diversity of objects, and, with literacy, breaking even into printed dreams. Today's secular disruption between the creative aspect of art and that of science is a barbarism that would have brought lifted eyebrows in a Cro-Magnon cave. It is a product of high technical specialization, the deliberate blunting of wonder, and the equally deliberate suppression of a phase of our humanity in the name of an authoritarian institution, science, which has taken on, in our time, curious puritanical overtones. Many scientists seem unaware of the historical reasons for this development or the fact that the creative aspect of art is not so remote from that of science as may seem, at first glance, to be the case.

I am not so foolish as to categorize individual scholars or scientists. I am, however, about to remark on the nature of science as an institution. Like all such structures it is apt to reveal certain behavioral rigidities and conformities which increase with age. It is no longer the domain of the amateur, though some of its greatest discoverers could be so defined. It is now a professional body, and with professionalism there tends to emerge a greater emphasis upon a coherent system of regulations. The deviant is more sharply treated, and the young tend to imitate their successful elders. In short, an "Establishment"—a trade union has appeared.

Similar tendencies can be observed among those of the humanities concerned with the professional analysis and interpretation of the works of the creative artist. Here too, a similar rigidity and exclusiveness make their appearance. It is not that in the case of both the sciences and the humanities standards are out of place. What I am briefly cautioning against is that too frequently they afford an excuse for stifling original thought or constricting much latent creativity within traditional molds.

Such molds are always useful to the mediocre conformist who instinctively castigates and rejects what he cannot imitate. Tradition, the continuity of learning, are, it is true, enormously important to the learned disciplines. What we must realize as scientists is that the particular institution we inhabit has its own irrational accretions and authoritarian dogmas which can be as unpleasant as some of those encountered in sectarian circles—particularly so since they are frequently unconsciously held and surrounded by an impenetrable wall of self-righteousness brought about because science is regarded as totally empiric and open-minded by tradition.

This type of professionalism, as I shall label it in order to distinguish it from what is best in both the sciences and humanities, is characterized by two assumptions: that the accretions of fact are cumulative and lead to progress, whereas the insights of art are, at best, singular, and lead nowhere, or, when introduced into the realm of science, produce obscurity and confusion. The convenient label "mystic" is, in our day, readily applied to men who pause for simple wonder, or who encounter along the borders of the known that "awful power" which Wordsworth characterized as the human imagination. It can, he says, rise suddenly from the mind's abyss and enwrap the solitary traveler like a mist.

We do not like mists in this era, and the word imagination is less and less used. We like, instead, a clear road, and we abhor solitary traveling. Indeed one of our great scientific historians remarked not long ago that the literary naturalist was obsolescent if not completely outmoded. I suppose he meant that with our penetration into the biophysical realm, life, like matter, would become increasingly represented by abstract symbols. To many it must appear that the more we can dissect life into its elements, the closer we are getting to its ultimate resolution. While I have some reservations on this score, they are not important. Rather, I should like to look at the symbols which in the one case denote science and in the other constitute those vaporings and cloud wraiths that are the abomination, so it is said, of the true scientists but are the delight of the poet and literary artist.

Creation in science demands a high level of imaginative insight and intuitive perception. I believe no one would deny this, even though it exists in varying degrees, just as it does, similarly, among writers, musicians, or artists. The scientist's achievement, however, is quantitatively transmissible. From a single point his discovery is verifiable by other men who may then, on the basis of corresponding data, accept the innovation and elaborate upon it in the cumulative fashion which is one of the great triumphs of science.

Artistic creation, on the other hand, is unique. It cannot be twice discovered, as, say, natural selection was discovered. It may be imitated stylistically, in a genre, a school, but, save for a few items of technique, it is not cumulative. A successful work of art may set up reverberations and is, in this, just as transmissible as science, but there is a qualitative character about it. Each reverberation in another mind is unique. As the French novelist François Mauriac has remarked, each great novel is a separate and distinct world operating under its own laws with a flora and fauna totally its own. There is communication, or the work is a failure, but the communication releases our own visions, touches some highly personal chord in our own experience.

The symbols used by the great artist are a key releasing our humanity from the solitary tower of the self. "Man," says Lewis Mumford, "is first and foremost the self-fabricating animal." I shall merely add that the artist plays an enormous role in this act of self-creation. It is he who touches the hidden strings of pity, who searches our hearts, who makes us sensitive to beauty, who asks questions about fate and destiny. Such questions, though they lurk always around the corners of the external universe which is the peculiar province of science, the rigors of the scientific method do not enable us to pursue directly.

And yet I wonder.

It is surely possible to observe that it is the successful analogy or symbol which frequently allows the scientist to leap from a generalization in one field of thought to a triumphant achievement in another. For example, Progressionism in a spiritual sense later became the model contributing to the discovery of organic evolution. Such analogies genuinely resemble the figures and enchantments of great literature, whose meanings similarly can never be totally grasped because of their endless power to ramify in the individual mind.

30

John Donne gave powerful expression to a feeling applicable as much to science as to literature when he said devoutly of certain Biblical passages: "The literall sense is always to be preserved; but the literall sense is not always to be discerned; for the literall sense is not always that which the very letter and grammar of the place presents." A figurative sense, he argues cogently, can sometimes be the most "literall intention of the Holy Ghost."

It is here that the scientist and artist sometimes meet in uneasy opposition, or at least along lines of tension. The scientist's attitude is sometimes, I suspect, that embodied in Samuel Johnson's remark that, wherever there is mystery, roguery is not far off.

Yet surely it was not roguery when Sir Charles Lyell glimpsed in a few fossil prints of raindrops the persistence of the world's natural forces through the incredible, mysterious aeons of geologic time. The fossils were a symbol of a vast hitherto unglimpsed order. They are, in Donne's sense, both literal and symbolic. As fossils they merely denote evidence of rain in a past era. Figuratively they are more. To the perceptive intelligence they afford the hint of lengthened natural order, just as the eyes of ancient trilobites tell us similarly of the unchanging laws of light. Equally, the educated mind may discern in a scratched pebble the retreating shadow of

vast ages of ice and gloom. In Donne's archaic phraseology these objects would bespeak the principal intention of the Divine Being—that is, of order beyond our power to grasp.

Such images drawn from the world of science are every bit as powerful as great literary symbolism and equally demanding upon the individual imagination of the scientist who would fully grasp the extension of meaning which is involved. It is, in fact, one and the same creative act in both domains.

Indeed evolution itself has become such a figurative symbol, as has also the hypothesis of the expanding universe. The laboratory worker may think of these concepts in a totally empirical fashion as subject to proof or disproof by the experimental method. Like Freud's doctrine of the subconscious, however, such ideas frequently escape from the professional scientist into the public domain. There they may undergo further individual transformation and embellishment. Whether the scholar approves or not, such hypotheses are now as free to evolve in the mind of the individual as are the creations of art. All the resulting enrichment and confusion will bear about it something suggestive of the world of artistic endeavor.

As figurative insights into the nature of things, such embracing conceptions may become grotesquely distorted or glow with added philosophical wisdom. As in the case of the trilobite eye or the fossil raindrop, there lurks behind the visible evidence vast shadows no longer quite of that world which we term natural. Like the words in Donne's Bible, enormous implications have transcended the literal expression of the thought. Reality itself has been superseded by a greater reality. As Donne himself asserted, "The substance of the truth is in the great images which lie behind."

It is because these two types of creation—the artistic and the scientific—have sprung from the same being and have their points of contact even in division that I have the temerity to assert that, in a sense, the "two cultures" are an illusion, that they are a product of unreasoning fear, professionalism, and misunderstanding. Because of the emphasis upon science in our society, much has been said about the necessity of educating the layman and even the professional student of the humanities upon the ways and the achievements of science. I admit that a barrier exists, but I am also concerned to express the view that there persists in the domain of science itself an occasional marked intolerance of those of its own membership who venture to pursue the way of letters. As I have remarked, this intolerance can the more successfully clothe itself in seeming objectivity because of the supposed open nature of the scientific society. It is not remarkable that this trait is sometimes more manifest in the younger and less secure disciplines.

There was a time, not too many centuries ago, when to be active in scientific investigation was to invite suspicion. Thus it may be that there now lingers among us, even in the triumph of the experimental method, a kind of vague fear of that other artistic world of deep emotion, of strange symbols, lest it seize upon us or distort the hard-won objectivity of our thinking—lest it corrupt, in other words, that crystalline and icy objectivity which, in our scientific guise, we erect as a model of conduct. This model, incidentally, if pursued to its absurd conclusion, would lead to a world in which the computer would determine all aspects of our existence, one in which the bomb would be as welcome as the discoveries of the physician.

Happily, the very great in science, or even those unique scientists such as Leonardo, who foreran the emergence of science as an institution, have been singularly free from this folly. Darwin decried it even as he recognized that he had paid a certain price in concentrated specialization for his achievement. Einstein, it is well known, retained a simple sense of wonder; Newton felt like a child playing with pretty shells on a beach. All show a deep humility and an emotional hunger which is the prerogative of the artist. It is with the lesser men, with the institutionalization of method, with the appearance of dogma and mapped-out territories, that an unpleasant suggestion of fenced preserves begins to dominate the university atmosphere.

As a scientist, I can say that I have observed it in my own and others' specialties. I have had occasion, also, to observe its effects in the humanities. It is not science *per se;* it is, instead, in both regions of thought, the narrow professionalism which is also plainly evident in the trade union. There can be small men in science just as there are small men in government or business. In fact it is one of the disadvantages of big science, just as it is of big government, that the availability of huge sums attracts a swarm of elbowing and contentious men to whom great dreams are less than protected hunting preserves.

The sociology of science deserves at least equal consideration with the biographies of the great scientists, for powerful and changing forces are at work upon science, the institution, as contrasted with science as a dream and an ideal of the individual. Like other aspects of society, it is a construct of men and is subject, like other social structures, to human pressures and inescapable distortions.

Let me give an illustration. Even in learned journals, clashes occasionally occur between those who would regard biology as a separate and distinct domain of inquiry and the reductionists who, by contrast, perceive in the living organism only a vaster and more random chemistry. Understandably, the concern of the reductionists is with the immediate. Thomas Hobbes was expressing a similar point of view when he castigated poets as "working on mean minds with words and distinctions that of themselves signifie nothing, but betray (by their obscurity) that there walketh . . . another kingdome, as it were a kingdome of fayries in the dark." I myself have been similarly criticized for speaking of a nature "beyond the nature that we know."

Yet consider for a moment this dark, impossible realm of "fayrie." Man is not totally compounded of the nature we profess to understand. He contains, instead, a lurking unknown future, just as the man-apes of the Pliocene contained in embryo the future that surrounds us now. The world of human culture itself was an unpredictable fairy world until, in some pre-ice-age meadow, the first meaningful sounds in all the world broke through the jungle babble of the past, the nature, until that moment, "known."

It is fascinating to observe that, in the very dawn of science, Francis Bacon, the spokesman for the empirical approach to nature, shared with Shakespeare, the poet, a recognition of the creativeness which adds to nature, and which emerges from nature as "an art which nature makes." Neither the great scholar nor the great poet had renounced this "kingdome of fayries."

Both had realized what Henri Bergson was later to express so effectively, that life inserts a vast "indetermination into matter." It is, in a sense, an intrusion from a realm which can never be completely subject to prophetic analysis by science. The novelties of evolution emerge, they cannot be predicted. They haunt, until their arrival, a world of unimaginable possibilities behind the living screen of events, as these last exist to the observer confined to a single point on the time scale.

Oddly enough, much of the confusion that surrounded my phrase, "a nature beyond the nature that we know," resolves itself into pure semantics. I might have pointed out what must be obvious even to the most dedicated scientific mind—that the nature which we know has been many times reinterpreted in human thinking, and that the hard, substantial matter of the nineteenth century has already vanished into a dark, bodiless void, a web of "events" in space-time. This is a realm, I venture to assert, as weird as any we have tried, in the past, to exorcise by the brave use of seeming solid words. Yet some minds exhibit an almost instinctive hostility toward the mere attempt to wonder or to ask what lies below that microcosmic world out of which emerge the particles which compose our bodies and which now take on this wraithlike quality.

Is there something here we fear to face, except when clothed in safely sterilized professional speech? Have we grown reluctant in this age of power to admit mystery and beauty into our thoughts, or to learn where power ceases? I referred earlier to one of our own forebears on a gravel bar, thumbing a pebble. If, after the ages of building and destroying, if after the measuring of light-years and the powers probed at the atom's heart if after the last iron is rust-eaten and the last glass lies shattered in the streets, a man, some savage, some remnant of what once we were, pauses on his way to the tribal drinking place and feels rising from within his soul the inexplicable mist of terror and beauty that is evoked from old ruins—even the ruins of the greatest city in the world—then, I say, all will still be well with man.

And if that savage can pluck a stone from the gravel because it shone like crystal when the water rushed over it, and hold it against the sunset, he will be as we were in the beginning, whole—as we were when we were children, before we began to split the knowledge from the dream. All talk of the two cultures is an illusion; it is the pebble which tells man's story. Upon it is written man's two faces, the artistic and the practical. They are expressed upon one stone over which a hand once closed, no less firm because the mind behind it was submerged in light and shadow and deep wonder.

Today we hold a stone, the heavy stone of power. We must perceive beyond it, however, by the aid of the artistic imagination, those humane insights and understandings which alone can lighten our burden and enable us to shape ourselves, rather than the stone, into the forms which great art has anticipated.

Reading and Thinking

1. The first two paragraphs of Eiseley's essay constitute his introduction. Note his thesis, the last sentence of the second paragraph. How does that sentence account for all that Eiseley has said up to that point? What does it promise the reader? What does Eiseley mean by "investment"?

2. Paragraphs 3–6 constitute the first section in the body of Eiseley's essay. What does Eiseley say about imagination, science, and literature in this section?

3. In paragraphs 4–5, Eiseley refers to at least eight other writers. Why does he refer to these writers?

4. In paragraphs 7–10, Eiseley makes use of his own story about another scientific explorer. What is the purpose of this story in the larger essay?

Thinking and Writing

1. In paragraphs 11–17, Eiseley tells a story about a stone ax. Trace this image of the ax throughout the essay, and write a one-page explanation of the purpose this image serves in developing Eiseley's main idea.

2. Notice that in paragraph 18, Eiseley moves from story to commentary. Look through the rest of the essay and find other occasions where Eiseley moves either from a written text to commentary or from story to commentary. Write a one-page assessment of the effectiveness of this kind of rhetorical move.

3. Finally, consider paragraphs 43–47, the essay's ending. Identify three interesting things that Eiseley does in that ending and explain why they are effective.

DISCOVERING DISCOVERY

AN OCCASION FOR NARRATION

In "The Illusion of the Two Cultures," Eiseley narrates his impressions of a stone hand ax that he picks up in his office one day. He makes extensive use of that story of discovery within his longer essay about the perceived split between the sciences and the humanities.

In this Occasion for narration, you will have a chance to incorporate several narratives of discovery together into a longer work with a larger thesis.

KERRIE BALDWIN
from *Stumbling Upon an Alien Fountain*

Imagine hurriedly walking through New York City's Washington Square Park (to be on time for an appointment or class) and halting, feet cemented to the asphalt, as you are dumbfounded by a beautiful stone creature gently spraying curved veins of sun-sparkling water out and down into a bubbling pool. You have never seen or heard of a "fountain," so you are convinced that this *creature* upon which you have stumbled is a miracle of nature. This first experience of a "fountain" is untainted—you see only the beauty that is before you, not the missing angels you might see sculpted in other fountains, on other occasions.

The possibility of such an experience, and of such experiences with every one of life's encounters, plays on the brain after reading Walker Percy's essay "The Loss of the Creature." It is easy to be deceived, however, by Percy's novel and captivating claim that human beings have lost the ability to truly "experience" the world because we attach to it "symbolic complexes"—that we use to measure experience—that is, we do not simply appreciate the world for its inherent beauty, but instead only derive satisfaction "by the degree to which [experience] conforms to the preformed complex." He cites as an example the Grand Canyon, which can no longer be seen for itself, but only measured against its representation in "picture postcard[s], geography book[s], tourist folders, and the words Grand Canyon." Percy claims that through the destruction of such "experience packages" (illustrated by his exhortation to renounce organized sightseeing trips to the Grand Canyon) we can recover the ability to see things as we ourselves perceive them—thus recovering the Self.

© William Mowder, 2003.

PREPARING TO WRITE: STUMBLING UPON AN ALIEN FOUNTAIN

1. In the first paragraph of this excerpt, Baldwin tries to get her readers to imagine that they have never seen a fountain. Why do you think Baldwin makes this playful move?

2. In the second paragraph, Baldwin summarizes Walker Percy's essay "The Loss of the Creature." Does that summary strike you as effective or relevant? Explain.

3. What does the word *deceived* in the second sentence of the second paragraph suggest about Baldwin's attitude toward Percy's ideas?

PREPARING TO WRITE: UNTITLED PHOTOGRAPH

1. William Mowder's photograph shows the fountain in Washington Square Park that Kerrie Baldwin refers to in her essay. But this photograph depicts a particular moment, not the ideal moment that Baldwin imagined. The fountain is occupied. Who are the principal actors within the fountain? Who has greater prominence—actors or fountain? Explain.

2. Who is observing the spectacle in the fountain? Are they part of the spectacle too? What do the spectators seem to be doing?

3. What part, if any, do the buildings play in this spectacle? For whom might they be most significant? Someone in the photograph or someone outside it? Explain in a paragraph.

MARCEL DUCHAMP

Marcel Duchamp (1887–1968) was born in France, but he became a U.S. citizen in 1955. He studied painting at the Académie Julian and exhibited his work for the first time in 1909 at the Salon des Indépendants and the Salon d'Automne in Paris. His earliest paintings were Impressionist in style, and those around 1911 were related to Cubism. He was associated with many experimental groups (Dada and Surrealism) in France and the United States.

Nude Descending a Staircase (No. 2) was painted in 1912 and was first exhibited in New York at the Armory Show of Contemporary Art in 1913. The painting was bought for $300 by a San Francisco dealer and then purchased in 1927 by Duchamp's collector-friend Walter Arensberg. Duchamp had, in the meantime, made Arensberg a hand-colored copy. That museum now owns the copy, the original, and a preparatory study of the painting.

© 2005 Artists Rights Society (ARS), New York/ADAGP, Paris.

PREPARING TO WRITE: NUDE DESCENDING A STAIRCASE (NO. 2)

1. Consider the colors in Duchamp's painting. How many do you see? How do they affect you? How many nudes do you see? Can you identify body parts? If so, how many? How does the counting exercise differ as you move from colors to bodies? Explain.

2. What is your primary impression of the painting? Record your impression and explain what you think Duchamp might be trying to suggest to his viewers.

Occasion

X. J. KENNEDY

X. J. Kennedy was born Joseph Charles Kennedy in Dover, New Jersey, in 1929. He studied at Seton Hall University, earned an M.A. from Columbia, and served in the U.S. Navy for four years. After additional study at the Sorbonne in Paris and the University of Michigan, Kennedy taught English at the University of North Carolina and Tufts University in Massachusetts. His first poetry collection, in 1961, won the Lamont Award. His other awards include a Guggenheim Fellowship, a National Endowment for the Arts grant, and a *Los Angeles Times* Book Prize. He is the former editor of the *Paris Review*. He has written numerous collections of verse for children, and he also writes textbooks.

"Nude Descending a Staircase" reflects Kennedy's interest in rhyme and metrical patterns. But it also shows him having a great time with Duchamp's painting. See if you can detect his playfulness as you read the poem.

Nude Descending a Staircase

Toe upon toe, a snowing flesh,
A gold of lemon, root and rind,
She sifts in sunlight down the stairs
With nothing on. Nor on her mind.

We spy beneath the banister
A constant thresh of thigh on thigh--
Her lips imprint the swinging air
That parts to let her parts go by.

One-woman waterfall, she wears
Her slow descent like a long cape
And pausing, on the final stair
Collects her motions into shape.

PREPARING TO WRITE: NUDE DESCENDING A STAIRCASE (POEM)

1. Identify the poem's rhyme scheme by placing a letter at the end of each line. The first stanza would be *abcb*. Complete the scheme for the other verses. What do the rhyming words suggest about emphasis and meaning?

2. What kind of movement, if any, do you detect from stanza to stanza in the poem? How does it correspond to the movement in the painting?

3. Who are the *we* of the second stanza of the poem? Where is this *we* physically located? Does the observer's angle of vision matter? Explain.

4. Kennedy identifies a number of body parts. He also identifies the subject of the painting as a *she*. Can you see a woman in the painting? What does Kennedy suggest by the phrase *one-woman waterfall*?

MOVING TOWARD ESSAY: ANALYSIS AND REFLECTION

1. Write a letter to a classmate explaining how you brought Kennedy's poem and Duchamp's image together in your mind to figure out something important about the painting. Tell the story of what Kennedy's poem did to change the way you see Duchamp's painting. How did Duchamp's painting change the way you understand Kennedy's poem?

2. Compare Baldwin's "word picture" of the fountain with the same fountain in Mowder's photograph. Having seen both, do you believe that you could ever again see the fountain itself as it really *is*, without this cast of interesting, odd characters playing across your mind? Explain.

3. In what ways are the relationships between Mowder's photograph and Baldwin's essay similar to the relationship between Kennedy's poem and Duchamp's painting *Nude Descending a Staircase*? Explain.

WRITING THOUGHTFULLY: IDEA AND ESSAY

1. Consider the Baldwin excerpt, the Mowder photograph, and the Duchamp/Kennedy pair as primary pieces of evidence that have something to do with shifting perspectives. Take into account all of the reflective writing that you have done that is related to what we might call seeing and knowing. Using a combination of stories and reflection (or commentary), develop your own idea about the relationship between seeing and knowing, or in other words, the way certain kinds of knowledge affect your ability to see and understand.

2. Go back to the two photographs in Seams of Time: An Occasion for Narration (p. 136) in this chapter. Consider those two photographs now as a pair. Let one influence the way you see the other, just as we imagine Duchamp's *Nude* influenced Kennedy's "Nude." Create new titles for the photographs based on this pairing. Select the photograph that speaks most clearly to you and, in an essay, convince your readers that your new title is more appropriate than the old one by telling the story of what you now see in the photograph that warrants the new emphasis.

CREATING OCCASIONS

1. Create two scenes that focus on an object or a public space—one scene drawn from your memory (a real-life recollection) and another that probes beneath the details of the scene to get to its essence, as Baldwin did with the fountain in her first paragraph.

2. Take the two scenes from the previous exercise. Write a short introduction for these scenes, giving your readers a sense of why you have created them. Then look for ways to integrate reflective commentary (explanatory clarification) within the scenes, between the scenes, or following the scenes (a combination could be the most effective) that will help you develop an idea of your own about the transforming or the inhibiting power of the imagination.

3. Eiseley makes especially good use of the hand ax in "The Illusion of the Two Cultures." For Eiseley, the ax represents a time in the past when utility and beauty seemed to go hand in hand, and it suggests that in the future the absence of that kind of blending of beauty and utility might lead to the misuse of power, that science without beauty might run amok. Select an image or an object from our culture that makes you suspect that scientific technology has or has not lost sight of beauty. Recreate that image so that your readers can see it and can also sense what story it conveys to you about the use and/or misuse of technology in our world.

4. Create your own interactive Occasion on *Comp21* using the textual, visual, and video libraries, as well as the Explicator analysis tools. From the main menu, choose "Build Your Own Occasion for Writing."

Occasion

chapter SIX

ILLUSTRATION

When you want to understand a general concept or an abstract idea, you probably ask for an example. And when you want to explain an idea, you probably provide examples as a strategy to make your thinking clear to others. Illustration, sometimes called exemplification, is a method of analysis useful for explaining and understanding things. Writers use examples to explain and develop ideas. They illustrate their ideas with specific examples because it is easier for readers to imagine a concrete example than an abstract concept. You understand the concept of "exercise" through the example of a thirty-minute aerobic workout or an hour's walk. And the notion of "a good meal" becomes clear with the example of a three-course dinner of lobster bisque soup, roasted salmon with garlic mashed potatoes, and a dessert of chocolate mousse and a cappuccino.

Readers appreciate illustration, or the use of examples, when writers explain their ideas. Examples clarify ideas by providing specific cases or situations. They bring ideas and concepts down to earth and close to home.

Illustrating is a natural process. You illustrate in your everyday life whenever someone asks you to give an example. The example provides a concrete or specific instance that clarifies, enabling readers to "see" what you mean. Examples make the abstract concrete and the general specific.

This work, American Alphabet by Heidi Cody, uses letters from various product logos. How many products can you identify? What does Cody's inclusion of these letters illustrate?

· · · · · · · · · ·

THE NATURE OF
ILLUSTRATION

To read more about Illustration with interactive examples and opportunities to work with interactive texts, click on "The Rhetorical Patterns of Inquiry" from the main menu of *Comp21*.

Illustrating is also a natural way to understand the world and ourselves. You understand what prejudice is by looking at specific instances of prejudicial action or examples of prejudicial thinking. You understand and explain your own ambitions by providing specific examples of what you hope to achieve and become.

In offering a "for example" or a "for instance" when you talk or write, you are providing examples to help listeners or readers understand what you mean. In suggesting to a friend that he or she has an unhealthy lifestyle, you would very likely have to explain your thinking with a few examples. "You get too little sleep," you might say. "You eat too much red meat and too few vegetables and whole grain foods, and you never exercise, except to walk to the refrigerator." Your notion is made clear through the examples of sleeping and eating habits that illustrate what you mean by "an unhealthy lifestyle."

To take a more academic example, you might explain how Benjamin Franklin was a "Renaissance man" (a person who can do many different kinds of things). To do so, you could mention that Franklin was, at different times in his life, a printer, a politician, a diplomat, a writer, and an inventor. Examples of a few of his many accomplishments that illustrate his wide-ranging "Renaissance" talents include his experiments with electricity by flying kites in electrical storms, his founding the first fire department and public library, his writing and publishing of the popular *Poor Richard's Almanack,* and his diplomatic work for the early American colonies as a founding father of the country, including his signing of the Declaration of Independence.

In the case of both Franklin and the friend with the unhealthy lifestyle, examples provide specific information that helps readers understand the point. If the examples are carefully chosen, and if there are enough of them, readers will be persuaded to accept what the writer claims—in the first case, that the friend is living an unhealthy lifestyle, and in the second, that Benjamin Franklin exemplifies an American "Renaissance man". Notice that it is both the number of examples used and their relevance that makes them convincing. Lots of bad examples won't be persuasive; neither will only a single example, unless it is particularly powerful and appropriate.

· · · · · · · · · ·

THE MEANING
OF ILLUSTRATION

If you think of the idea of an illustration literally, you think of a picture. And sometimes that is how a writer or speaker illustrates an idea—by providing either a visual image, a picture to illustrate what is being said, or by offering a word-picture, a description with numerous details to illustrate the concept. The diagrams in your biology textbook; the photographs in your psychology textbook; and the maps, charts, and timelines in your history textbook are all types of visual illustrations that help you see literally and mentally what an author is saying.

The word *illustrate* comes from the Latin word referring to light or illumination. The word *example* derives from *exemplum,* which refers to one thing from many, something that illustrates the more general category. Examples are instances, specific cases that have a larger resonance and that convey a more general significance. The example or illustration stands for more than itself alone. It serves to represent a larger notion, to convey a bigger idea. And so illustration, like other rhetorical strategies, is an aid to thinking.

. . . .

HOW ILLUSTRATION
WORKS: INDUCTIVE AND DEDUCTIVE THINKING

Illustration works through a process of moving back and forth between general ideas and specific examples. Specific examples share the general characteristics of the idea, concept, or principle a writer explains by means of using them. Examples enable readers to see how the idea exists in concrete instances in the real world. From those specific examples, readers can generalize to understand the idea.

This principle of abstracting an idea or generalization from particular instances is closely related to *inductive thinking*. When you think inductively, you start with particulars, with observations of what birds eat or how babies learn to talk. From those observations of particular birds eating and specific babies learning to talk, you make generalizations about how the process works in many or all circumstances. You use inductive thinking often in everyday life. Imagine seeing a person looking up into the sky, and then noticing two or three others doing the same, and still another pointing. From these instances of people looking up and pointing, you would infer that they see something unusual happening somewhere up high.

One danger of inductive thinking is jumping to conclusions from too few instances or examples. Another is reaching a conclusion or generalization based on an atypical set of examples.

Deductive thinking reverses inductive thinking. In deductive thinking, you begin with a generalization and then find specific examples to support the idea. If you notice that your portable telephone or laptop computer loses power, you infer that the battery needs to be recharged. The general idea that the phone or the laptop needs energy to keep working leads you to deduce that your machine is not functioning because it needs to have its battery recharged.

The classic example of deductive reasoning is the syllogism. A familiar example is the following syllogism: All men are mortal. Socrates is a man. Socrates is mortal. In syllogistic reasoning, the conclusion derives from the premises. In both deductive and inductive thinking, examples are an essential element. In inductive thinking, specific examples provide the basis or ground for generalizing, while in deductive thinking, examples serve to validate the general idea.

. . . .

USING ILLUSTRATION
IN WRITING

All good writing uses illustration. Specific examples, the particular illustrations that engage and interest readers, also ultimately persuade them. Writing that lacks examples can be vague and overly general. It can be boring. Examples add life to writing. Examples provide clarity to a writer's ideas. And examples make writing easier to follow and more enjoyable to read.

Some of the kinds of examples you can use to illustrate your ideas include the following:

- Facts
- Statistics
- Instances
- People, Places, Events
- Anecdotes or Stories

Consider the following sample paragraphs, each of which uses illustration to convey an idea. The first paragraph sample uses a single extended example; the second includes multiple examples. The paragraphs are taken from the same essay, "Can Hollywood Kick the Habit?" by Renee Graham, about the place of smoking in Hollywood movies. Here is the first paragraph, which was featured in the *Boston Globe* on August 20, 2002.

> In one of my favorite scenes from one of my favorite movies, "The Great Escape," wily prisoner of war James Garner sidles up to gullible German guard Robert Graf. Blowing cigarette smoke in the guard's direction—Graf practically swoons in the cloud—Garner offers Graf a cigarette, then slides a few more into the chest pocket of the guard's uniform. Accepting the cigarettes could be viewed as fraternizing, yet they are a pleasure these two men, made enemies by war, can share. Soon the two are talking casually in the lazy haze of smoke. Garner intends to bribe and blackmail the guard, but it all plays as if Garner were picking Graf up in a bar. For all intents and purposes, it's a subtle seduction scene, and one that would not have been as persuasive without the cigarettes.

As you can see, in this paragraph the author describes a single scene from one of her favorite films. Her choice of film and the particular scene within the film are designed to convey her point that cigarette smoking contributes to the scene's effectiveness and persuasiveness. The details of the example add to our interest in reading it. The example itself, expanded with specific details, clarifies the writer's point and also helps her to secure a reader's readiness to agree with her. It is convincing because it is appropriate to what the writer claims in her generalization. The example supports the writer's generalization that cigarettes are a key element in seduction scenes in movies.

In the second paragraph from the same article, the author explains how pervasive cigarettes have been as a prop in Hollywood films.

> In Hollywood, tobacco products remain a favorite prop. In scripted scenes, they serve as accent marks and exclamation points. For actors, they are as character-defining as a lisp or a way of walking—try to imagine Humphrey Bogart without a cigarette dangling from his lips. In a century of moviemaking, cigarettes have made tangible the doomed cool of James Dean, the carnivorous conniving of Bette Davis, and the urbane sophistication of super spy James Bond. When Olivia Newton-John's virginal Sandy in "Grease" turns teased and Spandex-clad bad girl, a cigarette becomes a potent accessory. And in 1992's "Basic Instinct," Sharon Stone became a star as the underwear-averse femme fatale, who when told by police she's not allowed to smoke in an interrogation room, utters the line, "What are you going to do? Charge me with smoking?"

In this sample paragraph, the author refers to a variety of films and actors. She uses many examples to illustrate her point about the pervasiveness of cigarettes in films. The writer's examples include references to recent films and to films made half a century ago. The examples also include both male and female actors, and they span a variety of film genres, or types. Like the first paragraph's single extended example, this paragraph provides examples that are appropriate, examples that support the claim the writer makes. Moreover, one of the virtues of this way of using illustration to convey a point is that readers can likely supply additional examples of their own, which, of course, serve to strengthen the author's argument.

· · · · · · · · · ·

ILLUSTRATION WITH
A PURPOSE

As you have seen from our discussion so far and from the examples and sample paragraphs, illustration serves a variety of purposes. Writers use illustration, as they use other rhetorical strategies, to explain and to persuade. Allied with both of these central rhetorical purposes are other goals, especially to clarify and to add interest.

Providing facts and statistics as examples can lend authority and persuasiveness to your writing. Including stories and anecdotes will add interest. Illustrating through description of particular people, places, and events will often clarify, engage, and persuade readers all at once.

As with other patterns, your decision whether to use facts and statistics or anecdotes and stories, or a combination of them, as well as your decision about which events, places, or people to describe or just what facts or statistics to include, will be determined by your audience and your purpose. For whom are you writing? Who will be reading your essay? And what is your purpose in writing it? Consider these questions when you choose your examples, for your goal is to get your reader to agree with what you are saying. The examples you select must be appropriate for the audience you address in your essay and your essay's underlying purpose.

. . . .

SELECTING EXAMPLES

A final concern about using examples to illustrate your ideas is that your examples should be representative. Representative examples are those that cover the territory—are broad enough in their range to fit your argument or idea. For example, if you are suggesting that Tiger Woods is on his way to becoming the greatest golfer the world has ever seen, you need to mention more than his accomplishments in a particular year or on a single golf course. Your examples need to be more wide-ranging than that. If you mean to argue that cell phones should be banned in public places, it isn't enough to illustrate with references to movie theaters or restaurants. You need to extend your examples to include other kinds of public places and spaces, such as libraries, schools, concert halls, and public parks.

Since your readers will be looking to see how you generalize from your examples, you need to select examples that share the characteristics of the concept you are explaining to your readers. Notice how the paragraphs about cigarette smoking in films contain examples that are representative, relating to a range of instances. They are not all about one kind of film, but rather range widely to illustrate the author's general idea about how pervasive cigarette smoking in films has been for a very long time.

. . . .

ILLUSTRATION
AND THE OTHER PATTERNS OF INQUIRY

Illustration is a common rhetorical strategy, but it is rarely used exclusively on its own. Rather, illustration is an essential element in all kinds of writing. Writers defining terms use examples to illustrate their meaning. Comparison and contrast, cause and effect, classification—all these patterns require writers to provide examples to illustrate the particular comparative and contrastive points, their causes and effects, their classificatory schemes. In developing any kind of analysis or argument, writers resort to illustration, most often simply to clarify their thinking for their readers.

When writers tell stories to illustrate an idea, those stories serve as illustrations, even though the writer's primary work in storytelling is that of narrative. And as in other types of writing—analysis, argument, description—narrative typically makes multiple uses of illustration. To see how illustration is used in narration and in the other rhetorical patterns, look back at the essays in the other chapters. You won't have to look very hard or long before you see writers narrating, describing, classifying, and so on, all illustrating with examples. Illustrating with examples is a writerly necessity. Illustration, in short, works.

. . . .

ILLUSTRATION
IN PURE FORM: AN ANNOTATED PARAGRAPH

Donald A. Norman is cofounder of the Nielsen Norman Group, an executive consulting firm that helps companies produce sensibly designed products and services. He is a professor of computer science at Northwestern University and professor emeritus at the University of California, San Diego, where he was founding chair of the Department of Cognitive Science and chair of the Department of Psychology. His books include *Memory and Attention, Things that Make Us Smart, The Invisible Computer,* and *The Design of Everyday Things,* from which the two paragraphs that follow have been taken.

direct quotation → "You would need an engineering degree from MIT to work this," someone once told me, shaking his head in puzzlement over his brand new digital watch. Well, I **— complicated** have an engineering degree from MIT. (Kenneth Olsen has two of them, and he can't figure out a microwave oven.) Give me a few hours and I can figure **— hours for a watch?** **Why should it? good question →** out the watch. But why should it take hours? I have talked with many people who can't use all the features of their washing machines or cameras, who can't figure **→ more examples** out how to work a sewing machine or a video cassette recorder, who habitually turn on the wrong stove burner.

Notice how Donald Norman begins his paragraph with a specific example about a friend's puzzlement over how to use a new digital watch. Notice, too, how the author provides additional examples to support his idea that it should not take hours to figure out how to use the appliances and "convenient" tools abundant in our everyday lives. The examples Norman provides clarify his idea; they also make us willing to think about what he is saying.

Exercises

1. Why do you think Norman mentions that he has an engineering degree from MIT? Taken alongside the parenthetical note that "Kenneth Olsen has two of them," what do these references illustrate? How do the particular examples help Norman make his point?

2. What do you think will follow this opening paragraph of his first chapter on the design of everyday things? Explain.

3. In this paragraph, only a few examples are annotated. Circle or highlight all the examples in the paragraph. What do they all have in common? What do they illustrate?

4. Write your own expansion of Norman's paragraph, including other examples of everyday items that are too complicated to use. Try to think beyond the types of things Norman mentions. Be sure to make it clear why your examples are too complicated.

ILLUSTRATION
IN PURE FORM: AN ANNOTATED PARAGRAPH

In this next paragraph from Norman's book, he goes into detail on a single example—the design of doors. As you read the paragraph, consider how it is related to his earlier paragraph with the varied examples.

Pure Form

nice contrast

personalize with question

4 common examples

doors—a major example

how doors can be used

Push? Pull? Slide?

more questions about how doors work

> If I were placed in the cockpit of a modern jet airline, my inability to perform gracefully and smoothly would neither surprise nor bother me. But I shouldn't have trouble with doors and switches, water faucets and stoves. "Doors?" I can hear the reader saying, "you have trouble opening doors?" Yes. I push doors that are meant to be pulled, pull doors that should be pushed, and walk into doors that should be slid. Moreover, I see others having the same troubles— unnecessary troubles. There are psychological principles that can be followed to make these things understandable and usable. Consider the door. There is not much you can do to a door: you can open it or shut it. Suppose you are in an office building, walking down a corridor. You come to a door. In which direction does it open? Should you pull or push, on the left or the right? Maybe the door slides. If so, in which direction? I have seen doors that slide up into the ceiling. A door poses only two essential questions: In which direction does it move? On which side should one work it? The answers should be given by the design, without any need for words or symbols, certainly without any need for trial and error.

This second, longer paragraph mentions a few other examples—switches, faucets, and stoves—but its focus is clearly on the design of doors. Norman finds much wrong with the design of doors, as it is often far from immediately evident just how we should open some of the doors we pass through every day. Notice how Norman uses his personal experience with doors to connect with his readers, implicitly inviting us to consider our own experience with doors. Finally, Norman makes clear his belief that doors should be designed so that how they open and close is logical and self-evident. We shouldn't have to guess, and we shouldn't have to try various ways to open them.

Exercises

1. Where does Norman make his point explicitly? Annotate this.

2. Why do you think he uses questions in his paragraph? How effective are his questions? Add a note in the margin about these questions.

3. While Norman's paragraph deals mostly with one type of contraption that is confusing—doors—he is able to provide specific examples of the difficulty with doors. List these specific examples.

4. Return to the first paragraph from Norman's book, on page 176. Choose one of the examples he cites, and write a paragraph listing and explaining specific difficulties with that item. Try to follow the bend of Norman's paragraph about doors.

ILLUSTRATION
IN ITS NATURAL HABITAT: AN ANNOTATED READING

Up till now, you have been presented with examples of paragraphs that include examples. Although the paragraphs were developed primarily through the use of examples, you will often encounter longer pieces that blend examples with other rhetorical strategies.

NATALIE GOLDBERG
from *Writing Down the Bones*

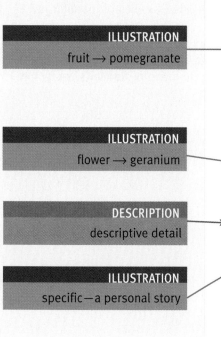

ILLUSTRATION
fruit → pomegranate

ILLUSTRATION
flower → geranium

DESCRIPTION
descriptive detail

ILLUSTRATION
specific—a personal story

Be specific. Don't say "fruit." Tell what kind of fruit—"It is a pomegranate." Give things the dignity of their names. Just as with human beings, it is rude to say, "Hey, girl, get in line." That "girl" has a name. (As a matter of fact, if she's at least twenty years old, she's a woman, not a "girl" at all.) Things, too, have names. It is much better to say "the geranium in the window" than "the flower in the window." "Geranium"—that one word gives us a much more specific picture. It penetrates more deeply into the beingness of that flower. It immediately gives us the scene by the window—red petals, green circular leaves, all straining toward sunlight.

About ten years ago I decided I had to learn the names of plants and flowers in my environment. I bought a book on them and walked down the tree-lined streets of Boulder, examining leaf, bark, and seed, trying to match them up with their descriptions and names in the book. Maple, elm, oak, locust. I usually

In this brief essay, Natalie Goldberg, a writer who often writes about writing, gives some advice to beginning writers. In addition to her book *Writing Down the Bones: Freeing the Writer Within,* she has also written *Living Color: A Writer Paints Her World,* as well as several novels, including *Banana Rose.* In the following essay, from *Writing Down the Bones,* Goldberg provides a number of specific examples that illustrate what she means when she advises writers to "be specific."

tried to cheat by asking people working in their yards the names of the flowers and trees growing there. I was amazed how few people had any idea of the names of the live beings inhabiting their little plot of land.

When we know the name of something, it brings us closer to the ground. It takes the blur out of our mind; it connects us to the earth. If I walk down the street and see "dogwood," "forsythia," I feel more friendly toward the environment. I am noticing what is around me and can name it. It makes me more awake.

If you read the poems of William Carlos Williams, you will see how specific he is about plants, trees, flowers—chicory, daisy, locust, poplar, quince, primrose, black-eyed Susan, lilacs—each has its own integrity. Williams says, "Write what's in front of your nose." It's good for us to know what is in front of our noses. Not just "daisy," but how the flower is in the season we are looking at it—"The days-eye hugging the earth/in August . . . brownedged,/green and pointed scales/armor his yellow." Continue to hone your awareness: to the name, to the month, to the day, and finally to the moment.

ARGUMENT
Is this true?

ARGUMENT
seeing/noticing

ILLUSTRATION
specifics—names—details

ILLUSTRATION
sharpening awareness

Williams also says: "No idea, but in things." Study what is "in front of your nose." By saying "geranium" instead of "flower," you are penetrating more deeply into the present and being there. The closer we can get to what's in front of our nose, the more it can teach us everything. "To see the World in a Grain of Sand, and a heaven in a Wild Flower . . ."

Goldberg's piece gets right to the point: "Be specific," she says in her first brief sentence. And then she immediately provides an example: rather than writing "fruit," identify a specific kind of fruit. Many more examples follow, as Goldberg illustrates what she argues for—the specificity that makes writing sharp and striking.

Besides including various examples of fruits and flowers to illustrate her argument about the need for being specific, Goldberg includes an anecdote of her personal experience. She tells how she began learning the specific names of particular things, so she could know them better. She argues that knowing the names of things, you get closer to their reality, their uniqueness. This, she suggests, enriches our lives as well as our writing.

In writing groups and classes too, it is good to quickly learn the names of all the other group members. It helps to ground you in the group and make you more attentive to each other's work.

Learn the names of everything: birds, cheese, tractors, cars, buildings. A writer is all at once everything—an architect, French cook, farmer—and at the same time, a writer is none of these things.

COMPARISON & CONTRAST
writer's two opposing tasks

Exercises

1. Why does Goldberg insist that it's better to say (or write) the word *geranium* than *flower?* What does *geranium* conjure up that *flower* doesn't?

2. Other than illustration, what rhetorical patterns does Goldberg make use of?

3. Why do you think she brings the American poet William Carlos Williams into her essay? How relevant are the references and the quotations from Williams? Explain.

4. What do you think Goldberg means by her last sentence? Is there a contradiction there? Explain.

RICHARD LEDERER

Richard Lederer (b. 1938) was born and raised in Philadelphia. After attending Haverford College, Harvard University, and the University of New Hampshire, he taught English at St. Paul's School, a private school in New Hampshire. He retired from full-time teaching to devote more time to writing, particularly books and essays concerned with the English language, including *Anguished English* and *Adventures of a Verbivore*. The essay that follows is taken from his popular book *Crazy English*.

English Is a Crazy Language

In the following essay, Lederer humorously illustrates the many oddities of the English language. His examples range from the apparent contradictions in the meaning of words to words whose sounds or meaning bear no relation to the dictionary meanings. Part of the essay's effectiveness is the way Lederer piles example upon example; part, too, is attributable to his use of questions throughout.

1   English is the most widely spoken language in the history of our planet, used in some way by at least one out of every seven human beings around the globe. Half of the world's books are written in English, and the majority of international telephone calls are made in English. English is the language of over sixty percent of the world's radio programs, many of them beamed, ironically, by the Russians, who know that to win friends and influence nations, they're best off using English. More than seventy percent of international mail is written and addressed in English, and eighty percent of all computer text is stored in English. English has acquired the largest vocabulary of all the world's languages, perhaps as many as two million words, and has generated one of the noblest bodies of literature in the annals of the human race.

Nonetheless, it is now time to face the fact that English is a crazy language.

In the crazy English language, the blackbird hen is brown, blackboards can be blue or green, and blackberries are green and then red before they are ripe.

Even if blackberries were really black and blueberries really blue, what are strawberries, cranberries, elderberries, huckleberries, raspberries, boysenberries, mulberries, and gooseberries supposed to look like?

To add to the insanity, there is no butter in buttermilk, no egg in eggplant, no grape in grapefruit, neither worms nor wood in wormwood, neither pine nor apple in pineapple, neither peas nor nuts in peanuts, and no ham in a hamburger. (In fact, if somebody invented a sandwich consisting of a ham patty in a bun, we would have a hard time finding a name for it.) To make matters worse, English muffins weren't invented in England, french fries in France, or danish pastries in Denmark. And we discover even more culinary madness in the revelations that sweetmeat is candy, while sweetbread, which isn't sweet, is made from meat.

In this unreliable English tongue, greyhounds aren't always grey (or gray); panda bears and koala bears aren't bears (they're marsupials); a woodchuck is a groundhog, which is not a hog; a horned toad is a lizard; glow-worms are fireflies, but fireflies are not flies (they're beetles); ladybugs and lightning bugs are also beetles (and to propagate, a significant proportion of ladybugs must be male); a guinea pig is neither a pig nor from Guinea (it's a South American rodent); and a titmouse is neither mammal nor mammaried.

Language is like the air we breathe. It's invisible, inescapable, indispensable, and we take it for granted. But when we take the time, step back, and listen to the sounds that escape from the holes in people's faces and explore the paradoxes and vagaries of English, we find that hot dogs can be cold, darkrooms can be lit, homework can be done in school, nightmares can take place in broad daylight, while morning sickness and daydreaming can take place at night, tomboys are girls, midwives can be men, hours—especially happy hours and rush hours—can last longer than sixty minutes, quicksand works *very* slowly, boxing rings are square, silverware can be made of plastic and tablecloths of paper, most telephones are dialed by being punched (or pushed?), and most bathrooms don't have any baths in them. In fact, a dog can go to the bathroom under a tree—no bath, no room; it's still going to the bathroom. And doesn't it seem at least a little bizarre that we go to the bathroom in order to go to the bathroom?

Why is it that a woman can man a station but a man can't woman one, that a man can father a movement but a woman can't mother one, and that a king rules a kingdom but a queen doesn't rule a queendom? How did all those Renaissance men reproduce when there don't seem to have been any Renaissance women?

A writer is someone who writes, and a stinger is something that stings. But fingers don't fing, grocers don't groce, hammers don't ham, and humdingers don't humding. If the plural of *tooth* is *teeth,* shouldn't the plural of *booth* be *beeth?* One goose, two geese—so one moose, two meese? One index, two indices—one Kleenex, two Kleenices? If people ring a bell today and rang a bell yesterday, why don't we say that they flang a ball? If they wrote a letter, perhaps they also bote their tongue. If the teacher taught, why isn't it also true that the preacher praught? Why is it that the sun shone yesterday while I shined my shoes, that I treaded water

and then trod on soil, and that I flew out to see a World Series game in which my favorite player flied out?

If we conceive a conception and receive at a reception, why don't we grieve a greption and believe a beleption? If a horsehair mat is made from the hair of horses and a camel's hair brush from the hair of camels, from what is a mohair coat made? If a vegetarian eats vegetables, what does a humanitarian eat? If a firefighter fights fire, what does a freedom fighter fight? If a weightlifter lifts weights, what does a shoplifter lift? If *pro* and *con* are opposites, is congress the opposite of progress?

Sometimes you have to believe that all English speakers should be committed to an asylum for the verbally insane. In what other language do people drive in a parkway and park in a driveway? In what other language do people recite at a play and play at a recital? In what other language do privates eat in the general mess and generals eat in the private mess? In what other language do men get hernias and women get hysterectomies? In what other language do people ship by truck and send cargo by ship? In what other language can your nose run and your feet smell?

How can a slim chance and a fat chance be the same, "what's going on?" and "what's coming off?" be the same, and a bad licking and a good licking be the same, while a wise man and a wise guy are opposites? How can sharp speech and blunt speech be the same and *quite a lot* and *quite a few* the same, while *overlook* and *oversee* are opposites? How can the weather be hot as hell one day and cold as hell the next?

If *button* and *unbutton* and *tie* and *untie* are opposites, why are *loosen* and *unloosen* and *ravel* and *unravel* the same? If *bad* is the opposite of *good, hard* the opposite of *soft,* and *up* the opposite of *down,* why are *badly* and *goodly, hardly* and *softly,* and *upright* and *downright* not opposing pairs? If harmless actions are the opposite of harmful actions, why are shameless and shameful behavior the same and pricey objects less expensive than priceless ones? If appropriate and inappropriate remarks and passable and impassable mountain trails are opposites, why are flammable and inflammable materials, heritable and inheritable property, and passive and impassive people the same and valuable objects less treasured than invaluable ones? If *uplift* is the same as *lift up,* why are *upset* and *set up* opposite in meaning? Why are *pertinent* and *impertinent, canny* and *uncanny,* and *famous* and *infamous* neither opposites nor the same? How can *raise* and *raze* and *reckless* and *wreckless* be opposites when each pair contains the same sound?

Why is it that when the sun or the moon or the stars are out, they are visible, but when the lights are out, they are invisible, and that when I wind up my watch, I start it, but when I wind up this essay, I shall end it?

English is a crazy language.

Reading and Thinking

1. What is the central idea of Lederer's essay? What is the main point of the opening paragraph?

2. What do the numerous examples Lederer provides in paragraphs 3–5 have in common? What purpose do they serve? Are there enough of them? Explain.

3. What do you think Lederer means by saying that "language is like the air we breathe?" How do people take language for granted?

Thinking and Writing

1. Lederer refers in paragraph 6 to "the paradoxes and vagaries" of English. Choose two of his examples from that paragraph and explain how those words are either vague or paradoxical or both.

2. Write a paragraph explaining why Lederer thinks that "English is a crazy language." Write a second paragraph identifying three principles of language that you think Lederer would approve of, and why you think he would approve of them.

3. Write a letter to someone who is learning English as a foreign language. Use half a dozen or so examples of your own or from Lederer's essay to convey an idea about the English language to this person.

Reading

CRAZY OBJECTS

AN OCCASION FOR ILLUSTRATION

In his essay, Richard Lederer uses humorous examples of the English paradoxes to entertain his readers and to illustrate his point that, indeed, English is a crazy language. In this Occasion you will have the chance to follow Lederer's lead with an essay of your own—not about language, but objects.

In the following pictures from his book *Catalog of Unfindable Objects,* the French artist Jacques Carelman provides examples of everyday objects that are deliberately unworkable. Delightfully outrageous, his images look very much like everyday objects we are familiar with, but their design makes them inherently contradictory.

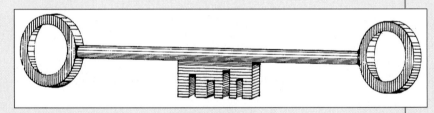

Double Key

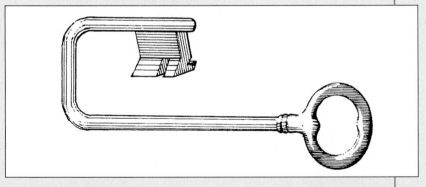

Key for Inaccessible Locks

Fork for Escargots

All images pp. 188–191: From *Le Catalogue d'objets introuvables* by Jacques Carelman. Copyright © 1997 le cherche midi éditeur. Used with permission.

Coffeepot for Masochists

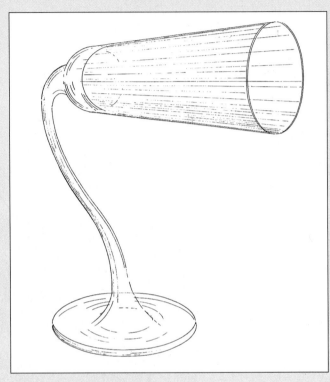

Glass for Short People

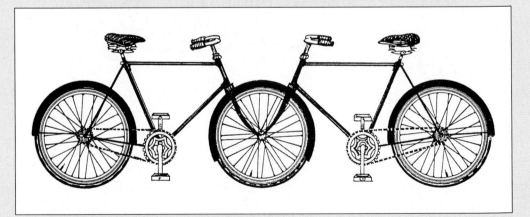

Converging Tandem Bicycle (Model for Fiancés)

Two-Piece Puzzle

Occasion

PREPARING TO WRITE: CRAZY OBJECTS

1. Look closely at each of Carelman's objects. Explain the inherent principle of each image.

2. Each object is accompanied by a caption (which has been translated from the original French), explaining what the object is and what its purpose is. Explain how each object is designed to fulfill its purpose.

MOVING TOWARD ESSAY: ANALYSIS AND REFLECTION

1. Consider the real-world equivalents of Carelman's objects: a key, a fork, a bicycle, a teapot, and so on. What is the fundamental purpose of each of these objects in its regular form? Make a list of the objects and note exactly what each object is designed to accomplish.

2. In a sentence or two, describe how the regular forms of the real-world equivalents help each object achieve its purpose. How does the shape of a puzzle, for example, help it to achieve its purpose? How does the particular shape, or form, of a fork allow it to do its job?

3. How do the forms of Carelman's objects relate to their stated purposes? How do the forms relate to the general purpose of the real-world equivalent?

4. Carelman's purpose in creating these "objects," as he calls them, is obviously to amuse. Do you find them amusing? If you do, explain why. What qualities of the objects make them funny? If you don't think they are funny, speculate why Carelman likely thinks they are funny.

Occasion

WRITING THOUGHTFULLY: IDEA AND ESSAY

1. What are Carelman's objects examples of? One way to consider the question is to ask yourself what they all have in common. You may want to consider the purpose of each object, the form of each object, particular features of each object, and/or how each object relates to its real-world equivalent.

2. Use your imagination to create your own example of an object that illustrates the principle you described in the previous question. Like Carelman, base your object on another object that has already been invented. If you can, sketch the object. In any case, describe it in words.

3. Construct an essay in which you explore the relationship between form, purpose, and humor (or lack thereof) in these objects and in general. In your essay, explain how your imaginary object is like the others, and use it and Carelman's objects (as well as their real-world equivalents) to illustrate your point.

CREATING OCCASIONS

1. Collaborate with a small group of classmates to work together on developing the ground rules for a new language. Formulate at least three rules for the grammar of the language. Then write four or five sentences illustrating the new language, while following the rules you create for the language.

2. Write an essay in which you provide your own thinking about why so many newly developed everyday objects are so hard to learn to use. Consider the extent to which the difficulties encountered are due to a lack of education or experience on the part of their users, to a lack of careful and thoughtful design on the part of their creators, to the increasing complexity of contemporary life, and/or to other possible explanations.

3. Create your own interactive Occasion on *Comp21* using the textual, visual, and video libraries, as well as the Explicator analysis tools. From the main menu, choose "Build Your Own Occasion for Writing."

READING

BRENT STAPLES

Brent Staples (b. 1951) is a journalist who has written for the *Chicago Sun-Times* and the *New York Times*. A native of Chester, Pennsylvania, where he grew up in a poor neighborhood, Staples attended Widener University and earned a Ph.D. in sociology from the University of Chicago. His 1994 memoir, *Parallel Time: Growing Up in Black and White,* explores his experiences as a black youth trying to escape the poverty and violence endemic in his environment. Staples is currently a member of the editorial board and a contributing editor of the *New York Times,* in which his opinion pieces occasionally appear.

Just Walk on By

In the following essay, Staples tells a series of stories and then reflects on their significance. The first story reveals the fear that he, as a black man, creates in others. He describes how people react to him and what he does to attempt to alleviate their fear. Staples's examples, rich with specific details, contribute to the strength of his essay.

1   My first victim was a woman—white, well dressed, probably in her late twenties. I came upon her late one evening on a deserted street in Hyde Park, a relatively affluent neighborhood in an otherwise mean, impoverished section of Chicago. As I swung onto the avenue behind her, there seemed to be a discreet, uninflammatory distance between us. Not so. She cast back a worried glance. To her, the youngish black man—a broad six feet two inches with a beard and billowing hair, both hands shoved into the pockets of a bulky military jacket—seemed menacingly close. After a few more quick glimpses, she picked up her pace and was soon running in earnest. Within seconds she disappeared into a cross street.

  That was more than a decade ago. I was twenty-two years old, a graduate student newly arrived at the University of Chicago. It was in the echo of that terrified woman's footfalls that I first began to know the unwieldy inheritance I'd come into—the ability to alter public space in ugly ways. It was clear that she thought herself the quarry of a mugger, a rapist, or worse. Suffering a bout of insomnia, however, I was stalking sleep, not defenseless wayfarers. As a softy who is scarcely able to take a knife to a raw chicken—

let alone hold one to a person's throat—I was surprised, embarrassed, and dismayed all at once. Her flight made me feel like an accomplice in tyranny. It also made it clear that I was indistinguishable from the muggers who occasionally seeped into the area from the surrounding ghetto. That first encounter, and those that followed, signified that a vast, unnerving gulf lay between nighttime pedestrians—particularly women—and me. And I soon gathered that being perceived as dangerous is a hazard in itself. I only needed to turn a corner into a dicey situation, or crowd some frightened, armed person in a foyer somewhere, or make an errant move after being pulled over by a policeman. Where fear and weapons meet—and they often do in urban America—there is always the possibility of death.

  In that first year, my first away from my hometown, I was to become thoroughly familiar with the language of fear. At dark, shadowy intersections, I could cross in front of a car stopped at a traffic light and elicit the *thunk, thunk, thunk, thunk* of the driver—black, white, male, or female—hammering down the door locks. On less traveled streets after dark, I grew accustomed to but never comfortable

Reading

with people crossing to the other side of the street rather than pass me. Then there were the standard unpleasantries with policemen, doormen, bouncers, cab-drivers, and others whose business it is to screen out troublesome individuals *before* there is any nastiness.

I moved to New York nearly two years ago and I have remained an avid night walker. In central Manhattan, the near-constant crowd cover minimizes tense one-on-one street encounters. Elsewhere—in SoHo, for example, where sidewalks are narrow and tightly spaced buildings shut out the sky—things can get very taut indeed.

5 After dark, on the warrenlike streets of Brooklyn where I live, I often see women who fear the worst from me. They seem to have set their faces on neutral, and with their purse straps strung across their chests bandolier-style, they forge ahead as though bracing themselves against being tackled. I understand, of course, that the danger they perceive is not a hallucination. Women are particularly vulnerable to street violence, and young black males are drastically overrepresented among the perpetrators of that violence. Yet these truths are no solace against the kind of alienation that comes of being ever the suspect, a fearsome entity with whom pedestrians avoid making eye contact.

It is not altogether clear to me how I reached the ripe old age of twenty-two without being conscious of the lethality nighttime pedestrians attributed to me. Perhaps it was because in Chester, Pennsylvania, the small, angry industrial town where I came of age in the 1960s, I was scarcely noticeable against a backdrop of gang warfare, street knifings, and murders. I grew up one of the good boys, had perhaps a half-dozen fistfights. In retrospect, my shyness of combat has clear sources.

As a boy, I saw countless tough guys locked away; I have since buried several, too. They were babies, really—a teenage cousin, a brother of twenty-two, a childhood friend in his mid-twenties—all gone down in episodes of bravado played out in the streets. I came to doubt the virtues of intimidation early on. I chose, perhaps unconsciously, to remain a shadow—timid, but a survivor.

The fearsomeness mistakenly attributed to me in public places often has a perilous flavor. The most frightening of these confusions occurred in the late 1970s and early 1980s, when I worked as a journalist in Chicago. One day, rushing into the office of a magazine I was writing for with a deadline story in hand, I was mistaken for a burglar. The office manager called security and, with an ad hoc posse, pursued me through the labyrinthine halls, nearly to my editor's door. I had no way of providing who I was. I could only move briskly toward the company of someone who knew me.

Another time I was on assignment for a local paper and killing time before an interview. I entered a jewelry store on the city's affluent Near North Side. The proprietor excused herself and returned with an enormous red Doberman pinscher straining at the end of a leash. She stood, the dog extended toward me, silent to my questions, her eyes bulging nearly out of her head. I took a cursory look around, nodded, and bade her good night.

10 Relatively speaking, however, I never fared as badly as another black male journalist. He went to nearby Waukegan, Illinois, a couple of summers ago to work on a story about a murderer who was born there. Mistaking the reporter for the killer, police officers hauled him from his car at gunpoint and but for his press credentials would probably have tried to book him. Such episodes are not uncommon. Black men trade tales like this all the time.

Over the years, I learned to smother the rage I felt at so often being taken for a criminal. Not to do so would surely have led to madness. I now take precautions to make myself less threatening. I move about with care, particularly late in the evening. I give a wide berth to nervous people on subway platforms during the wee hours, particularly when I have exchanged business clothes for jeans. If I happen to be entering a building behind some people who appear skittish, I may walk by, letting them clear the lobby before I return, so as not to seem to be following them. I have been calm and extremely congenial on those rare occasions when I've been pulled over by the police.

And on late-evening constitutionals I employ what has proved to be an excellent tension-reducing measure: I whistle melodies from Beethoven and Vivaldi and the more popular classical composers. Even steely New Yorkers hunching toward nighttime destinations seem to relax, and occasionally they even join in the tune. Virtually everybody seems to sense that a mugger wouldn't be warbling bright, sunny selections from Vivaldi's *Four Seasons*. It is my equivalent of the cowbell that hikers wear when they know they are in bear country.

Reading

Reading and Thinking

1. How does Staples begin his essay, and why do you think he begins as he does? How effective is his opening sentence and his opening paragraph? Explain.

2. What does Staples learn from the experience he describes? What central idea derived from his experience does Staples elaborate in his essay?

3. What examples of fearful behavior does Staples describe? What common elements unite them? What inferences do you think Staples expects his readers to make from them?

4. Why do you think Staples mentions his brother, his cousin, and his childhood friend? Why does he include the story of his being mistaken for a burglar?

5. What do you think of his strategy of whistling classical music tunes while walking dark streets in racially mixed or white neighborhoods?

Thinking and Writing

1. The subtitle of Staples's essay is "A Black Man Ponders His Power to Alter Public Space." Write a couple of paragraphs explaining how Staples "alters" public space. Comment, too, on the strategies he uses to prevent himself from being misunderstood as a threat to public safety, and to protect himself from possibly fatal consequences of being misunderstood.

2. Tell a story of a time when you were misunderstood—when you were perceived to be very different from who and what you truly are. Explain how you responded to others' misperceptions, what the consequences were, and what, in retrospect, you consider the meaning of the experience.

PRE-JUDGING PUBLIC SPACE

AN OCCASION FOR ILLUSTRATION

In "Just Walk On By," Brent Staples is aware that his presence in public often creates a certain impression—and therefore certain reactions—among others. Though in Staples's case the impression and reactions are based on racial prejudice, this Occasion will give you a chance to discuss a different kind of prejudice (in the sense of "pre-judging"): the kind that many businesses want you to do when they advertise their services. Included here are six hotel signs from different parts of the United States. As you look through the photographs and work toward your essay, think about how signs from all kinds of businesses advertise their products or services, and also consider the ways in which the signs interact with public space. Finally, think about how the ways businesses advertise relates to the different ways Staples describes being treated.

© Richard Eisele/CORBIS.

© Richard T. Nowitz/CORBIS.

PREPARING TO WRITE: HOTEL SIGNS

1. Look carefully at the design elements of each sign: the lettering it uses, its size and shape, and so on. Refer to chapter 2 to help you discuss the design of each sign. What does the design imply about the hotel it advertises?

2. Consider the context of each sign—the side of the road, for example. What is the purpose of each sign? Who is each sign talking to, and why?

3. What do the words on each sign seem to promise?

© Mark Stephenson/CORBIS.

© Richard Cummins/CORBIS.

© Rob Rowan; Progressive Image/CORBIS.

© Frank McMahon/CORBIS.

PRE-JUDGING PUBLIC SPACE: AN OCCASION FOR ILLUSTRATION   199

MOVING TOWARD ESSAY: ANALYSIS AND REFLECTION

1. How many different kinds of hotels do you think these signs advertise? Make a list of different kinds and briefly describe what you might expect a room in each one to look like. What would you expect the surroundings to look like? Explain what in the sign makes you picture the interior and exterior the way you do.

2. Aside from being hotel signs, what ideas does each sign illustrate? What do they all have in common? You may want to consider more than the design elements of the signs. Who might be likely to stay in each hotel?

3. What kinds of hotel signs are left out of this collection? Think of particular hotel signs you have seen recently. How do those signs differ from the signs included here?

WRITING THOUGHTFULLY: IDEA AND ESSAY

1. List several examples of signs for other types of businesses that you see every day. In a few paragraphs, explain what a couple of those signs seem to promise by their design and location. What particular elements of the signs—their design elements, their wording, and so on—help to establish that implied promise?

2. Consider other forms of public advertising, such as billboards. Take note of a number of billboards and consider the same questions you have been considering: what promises does each sign seem to make? Who is the intended audience? How do the elements of the sign's design work together to create a certain impression?

3. Write an essay in which you explore the use of advertising in public space. As you write, carefully consider your thinking from the previous questions, but also consider the criteria on which people make judgments—about which restaurant to eat in, which hotel to stay in, and where to get their hair cut, for example. How do the signs in this Occasion—those included in this book, and those you have noticed on your own—relate to the product or service they advertise? How accurately do they depict the product or service? What decision-making process do they hope to engender in their audience? How does that process relate to the one Staples describes about his role in public space—in particular, how he is perceived by others? You may wish to use specific examples from Staples's essay in your own. In any case, be sure to use the examples of signs and their role in public spaces to illustrate your point.

Occasion

workplac...
derstand...

The e...
masked a...
to assum...
thing "ni...
aggressiv...
ple, I wa...
the venee...
sponsibil...
do almos...
in male-f...
throws c...
ments ("...
while th...
we go, v...
like the...
ture's litt...
embarras...
coming a...
knowled...
gry or re...
them in...
great dea...

5   For c...
watch. T...
punk ma...
volta sw...
"Saturda...
ging off...
simper t...
lessly to...
up when...
hurt so...
therein,...

The a...
at least s...
is an aur...
psychiat...
using sel...
selfishne...
makes u...
Miller c...
when th...
who do...

4. **Comp21 Video Extension.** Extend this Occasion to include CNN® video footage using the Explicator video analysis tool on *Comp21*. From the main menu choose "Frames of Mind: Extending Occasions" and select "Pre-judging Public Space: An Occasion for Illustration" from the list.

CREATING OCCASIONS

1. Consider other times in which a kind of prejudice—pre-judging—plays a role in public spaces. Find several examples in public of particular things—objects or architecture, for example—that attempt to create an impression of something that may or may not live up to its impression. Take photographs or describe those elements that create the impression. Discuss in an essay how outward presentation can differ from the reality of a situation, place, person, or thing.

2. Work together with a few classmates to design a new sign for an existing hotel, motel, or restaurant chain. You should be familiar with the interior and exterior of whatever you choose. Try to make sure that the elements of your sign's design accurately depict what the potential consumer will encounter. Your job here will not be to advertise—that is, do not try to get your potential customers to patronize your establishment. Instead, try to give those customers an accurate way to judge what to expect. Sketch or describe the sign, and in a short essay, discuss how your approach compares with the approach you have seen in this Occasion.

3. Create your own interactive Occasion on *Comp21* using the textual, visual, and video libraries, as well as the Explicator analysis tools. From the main menu, choose "Build Your Own Occasion for Writing."

Occasion

OTHER TONGUES
AN OCCASION FOR CLASSIFICATION

In "Mother Tongue," Amy Tan investigates the different languages she uses at different times and in different circumstances throughout her daily life, classifying them by using the same methods discussed in this chapter. This Occasion for classification will give you the opportunity to do the same by studying the kinds of language used in advertisements. At first glance, the language used in each of these ads may appear to be the same: English. But as you look closer, you will begin to notice that there are different versions of English at work.

PREPARING TO WRITE: YO, VINNY

1. Write a sentence that characterizes the three types of shoes in the advertisement. Describe each shoe and the appropriate situations in which shoes like those might be worn. Who is the likely audience for this advertisement?

2. Though the names used in the advertisement are all variations of the same name, characterize the types of situations in which each name would be used. Provide a name or label for each type of situation.

3. How do the names accompanying each shoe, along with the images of the shoe, reinforce each other?

VINCENT

VINCE

YO, VINNY

Allen Edmonds
For All Walks of Life™
Made in USA

Styles from business to casual, sizes 6-16 and widths AAA-EEE. Truly the widest selection available. And when your shoes wear out, Recrafting® is the name to remember. For a catalog and nearest dealer, call 1-800-235-2348.

Shoes from top to bottom: Park Avenue, Bergamo, Broadstreet

allenedmonds.com

Occasion

UNWANTED

NAME: The Flu. **ALIASES:** Influenza, The Flu Bug

ADDRESS: World traveller. Usually found at airports, malls, offices and other public spaces. He is known to invite himself into homes for extended stays.

BEWARE: The Flu is contagious and should be considered dangerous. If you have come in contact with the Flu and think you have symptoms, talk to your doctor immediately. If your doctor says it's influenza, ask about RELENZA, to help start feeling better sooner.
CALL: 1-877-HELP-FLU

Influenza, commonly known as the flu, is a virus that lives primarily in the lungs. He brings symptoms such as high fever, fatigue, sore throat, cough, and body aches. New RELENZA is an inhaled antiviral medicine that can be used in patients as young as 12. The first dose should be taken within 2 days of feeling flu symptoms, so talk to your doctor immediately.

Patients with asthma or chronic lung disease may be at risk of wheezing and should consult their doctor. Side effects are generally mild and may include sinusitis, nausea and diarrhea, and occurred in 3% or less of patients. You should be shown how to use the inhaler. It may take a few days to start feeling better.

RELENZA®
ZANAMIVIR FOR INHALATION

Please see Brief Summary of Prescribing Information on the following page. www.Relenza.com

GlaxoWellcome

GET OFF (Okay, it may seem like I hate my parents, but I'm really demonstrating what a therapist would call "asserting my identity," so I can grow up to be a well-adjusted individual. Sure, I say I want freedom, but without parental supervision, I'm much more likely to smoke pot and stuff. I hope my parents don't try to act like my friends. What I really need is parents.) MY BACK.

Office of National Drug Control Policy · Partnership for a Drug-Free America®

TALK. KNOW. ASK. **PARENTS. THE ANTI-DRUG.**

For information contact us at 1-800-788-2800 or www.theantidrug.com

Occasion

PREPARING TO WRITE: UNWANTED

1. Notice the thumbtack at the top of the page of the "Unwanted" advertisement. What does the thumbtack suggest about the block of text and the photographs below it? What are the photographs intended to represent?

2. What is this an advertisement for? What is it an advertisement against? How does the visual representation characterize each?

3. Characterize the different types of language used in this advertisement. How many are there? Name them. Who is the presumed audience of each? How would you classify them?

PREPARING TO WRITE: GET OFF MY BACK

1. How many different types of language are used in the "Get Off My Back" advertisement? Who is the speaker of each type of language? Who is the audience? How many different intentions are displayed?

2. What is the language superimposed across the girl's face intended to imitate? Although the phrases "get off" and "my back" are usually used together, in this case they are separated, and they bracket other text. What does the bracketing suggest about the words in white?

3. Who is the intended audience? How do the different types of language work together to create the main point for that audience?

MOVING TOWARD ESSAY: ANALYSIS AND REFLECTION

1. Each advertisement uses several different types of language based on who the speaker is, who the audience is, and what the likely situation is. Make a comprehensive list of the different types of language used in all the advertisements. Some of the types of language you noticed and named in one may overlap with types from the others.

2. Which types of language used are appropriate for trying to get someone to buy a product or to buy into an idea? Which are not? Why?

3. Create two new categories—"direct language," in which the advertisement is addressing the viewer directly, and "indirect language," in which the advertisement may be addressing someone else.

WRITING THOUGHTFULLY: IDEA AND ESSAY

1. Consider the ways advertisers want their audience to react to the language of the advertisement. Use each of the three advertisements to create several new categories, this time based on the ways they use language to get a reaction. Consider the intent of each advertisement. What do they want their readers to buy (or buy into)? Identify the emotions the advertisements evoke in readers.

2. Within each of those categories, make a list of the different types of language used. Then write a sentence or two explaining how that type of language achieves the effects it does.

3. Write an essay explaining how advertisers use language to persuade their audience to do something, including to buy their products or use their services. Use classification to provide a way to organize and develop your thinking of the different kinds of language advertisers use and the different types of selling strategies they employ with that language.

CREATING OCCASIONS

1. Work with a small group of students to create your own advertisement for women's shoes or men's pants. Use a classification model, in the manner of the "Yo, Vinny" advertisement, the "Unwanted" advertisement, or the "Get Off My Back" advertisement, to structure your advertisement. Include both words and visual images.

2. Find up to ten examples of language used in public: signs, sides of buses, public announcements, and so on. Make a list of the language used in each. Classify the different types of language. Let your classifications lead you to a conclusion.

3. Create your own interactive Occasion on *Comp21* using the textual, visual, and video libraries, as well as the Explicator analysis tools. From the main menu, choose "Build Your Own Occasion for Writing."

BLOCK STRUCTURE

Sometimes writers organize their comparison-contrast discussion in a "block" structure by considering first one element of the comparison fully before considering the other one. The following paragraph example is taken from the essay "American Space, Chinese Place" by Yi-Fu Tuan.

> Americans have a sense of space, not of place. Go to an American home in exurbia, and almost the first thing you do is drift toward the picture window. How curious that the first compliment you pay your host inside his house is to say how lovely it is outside his house! He is pleased that you should admire his vistas. The distant horizon is not merely a line separating earth from sky, it is a symbol of the future. The American is not rooted in his place, however lovely: his eyes are drawn by the expanding space to a point on the horizon, which is his future. By contrast, consider the traditional Chinese home. Blank walls enclose it. Step behind the spirit wall and you are in a courtyard with perhaps a miniature garden around a corner. Once inside his private compound you are wrapped in an ambiance of calm beauty, an ordered world of buildings, pavement, rock, and decorative vegetation. But you have no distant view: nowhere does space open out before you. Raw nature in such a home is experienced only as weather, and the only open space is the sky above. The Chinese is rooted in his place. When he has to leave, it is not for the promised land on the terrestrial horizon, but for another world altogether along the vertical, religious axis of his imagination.

In this paragraph, Yi-Fu Tuan uses comparison and contrast to explain an idea about the way space and place are conceptualized. Tuan suggests that "space" and "place" are different concepts that reflect different cultural attitudes and perspectives. In using the block format—first describing American "space" and then Chinese "place," Tuan is able to sharpen the contrast between them. He makes the contrast to explain important cultural differences between how Americans and Chinese view their homes and their places in the cosmos.

In fact, the aspects of American space and Chinese place Tuan selects as the basis for his comparison are precisely those that enable him to sharpen his contrast between the two. Tuan highlights how Americans lack a sense of "place," of being rooted in a particular location, which is so important to the Chinese. The American preference is for "space"—for the openness of a big yard, the long vista with an unobstructed view. In this paragraph, Tuan does not go into further detail about how this American preference is rooted in American history. Nor does he explore here how even apartment dwellers in big cities reflect this preference, always looking for larger rooms and hoping to find affordable rooms with a view of a park, a cityscape, or an important monument. Such considerations, however, are implied in his paragraph.

Similarly, Tuan focuses on the Chinese view of place, particularly on how place is more than the room in which a person lives or the open space beyond the house. Place is, rather, the immediacy of one's surroundings, the harmony and order that put one at peace. By selecting these aspects of Chinese place to compare with American space, Tuan is able to explain his idea clearly and forcefully.

Exercise

Write a paragraph in which you contrast two different things. Some possibilities are two ways of looking at photographs, two ways of studying, two methods for learning a foreign language, two kinds of politicians, two kinds of commuting, two people, two places, or two films or television shows. Be sure to use the "block" structure, writing first about one thing and then about the other one.

ALTERNATING
STRUCTURE

Writers can also use an alternating structure, in which they move back and forth between items being compared or contrasted by taking up one aspect at a time. In the following paragraph, taken from John McPhee's book *Oranges,* the author contrasts Florida oranges with California oranges. Instead of discussing one type of orange completely before considering the other type, he moves back and forth between the two types of oranges to describe their differences.

McPhee selects a number of different characteristics as his basis for contrast. He considers the oranges' juiciness, texture, and sweetness and the climatic conditions under which they grow. His purpose is to help readers better understand and appreciate the distinctive features of each type of orange.

An orange grown in Florida usually has a thin and tightly fitting skin, and is also heavy with juice. Californians say that if you want to eat a Florida orange you have to get into a bathtub first. California oranges are light in weight and have thick skins that break easily and come off in hunks. The flesh inside is marvelously sweet, and the segments almost separate themselves. In Florida, it is said that you can run over a California orange with a ten-ton truck and not even wet the pavement. The differences from which these hyperboles arise will prevail in the two states even if the type of orange is the same. In arid climates, like California's, oranges develop a thick *albedo,* which is the white part of the skin. Florida is one of the two or three most rained-upon states in the United States. California uses the Colorado River and similarly impressive sources to irrigate its oranges, but of course irrigation can only do so much. The annual difference in rainfall between the Florida and California orange-growing areas is one million one hundred and forty thousand gallons per acre. For years, California was the leading orange-growing state, but Florida surpassed California in 1942, and grows three times as many oranges now. California oranges, for their part, can safely be called three times as beautiful.

Unlike Yi-Fu Tuan, John McPhee organizes his comparison and contrast of Florida and California oranges in an alternating structure. Instead of writing first all about the Florida orange and then turning to the California orange, McPhee weaves back and forth between them. He is careful to balance his comments about both kinds of oranges so as not to bias the reader more toward one type than the other. Rather, McPhee emphasizes the different advantages of each type, including thickness of skin and quantity of juice. McPhee's purpose is less to persuade than to explain. From his comparison of California and Florida oranges, we learn not only about the different features of the oranges, but why they develop these features. And we learn something, too, about the pride that Floridians and Californians take in oranges from their states.

Exercise

Write a paragraph in which you contrast two things that share some common features, as McPhee does with Florida and California oranges. Be sure to use the alternating structure, weaving back and forth between the two things. Possible topics include two professional athletes, two TV reality shows, two Internet dating sites, two teachers, two friends, two restaurants, two sports cars, or two neighborhoods.

A SPECIAL CASE
OF COMPARISON: ANALOGY

Analogy is a special type of comparison in which one thing is explained in terms of another. Writers use analogy to explain something unfamiliar to their readers by comparing it with something likely to be more familiar. For example, a science writer might compare how the heart functions to the way a water pump works. Or you might explain the game of football to someone by comparing it to war—the offense attacks the defense by attempting to invade its territory in order to score points.

Writers can also use analogy to help readers understand complex ideas. Here is an example of analogy from *The Disuniting of America,* in which the author, Arthur Schlesinger, Jr., makes a point about the importance of history:

> History is to the nation rather as memory is to the individual. As an individual deprived of memory becomes disoriented and lost, not knowing where he has been or where he is going, so a nation denied a conception of its past will be disabled in dealing with its present and its future.

COMPARISON AND CONTRAST
IN PURE FORM: AN ANNOTATED PARAGRAPH

Gretchen Rubin received her undergraduate and law degrees from Yale and was editor-in-chief of the *Yale Law Journal*. She clerked for U.S. Supreme Court Justice Sandra Day O'Connor and served as counsel to Federal Communications Commission Chairman Reed Hundt. She teaches at Yale Law School and the School of Management and is the author of *Power, Money, Fame, Sex: A User's Guide*. Her next book will be *Forty Ways to Look at John F. Kennedy*. "Churchill and Hitler" is excerpted from *Forty Ways to Look at Winston Churchill*.

"shared" suggests comparison

list of shared qualities

Churchill explained

"both"/"each" link the two men

Hitler explained

Although Churchill claimed that he shared only one thing with Hitler—"a horror of whistling"—they shared many of the qualities that buttress a leader's power. Each had charisma, confidence, eloquence, physical stamina, and a high tolerance for risk. Each was ruthless, driven, obsessed with military power, fascinated by science, self-educated, self-absorbed, with a strong historical imagination. They'd both proved themselves in battle, and both had a surprising passion for painting. They both sought to control every aspect of the war, from grand strategy to minor details (Churchill worrying about soldiers' beer ration, Hitler considering what music should be used as radio fanfares to announce German victories). Each leader had a deep faith in his destiny and in the destiny of his race. From his youth, Churchill believed himself fated to play a vital role in preserving the Empire and its traditions. He saw himself as a bulwark, the savior of something ancient and precious, the leader of a people who would once again triumph in defense of freedom. Hitler saw himself as a purifier and sole creator of something new. With the thousand-year Reich—which lasted twelve years, three months, and ten days—he wanted to destroy and transform, not preserve. Hitler's belief in his destiny was so profound that the near success of a 1944 assassination attempt actually comforted him; he believed his escape proved, once again, that Providence assured him victory. And after all, it's true that at the Reich's height, by diplomacy and war, Hitler—son of a minor official in rural Austria, a once-aimless drifter with little education—had achieved triumphs worthy of comparison to Napoleon.

Pure Form

In this paragraph, Daniel Goleman focuses on aspects such as the sizes of boys' and girls' play groups and the ways boys and girls react to disruptions in their games. He selects these aspects because through them he can make a point about gender differences: boys are independent and competitive while girls are more cooperative and emotionally supportive. Goleman uses the alternating structure format to contrast the different ways that boys and girls play. Goleman's first sentence sets up the terms of the comparison and identifies the key difference between boys' competitive and girls' cooperative play. The next three sentences provide an extended example to illustrate that difference. Following the example, two sentences explain why boys and girls engage so differently in play, and a third sentence links these differences in play with an analogous difference in the ways men and women communicate.

Exercise

The following paragraph has not been annotated. Add annotations of your own. Be sure to underline and circle key words and phrases in the paragraph and to jot additional notes in the margin. Keep your focus on the writer's main idea and how the comparative and contrastive details develop and support it.

The key is to distinguish education from training, to recognize that people require both, and to be unabashed about what is involved in the latter. Young children need to be trained in multiplication tables, reading, spelling, and writing, exactly as an athlete trains his body: it takes coaching, repetition, and practice. When children have acquired skills they can use by reflex, it gives them the confidence and the materials to profit from the next step, which is education proper: the process of learning to think and to know how to find and use information when needed. Above all, education involves refining capacities for judgment and evaluation; Heraclitus remarked that learning is only a means to an end, which is understanding—and understanding is the ultimate value in education.

In the first part of this long paragraph, Rubin identifies a number of different characteristics shared by Winston Churchill and Adolf Hitler, two leaders we would not normally think of as having much in common. Disputing Churchill's claim that he had only one thing in common with Hitler, Rubin emphasizes their common talents, goals, and passions.

In this first half of the paragraph, Rubin considers the two leaders together, using words such as *each* and *both*. In the second half of the paragraph, she shifts to a strategy in which she describes first Churchill and then Hitler. Rubin emphasizes how each leader envisioned himself, Churchill as a protector and savior of a civilization, Hitler as a purifier and creator of a new world order.

Rubin does not emphasize Churchill's and Hitler's differences in this paragraph, though differences were even more significant than these similarities. In a later paragraph in her book, however, Rubin describes those differences, explaining how each leader used his talents for leadership in different ways, for different purposes, and toward different ends.

Exercises

1. What similarities does Rubin identify between Hitler and Churchill?

2. Why do you think she compares these two important world leaders? How does the comparison with Hitler help illuminate her biographical subject, Churchill?

3. How does Rubin organize her comparison?

COMPARISON AND CONTRAST
IN ITS NATURAL HABITAT:
AN ANNOTATED READING

Dr. Leonard Shlain (b. 1937) is chairman of Laparoscopic Surgery at California Pacific Medical Center in San Francisco and associate professor of surgery there. A polymath with a wide range of interests, Shlain has published three books: *Art and Physics: Parallel Visions in Space, Time and Light; The Alphabet Versus the Goddess: The Conflict Between Word and Image;* and most recently, *Sex, Time & Power: How Women's Sexuality Shaped Human Evolution.* In addition to a number of awards for his books, he also holds several patents for surgical devices.

In the passage that follows, you will have a chance to look at an example of comparison and contrast used as one method among others in a larger context. The passage is taken from a book built on a series of extended contrasts between words and images, a conflict reflected in the book's title: *The Alphabet versus the Goddess: The Conflict Between Word and Image.* In these paragraphs, author Dr. Leonard Shlain compares the treatment of women in the ancient Greek city-states of Athens and Sparta.

As you read, notice how Shlain uses comparison and contrast—mainly contrast—to ex-

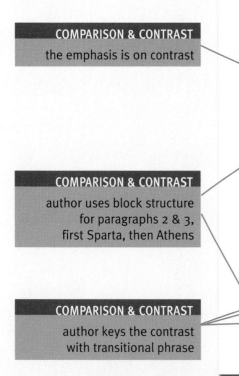

COMPARISON & CONTRAST

the emphasis is on contrast

COMPARISON & CONTRAST

author uses block structure for paragraphs 2 & 3, first Sparta, then Athens

COMPARISON & CONTRAST

author keys the contrast with transitional phrase

DR. LEONARD SHLAIN
Athens and Sparta

From the eighth century B.C. on, coincident with the spread of the written word, women were pushed to the periphery of Greek culture. This marginalization is nowhere better illustrated than in the disparity of women's roles in two diametrically opposing cultures: Sparta and Athens.

Sparta was a militaristic society that had little use for literacy. It produced not a single playwright, philosopher, or historian whose words are meaningful to us today. As Edith Hamilton points out, "The Spartans have left the world nothing in the way of art, literature, or science." Lycurgus, who formulated their law, did not commit it to writing. He ordered everyone to memorize it. Plutarch writes that there was even a Spartan law against committing any law to writing. The Spartan code of conduct glorified deprivation and cruelty; their government was oligarchic, with fascist leanings.

Athens, in contrast, produced history's greatest concentration of thinkers. Fortunately for posterity, bacco planters in particular dependent on slave labor and money borrowed from English creditors against future crops. John Adams, by contrast, had neither debts nor slaves and all his life abhorred the idea of either.

In keeping with his background, Adams was less than dazzled by the Virginia grandees. In Virginia, he would say, "all geese are swans." Jefferson, for his part, knew little or nothing of New Englanders and counted none as friends. A man of cultivated, even fastidious tastes, Jefferson was later to tell his Virginia neighbor James Madison that he had observed in Adams a certain "want of taste," this apparently in reference to the fact that Adams was known on occasion to chew tobacco and take his rum more or less straight.

Jefferson had been slower, more cautious and ambivalent than Adams about resolving his views on independence. As recently as August 1775, less than a year past, Jefferson had written to a Tory kinsman, John Randolph, of "looking with fondness towards a reconciliation with Great Britain." He longed for the "return of the happy period when, consistently with duty, I may withdraw myself totally from the public stage, and pass the rest of my days in domestic ease and tranquility, ban-

ishing every desire of afterwards even hearing what passes in the world." But in the same letter he declared that "rather than submit to the right of legislating for us assumed by the British parliament and which late experience has shown they will so cruelly exercise, [I] would lend my hand to sink the whole island in the ocean." His commitment now in the spring of 1776 was no less than Adams's own. And it was because of their common zeal for independence, their wholehearted, mutual devotion to the common cause of America, and the certainty that they were taking part in one of history's turning points, that the two were able to concentrate on the common purpose in a spirit of respect and cooperation, putting aside obvious differences, as well as others not so obvious and more serious than they could then have known.

Adams considered Jefferson his protégé at Philadelphia; Jefferson, impressed by Adams's clarity and vigor in argument, his "sound head," looked upon him as a mentor. They served on committees together, and as the pace quickened in the weeks after Jefferson's arrival, they were together much of the time. As would be said, each felt the value of the other in the common task.

Reading and Thinking

1. This reading selection is from a biography of Adams, yet McCullough talks more about Jefferson here than he does about Adams. What does he gain from this focus on Jefferson? What can you tell about McCullough's purpose in his discussion?

2. How does McCullough organize his comparison and contrast of Jefferson and Adams? What aspects does McCullough choose to focus on? How is the structure he uses effective in illuminating these aspects?

3. Identify one paragraph that emphasizes Jefferson, one that emphasizes Adams, and one that gives both equal treatment. Explain what the author accomplishes in each paragraph.

Thinking and Writing

1. Focus on the political and personal styles of Adams and Jefferson described in this passage. Develop a list of your own thoughts about each politician, paying attention to both the political and the personal. On the basis of your analysis, who do you think made the better statesman? Why? Write a short essay in which you develop your ideas about the relative effectiveness of these two early presidents. Do additional research if necessary.

2. Select two public figures who interest you. Write a brief story about each of these figures, then compare these two stories to see what they tell you about the similarities and differences between the figures. Finally, write an essay that includes your two stories and develops your ideas.

WHO'S FOR YOU?
AN OCCASION FOR
COMPARISON AND CONTRAST

In "John Adams and Thomas Jefferson," historian David McCullough compares and contrasts two great American figures, both of whom became president of the United States despite their differences. This Occasion will give you a chance to do your own comparison of two Americans—one who also became President and his rival for that office. Unlike McCullough, who based his comparison on extensive research, you will base your comparison on your analysis of two visual presentations: the campaign posters of Richard Nixon and Hubert Humphrey. As you study the posters and consider the questions for analysis and writing, keep in mind that the posters were specifically intended to give the viewer a particular sense of each candidate. Each poster reveals a bias leaning toward its own candidate. Ask yourself what the posters reveal about their creators and the candidates they advertise.

PREPARING TO WRITE: NIXON'S THE ONE!

1. Describe the Nixon poster, listing what you notice about the poster's frame, image(s), and printed text. Be sure to identify the details of each visual and verbal element.

2. Based on your observations of the poster, what message about Nixon is conveyed?

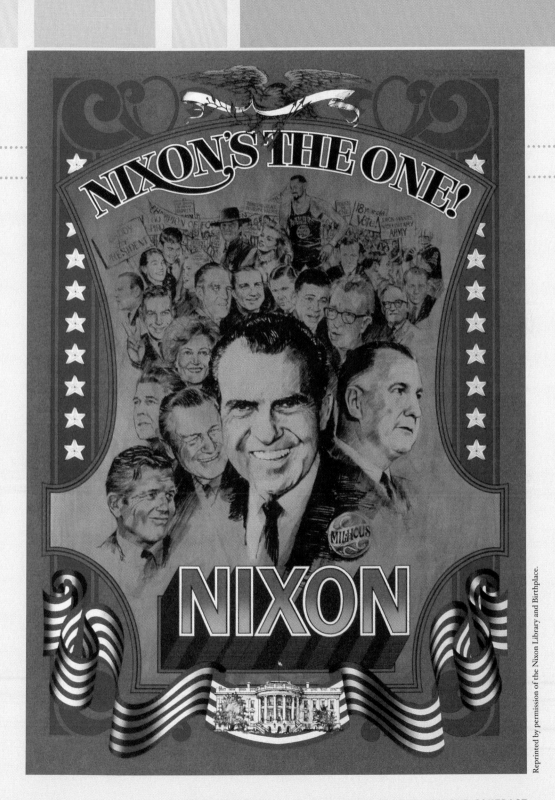

NIXON'S THE ONE!

NIXON

Some talk change. Others cause it.

Humphrey

Used by permission of the Humphrey Forum, University of Minnesota.

PREPARING TO WRITE: HUMPHREY

1. Describe the visual and verbal elements of the Humphrey poster, and comment on their meaning and implications. What, for example, do you think readers should infer from the poster's headline? How are viewers expected to interpret Humphrey's facial expression?

2. What is the overall message of the Humphrey poster? How do the size and shape of the words and the size and form of the picture convey that message?

MOVING TOWARD ESSAY: ANALYSIS AND REFLECTION

1. While the Nixon and Humphrey presidential election campaign posters each feature only the advertised candidate, the creators of each candidate's poster considered what they knew about their candidate's opponent, particularly how the public perceived him. With that in mind, consider how each poster compares or contrasts its promoted candidate with his opponent. Make brief notes for future work.

2. How important do you think such political campaign posters are in a presidential election campaign? To what extent has either television or Internet advertising affected the production and use of such posters? Find two political advertisements on television or the Internet. How do the advertisements you found differ from political campaign posters?

WRITING THOUGHTFULLY: IDEA AND ESSAY

1. Using your notes from "Preparing to Write," develop a more detailed written analysis of the two campaign posters. Consider your response to questions 1 and 2 from "Moving Toward Essay" as you consider the effectiveness of political advertising in different media. Finally, write a brief essay in which you develop your own idea about political advertising.

2. Using either the two campaign posters or David McCullough's comparison of Adams and Jefferson, explain in a short essay which of the two candidates (Nixon or Humphrey, Adams or Jefferson) would be your preferred choice for president. You may, of course, introduce any background historical knowledge you have about the pair.

3. *Comp21* **Video Extension.** Extend this Occasion to include CNN® video footage using the Explicator video analysis tool on *Comp21*. From the main menu choose "Frames of Mind: Extending Occasions" and select "Who's for You?: An Occasion for Comparison and Contrast" from the list.

CREATING OCCASIONS

1. Working together with a small group of classmates, write an advertisement for a candidate for political office (school, local, state, or national) by comparing or contrasting the candidate you support with a competitor.

2. Exchange advertisements with another group and compare and contrast the effectiveness of your advertisement with that of the other group.

3. Create your own interactive Occasion on *Comp21* using the textual, visual, and video libraries, as well as the Explicator analysis tools. From the main menu, choose "Build Your Own Occasion for Writing."

Occasion

CARL SAGAN

Carl Sagan (1934–1996) was professor of astronomy and space sciences at Cornell University, where he was also director of the Laboratory for Planetary Studies. Sagan was also a major contributor to the Mariner, Viking, and Voyager space missions. He published numerous scientific articles and many books, including *The Dragons of Eden* (1977), from which "The Cosmic Calendar" has been taken.

The Cosmic Calendar

In the following essay, Sagan uses analogy to explain the vast expanse of prehistoric time. In order to help his readers understand just how old the world is, Sagan uses the image of a calendar. On this scale, human beings do not make their appearance until 10:30 P.M. on December 31st. Through this comparative analogy with the calendar, Sagan helps his readers better understand just how little time in the history of the universe that human beings have been around.

1 The world is very old, and human beings are very young. Significant events in our personal lives are measured in years or less; our lifetimes in decades; our family genealogies in centuries; and all of recorded history in millennia. But we have been preceded by an awesome vista of time, extending for prodigious periods into the past, about which we know little—both because there are no written records and because we have real difficulty in grasping the immensity of the intervals involved.

Yet we are able to date events in the remote past. Geological stratification and radioactive dating provide information on archaeological, palenotological and geological events; and astrophysical theory provides data on the ages of planetary surfaces, stars, and the Milky Way Galaxy, as well as an estimate of the time that has elapsed since that extraordinary event called the Big Bang—an explosion that involved all of the matter and energy in the present universe. The Big Bang may be the beginning of the universe, or it may be a discontinuity in which information about the earlier history of the universe was destroyed. But it is certainly the earliest event about which we have any record.

Pre-December Dates

Big Bang	January 1
Origin of the Milky Way Galaxy	May 1
Origin of the solar system	September 9
Formation of the Earth	September 14
Origin of life on Earth	~September 25
Formation of the oldest rocks known on Earth	October 2
Date of oldest fossils (bacteria and blue-green algae)	October 9
Invention of sex (by microorganisms)	~November 1
Oldest fossil photosynthetic plants	November 12
Eukaryotes (first cells with nuclei) flourish	November 15

~ = *approximately*

Cosmic Calendar
DECEMBER

Sunday	Monday	Tuesday	Wednesday	Thursday	Friday	Saturday
	1 Significant oxygen atmosphere begins to develop on Earth.	**2**	**3**	**4**	**5** Extensive volcanism and channel formation on Mars.	**6**
7	**8**	**9**	**10**	**11**	**12**	**13**
14	**15**	**16** First worms.	**17** Precambrian ends. Paleozoic Era and Cambrian Period begin. Invertebrates flourish.	**18** First oceanic plankton. Trilobites flourish.	**19** Ordovician Period. First fish, first vertebrates.	**20** Silurian Period. First vascular plants. Plants begin colonization of land.
21 Devonian Period begins. First insects. Animals begin colonization of land.	**22** First amphibians. First winged insects.	**23** Carboniferous Period. First reptiles. First trees.	**24** Permian Period begins. First dinosaurs.	**25** Paleozoic Era ends. Mesozoic Era begins.	**26** Triassic Period. First mammals.	**27** Jurassic Period. First birds.
28 Cretaceous Period. First flowers. Dinosaurs become extinct.	**29** Mesozoic Era ends. Cenozoic Era and Tertiary Period begin. First cetaceans. First primates.	**30** Early evolution of frontal lobes in the brains of primates. First hominids. Giant mammals flourish.	**31** End of the Pliocene Period. Quatenary (Pleistocene and Holocene) Period. First humans.			

The most instructive way I know to express this cosmic chronology is to imagine the fifteen-billion-year lifetime of the universe (or at least its present incarnation since the Big Bang) compressed into the span of a single year. Then every billion years of Earth history would correspond to about twenty-four days of our cosmic year, and one second of that year to 475 real revolutions of the Earth about the sun. . . . I present the cosmic chronology in three forms: a list of some representative pre-December dates; a calendar for the month of December; and a closer look at the late evening of New Year's Eve. On this scale, the events of our history books—even books that make significant efforts to deprovincialize the present—are so compressed that it is necessary to give a second-by-second recounting of the last seconds of the cosmic year. Even then, we find events listed as contemporary that we have been taught to consider as widely separated in time. In the history of life, an equally rich tapestry must have been woven in other periods—for example, between 10:02 and 10:03 on the morning of April 6th or September 16th. But we have detailed records only for the very end of the cosmic year.

The chronology corresponds to the best evidence now available. But some of it is rather shaky. No one would be astounded if, for example, it turns out that plants colonized the land in the Ordovician rather than the Silurian Period; or that segmented worms appeared earlier in the Precambrian Period than indicated. Also, in the chronology of the last ten seconds of the cosmic year, it was obviously impossible for me to include all significant events; I hope I may be excused for not having explicitly mentioned advances in art, music and literature or the historically significant American, French, Russian, and Chinese revolutions.

The construction of such tables and calendars is inevitably humbling. It is disconcerting to find that in such a cosmic year the Earth does not condense out of

5

```
                    December 31

Origin of Proconsul and Ramapithecus, probable
    ancestors of apes and men                    ~1:30 P.M.
First humans                                     ~10:30 P.M.
Widespread use of stone tools                    11:00 P.M.
Domestication of fire by Peking man              11:46 P.M.
Beginning of most recent glacial period          11:56 P.M.
Seafarers settle Australia                       11:58 P.M.
Extensive cave painting in Europe                11:59 P.M.
Invention of agriculture                         11:59:20 P.M.
Neolithic civilization; first cities             11:59:35 P.M.
First dynasties in Sumer, Ebla, and Egypt;
    development of astronomy                     11:59:50 P.M.
Invention of the alphabet; Akkadian Empire       11:59:51 P.M.
Hammurabic legal codes in Babylon; Middle
    Kingdom in Egypt                             11:59:52 P.M.
Bronze metallurgy; Mycenaean culture; Trojan War;
    Olmec culture; invention of the compass      11:59:53 P.M.
Iron metallurgy; First Assyrian Empire; Kingdom of
    Israel; founding of Carthage by Phoenicia    11:59:54 P.M.
Asokan India; Ch'in Dynasty China;
    Periclean Athens; birth of Buddha            11:59:55 P.M.
Euclidean geometry; Archimedean physics;
    Ptolemaic astronomy; Roman Empire;
    birth of Christ                              11:59:56 P.M.
Zero and decimals invented in Indian arithmetic;
    Rome falls; Moslem conquests                 11:59:57 P.M.
Mayan civilization; Sung Dynasty China; Byzantine
    empire; Mongol invasion; Crusades            11:59:58 P.M.
Renaissance in Europe; voyages of discovery from
    Europe and from Ming Dynasty China; emergence
    of the experimental method in science        11:59:59 P.M.
Widespread development of science and technology;
    emergence of a global culture; acquisition of the     Now:
    means for self-destruction of the human species;  The first second
    first steps in spacecraft planetary exploration and   of New Year's
    the search for exraterrestrial intelligence          Day
```

interstellar matter until early September; dinosaurs, emerge on Christmas Eve; flowers arise on December 28th; and men and women originate at 10:30 P.M. on New Year's Eve. All of recorded history occupies the last ten seconds of December 31; and the time from the waning of the Middle Ages to the present occupies little more than one second. But because I have arranged it that way, the first cosmic year has just ended. And despite the insignificance of the instant we have so far occupied in cosmic time, it is clear that what happens on and near Earth at the beginning of the second cosmic year will depend very much on the scientific wisdom and the distinctly human sensitivity of mankind.

Reading and Thinking

1. According to Sagan's monthly cosmic calendar, how much time does the month of December represent? When do dinosaurs appear?

2. How does Sagan's placement of human and historical time on a calendar of geological time help readers understand his main idea? That is, how does Sagan's analogy enable him to convey his main point?

3. What purpose does each of the visuals serve? Why do you think Sagan places them in the order or sequence that he does? What would be gained or lost without these visuals?

Thinking and Writing

1. Explain the point Sagan makes in his introductory paragraph. Explain the idea he lays out in his concluding paragraph and his final sentence.

2. Think of a concept that interests you, one that you have tried to explain to others without much success. Develop an extended analogy to help with that explanation.

3. Gather evidence to create your own Occasion for writing in which you compare and contrast the benefits of living in today's world versus living in a previous era—the 1920s, 1940s, or 1960s, for example. Develop a graphic of some sort or create an extended analogy that will help you convey to your readers the differences and similarities that you see between the two time periods.

Please do not remove from aircraft   1095-12063   swissair +

Occasion

SAFETY
AN OCCASION FOR COMPARISON AND CONTRAST

In his essay "The Cosmic Calendar," Carl Sagan uses an extended analogy to explain the nearly incomprehensible span of cosmic time. Condensing all of time into a single year, Sagan is able to present a difficult subject in terms that are easier to understand. This Occasion will give you a chance to use comparison and contrast to discuss a different kind of analogy: parody. Like analogy, parody presents one thing in terms of another in order to shed light on the first. The purpose of parody, however, is not necessarily to make one subject easier to understand, but to shed light on the first subject by making fun of it in some way. Included here are two safety cards, the second a parody of the first. As you look at the cards and work toward an essay, try to keep in mind the differences and similarities between analogy and parody.

PREPARING TO WRITE: SAFETY ON BOARD

1. Look carefully at this flight card, normally found in the seat pocket of an airplane. What is its purpose? Under what circumstances would you expect this card to be used?

2. Look at each of the illustrations carefully. Using no more than five words each, briefly translate the meaning of each illustration.

3. How do the elements of this card's design help to convey its meanings? Consider its focal point, the figure-ground contrast in each of its smaller illustrations, the layout, and the various other ways the card makes information clear. You may wish to refer to chapter 2.

4. Why are there so few words on this card? Why might the creators of this card (and cards like them) have chosen to convey information through illustrations rather than in words?

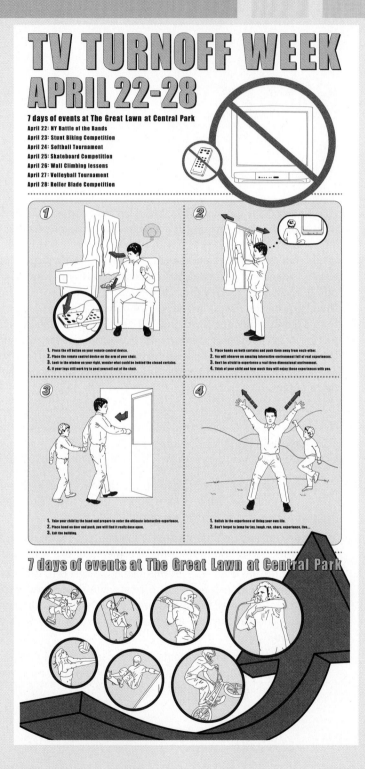

PREPARING TO WRITE: TV TURNOFF WEEK

1. Consider this poster advertising TV Turnoff Week. What is the purpose of this poster?

2. Look carefully at each of the illustrations. Considering the illustrations themselves, and ignoring the words already printed below each illustration, describe in your own words what each illustration seems to depict. What does the series of illustrations depict?

3. How do the illustrations address the card's main purpose? Explain.

MOVING TOWARD ESSAY: ANALYSIS AND REFLECTION

1. Describe the similarities between "TV Turnoff Week" and "Safety on Board" in terms of their visual presentation. What aspects of "TV Turnoff Week" are modeled after "Safety on Board" or cards like it?

2. Describe the differences between the visual aspects of "TV Turnoff Week" and "Safety on Board." What do those differences suggest about the particular differences between the purposes and likely audiences of each item?

3. What's at stake in each item? That is, how important is the message of each card?

WRITING THOUGHTFULLY: IDEA AND ESSAY

1. Considering your answers to previous questions, compare and contrast both the purposes of each card, and the ways that the cards use their presentations—visual and verbal—to make their points clear. In other words, explore the appropriateness of the visual presentation of each card, given its purpose and likely audience.

2. Why does "TV Turnoff Week" present its subject in terms of a flight safety card? How does such a parody comment on television, the proposed week without television, and on the events advertised in the poster? Try to determine what the creators might have hoped their viewers would think or do after viewing the card. Why might the creators have chosen to parody flight safety cards instead of other well-known visual representations such as street signs or movie posters, for example?

Occasion

3. Construct an essay in which you explore the usefulness of analogy and parody in commenting on their chosen subjects. In your essay, compare the effectiveness of the parody in "TV Turnoff Week" with the effectiveness of Carl Sagan's analogy of time. Describe the ways that each method works to shed light on its subject, and be sure to carefully explain what light is shed, exactly, in each case.

CREATING OCCASIONS

1. Find several advertisements in magazines, billboards, or on television that parody another form. Describe each in detail and discuss exactly what the parody implies.

2. Choose any piece of writing, photograph, advertisement, or painting that you admire. Create a parody of that piece that comments in a significant way on whatever subject you choose. Then, in a brief essay, discuss why your parody is appropriate.

3. Choose one of the following abstractions and write an essay explaining an important aspect of it using an analogy: love, time, peace, or self.

4. Create your own interactive Occasion on *Comp21* using the textual, visual, and video libraries, as well as the Explicator analysis tools. From the main menu, choose "Build Your Own Occasion for Writing."

READING

JOHN CANADAY

John Canaday (1907–1985) was born in Kansas and educated at the University of Texas and at Yale University. In addition to teaching art history at a number of U.S. universities, he also worked as an administrator and lecturer at the Philadelphia Museum of Art, where he directed the Division of Education. He also served as the art critic for the *New York Times* and is the author of more than twenty books, including art history and detective fiction.

Two Family Portraits: The Peales and the Bellellis

In the following essay from his book *What is Art?*, Canaday contrasts two paintings of families, one by the American painter Charles Willson Peale (1741–1827) and the other by the French impressionist artist Edgar Degas (1834–1917). Canaday describes each painting carefully, noting details about the structure and details used to convey an impression of the family portrayed. Canaday bases his interpretation of the two family portraits on the cumulative impression created by the details he observes in each painting. You might wish to look at each painting to gather your own impressions before reading what Canaday has to say.

I Peale began work on the group portrait of his family about 1773. Nine of the people in the picture are family members by birth or by marriage. The tenth is a matriarchal family nurse who stands in the background, hands folded, with all the dignity of a great natural monument. For good measure Peale includes three familial portrait busts on the shelf to the right, and as an afterthought adds the portrait head of a member who joined the family after the picture was half-finished, the dog Argus.

Charles Willson Peale, *The Peale Family*

Peale Family Group, ca. 1770–1773 and 1808, by Charles Willson Peale, oil on canvas, 56 1/2 by 89 1/2 inches, accession number 1867.298. © Collection of the New York Historical Society.

Reading

Argus, as a pup, was left to the Peales by a grateful old Revolutionary soldier who pulled him out from under his blouse in return for a free meal. The Revolution had come and gone since Peale began the picture. For many years he kept it unfinished in his studio as a kind of demonstration piece. In finishing it, he added the portrait of Argus, by then venerable, and the following inscription at center right: "C. W. Peale painted these Portraits *of his family* in 1773. wishing to finish every work he had undertaken—compleated this picture in 1809!"

A little arithmetic shows that the picture was completed thirty-six years after it was begun. This explains why Peale, who was sixty-eight years old at the time, appears in it as a young man of thirty-two. He stands to the left side, holding a palette and bending over to inspect a drawing on which his brother, St. George Peale, is at work.

The Peale Family is a delightful painting. John Adams, who saw it in 1776 in the painter's Philadelphia studio, wrote in a letter: "There was a pleasant, a happy cheerfulness in their countenances, and a familiarity in their air towards each other." And the intention of the picture is no more complicated than that. It presents an ideal façade of family life, informal, affectionate, harmonious, and secure. The canvas on the easel in the background, the picture-within-a-picture upon which Charles Willson Peale has been at work, originally bore the phrase *Concordia Animae* as a clue to the meaning of the whole painting. But Peale later eliminated these words, "the design being," he wrote to his son, "sufficient to tell the subject," as indeed it is. A glance at *The Peale Family* is enough to show that the ten people in it are happily united as a group. They are pleasantly disposed and share the limelight without competing for it (although Argus, it must be confessed, remains what he was when he was introduced into the composition, a postscript).

5   Compositionally, the subjects are divided into two groups, six figures clustered at the left and three at the right side, or, if you include the nurse, four. She stands in a nicely selected relationship to the family proper, expressive of her position in the household, closely allied with the other figures yet slightly removed, painted as she is in more subdued tones and standing as she does in the only attitude not physically bound to the rest by contact of a hand or a shoulder.

If all the figures had been massed together, they would have looked crowded and monotonous. Hence the division into two groups. But this is a family, a harmoniously united family, so it is necessary that we also be conscious of the two groups as a unit. And we are: the two halves are united by a slight overlapping and by a scattering of fruit across the table, a trivial detail, yet an important one in binding the two halves together— as well as a pretty bit of still life gratuitously offered. The halves are even more strongly held together by the fact that St. George (extreme left), sketching his mother as she holds a grandchild (extreme right), glances toward her as he draws. This play of interest across the breadth of the picture is a psychologically effective tie, nullifying any feeling of disunity that might have been produced by the physical division into two groups.

Within this firmly knit composition each figure is pleasantly varied. We are conscious of each one as an individual, but we cannot look long at one without being led to another. The composition is not brilliant or complicated, it need be neither to fulfill the painter's conception, which is direct and simple.

Peale's style has a suggestion of dryness in it, like a pinch of salt in a dish that might otherwise have been too bland. There are occasional awkwardnesses in drawing—the hands of the sister standing at the left, one resting on the shoulder of Charles Willson Peale, the other on the shoulder of his wife, are a touch oversize. These hands are not quite as fortunately incorporated as the rest. They remind us that the picture is a group of separate studies synthesized into a whole. Also, the arm of the grandmother cannot bear close examination. Instead of terminating as it should, it continues as a tubelike form and disappears into the shadows a moment too late to conceal from us that it is overlong, and handless. But these imperfections have their own appeal; they account for the suggestion of engaging provincialism that distinguishes the work of this early American painter from that of the facile English portrait painters he would have liked to emulate.

Pictures of this general type, which go by the name of "conversation pieces," are frequent in eighteenth-century and early nineteenth-century painting. Based on the assumption that life is a matter of agreeable surfaces, they are usually built around a theme with incidental reference to some pleasurable activity associated with the subjects, like the exercise in drawing that occupies St. George and Charles Willson here.

10   The picture is a happy interpretation of family life but not a very searching one, even for a pre-Freudian age. Families are more complicated than this. Family relationships produce frictions and irritations as minor evils, agonizing psychological conflicts as major ones. The brothers, sisters, and in-laws gathered around the Peale table were human beings, and certainly not immune to these difficulties. Just as certainly, in other aspects of their family life they rose to joys more intense than the casual affections so uniformly expressed in the group. Peale does not hint that these human beings have more than an agreeably tepid experience of life, nor does he make much effort, if any, to differentiate one from another psychologically. He was certainly aware of the psychological individuality of his sitters and of the crosscurrents of emotional relationships, but if it even occurred to him that it would be interesting to explore these in a painting, he rejected the idea as inappropriate in a family portrait.

The particular circumstances of individual relationships in all their psychological subtleties fascinated an-

other artist, a young Frenchman who painted a family group in 1859 when he was less than thirty years old. This, you may remember, is younger than Peale was when he began his family portrait. But at that age this Frenchman, Edgar Degas, was already an urbane cosmopolite. He was a doubter, a speculator upon human nature, and basically a pessimist. He spent the better part of a year in Italy in spite of his father's repeated insistence that he return to Paris, for Degas had begun work on a large painting of his aunt, Baroness Bellelli, his two young cousins, and the Baron. In this family there was a less happy state of affairs than the one Peale would have us believe existed in his. Degas reveals it through a composition as original as any in the history of painting, and, as Peale said of his own, "sufficient to tell the subject." "Sufficient" is an understatement. Superlatives are dangerous, but there is less danger than usual in describing *The Bellelli Family* as the finest psychological group portrait ever painted. The temperament of each of the four members is individualized for us, and, beyond that, their interrelationship is analyzed. Before you read the following paragraphs, you may want to ask yourself on the evidence of the picture what these people were like. In that case try to decide what the relationship of the father to the rest of the family might be, what the emotional tie of

Edgar Degas, *The Bellelli Family*

Réunion des Musées Nationaux/Art Resource, NY.

each of the little girls is to each of the parents, and what the difference is, temperamentally, between these two children. The chances are that you will learn as much from the picture itself as you will know when you have read the following summary, with the exception of specific historical facts.

From references in family letters we gather that the Baron was a man of uneven temperament, given to moods and, at least during the time Degas visited the family, conscious of frustrations and discouragements both in his personal life and in his career. His only son had died (the family is still in mourning in the portrait) and the Baron was marking time as a political exile from his native Naples. His disturbed life made him half a stranger in his own household, a condition aggravated by an increasing rift with his wife. Social conventions of respectability in the mid-nineteenth century placed limitations on a woman in the Baroness's situation. A reserved, intelligent, and patient woman—if we can accept the judgment of her young nephew—she seems to have shouldered even more of the responsibility for the home and the children than did the average wife of her time. Of the two little girls, the elder, Giovanna, was placid and closely attached to her mother, whereas the younger, Giuliana, was more energetic and restless, temperamentally sympathetic to her father but, by force of circumstance, more securely bound within the lives of her mother and sister.

The most casual observer must notice that in Degas's portrait the father is separated from the rest of the family by a series of vertical lines, which, violating normal compositional rules, separate a generous third of the picture from the rest. In addition, he sits unconventionally, with his back toward us and his profile in shadow. His features are painted less decisively than those of the other figures. He is the only one of the family who is not completely revealed to us as a person; we are left with the feeling that we do not know him as we know the mother and daughters. He has a life beyond this room; perhaps he leads a life more important to him than the life we are seeing here; he is an outsider.

But this vagueness, incompleteness, and isolation are reversed in the figure of the wife. She stands with decision, dignity, and forbearance, dominating the room by her quietness. Of all the figures, hers is the simplest and strongest in silhouette; that is why we return to her always, no matter how interesting the rest of the picture may be in its greater detail and variety.

Her right hand rests on the shoulder of Giovanna, the more placid daughter, who was like her and closest to her. This little girl is held within the larger silhouette of the mother's figure; her way of standing echoes her mother's, as does her general silhouette—and she stands quietly. She is the only one of the family who looks at us, although the others are aware of our presence. She looks at us unquestioningly, content to stay within her mother's support and protection.

But the other child, Giuliana, partially breaks away from the pair. She occupies the side of the picture separated from the father, yet we feel strongly her connection with him. She is the only one whose glance could, and in a moment might, meet her father's. She sits restlessly, one leg tucked up under her, as if impatient with sitting for her artist-cousin, unable to remain still, the volatile member of the group. Just as she is divided in her loyalty to her mother and her father, so she does not belong wholly to either in the composition of the painting.

It is apparent, then, that Degas set about expressing a specific set of circumstances with the help of appropriate compositional means. When we know the circumstances, the picture takes on some peripheral interest; but it is a great picture because it is expressive of the interrelationships of four people, whether or not we know the specific circumstances. The picture has a life of its own beyond the immediate reasons for its creation. If the identity of the painter and the family were unknown to us, any meaning *The Bellelli Family* might lose would be of little consequence.

The Bellellis are not important to us as individuals. It makes no difference how they looked. Their troubles were never of any significance except to themselves. The relationships so brilliantly revealed were neither unique nor on the grand scale. The picture's greatness lies in its ability to stir us to thought beyond the limited considerations of a single family's not unusual circumstances. And it does so because Degas has crystallized his material into forms of perfect order, rid of all confusions, incidentals, vagaries, and distractions. In the resultant clarity our sensibilities and understanding may expand.

Degas was one of the greatest of all pictorial composers, and *The Bellelli Family,* an early painting, is only one (though one of the best) of a succession of startlingly original compositions. Degas is preeminent in this unconventionality without freakishness. Other great masters of pictorial composition time and again demonstrate their ability to use conventional devices more skillfully than their contemporaries. But Degas invents compositions without direct precedent, and each of these compositions is so special to its subject that none is directly useful to followers hunting a formula. The composition of *The Peale Family* might be adapted to any number of group portraits, but that of *The Bellelli Family* could not.

Reading and Thinking

1. Why do you think that Peale and Degas painted their respective portraits of families? Who do you think may have commissioned them or been interested in purchasing them? Why?

2. How do the Peale and Bellelli family portraits compare with other paintings or photographs you have seen? If you were to create a portrait of your own family, how would you organize it, and what impression would you attempt to convey? Why?

Thinking and Writing

1. Write an analysis of the Peale and Bellelli family portraits, using your own observations along with those recorded by Canaday. In developing your analysis, you may wish to agree with Canaday's interpretation of the paintings, disagree with some of what he says, and/or introduce another perspective. Alternatively, you may wish to include a third family portrait by another artist to compare and contrast with Degas's and/or Peale's portraits.

2. Write an essay about the portrayal of two different families in television or movies—the Sopranos and the Simpsons, for example. Begin by creating two word-pictures of the family portraits. Include details from the TV series or from films to make your portraits sufficiently detailed and compelling.

3. Using the two created portraits, develop an interpretation of them that leads to an idea of your own about such families. Finally, write an essay about that idea, using comparison and contrast to structure, develop, and explain the idea.

KISSING COUSINS

AN OCCASION FOR

COMPARISON AND CONTRAST

John Canaday compares two paintings in his essay "Two Family Portraits: The Peales and the Bellellis," revealing something about the families as well as the art in the process. In this Occasion, you will have the chance to compare two works of art. Whereas Canaday compares two paintings of a similar subject and style, you will be comparing two sculptures of similar subjects—in fact, both share the title *The Kiss*—but of greatly contrasting styles. As you look at the photographs of the sculptures and work your way through the Occasion, pay particular attention to the way each sculptor uses the materials of the sculpture to achieve his purpose.

AUGUSTE RODIN

Auguste Rodin (1840–1917) was a prolific and innovative sculptor whose works have become familiar as benchmarks of modern realistic sculpture. Rodin portrayed the Gates of Hell, inspired by Dante's *Inferno,* as well as biblical figures such as John the Baptist and historical personages such as the French novelist Honoré de Balzac. He is best known, perhaps, for his realist marble monumental sculpture *The Thinker,* and the romantic portrayal of a couple kissing, *The Kiss.*

CONSTANTIN BRANCUSI

Constantin Brancusi (1876–1957) was a Romanian sculptor who lived and worked in France most of his adult life. Brancusi is best known for his highly simplified and abstract forms of represented objects, cast in wood, stone, steel, or bronze, such as his image of a bird in flight, which is little more than an elegant feather-like image cast in smooth polished bronze, capturing the essence of a flying bird. His sculpture *The Kiss* was completed in 1908.

Occasion

© 2005 Artists Rights Society (ARS), New York/ADAGP, Paris. Constantin Brancusi, *The Kiss*, 1916. Philadelphia Museum of Art: The Louise and Walter Arensberg Collection, 1950–1344. Used with permission.

© Christie's Images/CORBIS.

Auguste Rodin, *The Kiss*

Constantin Brancusi, *The Kiss*

PREPARING TO WRITE: RODIN'S *THE KISS*

1. Describe the relationship between the two figures in Rodin's sculpture. Comment on the color contrast between foreground and background.

2. What is the dominant impression created by Rodin's sculpture? How does he achieve this primary effect?

3. Rodin's sculpture is larger than life size and was sculpted in the nineteenth century. How do these facts affect your perception of and response to Rodin's work?

PREPARING TO WRITE: BRANCUSI'S *THE KISS*

1. Describe the details you notice about Brancusi's kissing couple.

2. Compare the overall form of Brancusi's sculpture with the overall form of Rodin's. If you could choose one geometric shape to describe each, what would it be?

3. Brancusi's work is made of limestone, is just over one foot tall, and was sculpted in the early twentieth century. What effect do these facts have on your impression of and response to Brancusi's sculpture? Why?

MOVING TOWARD ESSAY: ANALYSIS AND REFLECTION

1. To what extent does Brancusi's work derive from and comment on Rodin's? How would you characterize the relationship between these two works? Explain what you see.

2. Which of these sculptures would you prefer to place in your living room or in your yard? Why? Which better captures the essence of a kiss? Explain. Which do you think is most likely to survive? Why?

WRITING THOUGHTFULLY: IDEA AND ESSAY

1. Refer back to your initial analysis of the Rodin and Brancusi sculptures. Develop that analysis in greater detail. Compare their style and tone—that is, the attitude toward the subject taken by each sculptor. Consider the differences between the materials from which the sculptures are made and the effect of those differences on your sense of the sculptures and the kiss they convey.

Occasion

2. Based on your detailed analysis of the two sculptures, develop an idea about the artistic portrayal of a kiss—the joys, the difficulties, the accuracy. As you develop your idea, you might consider other artistic works: paintings, poems, novels, short stories, films, or photographs. Try searching the Internet using different key words or phrases to help you find other artistic portrayals of a kiss. Finally, write a short essay that develops your idea. Use as evidence the two sculptures and any other relevant evidence that you have found through reading and research.

3. Select a contemporary image of a couple kissing from an advertisement in a popular magazine or a newspaper. Write a piece comparing and contrasting the depiction of the kissing couple in the advertisement with that in either Brancusi's or Rodin's work, or both.

CREATING OCCASIONS

1. Do some research on different ways that couples are represented in contemporary print or television advertisements. You can do your research on the Internet, in the library, by taking notes as you watch TV commercials, and by scanning through newspapers and popular magazines. Focus on two particular representations of couples. Develop your own representation of the couples based on your findings. Compare and contrast those two portraits, looking as you do so for an interesting idea about such portrayals. Write an essay based on your findings. Be sure to make use of your own portraits and the comparative work that you did leading up to your idea. Use any other evidence that seems appropriate.

2. Create your own interactive Occasion on *Comp21* using the textual, visual, and video libraries, as well as the Explicator analysis tools. From the main menu, choose "Build Your Own Occasion for Writing."

chapter NINE

CAUSE and EFFECT

Cause and effect is a method of analysis useful for making sense of things. Writers use cause and effect to explain and develop ideas. Readers recognize the use of cause and effect in understanding what writers say. Cause and effect analysis may be used to explain the reasons why things are the way they are; to identify and explain effects or consequences of an event, action, decision, discovery, or invention; and to explain both causes and effects together.

Thinking causally is a natural mental process. You use causal thinking often, sometimes considering the causes of developments and sometimes thinking of outcomes from them. In fact, it is nearly impossible not to find yourself considering causes and effects, since your mind is designed to engage in the process of making the kinds of connections that causal relationships constitute.

The "domino effect" is one of the most commonly known examples of cause and effect. One thing happens, causing the next, and so on. Unlike most cause-and-effect relationships, the domino effect is quite simple and obvious.

© Grant Faint/Getty Images.

THE NATURE OF
CAUSE AND EFFECT

comp 21 To read more about Cause and Effect with interactive examples and opportunities to work with interactive texts, click on "The Rhetorical Patterns of Inquiry" from the main menu of *Comp21*.

Thinking causally is also a natural way to understand the world and the self. It is especially useful as a method of understanding. What was responsible for the demise and disappearance of dinosaurs? What led to the U.S. decision to go to war against Iraq? Why do so many people from all over the world either passionately hate or deeply love what the United States represents? What led you to many of your most important personal decisions? These and many other questions require causal analysis for understanding.

You use cause and effect in your everyday life when you make decisions about personal matters. Your decision to attend college resulted from a number of causes or influences. These very likely included such reasons as the better financial prospects of college graduates as compared with those who don't earn a college degree. You probably expect to get a better job than you have now or than you could acquire without a college degree. In addition to money, there may have been other reasons for your decision, such as encouragement from friends, expectation of family, or interest in learning. Still other possibilities might include new social opportunities or a chance to play on a college sports team. These are some of the reasons causing you and others to decide that college is the right choice.

But cause and effect analysis has other uses as well. Perhaps the most significant use of cause and effect is to make sense of the world, for example, to understand the reasons for the various kinds of political and economic crises occurring around the world. Why is there so much hatred and misunderstanding between Palestinians and Israelis, between Indians and Pakistanis, among believers in and practitioners of different religions? Cause and effect analysis can help you understand the present by analyzing events in the past that have brought us to where we are today. Causal analysis can also help you make decisions about the future by illuminating results of decisions made in the past.

MULTIPLE CAUSES

Most events, decisions, actions, discoveries, and inventions have multiple causes. It is rare that a single cause fully explains a complex phenomenon. In analyzing the causes of the last recession in the United States, for example, you might identify a number of contributory causes. These could include bank, accounting, and trading scandals; tight credit; business failures; an increasing trade deficit; and escalating national and personal consumer debt coupled with decreased savings. No one of these causes alone was responsible for the recession. Taken together, however, each contributed to the resulting effect.

In addition to a variety of multiple contributory causes that create a particular effect, there is also something called a causal chain. A *causal chain* is a set of linked causes in which one cause leads to another and then another until a result is achieved. Consider, for example, the simple case of being late for an examination for one of your courses. The day before the exam you meet with some classmates to review your class notes. You then go out for lunch, and you order clams. Later in the day, you feel sick to your stomach. You skip dinner and take a nap instead. You wake up and begin your final study session, but you quickly become fatigued, decide to go to bed early, and set the alarm for an early study session before the 10 A.M. exam. But you are careless, setting the alarm for P.M. instead of A.M., with the result that instead of waking up to the alarm at 6 A.M., you wake up at 9:30 and arrive half an hour late for the exam. What was the cause of your lateness? A chain of causes that began with the bad clams you ate for lunch and ended with the failure of the alarm to go off when you had planned.

. . . .

INTERACTIVE CAUSES

Another dimension of cause and effect analysis that is important to acknowledge is the interactive nature of many causes. That is, causes affect each other; they rarely operate independently. Consider the example of how you might wind up alienated from one of your friends. Very likely, in such a scenario, each of you would influence the other by creating a pattern of annoyance, argument, and misunderstanding that results in the breakup of your friendship. You say something that the friend doesn't appreciate, and he says something you don't care for. The next day, you do something to annoy your friend and he retaliates. Before long, your mutual friendship dissolves in angry criticism and recrimination.

Of course, not all interactive causes lead to unhappy consequences. To take the friendship example a bit further, imagine a situation in which you and your friend miss each other's friendship so much that you decide to look for ways to reconcile. Each of you makes a move to reestablish the friendship, one by calling, the other by e-mailing. Both of you talk with a mutual friend, who advises each of you how to reestablish the bond of friendship. The result is a renewal of your friendship created by an interactive set of causal actions.

. . . .

SPECULATING
ABOUT EFFECTS

About

Although the rhetorical strategy of cause and effect puts causes before effects, and though we often need to analyze causes of events and circumstances, we also need to consider effects. In fact, we often make decisions in our everyday lives based on effects we predict will occur. We may choose to postpone a trip abroad, for example, if there are government warnings about terrorist activity. We make choices about graduate study based on what we perceive as likely future financial benefits and job prospects.

Consider how the development of railroads in the United States and in Europe magnified the effects of the Industrial Revolution. The engines of trains needed coal and wood as fuel. The train cars were made of iron, and thus the mining of coal, wood, and iron ore needed to be increased dramatically. Forests had to be cut down and mines dug and manned. Other consequences of rapid development of railroads during the nineteenth century included swift transportation of goods, which allowed whole towns and areas to specialize in producing a single commodity, such as shoes or beer, and transport it elsewhere speedily for profit. In explaining this complex network of causes and effects linked with the development of railroads, you would need to rely on many rhetorical strategies to convey both information and analysis—on illustration, description, and narration, and perhaps on comparison, classification, or definition, all in the service of offering an explanation or developing a persuasive argument about the causes and/or the effects of railroads.

. . . .

USING
CAUSE AND EFFECT IN WRITING

Writers use cause and effect to make their understanding of things clear to their readers. Sometimes they use cause and effect as a major structural feature of a piece of writing. Sometimes they use cause and effect as one organizational pattern among others. Regardless of how extensive the use of cause and effect is in a piece of writing that you are reading or writing, it typically serves a larger rhetorical purpose—to inform or to persuade, for example. Writers don't use cause and effect for its sake only, but rather to explore or convey an idea, develop an analysis, or construct an argument.

CAUSES

The following paragraph by Anne Roiphe, from "Why Marriages Fail" in *Family Weekly,* uses causal analysis to point out the reasons marriages may end in divorce.

> Even though each broken marriage is unique, we can still find the common perils, the common causes for marital despair. Each marriage has crisis points and each marriage tests endurance, the capacity for both intimacy and change. Outside pressures such as job loss, illness, infertility, trouble with a child, care of aging parents, and all the other plagues of life hit marriage the way hurricanes blast our shores. Some marriages survive these storms and others don't. Marriages fail, however, not simply because of the outside weather but because the inner climate becomes too hot or too cold, too turbulent, or too stupefying.

In this paragraph, Roiphe uses causal analysis to account for why marriages fail. She identifies a series of external problems that affect marriages by putting a strain on the married couple's endurance and capacity to handle challenges and difficult situations. Any one of the pressures Roiphe identifies, from financial difficulties that ensue from the loss of a job to the emotional challenges involved in dealing with a sick child or an ailing parent, could put severe strains on a marriage. These pressures can cause the "inner climate" of some marriages to change so much that the couple divorces.

This passage is one short paragraph in an essay that explains in much more detail the causes of an increasing divorce rate in America. This paragraph does not consider the effects of divorce on the divorcing partners, on their children, or on society as a whole. Nor does this brief paragraph consider other aspects of marriage—how marital partners survive such external challenges, some in ways that strengthen rather than weaken the bonds of their marriage. Those issues are taken up elsewhere in her essay. Here the question is why some marriages fail, and Roiphe begins to supply some answers.

Exercise

Write a paragraph in which you explain the causes of some phenomenon. Possible topics include alcoholism (or controlled drinking of alcohol), failure (or success) in school, getting promoted in (or fired from) a job, arriving (or not) at a destination, a decline (or increase) in a school's enrollment, and a rise (or fall) of a civilization.

EFFECTS

Consider the following paragraph by David Halberstam from "Who We Are." This paragraph emphasizes effects rather than causes.

> Of the many results of the end of the Cold War—the amazing surge in the American economy, the rise of nationalism and tribalism in certain parts of the world—the most surprising and distressing was the trivialization of the American political agenda. This was reflected in the media, most especially in the decline of foreign reporting among the three main networks. Any serious look at the larger world was presumed to be boring. Fifty-six years after World War II ended I can still tell you the names of the great CBS radio reporters of that era . . . Who can

name five foreign correspondents for the networks today? Sadly, the people who make the biggest salaries, our new specialists in instant, artificial empathy, have, with some exceptions, by and large produced the most frivolous work—the sum of which has seemed to say that America was unthreatened, that there was no challenge to us, and that we need not know anything about the rest of the world. Not surprisingly, our national debates on important issues atrophied. During the last election, allegedly serious political commentators would sit around telling us which of the candidates seemed more likable, as if they were judging a campaign for high school class president.

Unlike Roiphe, who focuses on the causes of marital failure, Halberstam focuses on the effects of the conclusion of the Cold War. Instead of highlighting causes, Halberstam emphasizes effects. Halberstam first lists a string of effects, placing them between dashes in a single sentence. He does this in part to identify a range of consequences that occurred after the Cold War ended. He presents these effects also to prepare for and lead into the single big effect he wishes to emphasize—"the trivialization of the American political agenda." Once he identifies this effect about a third of the way through his paragraph, Halberstam then takes some pains to explain why this result occurred and why it is a matter of some importance.

Exercise

Write a paragraph in which you present the effects or consequences of an action or event, as Halberstam does with his analysis of the effects of the conclusion of the Cold War. You may wish to identify briefly a series of effects and then concentrate on one major effect, as Halberstam does. Or you may wish to identify a series of equally important effects, giving each of them the same amount of space and attention in your paragraph.

CAUSE AND EFFECT
WITH A PURPOSE

When you employ cause and effect in your writing, you need to decide whether you want to focus primarily on causes or primarily on effects, or whether you need to discuss both causes and effects. You also need to decide whether your use of cause and effect is primarily to provide information, to develop an argument, to offer an explanation, or to serve some other purpose. While you can use cause and effect to clarify your ideas, you may also hope that this strategy helps make your writing more interesting and more persuasive.

If your purpose is something more than mere explanation, you need to decide how best to present your analysis of causes and/or effects and how to relate this central writing work to other information, facts, details, and stories that you may be including. To think of this another way, you need to think about what effect you want your writing to have on readers, and then to select and organize your facts, details, stories, and other evidence in ways that will best convey your cause and effect analysis and best serve your overall purpose in writing.

Along with thinking about your purpose, which often will be to explain or to persuade, you also need to consider your audience. Who will be reading your essay? For whom are you writing it? The examples you select, the definitions of terms you provide, and the information you elect to omit and include will all be determined in part by your sense of your audience of readers and by the primary effect you wish your writing to have on that audience.

. . . .

CAUSE AND EFFECT
AND THE OTHER PATTERNS OF INQUIRY

Cause and effect is a useful rhetorical strategy when you need to analyze events, especially when you want to account for how a particular situation, historical or personal, came to be. It is also a useful strategy for predicting what will happen in the future.

But however useful cause and effect may be in helping writers explain and readers understand historical explanations, cause and effect is rarely used in isolation from other patterns. In providing historical explanation, for example, writers need to provide examples, to build arguments, to classify and compare, to describe, and to narrate. In short, as with using any of the patterns, working with cause and effect as a central rhetorical strategy typically necessitates the use of other rhetorical strategies in conjunction with it.

Examine the various examples of cause and effect in this chapter—from the brief paragraphs to the longer essays. In doing so, you will see how writers mix and blend various rhetorical strategies, even when they use cause and effect as their leading strategy and their organizing principle.

. . . .

CAUSE AND EFFECT
IN PURE FORM: AN ANNOTATED PARAGRAPH

Atul Gawande (b. 1965) is a surgeon at a Boston hospital and a staff writer on medicine and science for *The New Yorker* magazine. A graduate of Harvard Medical School and the Harvard School of Public Health, Gawande's writing has been selected to appear in *Best American Essays 2002* and *Best American Science Writing 2002*. His first book, *Complications,* describes the fallibility of physicians. Asking himself why doctors misdiagnose patients who die in three out of five cases, Gawande set himself to the task of explaining why misdiagnosis is so prevalent. The following paragraph, on the causes of error, is taken from that book.

identifying possible causes for mistakes

science will not allow these causes to have their effect

In a 1976 essay, the philosophers Samuel Gorovitz and Alasdair MacIntyre explored the nature of fallibility. Why would a meteorologist, say, fail to correctly predict where a hurricane was going to make landfall? They saw three possible reasons. One was ignorance: perhaps science affords only a limited understanding of how hurricanes behave. A second reason was ineptitude: the knowledge is available, but the weatherman fails to apply it correctly. Both of these are surmountable sources of error. We believe that science will overcome ignorance, and that training and technology will overcome ineptitude. The third possible cause of error the philosophers posited, however, was an insurmountable kind, one they termed "necessary fallibility."

exploring why fallibility occurs

1st cause

2nd cause

3rd cause

In this paragraph Atul Gawande summarizes three reasons philosophers Samuel Gorovitz and Alasdair MacIntyre present for human failure. These are ignorance, ineptitude, and necessary fallibility. The first two sources of error, Gawande implies, are correctible or "surmountable." What we know and understand about weather, including hurricanes, can be increased. Moreover, the meteorologist who fails to apply information correctly can do better the next time. Gawande suggests that ignorance and ineptitude are not inevitable. However, his third cause of error, necessary fallibility, suggests that there is no way to avoid certain kinds of error, and that, in fact, error is built into human understanding.

Exercises

1. What three reasons does Gawande identify for human failure? Why do you think he cites these reasons and identifies the philosophers who provide them?

2. What important distinction does Gawande make between the first two kinds of reasons for error and the third, necessary fallibility? What implications does the idea of necessary fallibility have for the training of doctors, lawyers, and airline pilots?

CAUSE AND EFFECT
IN ITS NATURAL HABITAT:
AN ANNOTATED READING

In this chapter you have been presented with passages featuring cause and effect analysis. Those paragraphs were organized and developed exclusively by means of cause and effect, but that is rarely the case in most of the writing you will encounter. Cause and effect seldom exists in such pure form throughout an entire essay or article. Most often it is used as one pattern among others for a particular rhetorical purpose.

In the passage that follows, you will have a chance to look at an example of cause and effect in a larger context. The passage, taken from an article about American technology by Edward Rothstein, appeared in the *New York Times* on May 31, 2003.

EDWARD ROTHSTEIN
The Double-Edged Ax of American Technology

What was so special about the American ax? In 1828 James Fenimore Cooper said it was admirable "for form, for neatness and precision of weight." In 1841 the British Parliament, impressed by its power, investigated its design. When Lincoln ran for president in 1860, his supporters marched with enormous symbolic models. And by the turn of the 20th century, it was the tool of choice in tall tales about Paul Bunyan, logger extraordinaire.

But the truly unusual character of the American ax, this book makes clear, is that it was considered unusual at all. It was treated not as a tool of destruction but as an

CAUSE & EFFECT
contrasts of effects

Rothstein, formerly the chief music critic for the *New York Times,* is critic-at-large for the *New York Times* and the music critic for *The New Republic.* He is author of *Emblems of Mind: The Inner Life of Music and Mathematics* and co-author of *Visions of Utopia.* His essays and music criticism have appeared in *The American Scholar, Commentary,* the *London Independent,* the *New York Review of Books,* and other magazines and journals. Rothstein holds a doctorate from the Committee on Social Thought at the University of Chicago.

As you read, notice how Rothstein analyzes causes and effects of American technology and uses causal explanation to explain and develop his ideas.

instrument of creation. Grasping its distinctively curved hickory handle, the solitary pioneer carved a home from the untamed woodlands. In the swings of the ax, Cooper wrote, have come conquests that "have left civilization in their train instead of havoc and desolation."

Or such, at any rate, is one version of the story. For as David E. Nye shows in *America as Second Creation,* every narrative of how a great invention helped create an American Eden inspired a counternarrative of how that same invention helped construct an American hell. The same ax championed as the creator of the log cabin was soon enough condemned as despoiler of the natural world, leaving behind stumps and wrecking the habitats of American Indians. The "heroic story of self-sufficiency," Mr. Nye writes, eventually became a "tale of thoughtless land exploitation."

DESCRIPTION
adds engaging detail

CAUSE & EFFECT
effects of the ax

CAUSE & EFFECT

use of contrast to describe effects of technologies: railroad and Industrial revolution as intrusions

COMPARISON & CONTRAST

more contrasts

COMPARISON & CONTRAST

contrasts Europe and America

And as with ax, so too with the mill, the canal, the railroad and the dam. On one hand, these technologies were championed for transforming the wilderness into "a prosperous and egalitarian society." On the other, they have been condemned for having increased economic inequality and for running roughshod over those less powerful. On one hand, they have been invocations of optimism and progress; on the other, they have been reminders of disruption and marginality.

In his earlier books, Mr. Nye, professor of American studies at Odense University in Denmark, has been a remarkable chronicler of how technological change has impressed itself on the American character. In this book, Mr. Nye draws on 40 years of scholarship, beginning with Leo Marx's influential *The Machine in the Garden* (1965), with its study of how the railroad and the Industrial Revolution were seen as intrusions on a pastoral realm celebrated by American writers. Hawthorne, Emerson, and their contemporaries reappear in Mr. Nye's book, with all their wariness. So do many of the tics of the contemporary academic discipline of American studies, which has itself been beset by precisely the same confrontations that Mr. Nye traces.

In fact, in outlining these warring narratives, Mr. Nye inadvertently provides a portrait of how Americans still think about themselves—and also, perhaps, how others still look at them—as bouncing between idealistic images and their extreme inversions.

Underlying the celebrations of American technology, Mr. Nye argues, is a vastly different experience. While European cities, for example, often developed around a central church with roads radiating outward, American cities often developed around a mill on a river and its expanding promise of commerce. While railroads developed in Europe and England to serve existing cities, in the United States railroads helped determine where cities would be developed.

And because there were no long traditions of land ownership or conquest, and because ownership often had to be assigned to land as yet unexplored, the rectangular grid became the defining order for the American landscape. Jefferson was a champion of the new grid system, which struck one French observer in 1836 as being more suited to the division of the heavens than of the earth. New towns were laid out on grids before they had inhabitants, and new grids extended across the continent with the railroad. One assumption, Mr. Nye points out, is that "the land was unused, empty and waiting for settlers."

There was also, Mr. Nye argues, an assumption that resources were abundant, that forests were unbounded and that prairies were open to unlimited farming. While America was inventing this sense of possibility, European consciousness was elsewhere: Malthus, in 1798, saw wars as the consequences of population growth and limited resources.

Counternarratives, of course, rejected American optimism, portraying each technology not as liberator but as oppressor. The mill "created not prosperity but poverty," Mr. Nye writes. "Its town was not harmonious but divided."

The railroad "confronted Americans with new forms of political power, class conflict, accidents, land swindles, pollution and unfamiliar environmental problems."

Mr. Nye clearly prefers these critiques to celebrations, but the counternarrative surely deserves its own countering. Mr. Nye writes, for example, "The railroad did not open the West; it closed it to poor settlers." But of course despite land speculation, eventually the railroad did open the West to vast migrations of populations seeking economic opportunity, just as the mill did far more than create poverty and division. Mr. Nye sometimes seems to defer to a new orthodoxy.

And the pattern of utopian expectation and dystopian warnings is also familiar, repeating itself again and again as technologies have erupted in innovation. Something similar happened during the last decade with the Internet, which was both hailed for

CAUSE & EFFECT
landscape as grid due to lack of land ownership

DESCRIPTION
describing grids

COMPARISON & CONTRAST
contrasts U.S. & Europe

CAUSE & EFFECT
examples/consequences/effects of the mill

effects of railroads

CAUSE & EFFECT
positive and negative effects of mills & railroad

CAUSE & EFFECT
effects of the Internet

ushering in a new era of human consciousness and attacked for increasing economic inequalities and polli-
nating pornography. Both were exaggerations.

For all its intriguing analysis, then, the great wonder
and great fear inspired by technology was better explored in one of Mr. Nye's earlier books, *American*

Edward Rothstein's piece is both an essay in which he develops an idea about the effects of
American technology and simultaneously a review of the book *America as Second Creation:
Technology and Narratives of New Beginnings* by David E. Nye. In analyzing the effects of
American technology, Edward Rothstein considers both positive and negative consequences. Rothstein begins with an example of American technology—the ax, which was
used to clear the land and consequently allowed for settlement of what previously had been
forest. The ax, for Rothstein, is a double-edged symbol of America's creative and civilizing
power on the one hand and of its dangerously destructive consequences on the other. For at
the same time that Americans were clearing forests to create farmland, they were destroying
the natural environment and upsetting complex ecosystems that had been in place for centuries. In developing a balanced overview of the consequences of American technological
achievement, Rothstein analyzes arguments put forth by Nye in his book, relying heavily on
comparison and contrast to organize, illustrate, and develop his ideas.

Technological Sublime. The immensity of transformation, the grandeur of possibility, the overwhelming dangers of failure, the grim worries over retribution: these are latent in the technological sublime. And they still haunt American life and debates about its future.

CAUSE & EFFECT
latent causes & effects

Natural Habitat

Exercises

1. What is the author's main idea? How does he use cause and effect to convey this idea?

2. How does Edward Rothstein organize his causal analysis about American technology? Does he emphasize primarily causes or effects?

READING

KENNETH POMERANZ

Kenneth Pomeranz is professor of history and chair of the history department at the University of California, Irvine. His first book, *The Making of a Hinterland: State, Society, and Economy in Inland North China, 1853–1937,* won the John King Fairbank award of the American Historical Association as the book of the year in modern East Asian history. His research interests include social and economic influences and environmental change in twentieth century China and the origin of a world economy.

America and the Coffee Bean

Taken from Pomeranz's book *The World That Trade Created,* the following essay is one of a number of short pieces about how a commodity, in this case coffee, became a staple of the American diet. As you read, try to identify Pomeranz's main idea and the way he uses causal analysis to explain that idea. Consider also the author's purpose.

1   Americans love coffee. For a long time now, we have been the world's largest coffee drinker. Indeed, our love of coffee rather than tea is often seen as a mark of national identity that distinguishes us from the British. Historians even see coffee-drinking as noble and patriotic. Most agree that the coffee habit was an intimate part of the creation of the nation: Colonists took up the beverage as an act of rebellion against the British.

    Every schoolchild has heard of the Boston Tea Party, in which American patriots, dressed as Indians, threw cases of Chinese tea into Massachusetts Bay. This is an inspiring story that infuses a consumption habit with glory. Unfortunately, as with too many glorious stories, it is not true. Quite simply, avarice and profit, not glory and patriotism, animated America's turn from tea to coffee.

    Tradition has it that the American colonists, as British subjects, loved tea rather than coffee. The truth is that Jamestown's John Smith—who earlier spent more than a year pressed into service of the Turkish vizier—is said to have brought the Turkish coffee habit to America as early as 1607. It is true, however, that colonial Americans drank more tea than coffee.

    Colonial imports of tea ballooned from a meager 2.5 million pounds in the 1790s to almost 90 million pounds 100 years later. But, at the same time, coffee consumption grew seven times as fast. By 1909, Americans downed an average of 1.25 pounds of tea and 11.5 pounds of coffee per person per year. That was 40 percent of all the coffee consumed in the world. By the 1950s, Americans drank a fifth more coffee annually than all of the rest of the world combined.

    How did this coffee mania come about?   5

    Not because of American patriotism or Anglophobia. Rather, the cause was, in a word, slavery. American shippers carried off the products of Haiti's huge slave labor force (the world's largest at the time) and supplied many of their basic necessities. Haiti's slaves produced huge amounts of sugar on large plantations. However, Haiti's yeoman and freedman population lacked the capital to carve out sugar plantations. Instead, the rural middle class opened up smaller and cheaper coffee farms to sell to the island's elite who were anxious to imbibe Paris fashion. Coffee became sufficiently profitable that production soon exceeded local demand.

    Yankee merchants came to the rescue. New England and Chesapeake traders had long been involved in a triangular trade with the sugar island that saw Americans deliver foodstuffs to feed Haitian slaves, as well as lumber and British manufactures in exchange for sugar and rum, which in part would be sold in Britain to obtain other manufactured goods. These shippers sometimes found themselves with carrying space to bring back consignment goods seeking new markets. Coffee, which withstood sea travel and was slow to spoil, was ideal freight.

The price of coffee plummeted. The drop in price from 18 shillings per pound in 1683 for Arabian coffee to 9 shillings in 1774 for Haitian coffee under British mercantilism and even further to 1 shilling in the independent United States made the beverage available to a far wider public. By 1790, coffee imports were a third greater than tea imports, and a decade later coffee shipments outstripped those of tea tenfold.

When Haiti's slaves, inspired by the American and French Revolutions, revolted in the 1790s—abolishing slavery and declaring independence in the process—coffee production slumped severely, prices shot up, and exports to the United States were cut in half. This might have spelled the end of America's love affair with the coffee bean if another country, also based on slavery, had not taken advantage of the situation and turned much of its arable land into coffee groves. The first Brazilian coffee reached New York in 1809. By mid-century Brazil was supplying two-thirds of the coffee consumed in the United States.

10   In the past, Lisbon's tight control of Brazil's com- merce had shut out Yankee traders from doing business with the vast Portuguese colony. But again the French Revolution intervened. Napoleon, bent on seizing Lisbon—one of the finest ports in Western Europe—convinced Portugal's King João VI to decamp to Rio de Janeiro and throw open Brazil's ports to the world. U.S. flagships now could enter Rio easily to load coffee, but what could they sell? Brazil—a continent-sized colony—was self-sufficient in provisions, unlike its Caribbean competitors. But it needed more slaves.

As world demand for coffee swelled in the 1830s, Brazilian planters sought more African chattel to work the coffee groves. Anti-slave sentiment—and eventually an act of Parliament—virtually ended the traditional British participation in the "peculiar institution." By the early 1840s, American ships carried one-fifth of Brazil's record slave imports across the Atlantic. By the last year of the slave trade—1850—one-half of the bound unfortunates came to Brazil in ships flying the Stars and Stripes.

Brazilian slaves toiled to grow the coffee to which America's teeming urban and industrial masses became addicted. Coffee became an integral part of the American way of life, not so much because Americans rejected the "Britishness" of tea but simply because slavery made coffee cheap—and profitable.

Reading and Thinking

1. Why do some historians suggest that coffee drinking can be considered "noble" and "patriotic"? What counterview does Pomeranz present? Which view seems more persuasive?

2. What reasons are mentioned for Americans' coffee mania? How are slavery, economics, and trade part of that explanation? How are those causes related to the others Pomeranz identifies?

Thinking and Writing

1. Write a summary of Pomeranz's argument. Be sure to include the various causes Pomeranz identifies for why Americans drink more coffee than tea. Explain the relationship between those causes.

2. Write an essay in which you explain your own reasons for drinking (or not drinking) coffee, tea, or another beverage.

HOW TO EAT

AN OCCASION FOR CAUSE AND EFFECT

Occasion

In "America and the Coffee Bean," Kenneth Pomeranz discusses the causes and effects of the American coffee habit, arguing that it has had unfavorable consequences. Countering the popular image of a benign and patriotic custom forged in response to British demands for taxes on tea, Pomeranz argues that the American coffee habit contributed to the spread of slavery throughout much of the eighteenth and nineteenth centuries. Similarly, in an effort to understand the recent boom in obesity in the United States, some critics have pointed to another seemingly benign symbol: the food pyramid. Arguing that the final form of the U.S. Department of Agriculture (USDA) food pyramid was the result of politics and not science, critics have suggested that the pyramid has ensured not good health, but rather the consumption of certain products whose manufacturers are well-represented on Capitol Hill.

In this Occasion, you will explore the implications of the design of the food pyramid as it relates to health in America. You will examine a USDA pyramid and an alternative food pyramid, and craft one of your own. You will also explore graphic representations of the increase of obesity in the United States. In the end you will determine exactly how food consumption patterns affect us on a personal and public level.

PREPARING TO WRITE: FOOD PYRAMIDS

1. Discuss why the U.S. Department of Agriculture chose the shape of a pyramid to convey its guidelines for healthy eating. What kind of symbolic weight does the shape have? How is it a practical vehicle for communicating ideas about diet? How has the shape fashioned our understanding of good health?

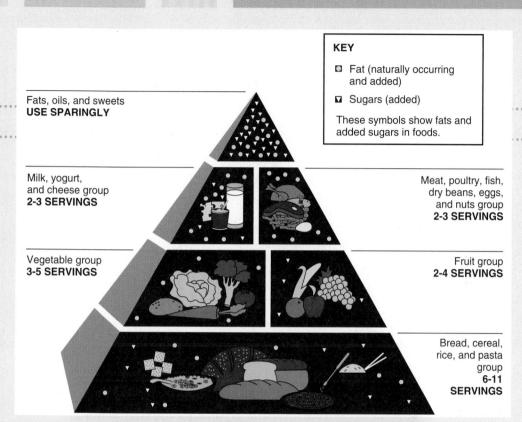

KEY

▢ Fat (naturally occurring and added)

☑ Sugars (added)

These symbols show fats and added sugars in foods.

Fats, oils, and sweets
USE SPARINGLY

Milk, yogurt,
and cheese group
2-3 SERVINGS

Meat, poultry, fish,
dry beans, eggs,
and nuts group
2-3 SERVINGS

Vegetable group
3-5 SERVINGS

Fruit group
2-4 SERVINGS

Bread, cereal,
rice, and pasta
group
**6-11
SERVINGS**

U.S. Department of Agriculture (USDA), Food Guide Pyramid, 1996

2. Look carefully at the USDA's Food Guide Pyramid and Dr. Walter Willet's Healthy Eating Pyramid (p. 320). Notice the design elements (color, icons, and so on) of each pyramid. Briefly describe how the elements and designs create an emotional effect.

3. Consider how each pyramid uses the visual principles of focal point, figure-ground contrast, and continuation discussed in chapter 2. How do the elements of the design cause your eye to move? How does that movement contribute to your understanding of the pyramid? Write your observations.

4. Consider the whole composition of each pyramid, paying special attention to the various other elements of visual design discussed in chapter 2. Look carefully at the elements and details of each pyramid you may have missed upon first glance. Add to your descriptive notes about each pyramid.

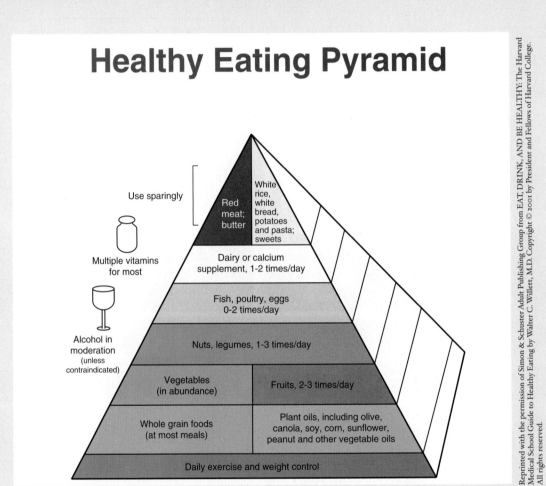

Healthy Eating Pyramid

Use sparingly

Multiple vitamins
for most

Alcohol in
moderation
(unless
contraindicated)

Red meat; butter

White rice, white bread, potatoes and pasta; sweets

Dairy or calcium supplement, 1-2 times/day

Fish, poultry, eggs 0-2 times/day

Nuts, legumes, 1-3 times/day

Vegetables (in abundance)

Fruits, 2-3 times/day

Whole grain foods (at most meals)

Plant oils, including olive, canola, soy, corn, sunflower, peanut and other vegetable oils

Daily exercise and weight control

Harvard University nutritionist Dr. Walter Willet's Healthy Eating Pyramid

Occasion

MOVING TOWARD ESSAY: ANALYSIS AND REFLECTION

1. What argument, or statement, does each pyramid make? Does the design of each pyramid seem to convey an attitude about health, about food, about particular food groups? How do the elements of its visual composition help convey that attitude?

2. As indicated at the beginning of this Occasion, critics have suggested that the food pyramid has had the unexpected effect of increasing the rate of obesity in America. The criticism has centered on several issues—the size of suggested servings, the foods that seem to be most heavily promoted, and the U.S. Department of Agriculture's conflict of interest in their dual role of promoting agricultural products and establishing an ideal diet. Identify those elements—portions, types of foods, and so on—from the USDA's Food Guide Pyramid that could have encouraged a diet that may lead to obesity.

3. Note the changes between the second and the first pyramid. What are the differences? Assuming the second pyramid was designed to reverse the effects of the first, what do those changes indicate about the first? Write a brief sales pitch promoting the Healthy Eating Pyramid as a more healthy alternative to the USDA Food Guide Pyramid.

4. Describe or draw a food pyramid that accurately reflects your eating habits. How have those habits affected your health?

5. Considering the USDA Food Guide Pyramid, the Healthy Eating Pyramid, and the pyramid you created, explore the relationship between what types and amounts of foods you eat and your health. Pay particular attention to the issue of weight.

WRITING THOUGHTFULLY: IDEA AND ESSAY

1. Identifying causes and promoting effects often requires a full consideration of as much data as possible. The graphs on the following page describe slightly different perspectives of the rise of obesity. Break down the information in the graphs. What do the different graphs tell you?

2. Which of the graphs could serve as support for a thesis suggesting rising obesity rates are caused by the USDA recommended servings? Which of the graphs could be used to refute such a notion? How?

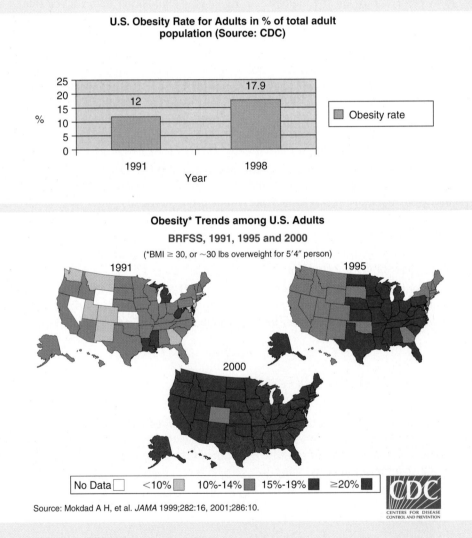

U.S. Obesity Rate for Adults in % of total adult population (Source: CDC)

Obesity* Trends among U.S. Adults

BRFSS, 1991, 1995 and 2000

(*BMI ≥ 30, or ~30 lbs overweight for 5′4″ person)

1991

1995

2000

No Data ☐   <10% ▨   10%-14% ▨   15%-19% ■   ≥20% ■

Source: Mokdad A H, et al. *JAMA* 1999;282:16, 2001;286:10.

3. Make a list of factors other than or in addition to the USDA's recommended food guide that could have caused the obesity crisis in America.

4. Pomeranz discusses collateral effects of the American coffee habit. What collateral effects could the obesity crisis have on American domestic and possibly foreign policy?

5. Write an essay delineating the causes of the obesity crisis in which you explore the relationship between diet and health, using the information gathered from the pyramids and the graphs. Assuming that we are in a health crisis in the United States, identify the causes of that crisis, either including or dismissing the USDA's recommended daily guide as a cause.

6. Write an essay exploring the impact of the obesity crisis in America. Think about how cigarettes are often cited as having an effect on federal health policy and oil consumption is often cited as having an impact on American foreign policy.

7. *Comp21* **Video Extension.** Extend this Occasion to include CNN® video footage using the Explicator video analysis tool on *Comp21*. From the main menu choose "Frames of Mind: Extending Occasions" and select "How to Eat: An Occasion for Cause and Effect" from the list.

CREATING OCCASIONS

1. On the Internet, in your local library or bookstore, or through interviews, research the development of the USDA food pyramids. Determine whether or not there is a viable relationship between the ways that food pyramids were developed and the rise in obesity in the United States.

2. A great deal has been written about the impact that bioengineered foods would have on humans, economies, and the environment. Most of the studies, policy pieces, and opinion articles that address the issue of bioengineered foods naturally fall into a cause and effect structure. On the Internet, or in your local library or bookstore, find coverage of the impact that bioengineered foods would have on humans, cultures, economies, or the environment and write a cause and effect argument regarding the use of bioengineered foods.

3. Prior to the Second Iraq War, politicians and pundits from both parties made many claims about the effects of the war in Iraq, the U.S. image abroad, domestic policy, the federal budget, and the state of affairs in the Middle East. Given the history of Iraq and the Middle East since the Second Iraq War, go to your library, the Internet, or a bookstore, locate opinion pieces written prior to the war, and evaluate the legitimacy of those claims.

4. Create your own interactive Occasion on *Comp21* using the textual, visual, and video libraries, as well as the Explicator analysis tools. From the main menu, choose "Build Your Own Occasion for Writing."

Occasion

READING

STEPHEN JAY GOULD

Perhaps most popularly known for his colloquial and often amusing essays about science, Stephen Jay Gould (1941–2002) was a professor of zoology and biology at Harvard University, where he taught the popular course "The Evolution of Earth and Its Life," among other courses, for over thirty years. Born in New York City, Gould graduated from Antioch College and received his doctorate from Columbia University in 1967. While he is the author of many books and articles of a purely scholarly nature, Gould was also the recipient of a number of popular awards, including the 1982 National Book Critics' Circle Award for *The Mismeasure of Man* and the 1981 American Book Award for Science for *The Panda's Thumb: More Reflections in Natural History*. He wrote regular columns in *Natural History* magazine, many of which have been collected in book-length volumes.

Sex, Drugs, Disasters, and the Extinction of the Dinosaurs

In "Sex, Drugs, Disasters, and the Extinction of the Dinosaurs," Gould not only illustrates several attempts at cause and effect analysis—in the form of theories of why the dinosaurs became extinct—but he clearly spells out a formula for a particular method of cause and effect analysis: what he calls "good science." Gould presents the three hypotheses while evaluating them on their merits. As you read, pay special attention to the different ways Gould treats cause and effect analysis: as an object of study, as a method of his own thinking, and as a process to be taught.

1   Science, in its most fundamental definition, is a fruitful mode of inquiry, not a list of enticing conclusions. The conclusions are the consequence, not the essence.

My greatest unhappiness with most popular presentations of science concerns their failure to separate fascinating claims from the methods that scientists use to establish the facts of nature. Journalists, and the public, thrive on controversial and stunning statements. But science is, basically, a way of knowing—in P. B. Medawar's apt words, "the art of the soluble." If the growing corps of popular science writers would focus on *how* scientists develop and defend those fascinating claims, they would make their greatest possible contribution to public understanding.

Consider three ideas, proposed in perfect seriousness to explain that greatest of all titillating puzzles—the extinction of dinosaurs. Since these three notions invoke the primarily fascinating themes of our culture—sex, drugs, and violence—they surely reside in the category of fascinating claims. I want to show why two of them rank as silly speculation, while the other represents science at its grandest and most useful.

Science works with testable proposals. If, after much compilation and scrutiny of data, new information continues to affirm a hypothesis, we may accept it provisionally and gain confidence as further evidence mounts. We can never be completely sure that a hypothesis is right, though we may be able to show with confidence that it is wrong. The best scientific hypotheses are also generous and expansive: They suggest extensions and implications that enlighten related, and even far distant, subjects. Simply consider how the idea of evolution has influenced virtually every intellectual field.

Useless speculation, on the other hand, is restrictive. It generates no testable hypothesis, and offers no way to obtain potentially refuting evidence. Please note that I am not speaking of truth or falsity. The speculation may well be true; still, if it provides, in principle, no material for affirmation or rejection, we can make nothing of it. It must simply stand forever as an intriguing idea. Useless speculation turns in on itself and leads nowhere; good science, containing both seeds for its potential refutation and implications for more and different testable knowledge, reaches out. But, enough preaching. Let's move on to dinosaurs, and the three proposals for their extinction.

1. *Sex.* Testes function only in a narrow range of temperature (those of mammals hang externally in a scrotal sac because internal body temperatures are too high for their proper function). A worldwide rise in temperature at the close of the Cretaceous period caused the testes of dinosaurs to stop functioning and led to their extinction by sterilization of males.

2. *Drugs.* Angiosperms (flowering plants) first evolved toward the end of the dinosaurs' reign. Many of these plants contain psychoactive agents, avoided by mammals today as a result of their bitter taste. Dinosaurs had neither means to taste the bitterness nor livers effective enough to detoxify the substances. They died of massive overdoses.

3. *Disasters.* A large comet or asteroid struck the earth some 65 million years ago, lofting a cloud of dust into the sky and blocking sunlight, thereby suppressing photosynthesis and so drastically lowering world temperatures that dinosaurs and hosts of other creatures became extinct.

Before analyzing these three tantalizing statements, we must establish a basic ground rule often violated in proposals for the dinosaurs' demise. *There is no separate problem of the extinction of dinosaurs.* Too often we divorce specific events from their wider contexts and systems of cause and effect. The fundamental fact of dinosaur extinction is its synchrony with the demise of so many other groups across a wide range of habitats, from terrestrial to marine.

The history of life has been punctuated by brief episodes of mass extinction. A recent analysis by University of Chicago paleontologists Jack Sepkoski and Dave Raup, based on the best and most exhaustive tabulation of data ever assembled, shows clearly that five episodes of mass dying stand well above the "background" extinctions of normal times (when we consider all mass extinctions, large and small, they seem to fall in a regular 26-million-year cycle). The Cretaceous debacle, occurring 65 million years ago and separating

the Mesozoic and Cenozoic eras of our geological time scale, ranks prominently among the five. Nearly all the marine plankton (single-celled floating creatures) died with geological suddenness; among marine invertebrates, nearly 15 percent of all families perished, including many previously dominant groups, especially the ammonites (relatives of squids in coiled shells). On land, the dinosaurs disappeared after more than 100 million years of unchallenged domination.

In this context, speculations limited to dinosaurs alone ignore the larger phenomenon. We need a coordinated explanation for a system of events that includes the extinction of dinosaurs as one component. Thus it makes little sense, though it may fuel our desire to view mammals as inevitable inheritors of the earth, to guess that dinosaurs died because small mammals ate their eggs (a perennial favorite among untestable speculations). It seems most unlikely that some disaster peculiar to dinosaurs befell these massive beasts—and that the debacle happened to strike just when one of history's five great dyings had enveloped the earth for completely different reasons.

The testicular theory, an old favorite from the 1940s, had its root in an interesting and thoroughly respectable study of temperature tolerances in the American alligator, published in the staid *Bulletin of the American Museum of Natural History* in 1946 by three experts on living and fossil reptiles—E. H. Colbert, my own first teacher in paleontology; R. B. Cowles; and C. M. Bogert.

The first sentence of their summary reveals a purpose beyond alligators: "This report describes an attempt to infer the reactions of extinct reptiles, especially the dinosaurs, to high temperatures as based upon reactions observed in the modern alligator." They studied, by rectal thermometry, the body temperatures of alligators under changing conditions of heating and cooling. (Well, let's face it, you wouldn't want to try sticking a thermometer under a 'gator's tongue.) The predictions under test go way back to an old theory first stated by Galileo in the 1630s—the unequal scaling of surfaces and volumes. As an animal, or any object, grows (provided its shape doesn't change), surface areas must increase more slowly than volumes—since surfaces get larger as length squared, while volumes increase much more rapidly, as length cubed. There-fore, small animals have high ratios of surface to volume, while large animals cover themselves with relatively little surface.

Among cold-blooded animals lacking any physiological mechanism for keeping their temperatures constant, small creatures have a hell of a time keeping warm—because they lose so much heat through their relatively large surfaces. On the other hand, large animals, with their relatively small surfaces, may lose heat so slowly that, once warm, they may maintain effectively constant temperatures against ordinary fluctuations of climate. (In fact, the resolution of the "hot-blooded dinosaur" controversy that burned so brightly a few years back may simply be that, while large dinosaurs possessed no physiological mechanism for constant temperature, and were not therefore warm-blooded in the technical sense, their large size and relatively small surface area kept them warm.)

Colbert, Cowles, and Bogert compared the warming rates of small and large alligators. As predicted, the small fellows heated up (and cooled down) more quickly. When exposed to a warm sun, a tiny 50-gram (1.76-ounce) alligator heated up one degree Celsius every minute and a half, while a large alligator, 260 times bigger at 13,000 grams (28.7 pounds), took seven and a half minutes to gain a degree. Extrapolating up to an adult 10-ton dinosaur, they concluded that a one-degree rise in body temperature would take eighty-six hours. If large animals absorb heat so slowly (through their relatively small surfaces), they will also be unable to shed any excess heat gained when temperatures rise above a favorable level.

The authors then guessed that large dinosaurs lived at or near their optimum temperatures; Cowles suggested that a rise in global temperatures just before the Cretaceous extinction caused the dinosaurs to heat up beyond their optimal tolerance—and, being so large, they couldn't shed the unwanted heat. (In a most unusual statement within a scientific paper, Colbert and Bogert then explicitly disavowed this speculative extension of their empirical work on alligators.) Cowles conceded that this excess heat probably wasn't enough to kill or even to enervate the great beasts, but since testes often function only within a narrow range of temperature, he proposed that this global rise might have sterilized all the males, causing extinction by natural contraception.

The overdose theory has recently been supported by UCLA psychiatrist Ronald K. Siegel. Siegel has gathered, he claims, more than 2,000 records of animals who, when given access, administer various drugs to themselves—from a mere swig of alcohol to massive doses of the big H. Elephants will swill the equivalent of twenty beers at a time, but do not like alcohol in concentrations greater than 7 percent. In a silly bit of anthropocentric speculation, Siegel states that "elephants drink, perhaps, to forget . . . the anxiety produced by shrinking rangeland and the competition for food."

Since fertile imaginations can apply almost any hot idea to the extinction of dinosaurs, Siegel found a way. Flowering plants did not evolve until late in the dinosaurs' reign. These plants also produced an array of aromatic, amino-acid-based alkaloids—the major group of psychoactive agents. Most mammals are "smart" enough to avoid these potential poisons. The alkaloids simply don't taste good (they are bitter); in any case, we mammals have livers happily supplied with the capacity to detoxify them. But, Siegel speculates, perhaps dinosaurs could neither taste the bitterness nor detoxify the substances once ingested. He recently told members of the American Psychological Association: "I'm not suggesting that all dinosaurs OD'd on plant drugs, but it certainly was a factor." He also argued that death by overdose may help explain why so many dinosaur fossils are found in contorted positions. (Do not go gently into that good night.)

Extraterrestrial catastrophes have long pedigrees in the popular literature of extinction, but the subject exploded again in 1979, after a long lull, when the father-son, physicist-geologist team of Luis and Walter Alvarez proposed that an asteroid, some 10 km in diameter, struck the earth 65 million years ago. (Comets, rather than asteroids, have since gained favor. Good science is self-corrective.)

The force of such a collision would be immense, greater by far than the megatonnage of all the world's nuclear weapons. In trying to reconstruct a scenario that would explain the simultaneous dying of di-

Reading

nosaurs on land and so many creatures in the sea, the Alvarezes proposed that a gigantic dust cloud, generated by particles blown aloft in the impact, would so darken the earth that photosynthesis would cease and temperatures drop precipitously. (Rage, rage against the dying of the light.) The single-celled photosynthetic oceanic plankton, with life cycles measured in weeks, would perish outright, but land plants might survive through the dormancy of their seeds (land plants were not much affected by the Cretaceous extinction, and any adequate theory must account for the curious pattern of differential survival). Dinosaurs would die by starvation and freezing; small, warm-blooded mammals, with more modest requirements for food and better regulation of body temperature, would squeak through. "Let the bastards freeze in the dark," as bumper stickers of our chauvinistic neighbors in sunbelt states proclaimed several years ago, during the Northeast's winter oil crisis.

All three theories, testicular malfunction, psychoactive overdosing, and asteroidal zapping, grab our attention mightily. As pure phenomenology, they rank about equally high on any hit parade of primal fascination. Yet, one represents expansive science, the others restrictive and untestable speculation. The proper criterion lies in evidence and methodology; we must probe behind the superficial fascination of particular claims.

How could we possibly decide whether the hypothesis of testicular frying is right or wrong? We would have to know things that the fossil record cannot provide. What temperatures were optimal for dinosaurs? Could they avoid the absorption of excess heat by staying in the shade, or in caves? At what temperatures did their testicles cease to function? Were late Cretaceous climates ever warm enough to drive the internal temperatures of dinosaurs close to this ceiling? Testicles simply don't fossilize, and how could we infer their temperature tolerances even if they did? In short, Cowles's hypothesis is only an intriguing speculation leading nowhere. The most damning statement against it appeared right in the conclusion of Colbert, Cowles, and Bogert's paper, when they admitted: "It is difficult to advance any definite arguments against this hypothesis." My statement may seem paradoxical—isn't a hy-

pothesis really good if you can't devise any arguments against it? Quite the contrary. It is simply untestable and unusable.

Siegel's overdosing has even less going for it. At least Cowles extrapolated his conclusion from some good data on alligators. And he didn't completely violate the primary guideline of siting dinosaur extinction in the context of a general mass dying—for rise in temperature could be the root cause of a general catastrophe, zapping dinosaurs by testicular malfunction and different groups for other reasons. But Siegel's speculation cannot touch the extinction of ammonites or oceanic plankton (diatoms make their own food with good sweet sunlight; they don't OD on the chemicals of terrestrial plants). It is simply a gratuitous, attention-grabbing guess. It cannot be tested, for how can we know what dinosaurs tasted and what their livers could do? Livers don't fossilize any better than testicles.

The hypothesis doesn't even make any sense in its own context. Angiosperms were in full flower ten million years before dinosaurs went the way of all flesh. Why did it take so long? As for the pains of a chemical death recorded in contortions of fossils, I regret to say (or rather I'm pleased to note for the dinosaurs' sake) that Siegel's knowledge of geology must be a bit deficient: Muscles contract after death and geological strata rise and fall with motions of the earth's crust after burial—more than enough reason to distort a fossil's pristine appearance.

The impact story, on the other hand, has a sound basis in evidence. It can be tested, extended, refined, and, if wrong, disproved. The Alvarezes did not just construct an arresting guess for public consumption. They proposed their hypothesis after laborious geochemical studies with Frank Asaro and Helen Michael had revealed a massive increase of iridium in rocks deposited right at the time of extinction. Iridium, a rare metal of the platinum group, is virtually absent from indigenous rocks of the earth's crust; most of our iridium arrives on extraterrestrial objects that strike the earth.

The Alvarez hypothesis bore immediate fruit. Based originally on evidence from two European localities, it led geochemists throughout the world to examine other sediments of the same age. They found ab-

20

normally high amounts of iridium everywhere—from continental rocks of the western United States to deep sea cores from the South Atlantic.

Cowles proposed his testicular hypothesis in the mid-1940s. Where has it gone since then? Absolutely nowhere, because scientists can do nothing with it. The hypothesis must stand as a curious appendage to a solid study of alligators. Siegel's overdose scenario will also win a few press notices and fade into oblivion. The Alvarezes' asteroid falls into a different category altogether, and much of the popular commentary has missed this essential distinction by focusing on the impact and its attendant results, and forgetting what really matters to a scientist—the iridium. If you talk just about asteroids, dust, and darkness, you tell stories no better and no more entertaining than fried testicles or terminal trips. It is the iridium—the source of testable evidence—that counts and forges the crucial distinction between speculation and science.

The proof, to twist a phrase, lies in the doing. Cowles's hypothesis has generated nothing in thirty-five years. Since its proposal in 1979, the Alvarez hypothesis has spawned hundreds of studies, a major conference, and attendant publications. Geologists are fired up. They are looking for iridium at all other extinction boundaries. Every week exposes a new wrinkle in the scientific press. Further evidence that the Cretaceous iridium represents extraterrestrial impact and not indigenous volcanism continues to accumulate. As I revise this essay in November 1984 (this paragraph will be out of date when [it] is published), new data include chemical "signatures" of other isotopes indicating unearthly provenance, glass spherules of a size and sort produced by impact and not by volcanic eruptions, and high-pressure varieties of silica formed (so far as we know) only under the tremendous shock of impact.

My point is simply this: Whatever the eventual outcome (I suspect it will be positive), the Alvarez hypothesis is exciting, fruitful science because it generates tests, provides us with things to do, and expands outward. We are having fun, battling back and forth, moving toward a resolution, and extending the hypothesis beyond its original scope.

As just one example of the unexpected, distant cross-fertilization that good science engenders, the Alvarez hypothesis made a major contribution to a theme that has riveted public attention in the past few months—so-called nuclear winter. In a speech delivered in April 1982, Luis Alvarez calculated the energy that a ten-kilometer asteroid would release on impact. He compared such an explosion with a full nuclear exchange and implied that all-out atomic war might unleash similar consequences.

This theme of impact leading to massive dust clouds and falling temperatures formed an important input to the decision of Carl Sagan and a group of colleagues to model the climatic consequences of nuclear holocaust. Full nuclear exchange would probably generate the same kind of dust cloud and darkening that may have wiped out the dinosaurs. Temperatures would drop precipitously and agriculture might become impossible. Avoidance of nuclear war is fundamentally an ethical and political imperative, but we must know the factual consequences to make firm judgments. I am heartened by a final link across disciplines and deep concerns—another criterion, by the way, of science at its best: A recognition of the very phenomenon that made our evolution possible by exterminating the previously dominant dinosaurs and clearing a way for the evolution of large mammals, including us, might actually help to save us from joining those magnificent beasts in contorted poses among the strata of the earth.

Reading and Thinking

1. Gould's essay can be broken into several parts: those discussing particular theories, those discussing science in general, and those discussing all three theories at once. Reread the essay, and mark the places where Gould begins a new "part." How does Gould help make the transition? Are his transitions effective? Explain.

2. Perhaps surprisingly, Gould's scientific essay contains many colorful (and sometimes amusing) words and phrases that help him to make his point more vivid. Notice in particular "burned so brightly" (para. 10), "exploded" (para. 15), "squeak" (para. 16), and "appendage" (para. 23). Explain how these word choices are especially effective at commenting on the subjects at hand. Look carefully through the essay for other particularly appropriate choices. Explain how Gould's word choices makes his subjects more vivid.

3. Write a brief paragraph summarizing Gould's ideas about scientific hypotheses. How does Gould define "good science"? How is "good science" different from "useless speculation"?

Thinking and Writing

1. In paragraphs 14 and 16, Gould cites lines from the poem "Do Not Go Gentle into That Good Night" by Dylan Thomas. Look up the poem, and write a short paper discussing Gould's use of the poem in "Sex, Drugs, Disasters, and the Extinction of the Dinosaurs." What effect did the poem have on your understanding of the essay? How does the poem help Gould make his point?

2. Gould's essay considers three theories about the cause or causes of a specific event: the extinction of the dinosaurs. However, in paragraph 5, Gould suggests that the extinction of the dinosaurs is deeply interrelated with other extinctions—so much so that "there is no separate problem of the extinction of dinosaurs." In a brief essay, explain how the interrelated effects of the extinction of the dinosaurs and the other events that Gould discusses in paragraphs 5–7 must be accounted for in any hypothesis of cause.

3. Find another event from either geologic or political history and form a hypothesis about its cause or causes. Be sure to treat the subject as carefully as Gould treats extinction. Write a brief essay explaining your hypothesis.

4. Considering your hypothesis in the previous question, explain in another brief essay how your hypothesis is "good science" according to Gould's definition.

THE CAUSES OF CAUSES
AN OCCASION FOR CAUSE AND EFFECT

While Stephen Jay Gould's essay discusses the possible causes of a particular event, much of the essay is devoted to evaluating the validity of cause and effect analysis. Gould spells out particular criteria for scientific hypotheses and looks at three separate cause and effect analyses. This Occasion will give you the opportunity to make and evaluate such hypotheses. The ingenious chart to the right was reprinted in *Discover* magazine from the book *Understanding Healthcare* by Richard Saul Wurman. The chart was designed by Dr. Wurman and Nigel Holmes. Its title, "Top 10 Causes of Death in the U. S. by Age," tells much of the story. However, as you look more closely at the chart, you will find that the information encoded in it can be as provocative as it is definitive.

PREPARING TO WRITE: TOP 10 CAUSES OF DEATH IN THE U.S. BY AGE

1. What does this chart show? Explain how it works.

2. Note the icons representing each possible cause of death. Considering that each icon is a simplified visual representation of a complex phenomenon, how well do you think they represent the causes of death? Choose two or three icons and improve upon them. Sketch or describe your new icon. Explain why it is a more accurate representation of the phenomenon.

DEFINITIONS

Accidents are unintentional injuries, including motor vehicle accidents and medical errors (see below).

Benign neoplasms are tumors that do not spread throughout the body.

Cancer includes all forms of malignant neoplasms (tumors that grow and spread throughout the body).

Cerebrovascular diseases include stroke (damage to the brain by an interruption of its blood supply), atherosclerosis (narrowing of the arteries), and aneurysm (permanent swelling in an artery).

Diabetes mellitus is the more common form of diabetes (the other is diabetes insipidus) and has two types. Insulin-dependent type I is the more severe and usually first appears in people under 35. Non-insulin-dependent type II occurs mainly in people over 40.

Nephritis is inflammation of the kidneys.

Septicemia is blood poisoning.

Influenza has surpassed AIDS as a lethal killer and contributes to an average of 36,000 annual deaths in the United States.

Source: Centers for Disease Control and Prevention, 2003

Top 10 Causes of Death in the U.S. by Age

Reprinted by kind permission of Dr. Richard Saul Wurman from *Understanding Healthcare* (TOP, 2004) by Richard Saul Wurman. Designed by Nigel Holmes with art direction by Richard Saul Wurman.

Occasion

THE CAUSES OF CAUSES: AN OCCASION FOR CAUSE AND EFFECT   331

3. This chart ranks causes of death within certain age ranges. What is the standard for ranking the deaths? In other words, what does it mean that accidents are the number one cause of death of people below the age of four? Why do you suppose that standard was chosen? What useful function could this chart support? What other standards of ranking might have been used? How would the different standards change the usefulness of the chart?

4. Look carefully at the age ranges represented by each row. The first range spans four years, the second and third ranges nine years each, the fourth range nineteen years, and so on. Why do you suppose the age ranges differ from row to row? How do such differences affect your understanding of the chart?

MOVING TOWARD ESSAY: ANALYSIS AND REFLECTION

1. What else could be represented on this chart? What other populations could be represented, for example? How might any of the represented causes of death be divided into subgroups? What effect would new divisions have on the information presented on this chart?

2. Look at the chart from a different perspective by tracing a particular rank through every age range. For example, the tenth most common cause of death for people under four years old is lower respiratory diseases. For the five-to-fourteen age bracket, it is cardiovascular diseases. For the fifteen-to-twenty-four bracket, it is HIV. Summarize the trend you discover and offer a brief speculation as to its cause.

3. Consider the chart from yet another angle. This time, find any particular cause of death and follow it through the different age ranges. Imagine (or draw) a line connecting the icon in each age range to the same icon in the next range. The farther to the left the line appears, the more prominent the cause of death. (If you turn the chart sideways and read from right to left, you will see the relative ranking of the cause of death as ages progress.) Summarize the trend, or trends, you discover.

Occasion

WRITING THOUGHTFULLY: IDEA AND ESSAY

1. Isolate one or more trends by tracking any particular cause of death through every age range. Given the information included on this chart, formulate three hypotheses that could explain each trend you have isolated. In a short essay, explore the ways each hypothesis could explain the trend.

2. Explain how each hypothesis from your short essay is testable. (You may wish to refer back to Gould's essay for a discussion of testability.) Explain the test or tests that might prove or disprove each hypothesis. If one or more of your hypotheses isn't testable, you need to modify or replace it. According to Gould, a hypothesis is "good science" if it is testable, even if it is incorrect.

3. Revise your essay to include a discussion of exactly what further information or data you would need to know to determine whether any of your hypotheses accurately describes the cause of the trend you outlined. Either conduct the research yourself and select the most plausible explanation for the trend, or suggest in detail what future researchers would need to find out to choose the likeliest explanation. Discuss the usefulness of understanding the causes of the trends you discuss.

CREATING OCCASIONS

1. The chart reprinted here is from the book *Understanding Healthcare* by Richard Saul Wurman. Wurman's Web page at www.wurman.com includes a number of other charts and graphics with different information about healthcare and a variety of subjects. Choose any of the charts available and study it carefully. Aside from the information explicitly shown, mine the chart for other trends. Create a hypothesis explaining the trend and discuss how your hypothesis is valid according to Gould's definition of "good science."

2. In the library or on the Internet, find any graphic representation, such as a table, graph, or chart, presenting information on a subject that interests you. Study the graphic carefully, looking especially for information beyond the obvious. Include the graphic at the beginning of an essay in which you explain to your readers the different ways that the information can be read. What causes and effects are illuminated by looking at the graphic in various ways?

3. Create your own interactive Occasion on *Comp21* using the textual, visual, and video libraries, as well as the Explicator analysis tools. From the main menu, choose "Build Your Own Occasion for Writing."

MALCOLM GLADWELL

Malcolm Gladwell (b. 1963) was born in England and graduated with a degree in history from the University of Toronto. A former business and science writer at the *Washington Post,* he was named the newspaper's New York City bureau chief. Gladwell is currently a staff writer for *The New Yorker* magazine.

The Tipping Point

In "The Tipping Point," excerpted from his book of the same title, Gladwell describes the phenomenon of "tipping," the process by which a sequence of events proceeds to the point of becoming an epidemic. In his essay, Gladwell identifies three factors that lead up to the tipping point of a physical or social epidemic. As you read his essay, try to identify each of these different causes.

1   In the mid-1990s, the city of Baltimore was attacked by an epidemic of syphilis. In the space of a year, from 1995 to 1996, the number of children born with the disease increased by 500 percent. If you look at Baltimore's syphilis rates on a graph, the line runs straight for years and then, when it hits 1995, rises almost at a right angle.

What caused Baltimore's syphilis problem to tip? According to the Centers for Disease Control [CDC], the problem was crack cocaine. Crack is known to cause a dramatic increase in the kind of risky sexual behavior that leads to the spread of things like HIV and syphilis. It brings far more people into poor areas to buy drugs, which then increases the likelihood that they will take an infection home with them to their own neighborhood. It changes the patterns of social connections between neighborhoods. Crack, the CDC said, was the little push that the syphilis problem needed to turn into a raging epidemic.

John Zenilman of Johns Hopkins University in Baltimore, an expert on sexually transmitted diseases, has another explanation: the breakdown of medical services in the city's poorest neighborhoods. "In 1990–91, we had thirty-six thousand patient visits at the city's sexually transmitted disease clinics," Zenilman says. "Then the city decided to gradually cut back because of budgetary problems. The number of clinicians [med-ical personnel] went from seventeen to ten. The number of physicians went from three to essentially nobody. Patient visits dropped to twenty-one thousand. There also was a similar drop in the amount of field outreach staff. There was a lot of politics — things that used to happen, like computer upgrades, didn't happen. It was a worst-case scenario of city bureaucracy not functioning. They would run out of drugs."

When there were 36,000 patient visits a year in the STD clinics of Baltimore's inner city, in other words, the disease was kept in equilibrium. At some point between 36,000 and 21,000 patient visits a year, according to Zenilman, the disease erupted. It began spilling out of the inner city, up the streets and highways that connect those neighborhoods to the rest of the city. Suddenly, people who might have been infectious for a week before getting treated were now going around infecting others for two or three or four weeks before they got cured. The breakdown in treatment made syphilis a much bigger issue than it had been before.

There is a third theory, which belongs to John Potterat, one of the country's leading epidemiologists. His culprits are the physical changes in those years affecting East and West Baltimore, the heavily depressed neighborhoods on either side of Baltimore's downtown, where the syphilis problem was centered. In the mid-1990s, he points out, the city of Baltimore embarked on a highly publicized policy of dynamiting the old 1960s-style public housing high-rises in East and West Baltimore. Two of the most publicized demolitions—Lexington Terrace in West Baltimore and Lafayette Courts in East Baltimore—were huge projects, housing hundreds of families, that served as centers for crime and infectious disease. At the same time, people began to move out of the old row houses in East and West Baltimore, as those began to deteriorate as well.

"It was absolutely striking," Potterat says, of the first time he toured East and West Baltimore. "Fifty percent of the row houses were boarded up, and there was also a process where they destroyed the projects. What happened was a kind of hollowing out. This fueled the diaspora. For years syphilis had been confined to a specific region of Baltimore, within highly confined sociosexual networks. The housing dislocation process served to move these people to other parts of Baltimore, and they took their syphilis and other behaviors with them."

What is interesting about these three explanations is that none of them is at all dramatic. The CDC thought that crack was the problem. But it wasn't as if crack came to Baltimore for the first time in 1995. It had been there for years. What they were saying is that there was a subtle increase in the severity of the crack problem in the mid-1990s, and that change was enough to set off the syphilis epidemic. Zenilman, likewise, wasn't saying that the STD clinics in Baltimore were shut down. They were simply scaled back, the number of clinicians cut from seventeen to ten. Nor was Potterat saying that all Baltimore was hollowed out. All it took, he said, was the demolition of a handful of housing projects and the abandonment of homes in key downtown neighborhoods to send syphilis over the top. It takes only the smallest of changes to shatter an epidemic's equilibrium.

The second, and perhaps more interesting, fact about these explanations is that all of them are describing a very different way of tipping an epidemic. The CDC is talking about the overall context for the disease—how the introduction and growth of an addictive drug can so change the environment of a city that it can cause a disease to tip. Zenilman is talking about the disease itself. When the clinics were cut back, syphilis

was given a second life. It had been an acute infection. It was now a chronic infection. It had become a lingering problem that stayed around for weeks. Potterat, for his part, was focused on the people who were carrying syphilis. Syphilis, he was saying, was a disease carried by a certain kind of person in Baltimore—a very poor, probably drug-using, sexually active individual. If that kind of person was suddenly transported from his or her old neighborhood to a new one—to a new part of town, where syphilis had never been a problem before—the disease would have an opportunity to tip.

There is more than one way to tip an epidemic, in other words. Epidemics are a function of the people who transmit infectious agents, the infectious agent itself, and the environment in which the infectious agent is operating. And when an epidemic tips, when it is jolted out of equilibrium, it tips because something has happened, some change has occurred in one (or two or three) of those areas. These three agents of change I call the Law of the Few, the Stickiness Factor, and the Power of Context.

I.

When we say that a handful of East Village kids started the Hush Puppies epidemic, or that the scattering of the residents of a few housing projects was sufficient to start Baltimore's syphilis epidemic, what we are really saying is that in a given process or system some people matter more than others. This is not, on the face of it, a particularly radical notion. Economists often talk about the 80/20 Principle, which is the idea that in any situation roughly 80 percent of the "work" will be done by 20 percent of the participants. In most societies, 20 percent of criminals commit 80 percent of crimes. Twenty percent of motorists cause 80 percent of all accidents. Twenty percent of beer drinkers drink 80 percent of all beer. When it comes to epidemics, though, this disproportionality becomes even more extreme: a tiny percentage of people do the majority of the work.

Potterat, for example, once did an analysis of a gonorrhea epidemic in Colorado Springs, Colorado, looking at everyone who came to a public health clinic for treatment of the disease over the space of six months. He found that about half of all the cases came, essentially, from four neighborhoods representing about 6 percent of the geographic area of the city. Half of those in that 6 percent, in turn, were socializing in the same six bars. Potterat then interviewed 768 people in that tiny subgroup and found that 600 of them either didn't give gonorrhea to anyone else or gave it to only one other person. These people he called nontransmitters. The ones causing the epidemic to grow—the ones who were infecting two and three and four and five others with their disease—were the remaining 168. In other words, in all of the city of Colorado Springs—a town of well in excess of 100,000 people—the epidemic of gonorrhea tipped because of the activities of 168 people living in four small neighborhoods and basically frequenting the same six bars.

Who were those 168 people? They aren't like you or me. They are people who go out every night, people who have vastly more sexual partners than the norm, people whose lives and behavior are well outside of the ordinary. In the mid-1990s, for example, in the pool halls and rollerskating rinks of East St. Louis, Missouri, there was a man named Darnell "Boss Man" McGee. He was big—over six feet—and charming, a talented skater, who wowed young girls with his exploits on the rink. His specialty was thirteen- and fourteen-year-olds. He bought them jewelry, took them for rides in his Cadillac, got them high on crack, and had sex with them. Between 1995 and 1997, when he was shot dead by an unknown assailant, he slept with at least 100 women and—it turned out later—infected at least 30 of them with HIV.

In the same two-year period, fifteen hundred miles away, near Buffalo, New York, another man—a kind of Boss Man clone—worked the distressed downtown streets of Jamestown. His name was Nushawn Williams, although he also went by the names "Face," "Sly," and "Shyteek." Williams juggled dozens of girls, maintaining three or four different apartments around the city, and all the while supporting himself by smuggling drugs up from the Bronx. (As one epidemiologist familiar with the case told me flatly, "The man was a genius. If I could get away with what Williams did, I'd never have to work a day again in my life.") Williams, like Boss Man, was a charmer. He would buy his girlfriends roses, let them braid his long hair, and host all-night marijuana and malt liquor–fueled orgies at his apartments. "I slept with him three or four times in one night," one of his partners re-

membered. "Me and him, we used to party together all the time. . . . After Face had sex, his friends would do it too. One would walk out, the other would walk in." Williams is now in jail. He is known to have infected at least sixteen of his former girlfriends with the AIDS virus. And most famously, in the book *And the Band Played On* Randy Shilts discusses at length the so-called Patient Zero of AIDS, the French-Canadian flight attendant Gaetan Dugas, who claimed to have 2,500 sexual partners all over North America, and who was linked to at least 40 of the earliest cases of AIDS in California and New York. These are the kinds of people who make epidemics of disease tip.

Social epidemics work in exactly the same way. They are also driven by the efforts of a handful of exceptional people. In this case, it's not sexual appetites that set them apart. It's things like how sociable they are, or how energetic or knowledgeable or influential among their peers. In the case of Hush Puppies, the great mystery is how those shoes went from something worn by a few fashionforward downtown Manhattan hipsters to being sold in malls across the country. What was the connection between the East Village and Middle America? The Law of the Few says the answer is that one of these exceptional people found out about the trend, and through social connections and energy and enthusiasm and personality spread the word about Hush Puppies just as people like Gaetan Dugas and Nushawn Williams were able to spread HIV.

2.

In Baltimore, when the city's public clinics suffered cutbacks, the nature of the syphilis affecting the city's poor neighborhoods changed. It used to be an acute infection, something that most people could get treated fairly quickly before they had a chance to infect many others. But with the cutbacks, syphilis increasingly became a chronic disease, and the disease's carriers had three or four or five times longer to pass on their infection. Epidemics tip because of the extraordinary efforts of a few select carriers. But they also sometimes tip when something happens to transform the epidemic agent itself.

This is a well-known principle in virology. The strains of flu that circulate at the beginning of each winter's flu epidemic are quite different from the strains of flu that circulate at the end. The most famous flu epidemic of all—the pandemic of 1918—was first spotted in the spring of that year and was, relatively speaking, quite tame. But over the summer the virus underwent some strange transformation and over the next six months ended up killing between 20 and 40 million people worldwide. Nothing had changed in the way in which the virus was being spread. But the virus had suddenly become much more deadly.

The Dutch AIDS researcher Jaap Goudsmit argues that this same kind of dramatic transformation happened with HIV. Goudsmit's work focuses on what is known as *Pneumocystis carinii* pneumonia, or PCP. All of us carry the bacterium in our bodies, probably since birth or immediately thereafter. In most of us it is harmless. Our immune systems keep it in check easily. But if something, such as HIV, wipes out our immune system, it becomes so uncontrollable that it can cause a deadly form of pneumonia. PCP is so common among AIDS patients, in fact, that it has come to be seen as an almost certain indication of the presence of the virus. What Goudsmit did was go back in the medical literature and look for cases of PCP, and what he found is quite chilling. Just after World War II, beginning in the Baltic port city of Danzig and spreading through central Europe, there was an epidemic of PCP that claimed the lives of thousands of small children.

Goudsmit has analyzed one of the towns hit hardest by the PCP epidemic, the mining town of Heerlen in the Dutch province of Limburg. Heerlen had a training hospital for midwives called the Kweekschool voor Vroedvrouwen, a single unit of which—the so-called Swedish barrack—was used in the 1950s as a special ward for underweight or premature infants. Between June 1955 and July 1958, 81 infants in the Swedish barrack came down with PCP and 24 died. Goudsmit thinks that this was an early HIV epidemic, and that somehow the virus got into the hospital, and was spread from child to child by the then, apparently common, practice of using the same needles over and over again for blood transfusions or injections of antibiotics. He writes:

> Most likely at least one adult—probably a coal miner from Poland, Czechoslovakia, or Italy—brought the virus to Limburg. This one adult could have died

from AIDS with little notice. . . . He could have transmitted the virus to his wife and offspring. His infected wife (or girlfriend) could have given birth in a Swedish barrack to a child who was HIV infected but seemingly healthy. Unsterilized needles and syringes could have spread the virus from child to child.

The truly strange thing about this story, of course, is that not all of the children died. Only a third did. The others did what today would seem almost impossible. They defeated HIV, purged it from their bodies, and went on to live healthy lives. In other words, the strains of HIV that were circulating back in the 1950s were a lot different from the strains of HIV that circulate today. They were every bit as contagious. But they were weak enough that most people—even small children—were able to fight them off and survive them. The HIV epidemic tipped in the early 1980s, in short, not just because of the enormous changes in sexual behavior in the gay communities that made it possible for the virus to spread rapidly. It also tipped because HIV itself changed. For one reason or another, the virus became a lot deadlier. Once it infected you, you stayed infected. It stuck.

This idea of the importance of stickiness in tipping has enormous implications for the way we regard social epidemics as well. We tend to spend a lot of time thinking about how to make messages more contagious—how to reach as many people as possible with our products or ideas. But the hard part of communication is often figuring out how to make sure a message doesn't go in one ear and out the other. Stickiness means that a message makes an impact. You can't get it out of your head. It sticks in your memory. When Winston filter-tip cigarettes were introduced in the spring of 1954, for example, the company came up with the slogan "Winston tastes good like a cigarette should." At the time, the ungrammatical and somehow provocative use of "like" instead of "as" created a minor sensation. It was the kind of phrase that people talked about, like the famous Wendy's tag line from 1984 "Where's the beef?" In his history of the cigarette industry, Richard Kluger writes that the marketers at R. J. Reynolds, which sells Winston, were "delighted with the attention" and "made the offending slogan the lyric of a bouncy little jingle on television and radio, and wryly defended their syntax as a colloquialism rather than bad grammar." Within months of its introduction, on the strength of that catchy phrase, Winston tipped, racing past Parliament, Kent, and L&M into second place, behind Viceroy, in the American cigarette market. Within a few years, it was the bestselling brand in the country. To this day, if you say to most Americans "Winston tastes good," they can finish the phrase, "like a cigarette should." That's a classically sticky advertising line, and stickiness is a critical component in tipping. Unless you remember what I tell you, why would you ever change your behavior or buy my product or go to see my movie?

20   The Stickiness Factor says that there are specific ways of making a contagious message memorable; there are relatively simple changes in the presentation and structuring of information that can make a big difference in how much of an impact it makes.

3.

Every time someone in Baltimore comes to a public clinic for treatment of syphilis or gonorrhea, John Zenilman plugs his or her address into his computer, so that the case shows up as a little black star on a map of the city. It's rather like a medical version of the maps police departments put up on their walls, with pins marking where crimes have occurred. On Zenilman's map the neighborhoods of East and West Baltimore, on either side of the downtown core, tend to be thick with black stars. From those two spots, the cases radiate outward along the two central roadways that happen to cut through both neighborhoods. In the summer, when the incidence of sexually transmitted disease is highest, the clusters of black stars on the roads leading out of East and West Baltimore become thick with cases. The disease is on the move. But in the winter months, the map changes. When the weather turns cold, and the people of East and West Baltimore are much more likely to stay at home, away from the bars and clubs and street corners where sexual transactions are made, the stars in each neighborhood fade away.

The seasonal effect on the number of cases is so strong that it is not hard to imagine that a long, hard winter in Baltimore could be enough to slow or lessen substantially—at least for the season—the growth of the syphilis epidemic.

Epidemics, Zenilman's map demonstrates, are strongly influenced by their situation—by the circumstances and conditions and particulars of the environments in which they operate. This much is obvious. What is interesting, though, is how far this principle can be extended. It isn't just prosaic factors like the weather that influence behavior. Even the smallest and subtlest and most unexpected of factors can affect the way we act. One of the most infamous incidents in New York City history, for example, was the 1964 stabbing death of a young Queens woman by the name of Kitty Genovese. Genovese was chased by her assailant and attacked three times on the street, over the course of half an hour, as thirty-eight of her neighbors watched from their windows. During that time, however, none of the thirty-eight witnesses called the police. The case provoked rounds of self-recrimination. It became symbolic of the cold and dehumanizing effects of urban life. Abe Rosenthal, who would later become editor of the *New York Times,* wrote in a book about the case:

> Nobody can say why the thirty-eight did not lift the phone while Miss Genovese was being attacked, since they cannot say themselves. It can be assumed, however, that their apathy was indeed one of the big-city variety. It is almost a matter of psychological survival, if one is surrounded and pressed by millions of people, to prevent them from constantly impinging on you, and the only way to do this is to ignore them as often as possible. Indifference to one's neighbor and his troubles is a conditioned reflex in life in New York as it is in other big cities.

This is the kind of environmental explanation that makes intuitive sense to us. The anonymity and alienation of big-city life makes people hard and unfeeling. The truth about Genovese, however, turns out to be a little more complicated—and more interesting. Two New York City psychologists—Bibb Latane of Columbia University and John Darley of New York University—subsequently conducted a series of studies to try to understand what they dubbed the "bystander problem." They staged emergencies of one kind or another in different situations in order to see who would come and help. What they found, surprisingly, was that the one factor above all else that predicted helping behavior was how many witnesses there were to the event.

In one experiment, for example, Latane and Darley had a student alone in a room stage an epileptic fit. When there was just one person next door, listening, that person rushed to the student's aid 85 percent of the time. But when subjects thought that there were four others also overhearing the seizure, they came to the student's aid only 31 percent of the time. In another experiment, people who saw smoke seeping out from under a doorway would report it 75 percent of the time when they were on their own, but the incident would be reported only 38 percent of the time when they were in a group. When people are in a group, in other words, responsibility for acting is diffused. They assume that someone else will make the call, or they assume that because no one else is acting, the apparent problem— the seizure-like sounds from the other room, the smoke from the door—isn't really a problem. In the case of Kitty Genovese, then, social psychologists like Latane and Darley argue, the lesson is not that no one called despite the fact that thirty-eight people heard her scream; it's that no one called *because* thirty-eight people heard her scream. Ironically, had she been attacked on a lonely street with just one witness, she might have lived.

The key to getting people to change their behavior, in other words, to care about their neighbor in distress, sometimes lies with the smallest details of their immediate situation. The Power of Context says that human beings are a lot more sensitive to their environment than they may seem.

4.

The three rules of the Tipping Point—the Law of the Few, the Stickiness Factor, the Power of Context—offer a way of making sense of epidemics. They provide us with direction for how to go about reaching a Tipping Point. How do these three rules help us understand teenage smoking, for example, or the phenomenon of word of mouth, or crime, or the rise of a bestseller? The answers may surprise you.

Reading and Thinking

1. What does Gladwell identify as causes of the 1996 Baltimore syphilis epidemic? What point does he make about each of these contributing causes? Would any of these causes alone have been sufficient to start the epidemic? Explain.

2. What three causes does Gladwell identify for the tipping point? Provide an example of each of these types of causal explanation.

3. What connections does Gladwell make between physical/medical epidemics, such as syphilis, HIV, and the flu, on one hand, and social epidemics on the other? What is a social epidemic?

Thinking and Writing

1. Write a summary of Gladwell's essay. Be sure to include the three types of reasons he offers for an event or situation to tip and become an epidemic. Include one example of each category of explanation for such a tipping point.

2. Write an essay in which you explain the different causes of a social event, such as the rise of teenage smoking or the popularity of a bestselling book or popular movie.

3. Write an essay in which you explain the reasons for the emergence of a new trend, such as the use of cell phones for instant messaging or a new form of music.

PROPAGANDA

AN OCCASION FOR CAUSE AND EFFECT

In "The Tipping Point," Malcolm Gladwell discusses a number of interrelated causes that can "tip" and become what he calls "epidemics," or widespread change. All of Gladwell's examples revolve around accidental causes. This Occasion will give you a chance to explore widespread changes from a different perspective by looking at several posters created by the U.S. government with the intention of creating such changes. You will have the opportunity to explore causes and effects yourself and to discuss different ways cause and effect analysis can be used persuasively to try to change minds and behaviors.

During World War II, when the United States was fighting against both Nazi Germany and Japan, several branches of the U.S. government commissioned posters to persuade Americans of their duty to contribute to the war effort in various ways. In some cases, the posters asked Americans to contribute by doing something, as in the first pair of posters. In others, the posters asked Americans not to do something that might harm the war effort, as in the second pair. In every case, the posters imply that certain actions cause certain effects.

PREPARING TO WRITE: WAR POSTERS

1. Look carefully at each of the first two posters, "For Freedom's Sake" and "Don't Let That Shadow. . . ." What feeling or emotion do the images try to evoke? Explain. You may want to consider features of the posters' visual design, such as focal point, figure-ground contrast, and color (see chapter 2). You may also want to consider the context and narrative in each picture. What do the positions, postures, and situations of the central figures imply?

2. Describe the differences between the first two posters.

3. Consider the posters "Wanted" and "if you talk too much." Describe the visual similarities between the two. Consider the layout of each poster, as well as how the text is presented.

4. Describe the differences between the two posters on the right. In addition to the visual elements of each poster and the layout of the text, you may want to consider what each poster suggests about its central figure. Who is the audience of each poster?

5. Consider each of the posters as an effect. Briefly speculate about the cause of each. Why did the creators feel the posters were necessary? Look up *war bonds* in a dictionary, encyclopedia, or on a legitimate historical site on the Internet.

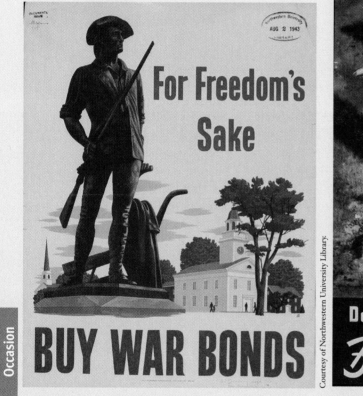

WANTED!

FOR MURDER

Her careless talk costs lives

if you talk too much

THIS MAN MAY DIE

SARRA

MOVING TOWARD ESSAY: ANALYSIS AND REFLECTION

1. Each of the four posters in this Occasion implies that certain effects will, or could, follow specific causes. Isolate the cause and effect that each poster suggests. Create a chart with a row for each poster, a column for cause, and a column for effect. Limit your responses to what appears on each poster.

2. Each poster wants its viewers to do something or not do something specific. Add a column to your list, indicating what each poster specifically asks of its audience.

3. None of the posters explains *how* exactly the cause it mentions could lead to the effect, nor how the action it would like its viewers to take might lead to a different effect. Write a paragraph for each of the four posters, speculating on how the creators of the posters may have envisioned these processes between cause and effect. Be as specific as possible.

WRITING THOUGHTFULLY: IDEA AND ESSAY

1. Write an essay in which you explore how propaganda is intended to work. Use your work from the previous questions about the posters as well as any other propaganda that you find in the library or on the Internet. What thoughts or emotions does each poster appeal to? How is the viewer supposed to feel? What action or actions are they supposed to take? How will those actions lead to other actions and so on? Specifically, pay attention to how the creators of the posters try to ensure that their posters achieve the results they are intended to achive.

2. Write an essay, using your answers to the previous questions as evidence, in which you explore the ways these posters exploit the dos and don'ts, wills and won'ts of society and behavior. Consider, for example, how some of the posters suggest that citizens should do something to achieve certain effects. Other posters suggest that citizens should *not* do something to avoid certain effects. In each of these cases, the posters use the viewers' emotions along with promises or threats to achieve certain effects.

3. Find several other examples of propaganda posters from other places and times, and with a number of different purposes. Be sure to include posters from different countries, created at the same time with similar purposes, but from completely different perspectives. Explore how each of the posters works in its specific context, and then write a paper in which you explore the general ways that propaganda works in all or most circumstances. Include your work on previous questions as evidence, but be sure to expand your generalizations to include the new posters you have found. Try to create a "grammar" of propaganda posters—their elements and rules—that applies to many circumstances.

CREATING OCCASIONS

1. Locate several magazine advertisements or billboards that use similar techniques to entreat viewers to buy their product. In each, isolate the implication of cause and effect and discuss whether the advertisement explains how the cause leads to the effect. How do the implications of cause and effect match up with reality?

2. Locate two political speeches or television advertisements on opposing views. Carefully comb through the advertisement or speech, and discuss the moments when each implies a cause and effect relationship without explaining how, exactly, the cause leads to the effect. Speculate as to why each advertisement or speech makes use of those moments.

3. Create your own interactive Occasion on *Comp21* using the textual, visual, and video libraries, as well as the Explicator analysis tools. From the main menu, choose "Build Your Own Occasion for Writing."

Occasion

PROCESS ANALYSIS

Process analysis is a how-to. Analyzing—or breaking down—a process helps explain how something has been, or can be, accomplished. The process is described in a sequence of steps that lead, one step at a time, to a particular result. To make an omelette, for example, you go through a sequence of steps. Put butter in a frying pan and heat it. Crack three eggs in a small bowl and stir. Add a couple of ounces of milk or cream, if desired. Stir in small bits of bacon, ham, cheese, or other meats and vegetables to taste. Place the beaten eggs plus extras into the frying pan over a moderate flame and heat until the eggs congeal and are cooked as desired. Then flip the omelette over on itself to cover only half the frying pan. When cooked sufficiently, slide onto a plate. Garnish and season as desired.

Process analysis is a natural way of thinking. We use process analysis often in our everyday lives. Making an omelette is one of many kinds of examples. Giving and receiving directions, ordering food from a menu, using a computer program, and learning how to operate a digital camera and to program a high-tech cell phone are just a few of many ways we use process on a day-to-day basis.

Writers use process analysis to explain and clarify their thinking. Readers understand process analysis and follow the sequence of steps or stages that writers provide to better comprehend what is being described or explained.

· · · · · · · · · ·

Henry Ford, founder of the Ford Motor Company, is credited with revolutionizing manufacturing by creating the assembly line, which divided the process of creating cars into relatively simple steps and assigned particular workers to each step.

© CORBIS.

THE NATURE OF
PROCESS ANALYSIS

To read more about Process Analysis with interactive examples and opportunities to work with interactive texts, click on "The Rhetorical Patterns of Inquiry" from the main menu of *Comp21*.

Using process analysis is a natural way to understand the world and ourselves. We understand how things are done—how a road is paved, how a book is made, or how butterflies emerge from caterpillars—through following the processes by which they develop. We also understand how we ourselves become who we are by reflecting on the series of actions, decisions, and choices we make along the way of becoming who we are.

The uses of process analysis are many and varied. We use process analysis when we explain to a friend how to operate a video recorder. We use process analysis when we plan out a research project required for a course, when we give someone instructions on how to pitch a tent or cook a casserole, and when we offer advice on how to write a résumé or how to start a business. It is also important in the business world. Successful companies create and follow sensible and thorough processes to achieve good results. Successful leaders and managers create processes for their employees and subordinates to follow so that everyone knows how things should be done.

Process analysis is a practical thinking tool. It is one of many ways of organizing and developing ideas. It helps writers and speakers make their ideas clear, and it helps readers and listeners follow what writers and speakers are saying. Like any analytical tool, you can develop your skill in using process analysis by looking for and creating opportunities to practice it.

· · · · · · · · · ·

BREAKING THINGS
DOWN INTO STEPS

The central feature of process analysis is chronological sequence. The steps of a process, whether in a set of how-to instructions or in an after-the-fact explanation, have a fixed order. To bake a cake, drive a car, or install a computer program, you follow particular steps in a particular sequence. The fixed order of steps in a process helps ensure that the same result occurs each time.

The more complex the process, however, and the more human the decisions that must be made along the way, the greater the chance that the process will not always achieve the expected or desired result. When you undertake a complex task, you can become overwhelmed with its complexity and scale unless you break it down into small, manageable parts or steps. If you are assigned to write a ten- or fifteen-page research paper, you approach such a project by breaking it down into a series of steps. First you decide on a topic, which you subsequently narrow to something manageable and appropriate for a research paper of a certain length. Next you survey library and Internet sources. Then you begin thinking about a key question you would like your research to answer. After you begin reading and notetaking, you may reformulate your research question and refine your topic further. Once you are confident that you have a workable topic and a good question, you continue reading to try to find an answer to that question. At this point, you can develop a preliminary, tentative thesis.

In doing research for a big project, you divide your labor into discrete tasks—reading and notetaking, drafting and revising, and editing and proofreading your paper. But you do all this after the other preliminary steps described earlier. In addition, you may take intermediate steps, such as outlining or otherwise planning an organizational structure for your paper, and working on one section at a time.

In following a process as complex as writing a paper, you may have great success with the stages or steps in writing one paper, mixed success with another paper, and very little success with a third. The virtue of using a consistent process is that you can *repeat the process* as many times as necessary until you achieve the result you desire or until you have to meet a deadline and run out of time.

When you explain a complex task to someone—giving them directions, for example, about cooking a complicated dish, searching for a new job, or planning a month-long trip abroad—you break down the advice into doable steps. In planning a trip, for example, you might advise your friend first to decide on a particular continent, country, or other geographic region, perhaps after doing some research in the library and conversing with experienced travelers. Another aspect of your advice could concern how to travel—both how to get the best airfare going there and how to get around once there. Advice about accommodations would constitute another aspect or element of the process. You would also very likely provide advice about how to eat well and affordably, how to find good but affordable entertainment, and where to get the latest information about special events and attractions in the places your friend will visit.

PROCESS ANALYSIS
IN PURE FORM: AN ANNOTATED PARAGRAPH

In this paragraph from his book *Sociology,* author Neil Smelser describes the process by which women joined the workforce in the United States. As you read, notice how he keeps his readers posted as to the chronology of the process he describes.

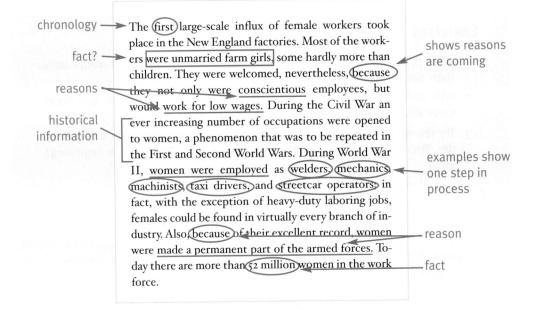

chronology →

fact? →

reasons →

historical information →

shows reasons are coming

examples show one step in process

reason

fact

The first large-scale influx of female workers took place in the New England factories. Most of the workers were unmarried farm girls, some hardly more than children. They were welcomed, nevertheless, because they not only were conscientious employees, but would work for low wages. During the Civil War an ever increasing number of occupations were opened to women, a phenomenon that was to be repeated in the First and Second World Wars. During World War II, women were employed as welders, mechanics, machinists, taxi drivers, and streetcar operators; in fact, with the exception of heavy-duty laboring jobs, females could be found in virtually every branch of industry. Also, because of their excellent record, women were made a permanent part of the armed forces. Today there are more than 52 million women in the work force.

This second paragraph, unlike the first how-to paragraph, exemplifies the how-it-was-done type of process analysis. Ruth Reichl's paragraph about "Everything Stew" described how to make an unusual meal, while Smelser's explains how a particular historical situation occurred over time. Notice how Smelser links his observation about women's work during the Civil War with what is to come, preparing readers for the follow-up details about women's work responsibilities in the First and Second World Wars. The concluding sentence suggests that once women became part of the work force out of necessity, their talents were recognized, and they became widely employed in both the military and in other lines of work.

Exercises

1. How does Smelser cue the reader about the chronology of the paragraph?
2. What words in the paragraph present a positive attitude toward women?
3. What are the implication and the effect of the last sentence?

PROCESS ANALYSIS
IN ITS NATURAL HABITAT: AN ANNOTATED READING

Up till now, you have been presented with examples of paragraphs that include process analysis. Although those paragraphs were developed primarily through the use of process analysis, you will often encounter paragraphs and longer pieces that blend process with other patterns. Process analysis is typically used as one rhetorical strategy among others.

Andy Rooney (b. 1919), best known for his weekly humorous opinion segments on "60 Minutes" discussing cultural and current events, is a well-known television writer, producer, and author. His sardonic and sometimes biting remarks, which once kept him off the air for a few months, have made him a legend in broadcast television. Rooney writes a bi-weekly column for the Tribune Media Services and wrote *A Few Minutes with Andy Rooney* (1981), a collection of his television pieces and newspaper columns.

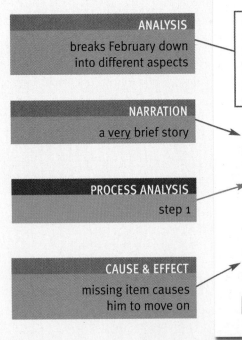

ANALYSIS
breaks February down into different aspects

NARRATION
a <u>very</u> brief story

PROCESS ANALYSIS
step 1

CAUSE & EFFECT
missing item causes him to move on

ANDY ROONEY
How to Put Off Doing a Job

February is one of the most difficult times of the year to put off doing some of the things you've been meaning to do. There's no vacation coming up, there are no long weekends scheduled in the immediate future; it's just this long, grim February. Don't tell me it's a short month. February is the longest by a week.

Because I have so many jobs that I don't like to do, I've been reviewing the notebook I keep with notes in it for how to put off doing a job. Let's see now, what could I use today?

—Go to the store to get something. This is one of my most dependable putter-offers. If I start a job and find I need some simple tool or a piece of hardware, I stop right there. I put on some better clothes, get in the car and drive to the store. If that store doesn't have what I'm looking for, I go to another. Often I'm attracted to some item that has nothing whatsoever to do with the job I was about to start and I buy that instead. For instance, if I go to the hardware store to buy a new

In "How to Put Off Doing a Job," Rooney uses process analysis to show the steps of how to not do something, the opposite of a "typical" process analysis. Rooney effectively uses process analysis for humorous effect to tell his readers how to avoid doing a task. As you read through his essay, notice how many other patterns Rooney employs. Try to find examples of other patterns in this essay that have not been annotated and explain how they strengthen Rooney's use of process analysis.

snow shovel so I can clean out the driveway, but then I see a can of adhesive spray that will keep rugs in place on the floor, I'm apt to buy the adhesive spray. That ends the idea I had to shovel out the driveway.

> **ILLUSTRATION**
> "For instance" indicates example

—Tidy up the work area before starting a job. This has been useful to me over the years as a way of not getting started. Things are such a mess in my workshop, on my desk, in the kitchen and in the trunk of the car that I decide I've got to go through some of the junk before starting to work.

> **PROCESS ANALYSIS**
> step 2

> **DESCRIPTION**
> "such a mess"

—Make those phone calls. There's no sense trying to do a job if you have other things on your mind, so get them out of the way first. This is a very effective way of not getting down to work. Call friends you've been meaning to call, or the distant relative you've been out of touch with. Even if someone is in California, Texas, or Chicago and you're in Florida, call. Paying for a long-distance call is still easier and less unpleasant than actually getting down to work.

> **PROCESS ANALYSIS**
> step 3

> **ILLUSTRATION**
> more examples

> **COMPARISON & CONTRAST**
> "easier and less unpleasant" are comparators

—Study the problem. It's foolish to jump right into a job before you've thought it through. You might be

> **PROCESS ANALYSIS**
> step 4

doing the wrong thing. There might be an easier way to accomplish what you want to do, so think it over carefully from every angle. Perhaps someone has written a how-to book about the job you have in front of you. Buy the book and then sit down and read it. Ask friends who have had the same job for advice about the best way to do it.

Once you've studied the problem from every angle, don't make a quick decision. Sleep on it.

—Take a coffee break. Although the term "coffee break" assumes that you are drinking coffee in an interim period between stretches of solid work, this is not necessarily so. Don't be bound by old ideas about when it's proper to take a coffee break. If taking it be-

PROCESS ANALYSIS
Is this a separate step?

PROCESS ANALYSIS
next step

DEFINITION
defines coffee break

While most process analysis essays discuss how *to* do something, Andy Rooney turns expectations upside-down in "How to Put Off Doing a Job" by analyzing the process for *not* doing something. It is always difficult to talk about what is not there—in this case work—because by not being there, there is nothing to discuss. In Rooney's case, he might have been stuck with a four word essay, "Just don't do it," had he not spend his process analysis talking about the process of *alternative* activities. Notice that Rooney does not break the process of avoiding work into steps (which is nearly impossible), but instead provides smaller process analyses for all the things to do *instead* of work, passing those smaller process analyses off as steps in the larger "process" of not doing a job.

Much of the humor is born from subversion of expectations, and much of the humor stems from the fact that, intuitively, readers know that to put off doing a job is extraordinarily easy: you simply do not do it. An entire essay on the subject is necessarily silly, and Rooney's tone throughout—for which he is famous—simply drives the silliness home. But though the essay is humorous, it nonetheless shares something with the reader about life and common experience. In the process, Rooney is able to illustrate something about parody, about process analysis, and about the other patterns of inquiry.

fore you get started is going to help keep you from doing the work, by all means take your coffee break first.

—As a last resort before going to work, think this thing over. Is this really what you want to do with your life? Philosophize. Nothing is better for putting off doing something than philosophizing. Are you a machine, trapped in the same dull, day-after-day routine that everyone else is in? Or are you a person who makes up his or her own mind about things? Are you going to do these jobs because that's what's expected of you, or are you going to break the mold and live the way you feel like living?

Try these as ways for not getting down to work.

PROCESS ANALYSIS
last step

Natural Habitat

Exercises

1. Think of a negative process—a process in which the action is, instead, a lack of action. Quitting smoking cigarettes, for example, requires that the quitter not smoke. Isolate a negative process in your life (they happen all the time), and write a brief essay outlining the process. You may wish to discuss alternative activities, as Rooney does in "How to Put Off Doing a Job," or you may find a better solution.

2. Respond to Rooney from the point of view of his boss. Imagine the job Rooney is putting off and offer a response that explains to Rooney exactly how *to* do the job. Rooney mentions a number of jobs in his essay, and you may want to choose from them.

READING

HENRY LOUIS GATES, JR.

Henry Louis Gates, Jr., (b. 1950) grew up in a small West Virginia town and received degrees from Yale and Cambridge Universities. Chair of the department of Afro-American studies at Harvard, Gates has written and edited a number of scholarly works such as *Loose Canons: Notes on the Culture Wars, The Signifying Monkey: A Theory of Afro-American Literary Criticism,* and *The Norton Anthology of African American Literature.* He has also written books and articles aimed at a popular audience, including *Colored People,* a memoir, and *Thirteen Ways of Looking at a Black Man.* His *Wonders of the African World* was the basis for a PBS documentary series he hosted about life in Africa.

In the Kitchen

In the following autobiographical essay "In the Kitchen," Gates memorializes his mother by writing about hair—his mother's hair, his own hair, and the hair of the women his mother straightens in her kitchen. Through his discussion of hair, Gates also suggests something about standards of beauty. Wavy hair is considered good and kinky hair bad, a standard based on one culture's perception of beauty over another's. But Gates doesn't linger over cultural and aesthetic differences for long. Instead he takes pleasure in describing the processes African Americans use to straighten their hair, and he celebrates a few people with heads of hair worth noticing.

1 We always had a gas stove in the kitchen, in our house in Piedmont, West Virginia, where I grew up. Never electric, though using electric became fashionable in Piedmont in the sixties, like using Crest toothpaste rather than Colgate, or watching Huntley and Brinkley rather than Walter Cronkite. But not us: gas, Colgate, and good ole Walter Cronkite, come what may. We used gas partly out of loyalty to Big Mom, Mama's Mama, because she was mostly blind and still loved to cook, and could feel her way more easily with gas than with electric. But the most important thing about our gas-equipped kitchen was that Mama used to do hair there. The "hot comb" was a fine-toothed iron instrument with a long wooden handle and a pair of iron curlers that opened and closed like scissors. Mama would put it in the gas fire until it glowed. You could smell those prongs heating up.

I liked that smell. Not the smell so much, I guess, as what the smell meant for the shape of my day. There was an intimate warmth in the women's tones as they talked with my Mama, doing their hair. I knew what the women had been through to get their hair ready to be "done," because I would watch Mama do it to herself. How that kink could be transformed through grease and fire into that magnificent head of wavy hair was a miracle to me, and still is.

Mama would wash her hair over the sink, a towel wrapped around her shoulders, wearing just her slip and her white bra. (We had no shower—just a galvanized tub that we stored in the kitchen—until we moved down Rat Tail Road into Doc Wolverton's house, in 1954.) After she dried it, she would grease her scalp thoroughly with blue Bergamot hair grease, which came in a short, fat jar with a picture of a beautiful colored lady on it. It's important to grease your scalp real good, my Mama would explain, to keep from burning yourself. Of course, her hair would return to its natural kink almost as soon as the hot water and shampoo hit it. To me, it was another miracle how hair so "straight" would so quickly become kinky again the second it even approached some water.

My Mama had only a few "clients" whose heads she "did"—did, I think, because she enjoyed it, rather than for the few pennies it brought in. They would sit on one of our red plastic kitchen chairs, the kind with the shiny metal legs, and brace themselves for the process. Mama would stroke that red-hot iron—which by this time had been in the gas fire for half an hour or more—slowly but firmly through their hair, from scalp to strand's end. It made a scorching, crinkly sound, the hot iron did, as it burned its way through kink, leaving in its wake straight strands of hair, standing long and tall but drooping over at the ends, their shape like the top of a heavy willow tree. Slowly, steadily, Mama's hands would transform a round mound of Odetta kink into a darkened swamp of everglades. The Bergamot made the hair shiny; the heat of the hot iron gave it a brownish-red cast. Once all the hair was as straight as God allows kink to get, Mama would take the well-heated curling iron and twirl the straightened strands into more or less loosely wrapped curls. She claimed that she owed her skill as a hairdresser to the strength in her wrists, and as she worked her little finger would poke out, the way it did when she sipped tea. Mama was a southpaw, and wrote upside down and backward to produce the cleanest, roundest letters you've ever seen.

5   The "kitchen" she would all but remove from sight with a handheld pair of shears, bought just for this purpose. Now, the kitchen was the room in which we were sitting—the room where Mama did hair and washed clothes, and where we all took a bath in that galvanized tub. But the word has another meaning, and the kitchen that I'm speaking of is the very kinky bit of hair at the back of your head, where your neck meets your shirt collar. If there was ever a part of our African past that resisted assimilation, it was the kitchen. No matter how hot the iron, no matter how powerful the chemical, no matter how stringent the mashed-potatoes-and-lye formula of a man's "process," neither God nor woman nor Sammy Davis, Jr., could straighten the kitchen. The kitchen was permanent, irredeemable, irresistible kink. Unassimilably African. No matter what you did, no mat-

ter how hard you tried, you couldn't dekink a person's kitchen. So you trimmed if off as best you could.

When hair had begun to "turn," as they'd say—to return to its natural kinky glory—it was the kitchen that turned first (the kitchen around the back, and nappy edges at the temples). When the kitchen started creeping up the back of the neck, it was time to get your hair done again.

Sometimes, after dark, a man would come to have his hair done. It was Mr. Charlie Carroll. He was very light-complected and had a ruddy nose—it made me think of Edmund Gwenn, who played Kris Kringle in "Miracle on 34th Street." At first, Mama did him after my brother, Rocky, and I had gone to sleep. It was only later that we found out that he had come to our house so Mama could iron his hair—not with a hot comb or a curling iron but with our very own Proctor-Silex steam iron. For some reason I never understood, Mr. Charlie would conceal his Frederick Douglass-like mane under a big white Stetson hat. I never saw him take it off except when he came to our house, at night, to have his hair pressed. (Later, Daddy would tell us about Mr. Charlie's most prized piece of knowledge, something that the man would only confide after his hair had been pressed, as a token of intimacy. "Not many people know this," he'd say, in a tone of circumspection, "but George Washington was Abraham Lincoln's daddy." Nodding solemnly, he'd add the clincher: "A white man told me." Though he was in dead earnest, this became a humorous refrain around our house—"a white man told me"—which we used to punctuate especially preposterous assertions.)

My mother examined my daughters' kitchens whenever we went home to visit, in the early eighties. It became a game between us. I had told her not to do it, because I didn't like the politics it suggested—the notion of "good" and "bad" hair. "Good" hair was "straight," "bad" hair kinky. Even in the late sixties, at the height of Black Power, almost nobody could bring themselves to say "bad" for good and "good" for bad. People still said that hair like white people's hair was "good," even if they encapsulated it in a disclaimer, like "what we used to call 'good.'"

Maggie would be seated in her high chair, throwing food this way and that, and Mama would be cooing about how cute it all was, how I used to do just like Maggie was doing, and wondering whether her flinging her food with her left hand meant that she was going to be left-handed like Mama. When my daughter was just about covered with Chef Boyardee Spaghetti-O's, Mama would seize the opportunity: wiping her clean, she would tilt Maggie's head to one side and reach down the back of her neck. Sometimes Mama would even rub a curl between her fingers, just to make sure that her bifocals had not deceived her. Then she'd sigh with satisfaction and relief: No kink . . . yet. Mama! I'd shout, pretending to be angry. Every once in a while, if no one was looking, I'd peek, too.

I say "yet" because most black babies are born with soft, silken hair. But after a few months it begins to turn, as inevitably as do the seasons or the leaves on a tree. People once thought baby oil would stop it. They were wrong.

Everybody I knew as a child wanted to have good hair. You could be as ugly as homemade sin dipped in misery and still be thought attractive if you had good hair. "Jesus moss," the girls at Camp Lee, Virginia, had called Daddy's naturally "good" hair during the war. I know that he played that thick head of hair for all it was worth, too.

My own hair was "not a bad grade," as barbers would tell me when they cut it for the first time. It was like a doctor reporting the results of the first full physical he has given you. Like "You're in good shape" or "Blood pressure's kind of high—better cut down on salt."

I spent most of my childhood and adolescence messing with my hair. I definitely wanted straight hair. Like Pop's. When I was about three, I tried to stick a wad of Bazooka bubble gum to that straight hair of his. I suppose what fixed that memory for me is the spanking I got for doing so: he turned me upside down, holding me by my feet, the better to paddle my behind. Little nigger, he had shouted, walloping away. I started to laugh about it two days later, when my behind stopped hurting.

When black people say "straight," of course, they don't usually mean literally straight—they're not describing hair like, say, Peggy Lipton's (she was the white girl on "The Mod Squad"), or like Mary's of Peter, Paul & Mary fame; black people call that "stringy" hair. No,

"straight" just means not kinky, no matter what contours the curl may take. I would have done *anything* to have straight hair—and I used to try everything, short of getting a process.

Of the wide variety of techniques and methods I came to master in the challenging prestidigitation of the follicle, almost all had two things in common: a heavy grease and the application of pressure. It's not an accident that some of the biggest black-owned companies in the fifties and sixties made hair products. And I tried them all, in search of that certain silken touch, the one that would leave neither the hand nor the pillow sullied by grease.

I always wondered what Frederick Douglass put on *his* hair, or what Phillis Wheatley put on hers. Or why Wheatley has that rag on her head in the little engraving in the frontispiece of her book. One thing is for sure: you can bet that when Phillis Wheatley went to England and saw the Countess of Huntingdon she did not stop by the Queen's coiffeur on her way there. So many black people still get their hair straightened that it's a wonder we don't have a national holiday for Madame C. J. Walker, the woman who invented the process of straightening kinky hair. Call it Jheri-Kurled or call it "relaxed," it's still fried hair.

I used all the greases, from sea-blue Bergamot and creamy vanilla Duke (in its clear jar with the orange-white-and-green label) to the godfather of grease, the formidable Murray's. Now, Murray's was some *serious* grease. Whereas Bergamot was like oily jello, and Duke was viscous and sickly sweet, Murray's was light brown and *hard*. Hard as lard and twice as greasy, Daddy used to say. Murray's came in an orange can with a press-on top. It was so hard that some people would put a match to the can, just to soften the stuff and make it more manageable. Then, in the late sixties, when Afros came into style, I used Afro Sheen. From Murray's to Duke to Afro Sheen: that was my progression in black consciousness.

We used to put hot towels or washrags over our Murray-coated heads, in order to melt the wax into the scalp and the follicles. Unfortunately, the wax also had the habit of running down your neck, ears, and forehead. Not to mention your pillowcase. Another problem was that if you put two palmfuls of Murray's on

Reading

your head your hair turned white. (Duke did the same thing.) The challenge was to get rid of that white color. Because if you got rid of the white stuff you had a magnificent head of wavy hair. That was the beauty of it: Murray's was so hard that it froze your hair into the wavy style you brushed it into. It looked really good if you wore a part. A lot of guys had parts *cut* into their hair by a barber, either with the clippers or with a straight-edge razor. Especially if you had kinky hair—then you'd generally wear a short razor cut, or what we called a Quo Vadis.

We tried to be as innovative as possible. Everyone knew about using a stocking cap, because your father or your uncle wore one whenever something really big was about to happen, whether sacred or secular: a funeral or a dance, a wedding or a trip in which you confronted official white people. Any time you were trying to look really sharp, you wore a stocking cap in preparation. And if the event was really a big one, you made a new cap. You asked your mother for a pair of her hose, and cut it with scissors about six inches or so from the open end—the end with the elastic that goes up to the top of the thigh. Then you knotted the cut end, and it became a beehive-shaped hat, with an elastic band that you pulled down low on your forehead and down around your neck in the back. To work well, the cap had to fit tightly and snugly, like a press. And it had to fit that tightly because it was a press: it pressed your hair with the force of the hose's elastic. If you greased your hair down real good, and left the stocking cap on long enough, voilà: you got a head of pressed-against-the-scalp waves. (You also got a ring around your forehead when you woke up, but it went away.) And then you could enjoy your concrete do. Swore we were bad, too, with all that grease and those flat heads. My brother and I would brush it out a bit in the mornings, so that it looked—well, "natural." Grown men still wear stocking caps—especially older men, who generally keep their stocking caps in their top drawers, along with their cufflinks and their see-through silk socks, their "Maverick" ties, their silk handkerchiefs, and whatever else they prize the most.

20   A Murrayed-down stocking cap was the respectable version of the process, which, by contrast, was most definitely not a cool thing to have unless you were an entertainer by trade. Zeke and Keith and Poochie and a few other stars of the high-school basketball team all used to get a process once or twice a year. It was expensive, and you had to go somewhere like Pittsburgh or D.C. or Uniontown—somewhere where there were enough colored people to support a trade. The guys would disappear, then reappear a day or two later, strutting like peacocks, their hair burned slightly red from the lye base. They'd also wear "rags"—cloths or handkerchiefs—around their heads when they slept or played basketball. Do-rags, they were called. But the result was straight hair, with just a hint of wave. No curl. Do-it-yourselfers took their chances at home with a concoction of mashed potatoes and lye.

The most famous process of all, however, outside of the process Malcolm X describes in his "Autobiography," and maybe the process of Sammy Davis, Jr., was Nat King Cole's process. Nat King Cole had patent-leather hair. That man's got the finest process money can buy, or so Daddy said the night we saw Cole's TV show on NBC. It was November 5, 1956. I remember the date because everyone came to our house to watch it and to celebrate one of Daddy's buddies' birthdays. Yeah, Uncle Joe chimed in, they can do shit to his hair that the average Negro can't even *think* about—secret shit.

Nat King Cole was *clean.* I've had an ongoing argument with a Nigerian friend about Nat King Cole for twenty years now. Not about whether he could sing—any fool knows that he could—but about whether or not he was a handkerchief head for wearing that patent-leather process.

Sammy Davis, Jr.'s process was the one I detested. It didn't look good on him. Worse still, he liked to have a fried strand dangling down the middle of his forehead, so he could shake it out from the crown when he sang. But Nat King Cole's hair was a thing unto itself, a beautifully sculpted work of art that he and he alone had the right to wear. The only difference between a process and a stocking cap, really, was taste; but Nat King Cole, unlike, say, Michael Jackson, looked *good* in his. His head looked like Valentino's head in the twenties, and some say it was Valentino the process was imitating. But Nat King Cole wore a process because it suited his face, his demeanor, his name, his style. He was as clean as he wanted to be.

I had forgotten all about that patent-leather look until one day in 1971, when I was sitting in an Arab restaurant on the island of Zanzibar surrounded by men in fezzes and white caftans, trying to learn how to eat curried goat and rice with the fingers of my right hand and feeling two million miles from home. All of a sudden, an old transistor radio sitting on top of a china cupboard stopped blaring out its Swahili music and started playing "Fly Me to the Moon," by Nat King Cole. The restaurant's din was not affected at all, but in my mind's eye I saw it: the King's magnificent sleek black tiara. I managed, barely, to blink back the tears.

Reading and Thinking

1. What kinds of memories does Gates have with his mother's work on her friends' hair? How does Gates help his readers understand both the importance for the women of having their hair done and the difficulty of it?

2. List the steps of the hair straightening process. What other processes does Gates describe? Why do you think Gates includes these other processes? How are they related to his mother's work?

3. Why does Gates title his essay "In the Kitchen"? What are the various meanings and associations of the word *kitchen* as mentioned in the essay?

4. What social and political issues does Gates touch on in his essay? What does he— and what do you—think about changing the natural features of a person's hair? Of a person's appearance more generally?

Thinking and Writing

1. Recall a memory from your childhood or adolescence in which something was done in your house or your neighborhood. Write a few paragraphs describing how it was done.

2. Think about the purpose of what you chose to describe. Why was it done in your home or neighborhood? Why was it done in the particular manner it was?

3. Now describe another process that can be related, in some way, to what you first described. Identify the connection between the two processes.

4. Let an idea emerge from your reflection on the connections between the two processes you describe. Think about the purpose, value, and significance of those processes. Write a draft of the essay.

5. Write an essay in which you describe how you or someone you know tried to change appearance.

THE MONOPOLY OF IDEAS

AN OCCASION FOR PROCESS ANALYSIS

Occasion

In the essay "In the Kitchen," Henry Louis Gates, Jr., investigates a process and learns something about the larger issues that surround it. While analyzing the almost ritualistic process of straightening hair, Gates finds himself pondering the issues of racial identity and questioning where his own responsibilities lie as an individual in relation to those as a member of a group. This Occasion will give you a chance to analyze a process and to consider the larger social implications of that process.

PREPARING TO WRITE: MONOPOLY BOARD

1. Look closely at the game board and consider the various aspects of visual presentation (you may want to consult chapter 2). What is the focal point? What principles of continuation are suggested by the board's layout?

2. Considering your answers to question 1, describe how the setup of the game board—even if you didn't know the rules of the game—suggests the process of playing. How do the corners relate to the sides? How do the various colors relate to one another? How does the general layout, rectangles around the outside with space in the middle, suggest a certain process of movement?

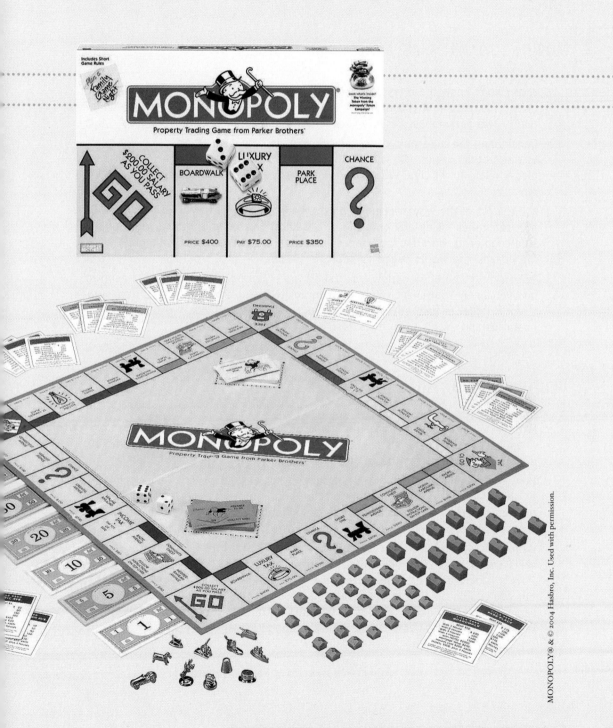

MONOPOLY® & © 2004 Hasbro, Inc. Used with permission.

Occasion

MOVING TOWARD ESSAY: ANALYSIS AND REFLECTION

1. If you don't know the rules of Monopoly, look them up and summarize them in one or two paragraphs. If you do know the rules, restate them in your own words in one or two paragraphs. Be sure to include the object of the game.

2. Considering the rules and all the pieces, explain how each Monopoly piece relates to the process of play. What is the meaning of the dog or the hat? How do these pieces relate to real life? What do they symbolize? Why houses and hotels? Why money?

3. Make a list of the words included on the game board. Sort that list into three or four categories, using any principle of classification that you think is appropriate (see chapter 7). Now list the images shown on the board and sort them. What do the images and words suggest about the game?

4. To win the game of Monopoly, what skills are important? What obstacles need to be overcome? What events must be manipulated, and how must they be manipulated, in order to gain advantage over your opponents? Make an extended list of obstacles and events, with brief descriptions after each.

WRITING THOUGHTFULLY: IDEA AND ESSAY

1. Write an essay describing what the game of Monopoly teaches its participants. How does the process of the game reinforce those lessons? Are those lessons, in your opinion, appropriate (as the game suggests) for players "ages 8 to adult"?

2. How is the game of Monopoly—especially the process of playing and winning—like or unlike life? Focus your essay on one or more particular aspects of life that can be illuminated by their similarities and/or differences to the game. Where might the skills of Monopoly help a person function? Where might they not?

3. Write an essay in which you invent a new game that teaches and reinforces the skills and attitudes that you would like to teach. What is the name of the game? How is it played? You needn't invent the rules and process of playing completely, but you should be able to describe the steps in such a way as to examine how each step teaches and/or reinforces the attitude or skill you would like to teach. How does your new game compare to Monopoly? Explain.

Occasion

CREATING OCCASIONS

1. Find any other board game, sport, or competitive activity that interests you. Break its process down into repeatable steps and describe each step. Explore what skills and attitudes the steps teach and reinforce, and evaluate the game or activity based on your exploration.

2. Investigate the history of monopolies in American business and law and find a recent case or two involving government action against monopolies. Write an essay summarizing that history, and discuss why you agree or why you do not agree with particular attitudes or actions relating to monopolies. Carefully consider the process involved in becoming a monopoly and the processes enhanced and/or harmed by monopolies.

 3. Create your own interactive Occasion on *Comp21* using the textual, visual, and video libraries, as well as the Explicator analysis tools. From the main menu, choose "Build Your Own Occasion for Writing."

JESSICA MITFORD

Jessica Mitford (1917–1996) is best known for her book *The American Way of Death,* a critical examination of the American funeral industry. She has also written *Kind and Usual Punishment,* a book about prisons, and *A Fine Old Conflict,* a book about communism. Her last book was *The American Way of Birth.*

Behind the Formaldehyde Curtain

In the following excerpt from her book on the funeral industry, Mitford explains the process of embalming and restoring a cadaver. Mitford describes the process in painstaking detail, and with a great deal of wit and humor, as she satirizes the mortuary practices of the American funeral industry. As you read, look for words and phrases that convey Mitford's ironic tone and her critical perspective.

1   Embalming is indeed a most extraordinary procedure, and one must wonder at the docility of Americans who each year pay hundreds of millions of dollars for its perpetuation, blissfully ignorant of what it is all about, what is done, how it is done. Not one in ten thousand has any idea of what actually takes place. Books on the subject are extremely hard to come by. They are not to be found in most libraries or bookshops.

In an era when huge television audiences watch surgical operations in the comfort of their living rooms, when, thanks to the animated cartoon, the geography of the digestive system has become familiar territory even to the nursery school set, in a land where the satisfaction of curiosity about almost all matters is a national pastime, the secrecy surrounding embalming can, surely, hardly be attributed to the inherent gruesomeness of the subject. Custom in this regard has within this century suffered a complete reversal. In the early days of American embalming, when it was performed in the home of the deceased, it was almost mandatory for some relative to stay by the embalmer's side and witness the procedure. Today, family members who might wish to be in attendance would certainly be dissuaded by the funeral director. All others, except apprentices, are excluded by law from the preparation room.

A close look at what does actually take place may explain in large measure the undertaker's intractable reticence concerning a procedure that has become his major *raison d'etre.* Is it possible he fears that public information about embalming might lead patrons to wonder if they really want this service? If the funeral men are loath to discuss the subject outside the trade, the reader may, understandably, be equally loath to go on reading at this point. For those who have the stomach for it, let us part the formaldehyde curtain. . . .

The body is first laid out in the undertaker's morgue—or rather, Mr. Jones is reposing in the preparation room—to be readied to bid the world farewell.

5   The preparation room in any of the better funeral establishments has the tiled and sterile look of a surgery, and indeed the embalmer-restorative artist who does his chores there is beginning to adopt the term "dermasurgeon" (appropriately corrupted by some mortician-writers as "demisurgeon") to describe his calling. His equipment, consisting of scalpels, scissors, augers, forceps, clamps, needles, pumps, tubes, bowls and basins, is crudely imitative of the surgeon's as is his technique, acquired in a nine- or twelve-month post-high-school course in an embalming school. He is supplied by an advanced chemical industry with a bewildering array of fluids, sprays, pastes, oils, powders,

creams, to fix or soften tissue, shrink or distend it as needed, dry it here, restore the moisture there. There are cosmetics, waxes and paints to fill and cover features, even plaster of Paris to replace entire limbs. There are ingenious aids to prop and stabilize the cadaver: a Vari-Pose Head Rest, the Edwards Arm and Hand Positioner, the Repose Block (to support the shoulders during the embalming), and the Throop Foot Positioner, which resembles an old-fashioned stocks.

Mr. John H. Eckels, president of the Eckels College of Mortuary Science, thus describes the first part of the embalming procedure: "In the hands of a skilled practitioner, this work may be done in a comparatively short time and without mutilating the body other than by slight incision—so slight that it scarcely would cause serious inconvenience if made upon a living person. It is necessary to remove all the blood, and doing this not only helps in the disinfecting, but removes the principal cause of disfigurements due to discoloration."

Another textbook discusses the all-important time element: "The earlier this is done, the better, for every hour that elapses between death and embalming will add to the problems and complications encountered. . . ." Just how soon should one get going on the embalming? The author tells us, "On the basis of such scanty information made available to this profession through its rudimentary and haphazard system of technical research, we must conclude that the best results are to be obtained if the subject is embalmed before life is completely extinct—that is, before cellular death has occurred. In the average case, this would mean within an hour after somatic death." For those who feel that there is something a little rudimentary, not to say haphazard, about this advice, a comforting thought is offered by another writer. Speaking of fears entertained in early days of premature burial, he points out, "One of the effects of embalming by chemical injection, however, has been to dispel fears of live burial." How true; once the blood is removed, chances of live burial are indeed remote.

To return to Mr. Jones, the blood is drained out through the veins and replaced by embalming fluid pumped in through the arteries. As noted in *The Principles and Practices of Embalming,* "every operator has a fa-

vorite injection and drainage point—a fact which becomes a handicap only if he fails or refuses to forsake his favorites when conditions demand it." Typical favorites are the carotid artery, femoral artery, jugular vein, subclavian vein. There are various choices of embalming fluid. If Flextone is used, it will produce a "mild, flexible rigidity. The skin retains a velvety softness, the tissues are rubbery and pliable. Ideal for women and children." It may be blended with B. and G. Products Company's Lyf-Lyk tint, which is guaranteed to reproduce "nature's own skin texture . . . the velvety appearance of living tissue." Suntone comes in three separate tints: Suntan; Special Cosmetic Tint, a pink shade "especially indicated for young female subjects"; and Regular Cosmetic Tint, moderately pink.

About three to six gallons of a dyed and perfumed solution of formaldehyde, glycerin, borax, phenol, alcohol and water is soon circulating through Mr. Jones, whose mouth has been sewn together with a "needle directed upward between the upper lip and gum and brought out through the left nostril," with the corners raised slightly "for a more pleasant expression." If he should be bucktoothed, his teeth are cleaned with Bon Ami and coated with colorless nail polish. His eyes, meanwhile, are closed with flesh-tinted eye caps and eye cement.

The next step is to have at Mr. Jones with a thing called a trocar. This is a long, hollow needle attached to a tube. It is jabbed into the abdomen, poked around the entrails and chest cavity, the contents of which are pumped out and replaced with "cavity fluid." This is done, and the hole in the abdomen sewed up, Mr. Jones's face is heavily creamed (to protect the skin from burns which may be caused by leakage of the chemicals), and he is covered with a sheet and left unmolested for a while. But not for long—there is more, much more, in store for him. He has been embalmed, but not yet restored, and the best time to start restorative work is eight to ten hours after embalming, when the tissues have become firm and dry.

The object of all this attention to the corpse, it must be remembered, is to make it presentable for viewing in an attitude of healthy repose. "Our customs require the presentation of our dead in the semblance of normality . . . unmarred by the ravages of illness, disease or mutilation," says Mr. J. Sheridan Mayer in his *Restorative Art.* This is rather a large order since few people die in the full bloom of health, unravaged by illness and unmarked by some disfigurement. The funeral industry is equal to the challenge: "In some cases the gruesome appearance of a mutilated or disease-ridden subject may be quite discouraging. The task of restoration may seem impossible and shake the confidence of the embalmer. This is the time for intestinal fortitude and determination. Once the formative work is begun and affected tissues are cleaned or removed, all doubts of success vanish. It is surprising and gratifying to discover the results which may be obtained."

The embalmer, having allowed an appropriate interval to elapse, returns to the attack, but now he brings into play the skill and equipment of sculptor and cosmetician. Is a hand missing? Casting one in plaster of Paris is a simple matter. "For replacement purposes, only a cast of the back of the hand is necessary; this is within the ability of the average operator and is quite adequate." If a lip or two, a nose or an ear should be missing, the embalmer has at hand a variety of restorative waxes with which to model replacements. Pores and skin texture are simulated by stippling with a little brush, and over this cosmetics are laid on. Head off? Decapitation cases are rather routinely handled. Ragged edges are trimmed, and head joined to torso with a series of splints, wires and sutures. It is a good idea to have a little something at the neck—a scarf or high collar—when time for viewing comes. Swollen mouth? Cut out tissue as needed from inside the lips. If too much is removed, the surface contour can easily be restored by padding with cotton. Swollen necks and cheeks are reduced by removing tissue through vertical incisions made down each side of the neck. "When the deceased is casketed, the pillow will hide the suture incisions . . . as an extra precaution against leakage, the suture may be painted with liquid sealer."

The opposite condition is more likely to be present itself—that of emaciation. His hypodermic syringe now loaded with massage cream, the embalmer seeks out and fills the hollowed and sunken areas by injection. In this procedure the backs of the hands and fingers and the under-chin area should not be neglected.

Positioning the lips is a problem that recurrently challenges the ingenuity of the embalmer. Closed too tightly, they tend to give a stern, even disapproving expression. Ideally, embalmers feel, the lips should give the impression of being ever so slightly parted, the upper lip protruding slightly for a more youthful appearance. This takes some engineering, however, as the lips tend to drift apart. Lip drift can sometimes be remedied by pushing one or two straight pins through the inner margin of the lower lip and then inserting them between the two front upper teeth. If Mr. Jones happens to have no teeth, the pins can just as easily be anchored in his Armstrong Face Former and Denture Replacer. Another method to maintain lip closure is to dislocate the lower jaw, which is then held in its new position by a wire run through holes which have been drilled through the upper jaws at the midline. As the French are fond of saying, *il faut souffrir pour être belle.*

If Mr. Jones has died of jaundice, the embalming fluid will very likely turn him green. Does this deter the embalmer? Not if he has intestinal fortitude. Masking pastes and cosmetics are heavily laid on, burial garments and casket interiors are color-correlated with particular care, and Jones is displayed beneath rose-colored lights. Friends will say, "How *well* he looks." Death by carbon monoxide, on the other hand, can be rather a good thing from the embalmer's viewpoint: "One advantage is the fact that this type of discoloration is an exaggerated form of a natural pink coloration." This is nice because the healthy glow is already present and needs but little attention.

The patching and filling completed, Mr. Jones is now shaved, washed and dressed. Cream-based cosmetic, available in pink, flesh, suntan, brunette and blonde, is applied to his hands and face, his hair is shampooed and combed (and, in the case of Mrs. Jones, set), his hands manicured. For the horny-handed son of toil special care must be taken; cream should be applied to remove ingrained grime, and the nails cleaned. "If he were not in the habit of having them manicured in life, trimming and shaping is advised for better appearance—never questioned by kin."

Jones is now ready for casketing (this is the present participle of the verb "to casket"). In this operation his right shoulder should be depressed slightly "to turn the body a bit to the right and soften the appearance of lying flat on the back." Positioning the hands is a matter of importance, and special rubber positioning blocks may be used. The hands should be cupped slightly for a more life-like, relaxed appearance. Proper placement of the body requires a delicate sense of balance. It should lie as high as possible in the casket, yet not so high that the lid, when lowered, will hit the nose. On the other hand, we are cautioned, placing the body too low "creates the impression that the body is in a box."

Jones is next wheeled into the appointed slumber room where a few last touches may be added—his favorite pipe placed in his hand or, if he was a great reader, a book propped into position. (In the case of little Master Jones a Teddy bear may be clutched.) Here he will hold open house for a few days, visiting hours 10 A.M. to 9 P.M.

Reading and Thinking

1. What is Mitford's purpose in this selection? What techniques does she use to achieve her purpose? What is Mitford's attitude toward embalming? What patterns does she use to make her attitude clear?

2. What key mortuary terms interest Mitford? How does she use, explain, analyze, and respond to them? What euphemisms, in particular, attract her attention? Why?

3. What steps are involved in the process of embalming? Where does Mitford interrupt her description of the sequence of embalming steps? Why, and with what effects?

4. For what purpose and to what effect does Mitford quote from textbooks of mortuary science? What kinds of word choices and sentence structures help Mitford establish and convey her ironic tone? What other patterns does she use to strengthen the ironic tone of the piece?

Thinking and Writing

1. Why do you think Mitford only gives brief attention to the wake and funeral of Mr. Jones? Why do you think she goes into greater detail about his embalming? Explain.

2. Write an essay in which you analyze the various patterns Mitford uses in this piece. Explain her purpose in using these strategies. What idea about the mortuary profession is she trying to convey?

3. Write an essay about a process you dislike or disapprove of. Try to employ some of Mitford's rhetorical techniques to convey your point of view through irony.

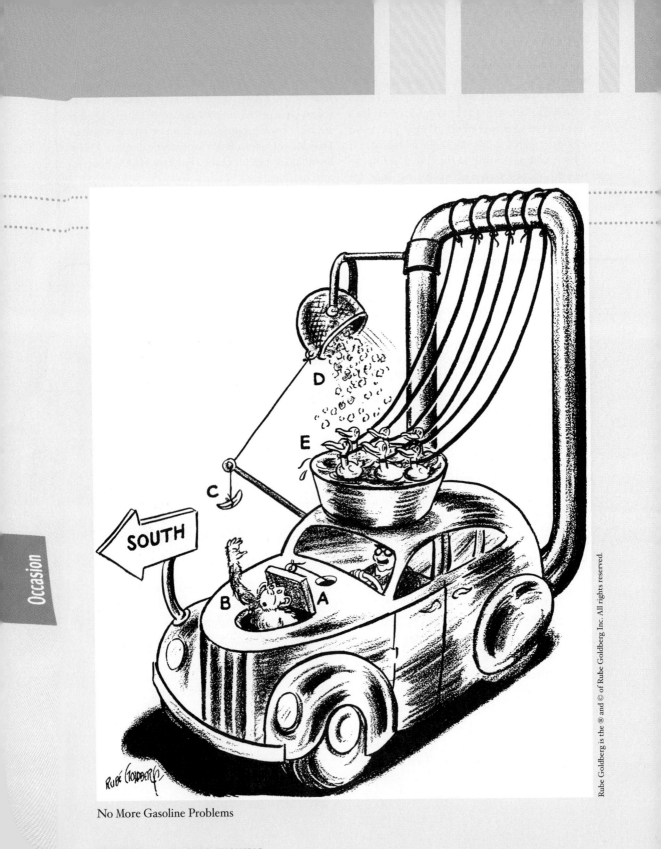

No More Gasoline Problems

Occasion

CHAPTER 10: PROCESS ANALYSIS

RIDICULOUSNESSING

AN OCCASION FOR PROCESS ANALYSIS

In "Behind the Formaldehyde Curtain," Jessica Mitford uses her analysis of the processes in the "death industry" to suggest something about the usefulness, naturalness, and necessity of embalming and burying of our loved ones. Throughout the essay, Mitford's word choice and tone implies that there might be something ridiculous about the process. This Occasion begins with cartoons depicting ridiculous inventions for otherwise simple processes by the famous cartoonist and "inventor" Rube Goldberg.

Best known for his cartoons of funny inventions—which often require excessive effort for a relatively mundane result—Goldberg's cartoons are often accompanied by text explaining how the invention works step by step. Here, however, the text has been omitted and you will be supplying your own. As you study the cartoons and work through the exercises toward your own process analysis essay, consider the different ways that Goldberg and Mitford use process analysis toward a larger purpose. In the end, your essay may make a similar commentary.

PREPARING TO WRITE: RUBE GOLDBERG CARTOONS

1. Look closely at each of the cartoons. How does your eye move across the cartoon?
2. Each cartoon includes several different elements. Choose one or two of the cartoons and list the particular elements.
3. Follow each cartoon completely. Try to understand exactly how each invention works.

The Latest Simple Flyswatter

A Self-Working Corkscrew

MOVING TOWARD ESSAY: ANALYSIS AND REFLECTION

1. Choose one of the inventions. What is the function of each part? Make a list describing each part and its function.

2. Carefully consider how the function of each part relates both to the parts before and after it (in a cause and effect relationship), and how it relates to the process as a whole. Add some notes to your list describing the function.

3. Describe how the process of saving gasoline, unscrewing a cork, or turning out the light is normally performed. What does Goldberg's invention add to the process? Explain.

WRITING THOUGHTFULLY: IDEA AND ESSAY

1. Using either the cartoon you analyzed in previous questions or a different cartoon, write an essay describing what makes it funny. If you don't think any of the cartoons are funny, explain why the intended humor falls short. Be sure to include your analysis of Goldberg's process as well as the analysis of the usual real-life process.

2. Consider Goldberg's cartoons as a work of social commentary. For example, what does the invention with the car say about the world in which Goldberg lived? Be sure to discuss each step. Your paper will be a process analysis with a purpose—to show what the process says about the world.

3. Imagine you are a modern-day Rube Goldberg. Select any regular task or process and create your own ridiculous invention, describing it in words. Write an essay around that process analysis, describing what your invention says about today's modern world.

4. *Comp21* **Video Extension**. Extend this Occasion to include CNN® video footage using the Explicator video tool on *Comp21*. From the main menu choose "Frames of Mind: Extending Occasions" and select "Ridiculousnessing: An Occasion for Process Analysis" from the list.

CREATING OCCASIONS

1. Spend some time paying attention to daily life and the processes that underlie daily activities. Choose one process that is seldom considered, such as how your textbooks are made or how the dishes at the dining hall are cleaned. Do some research into the process, and write a brief set of directions intended to help others understand the process. Explain why you think most people are unaware of the process.

2. Create your own interactive Occasion on *Comp21* using the textual, visual, and video libraries, as well as the Explicator analysis tools. From the main menu, choose "Build Your Own Occasion for Writing."

ALEXANDER PETRUNKEVITCH

Alexander Petrunkevitch (1875–1964) was born in Russia and moved to the United States in his early twenties. A professor of zoology at Yale University, he had a particular interest in spiders and produced two books about them: *Index Catalog of Spiders of North, Central, and South America* and *An Inquiry into the Natural Classification of Spiders*. A frequent contributor of articles to popular magazines, Petrunkevitch also wrote works of history and philosophy.

The Spider and the Wasp

The following essay, originally published in *Scientific American,* describes the life and death relationship between a particular species of spider and its archenemy species of wasp. Petrunkevitch explains the process of how the wasp preys on the spider to ensure the survival of its species. It's a surprising, even astonishing story. As we read, we can hardly believe that the tarantula allows itself to be captured and killed the way Petrunkevitch describes. But beyond explaining the fascinating process of the wasp capturing its prey, Petrunkevitch raises questions about the ways intelligence and instinct collaborate on a seemingly predetermined outcome.

1   In the feeding and safeguarding of their progeny insects and spiders exhibit some interesting analogies to reasoning and some crass examples of blind instinct. The case I propose to describe here is that of the tarantula spiders and their archenemy, the digger wasps of the genus Pepsis. It is a classic example of what looks like intelligence pitted against instinct—a strange situation in which the victim, though fully able to defend itself, submits unwittingly to its destruction.

Most tarantulas live in the tropics, but several species occur in the temperate zone and a few are common in the southern U.S. Some varieties are large and have powerful fangs with which they can inflict a deep wound. These formidable looking spiders do not, however, attack man; you can hold one in your hand, if you are gentle, without being bitten. Their bite is dangerous only to insects and small mammals such as mice; for man it is no worse than a hornet's sting.

Tarantulas customarily live in deep cylindrical burrows, from which they emerge at dusk and into which they retire at dawn. Mature males wander about after dark in search of females and occasionally stray into houses. After mating, the male dies in a few weeks, but a female lives much longer and can mate several years in succession. In a Paris museum is a tropical specimen which is said to have been living in captivity for 25 years.

A fertilized female tarantula lays from 200 to 400 eggs at a time; thus it is possible for a single tarantula to produce several thousand young. She takes no care of them beyond weaving a cocoon of silk to enclose the eggs. After they hatch, the young walk away, find convenient places in which to dig their burrows and spend the rest of their lives in solitude. The eyesight of tarantulas is poor, being limited to a sensing of change in the intensity of light and to the perception of moving objects. They apparently have little or no sense of hearing, for a hungry tarantula will pay no attention to a loudly chirping cricket placed in its cage unless the insect happens to touch one of its legs.

But all spiders, and especially hairy ones, have an extremely delicate sense of touch. Laboratory experiments prove that tarantulas can distinguish three types of touch: pressure against the body wall, stroking of

5

the body hair, and riffling of certain very fine hairs on the legs called trichobothria. Pressure against the body, by the finger or the end of a pencil, causes the tarantula to move off slowly for a short distance. The touch excites no defensive response unless the approach is from above where the spider can see the motion, in which case it rises on its hind legs, lifts its front legs, opens its fangs and holds this threatening posture as long as the object continues to move.

The entire body of a tarantula, especially its legs, is thickly clothed with hair. Some of it is short and wooly, some long and stiff. Touching this body hair produces one of two distinct reactions. When the spider is hungry, it responds with an immediate and swift attack. At the touch of a cricket's antennae the tarantula seizes the insect so swiftly that a motion picture taken at the rate of 64 frames per second shows only the result and not the process of capture. But when the spider is not hungry, the stimulation of its hairs merely causes it to shake the touched limb. An insect can walk under its hairy belly unharmed.

The trichobothria, very fine hairs growing from dislike membranes on the legs, are sensitive only to air movement. A light breeze makes them vibrate slowly, without disturbing the common hair. When one blows gently on the trichobothria, the tarantula reacts with a quick jerk of its four front legs. If the front and hind legs are stimulated at the same time, the spider makes a sudden jump. This reaction is quite independent of the state of its appetite.

These three tactile responses—to pressure on the body wall, to moving of the common hair, and to flexing of the trichobothria—are so different from one another that there is no possibility of confusing them. They serve the tarantula adequately for most of its needs and enable it to avoid most annoyances and dangers. But they fail the spider completely when it meets its deadly enemy, the digger wasp Pepsis.

These solitary wasps are beautiful and formidable creatures. Most species are either a deep shiny blue all over, or deep blue with rusty wings. The largest have a wing span of about four inches. They live on nectar. When excited, they give off a pungent odor—a warning that they are ready to attack. The sting is much worse than that of a bee or common wasp, and the pain and swelling last longer. In the adult stage the wasp lives only a few months. The female produces but a few eggs, one at a time at intervals of two or three days. For each egg the mother must provide one adult tarantula, alive but paralyzed. The mother wasp attaches the egg to the paralyzed spider's abdomen. Upon hatching from the egg, the larva is many hundreds of times smaller than its living but helpless victim. It eats no other food and drinks no water. By the time it has finished its single Gargantuan meal and become ready for wasphood, nothing remains of the tarantula but its indigestible chitinous skeleton.

The mother wasp goes tarantula-hunting when the egg in her ovary is almost ready to be laid. Flying low over the ground late on a sunny afternoon, the wasp looks for its victim or for the mouth of a tarantula burrow, a round hole edged by a bit of silk. The sex of the spider makes no difference, but the mother is highly discriminating as to species. Each species of Pepsis requires a certain species of tarantula, and the wasp will not attack the wrong species. In a cage with a tarantula which is not its normal prey, the wasp avoids the spider and is usually killed by it in the night.

Yet when a wasp finds the correct species, it is the other way about. To identify the species the wasp apparently must explore the spider with her antennae. The tarantula shows an amazing tolerance to this exploration. The wasp crawls under it and walks over it without evoking any hostile response. The molestation is so great and so persistent that the tarantula often rises on all eight legs, as if it were on stilts. It may stand this way for several minutes. Meanwhile the wasp, having satisfied itself that the victim is of the right species, moves off a few inches to dig the spider's grave. Working vigorously with legs and jaws, it excavates a hole 8 to 10 inches deep with a diameter slightly larger than the spider's girth. Now and again the wasp pops out of the hole to make sure that the spider is still there.

When the grave is finished, the wasp returns to the tarantula to complete her ghastly enterprise. First she feels it all over once more with her antennae. Then her behavior becomes more aggressive. She bends her abdomen, protruding her sting, and searches for the soft membrane at the point where the spider's legs join its body—the only spot where she can penetrate the horny skeleton. From time to time, as the exasperated spider slowly shifts ground, the wasp turns on her back and slides along with the aid of her wings, trying to get under the tarantula for a shot at the vital spot. During all this maneuvering, which can last for several minutes, the tarantula makes no move to save itself. Finally the wasp corners it against some obstruction and grasps one of its legs in her powerful jaws. Now at last the harassed spider tries a desperate but vain defense. The two contestants roll over and over on the ground. It is a terrifying sight and the outcome is always the same. The wasp finally manages to thrust her sting into the soft spot and holds it there for a few seconds while she pumps in the poison. Almost immediately the tarantula falls paralyzed on its back. Its legs stop twitching; its heart stops beating. Yet it is not dead, as is shown by the fact that if taken from the wasp it can be restored to some sensitivity by being kept in a moist chamber for several months.

After paralyzing the tarantula, the wasp cleans herself by dragging her body along the ground and rubbing her feet, sucks the drop of blood oozing from the wound in the spider's abdomen, then grabs a leg of the flabby, helpless animal in her jaws and drags it down to the bottom of the grave. She stays there for many minutes, sometimes for several hours, and what she does all that time in the dark we do not know. Eventually she lays her egg and attaches it to the side of the spider's abdomen with a sticky secretion. Then she emerges, fills the grave with soil carried bit by bit in her jaws, and finally tramples the ground all around to hide any trace of the grave from prowlers. Then she flies away, leaving her descendant safely started in life.

In all this the behavior of the wasp evidently is qualitatively different from that of the spider. The wasp acts like an intelligent animal. This is not to say that instinct plays no part or that she reasons as man does. But her actions are to the point; they are not automatic and can be modified to fit the situation. We do not know for certain how she identifies the tarantula—probably it is by some olfactory or chemo-tactile sense—but she does it purposefully and does not blindly tackle a wrong species.

On the other hand, the tarantula's behavior shows only confusion. Evidently the wasp's pawing gives it no pleasure, for it tries to move away. That the wasp is not simulating sexual stimulation is certain because male and female tarantulas react in the same way to its advances. That the spider is not anesthetized by some odorless secretion is easily shown by blowing lightly at the tarantula and making it jump suddenly. What, then, makes the tarantula behave as stupidly as it does?

No clear, simple answer is available. Possibly the stimulation by the wasp's antennae is masked by a heavier pressure on the spider's body, so that it reacts as when prodded by a pencil. But the explanation may be much more complex. Initiative in attack is not in the nature of tarantulas; most species fight only when cornered so that escape is impossible. Their inherited patterns of behavior apparently prompt them to avoid problems rather than attack them. For example, spiders always weave their webs in three dimensions, and when a spider finds that there is insufficient space to attach certain threads in the third dimension, it leaves the place and seeks another, instead of finishing the web in a single plane. This urge to escape seems to arise under all circumstances, in all phases of life, and to take the place of reasoning. For a spider to change the pattern of its web is as impossible as for an inexperienced man to build a bridge across a chasm obstructing his way.

In a way the instinctive urge to escape is not only easier but often more efficient than reasoning. The tarantula does exactly what is most efficient in all cases except in an encounter with a ruthless and determined attacker dependent for the existence of her own species on killing as many tarantulas as she can lay eggs. Perhaps in this case the spider follows its usual pattern of trying to escape, instead of seizing and killing the wasp, because it is not aware of its danger. In any case, the survival of the tarantula species as a whole is protected by the fact that the spider is much more fertile than the wasp.

Reading and Thinking

1. What main idea does Petrunkevitch convey through his description of the relationship between and the behavior of the tarantula and the Pepsis wasp? How do you respond to this behavior and to Petrunkevitch's idea?

2. Why does Petrunkevitch provide details early on about the tarantula's senses of sight and touch? Why does he include information about its body hair?

3. Identify three details that Petrunkevitch includes in the process that strike you especially forcefully. Explain why you selected those details and what their effect is on you.

4. What contrasts between spider and wasp does Petrunkevitch accentuate? How are those contrasts related to his main idea?

Thinking and Writing

1. Summarize the steps of the process Petrunkevitch describes in the hunter/hunted relationship of wasp and spider.

2. Describe another process of hunter and hunted from any aspect of the animal world, including the human realm. Be sure to provide sufficient detail to enable your readers to "see" as well as understand the process.

3. Compare Petrunkevitch's use of process analysis with that of either Jessica Mitford in "Behind the Formaldehyde Curtain" (p. 372) or Henry Louis Gates's "In the Kitchen" (p. 362). Discuss the structure of the two essays, the tone of each, and the patterns each author uses to convey his or her ideas.

THE PROCESS OF PROCESS
AN OCCASION FOR PROCESS ANALYSIS

In "The Spider and the Wasp," Alexander Petrunkevitch takes great pains to describe several loosely interrelated processes, including that of the life spans of the tarantula and the Pepsis wasp, spending the most time describing the process of the two species' deep interrelationship. At the beginning of the essay, Petrunkevitch suggests that there is more to the process analysis than simply a recounting of what happens. He writes that the process is a "classic example of what looks like intelligence pitted against instinct." Though Petrunkevitch does not have answers to all the questions raised, he uses process analysis to speculate about the answers.

In this Occasion, you will have the opportunity to consider a similar dichotomy—two things pitted against each other—by considering the different ways a natural item (in this case a lemon) becomes other, less natural items, such as a lemon cream pie, lemonade, or "lemon" cleaning products. As you consider the pictures and work through the questions, keep in mind that everything you are looking at has several processes associated with it, in much the same way that Petrunkevitch's spider and wasp each has its own set of processes, separate from one another but ultimately interrelated. Be sure to keep the interrelationships in mind as you write. You may not know about every process involved, but speculate, as Petrunkevitch does, and try to be reasoned and careful in your analysis.

PREPARING TO WRITE: IMAGES OF LEMON

1. Look at the lemon to the right and the products associated with it. Consider how each product relates to lemons. Make a quick list.

© Hemera Photo Objects.

© Royalty-Free/CORBIS.

© Hemera Photo Objects.

Courtesy of SC Johnson; photo © Steven Lunetta Photography.

Courtesy of Colgate-Palmolive; photo © Steven Lunetta Photography.

Occasion

© Hemera Photo Objects.

2. How does each of the products claim that it is—in one way or another—a product of a lemon? In other words, what does each product seem to suggest about its relationship to lemons?

3. How does the appearance (or packaging) of each product suggest its relationship to lemons? Discuss uses of language, such as the use of the word *lemon,* but also consider other elements of visual design discussed in chapter 2.

MOVING TOWARD ESSAY

1. Classify the products into two categories, depending on the process that begins with lemons and ends with the products. You may wish to classify them by unnatural vs. natural or homemade vs. factory-made, or use another system of classification you think is appropriate after consideration of the processes involved. Make a list with your conclusions.

2. Choose one product from each of your categories and research the process through which a lemon ends up as that product. Find out as much information as possible and restate the process in your own words. How accurately are you able to explain the process to your readers?

WRITING THOUGHTFULLY: IDEA AND ESSAY

1. Each of the products uses the word *lemon* in its name or description. Having investigated the processes, use your own process analysis to argue whether the product's use of the word *lemon* is appropriate.

2. Research the process of growing and marketing lemons. Who grows them? Where? What practices are used to get lemons from seeds to the grocery store? Recount the processes you find out about. How do natural and unnatural processes relate as lemons are created, marketed, shipped, and sold?

3. Choose one of the products. Research the processes that will take place once the consumer obtains the product. In an essay, relate those processes with the processes you have already discussed. At what point is one thing transformed into another thing? Does it ever stop? Make an argument for identifying a particular point at which one thing—in this case, lemons—becomes another.

CREATING OCCASIONS

1. Find any natural item or substance (such as mint or fiber) out of which many products, both natural and unnatural, are created. Research the process each of the items goes through to become the product. Restate the process in your own words and discuss whether knowledge of the process makes any difference to your ideas about the natural item or its products. Why or why not?

2. Reverse the process from the above question. Find several products that boast "natural" uses of any naturally occurring substance or item and research the process by which that substance or item becomes that product. Recount the process in an essay, using it as evidence to discuss your conclusion about the appropriateness of the word *natural* in product description. What is *natural*?

3. Create your own interactive Occasion on *Comp21* using the textual, visual, and video libraries, as well as the Explicator analysis tools. From the main menu, choose "Build Your Own Occasion for Writing."

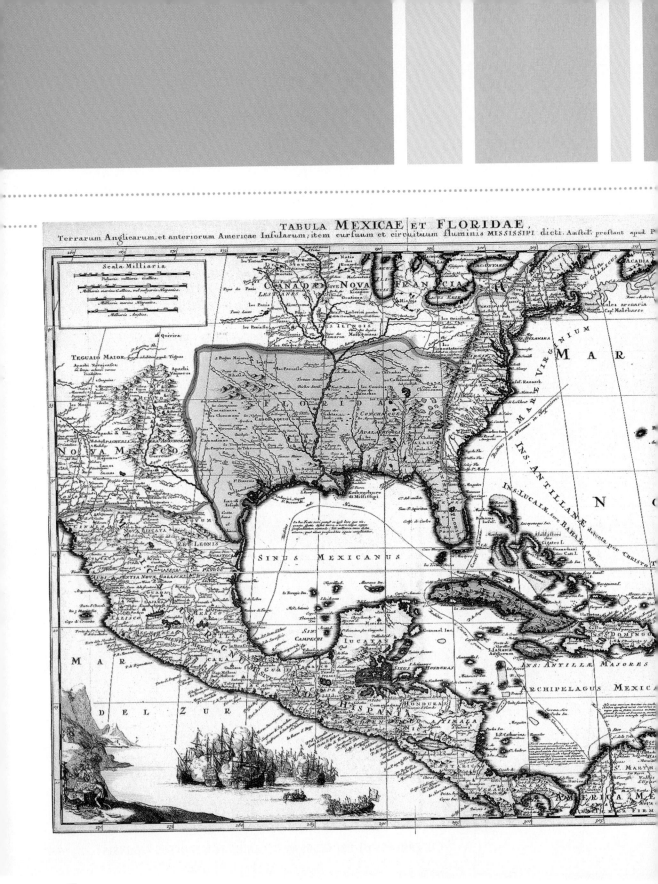

DEFINITION

You may recognize this map of what is now the southeastern United States. Compare it to a current map of the same area. How might the political definitions, or boundaries, affect real issues such as voting rights, resource usage, taxation, or government benefits?

Definition is an act of clarification. Such clarification is inevitably an act of persuasion, an attempt by a writer to account for one of the many concepts that lie behind our conversations with one another. The concepts themselves, of course, are varied and never-ending: birth, identity, responsibility, bird, lying, tree, persuasion, earth, love, ring, selling out, trust, loss, person, work, aging, death, and so on.

These concepts are never as clear as the dictionary might suggest; they need context and clarification. A young woman in love, operating under a personalized notion of what love means, might find herself disappointed by a young man whose idea of love differs radically from hers. An extended conversation about the various aspects of love—excitement, commitment, trust, disappointment, betrayal, and reconciliation—might very well lead to a clearer understanding of just what those two people mean when they say "I love you." There is unlikely to be satisfaction between the two parties unless they can agree and act on the meaning of love.

But even the clarifying resolution of those two lovers would not likely satisfy others who use the term. So these acts of clarification, these attempts to define, go on and on as we seek to understand ourselves and the world we live in, as we go on to reach agreement about the naming of things. Acts of definition are indeed attempts to establish the criteria for distinguishing one concept from another. We attempt to establish eternal and precise naming rules, but the laws of usage never allow us to fix meaning. There is always clarifying work to do.

THE NATURE OF
DEFINITION

To read more about Definition with interactive examples and opportunities to work with interactive texts, click on "The Rhetorical Patterns of Inquiry" from the main menu of *Comp21*.

The *Oxford English Dictionary* (OED)—some would say the most definitive and authoritative dictionary of the English language—offers these definitions of *definition*:

1. The setting of bounds or limits; limitation, restriction.
2. The action of determining a controversy or question at issue; determination, decision; a formal decision or pronouncement of an ecclesiastical authority.
3. The action of defining, or stating exactly what a thing is, or what a word means.
4. a. A precise statement of the essential nature of a thing; a statement or form of words by which anything is defined.
   b. A declaration or formal explanation of the signification of a word or phrase.
   c. Definition in use: a definition which does not provide an equivalent for the expression to be defined, but instead replaces the whole context in which that expression occurs by an equivalent not containing that expression; a contextual definition.
5. a. The action of making definite; the condition of being made, or of being definite, in visual form or outline; distinctness; the defining power of a lens or optical instrument, i.e. its capacity to render an object or image distinct to the eye.
   b. Definiteness, precision, exactitude.
   c. The degree of distinctness of the details in a photograph, film, television picture, etc.

Within these definitions is an inherent tug of war: a desire to be precise and definitive working against a desire to be clear enough to leave nothing essential out. Definition is a clarifying attempt that must at once be precise and inclusive.

. . . .

DENOTATION
AND CONNOTATION

There are traditionally two kinds of definitions: those that denote with precision and those that connote, expanding the definition. Denotation is a word's dictionary definition. Connotation includes other implications. The denotative definition of a word distinguishes it from other words. It names something as precisely as possible. Consider the noun *hammer,* defined by the *OED* as "An instrument having a hard solid head, usu. of metal, set transversely to the handle, used for beating, breaking, driving nails, etc." That is a clean, unambiguous definition of what we mean by the instrument named *hammer.*

But that is not, of course, all there is to say about the noun *hammer. Hammer* is a suggestive word; it signifies something besides its physical nature and its typical functions. The *OED* goes on about *hammer:* "A person or agency that smites, beats down, or crushes as with blows of a hammer." This movement into figurative (suggestive) language alerts us to the difficulty of trying to pin a word down. There is even more, of course, to hammers. A hammer can suggest something about physics, something about balance and force, something about power. Misdirected hammers can instantaneously make the body swell, pound, turn purple in response to their misdirection and misapplication. Hammers can suggest their limitations as well.

The distinction between denotation and connotation suggests that we can actually be definitive and suggestive at the same time. Definition, like a good idea, is always subject to further analysis, refinement, and amplification.

. . . .

USING DEFINITION
IN WRITING

About

We define to clarify and persuade, to make clear to someone else what something means. We use definition to build up arguments.

Definition itself is the fundamental building block of all discourse. Every written document is an extended act of clarification, an attempt to stake out and account for a claim about the meaning of something: a law clarifying actions that are appropriate and inappropriate within a given society, a love note that attempts to account for the feelings of a lover, a paper that identifies a particular animal in terms of its genus and species.

We define to reach agreement about words and ideas that have already been defined. Definitions are mutable, subject to change and alteration. These changes evolve over time through usage and consensus. New meanings crop up, as do new words. Eventually these changes, brought about by popular usage, find their way into dictionaries, reminding us that our language, whatever it might be, is alive, ever-changing, and subject to misunderstanding.

When writers use a term or clarify a concept, they do so both to clarify and persuade. They write to seek agreement. Often they write to change the meaning of things. To effect such a change, they must have their audience's agreement. They must persuade others that their definition has merit.

. . . .

WAYS TO DEFINE

SAYING WHAT SOMETHING IS NOT

Good writers mark off characteristics that create confusion about what they're trying to define. They make clear to others that they are not talking about X or Y but are instead talking about Z. Don't be confused, they say to their audience, by thinking that X has anything at all to do with Z. They trust that by getting X out of the way, they can establish a clearer definition of Z.

Consider this student writer's attempt to get his audience to understand the power he feels when he wins from his cousin the right to pull the card that will destroy the house of cards built by their uncle. Gian Neffinger wants his readers to know that this particular kind of power has nothing whatsoever to do with malice.

> It was a unique phenomenon, the fall of a house of cards. Having not actually witnessed it, you might guess it would be fun to watch, but for all the wrong reasons. Mother never understood at all; she thought we were just being beastly, destroying the card house just as we destroyed our Lego airplanes and our matchbox cars and our new Sunday slacks. It was not anything malicious at all. "Malicious" is laughing at the blood dribbling from Tyler Evans' nose after my friend Pete clocked him. But Andy and I never had anything against Uncle Pete's houses; in fact we liked them. Malice had nothing to do with it.

Neffinger and his cousin Andy fought for the sense of power that came from pulling the card. The puller had the power to make the structure fall. The pulling, Neffinger reveals in his longer essay, could be ever so delicate, reflecting the fragility of the structure. The beauty of the house's intricate relationships, he explains, is most apparent at the moment of its destruction. That power to reveal is the power that Neffinger works to clarify in his essay.

Writers mark off and set aside that which might confuse their audience. They clear away some of their preconceptions and learned associations, so that they can more precisely reveal what they want readers to understand about the thing being defined.

USING SYNONYMS

Just as writers want to clear away clutter and unwanted associations, they also want to make sure that nothing pertinent is left out of the definition. They call on the reader's stock of associations so as to make deliberate connections between the word being defined and a synonym that generally means the same thing but not precisely and not adequately. Writers can use a synonym both to clarify the word under consideration and to suggest something about it that might be overlooked.

The following passage, from Mary Sheedy Kurcinka's *Raising a Spirited Child,* relates a conversation between a group of parents who are trying to figure out how to define and understand their "spirited children." Kurcinka explains the day's work and then illustrates it:

> Today the topic is labels. Everyone is given three cards. The parents are asked to write on each card a word or phrase that describes something their child does that drives them crazy. A few immediately ask for more cards insisting that three is not nearly enough. Everyone laughs. Everyone feels good to know that other people might also entertain a few unpleasant thoughts. The cards are completed in seconds.
>
> "Who would like to share their words or phrases?" I ask.
>
> Dead silence. Bodies shift in their chairs, they look at each other and cough. The thought of publicly admitting these horrible thoughts is almost unbearable.
>
> It's Mike, low-key, observant Mike, the father of two—one spirited, one not—who breaks the silence. "Argumentative," he announces. "John will argue about anything. Yesterday he tried to tell me the sun wasn't shining. I'm not blind, the sun was shining. 'Look out the window,' I told him, 'the sun is shining.' Do you know what John's answer was? 'Well, it isn't in China.'"
>
> The others laugh, nodding in recognition, remembering their own dead-end debates. As the laughter dies down, Nancy flips one of her cards over.

And the defining continues. Finally, the group produces a list of words, synonyms for what they understand, from their own experiences, about the meaning of the label "spirited child." Here is the list:

demanding	argumentative
stubborn	never stops
noisy	unpredictable
nosy	angry
loud	aggressive
whiny	explosive
easily frustrated	picky
wild	single-minded
disruptive	easily bored
self-critical	obnoxious
manipulative	up/down extremes

Kurcinka does not end the session on a negative note; there is more to the defining. She asks the parents to remember their favorite images of their spirited children and to redesign the negative associations in light of this more positive image. Here is an excerpt from their modified list:

Old Negative Labels / New Exciting Labels
demanding ⟶ holds high standards
unpredictable ⟶ flexible, a creative problem solver
loud ⟶ enthusiastic and zestful
argumentative ⟶ opinionated, strongly committed to one's goals
stubborn ⟶ assertive, a willingness to persist in the face of one's difficulties

This investigative session suggests the practical value of attending to the definition of words and concepts. We see a group of concerned parents learning to think in new ways about their so-called spirited children, learning to re-conceive the meaning of *spirited child* through the creative use of synonyms. Over time, they reach a new consensus, not only about the meaning of a concept but also about how better to cope with such a child.

Any good dictionary will list synonyms for selected words. These synonyms generally follow the definitions of the primary word. Consider these synonyms for the word *spontaneous,* taken from the *American Heritage Dictionary:* "impulsive, instinctive, involuntary, automatic." Each of these words is then defined so that readers can note similarities and distinctions. Together, these words help round out the meaning of *spontaneous,* suggesting a range of connections.

BUILDING YOUR OWN DEFINITION

Finally, writers must say precisely what it is that they want their audience to know about a given word or concept. They have the latitude to work within the range of definitions that have already been established and recorded in the dictionary. But as you have seen, the meanings of words shift over time through usage and then consensus. Eventually, changes make their way into dictionaries. Writers can make a new claim about the meanings of elusive but important concepts, such as *terrorism, democracy, religion, freedom,* or *gender,* concepts whose meanings shape the world in which we live.

The act of defining always presents an interesting challenge, an opportunity to investigate meanings that are already established and to extend those meanings into other logical and persuasive directions. Often writers must provide both the logic and the evidence to support their more complex definition. They do so by isolating the established rules by which the thing is already defined, isolating criteria that are important to the point being made, and establishing criteria of their own based on what they are trying to help their audience understand.

Writers are always in the business of making meaning. They want their readers to know what they have discovered about a concept that may have escaped notice or that might be crucial to a course of action they are promoting.

DEFINITION
WITH A PURPOSE

Often, your purpose, or given vantage post, determines the way you define a term or a concept. Consider the word *criticism.* For artists and scholars whose work is being assessed by others, the word *criticism* often brings to mind the critic himself, the one who judges their work, whether it be film, visual art, sculpture, drama, or writing. A person whose work has received positive critical acclaim might be inclined to define *criticism* in relatively neutral terms: the act of criticizing or passing judgment. But a person whose work has fared less well with the critic might consider *criticism* in a different light: the act of criticizing or passing negative judgment. A teenager scolded by his parents would likely share the negative view of the artist whose work was deemed flawed by the critic. *Criticism* for the hassled teenager would mean the harassment that parents always seem to hand out. But the critic himself would consider *criticism* in yet another way: "the act of estimating the quality and character of literary or artistic work" (*OED*), and the well-intentioned parent might define it as the act of estimating the appropriateness of one's social behavior.

As you can see from these examples, the use of words never offers the latitude to consider definitions in isolation from one another. The critic and the criticized have to face one another either figuratively or literally. After all, language is the medium of exchange; we cannot communicate effectively without it. Even those who cannot

fortress island could not be something a man gives up without ambivalent thoughts.

I went out there with him a while ago. Any child could imagine a prison more like a prison than Alcatraz looks, for what bars and wires there are seem perfunctory, beside the point; the island itself was the prison, and the cold tide its wall. It is precisely what they called it: the Rock. Bill Doherty and Duke lowered the dock for us, and in the station wagon on the way up the cliff Bill Doherty told Mr. Scott about small repairs he had made or planned to make. Whatever repairs get made on Alcatraz are made to pass the time, a kind of caretaker's scrimshaw, because the government pays for no upkeep at all on the prison; in 1963 it would have cost five million dollars to repair, which is why it was abandoned, and the $24,000 a year that it costs to maintain Alcatraz now is mostly for surveillance, partly to barge in the 400,000 gallons of water that Bill Doherty and the Harts use every year (there is no water at all on Alcatraz, one impediment to development), and the rest to heat two apartments and keep some lights burning. The buildings seem quite literally abandoned. The key locks have been ripped from the cell doors and the big electrical locking mechanisms disconnected. The tear-gas vents in the cafeteria are empty and the paint is buckling everywhere, corroded by the sea air, peeling off in great scales of pale green and ocher. I stood for a while in Al Capone's cell, five by nine feet, number 200 on the second tier of B Block, not one of the view cells, which were awarded on seniority, and I walked through the solitary block, totally black when the doors were closed. "Snail Mitchel," read a pencil scrawl on the wall of Solitary 14. "The only man that ever got shot for walking too slow." Beside it was a calendar, the months penciled on the wall with the days scratched off, May, June, July, August of some unnumbered year.

Mr. Scott, whose interest in penology dates from the day his office acquired Alcatraz as a potential property, talked about escapes and security routines and pointed out the beach where Ma Barker's son Doc was killed trying to escape. (They told him to come back up, and he said he would rather be shot, and he was.) I saw the shower room with the soap still in the dishes. I picked up a yellowed program from an Easter service *(Why seek ye the living among the dead? He is not here, but is risen)* and I struck a few notes on an upright piano with the ivory all rotted from the keys and I tried to imagine the prison as it had been, with the big lights playing over the windows all night long and the guards patrolling the gun galleries and the silverware clattering into a bag as it was checked in after meals, tried dutifully to summon up some distaste, some night terror of the doors locking and the boat pulling away. But the fact of it was that I liked it out there, a ruin devoid of human vanities, clean of human illusions, an empty place reclaimed by the weather where a woman plays an organ to stop the wind's whining and an old man plays ball with a dog named Duke. I could tell you that I came back because I had promises to keep, but maybe it was because nobody asked me to stay.

Reading and Thinking

1. Most Americans have a sense of what Alcatraz is—a famous prison off the coast of San Francisco. How does Didion, in her first paragraph, confound our precise definition by making us think not of Alcatraz the prison but of Alcatraz Island?

2. What do you think Didion means when she tells us that to like a place like Alcatraz Island, "you have to want a moat." What is a *moat?* Why a moat and not an enormous drawbridge extending from the island to the mainland? Consider too the verb *moated:* to be moated on our island.

3. Account for the various ways that Didion complicates our sense of Alcatraz Island in the lengthy second paragraph. How does her expanding definition of the island balance the tension, or create more tension, between a concept of *home* and a concept of a *fortress island?* To what extent does the essay resolve that tension? Explain.

Thinking and Writing

1. In paragraph 3 Didion focuses our attention on Alcatraz the prison. She does so by renaming the island: "It is precisely what they called it: the Rock." What exactly does that word *Rock* come to mean in Didion's skillful hands? Following Didion's style, write out your definition of *Rock.* Then, look up the word *rock* in a dictionary. Compare definitions.

2. Select the most compelling of Didion's images, the ones that account for her interest in remaining on the island. Explain in a paragraph or two how those images contribute to her definition of the island itself. Do they clarify or complicate the definition? Or do they clarify while they complicate? Explain.

ISLANDS OF FREEDOM
AN OCCASION FOR DEFINITION

Joan Didion's "Rock of Ages" applies techniques of definition to ideas about Alcatraz Island. This Occasion turns to a similar image that will give you a chance to explore the definitions of related concepts. Look at the single image of a floating island. This island is not a grounded island as is Alcatraz. It is adrift at sea. As you consider this image, your interest will eventually shift from the nature of the island itself to a sense of what it signifies about a concept woven into the very fabric of America. Our chief concern will be to notice how place and historical context can change our sense of a word or a concept.

PREPARING TO WRITE: FLOATING ISLAND

1. Consider this item to be a floating sculpture. What do you see in the sculpture?

2. Did you name the water? What does the floating nature of the sculpture suggest about the relationship among the words *free*, *flag*, and *bench*?

3. What happens in your mind as you begin to translate the words *free*, *flag*, and *bench* into related concepts? Ask yourself a series of questions: What does it mean to be *free?* To be a free *American?* To be a stationary object (*bench*) that floats untethered? How do these concepts relate to one another?

Occasion

MOVING TOWARD ESSAY: ANALYSIS AND REFLECTION

1. Consider the word *freedom*. What does it actually mean to be free in America?

2. How does the history of the United States complicate the meaning of freedom for an American? As you move from a consideration of Americans in general to particular Americans, does your sense of American freedom shift? Consider soldier, protester, prisoner, slave, or any ethnic group.

3. What does the image below suggest about the meaning of freedom for Native Americans?

© Bettman/CORBIS.

4. The image above shows the occupation of Alcatraz by Native Americans in 1969. How does that historical fact alter your sense of what freedom might mean to Native Americans? Explain.

WRITING THOUGHTFULLY: IDEA AND ESSAY

1. Write a letter to the anonymous sculptor who created "Floating Island." In the letter, reveal how the sculpture speaks to you about freedom in America. Try to adopt the same measured tone that Naylor uses in her essay "The Meanings of a Word" (p. 406).

Occasion

2. Return to the floating sculpture and look at it in a clearer context:

This island floats in Boston Harbor very near the former site of the museum that commemorated the Boston Tea Party. Focusing on the concept *freedom in America,* write a short narrative account of how your mind has traveled from your initial viewing of the isolated art object to this revised image. How does your sense of the sculpture and of the concept of freedom change during your mind's journey?

3. *Comp21* **Video Extension.** Extend this Occasion to include CNN® video footage using the Explicator video analysis tool on *Comp21.* From the main choose "Frames of Mind: Extending Occasions" and select "Islands of Freedom: An Occasion for Definition" from the list.

CREATING OCCASIONS

1. Write a brief essay that explores the relationship between a single term and a particular historical context. Your task is to show your readers how the dictionary definition of a term either can be or must be altered to accommodate historical and contextual considerations.

2. Create your own interactive Occasion on *Comp21* using the textual, visual, and video libraries, as well as the Explicator analysis tools. From the main menu, choose "Build Your Own Occasion for Writing."

MATTHEW GOULISH

Matthew Goulish, who graduated from Kalamazoo College, is a performer and a writer. He has collaborated on the creation of seven performances with the group Goat Island. A founding member of that group, Goulish also teaches at the School of the Art Institute of Chicago. His book *39 Microlectures in Proximity of Performance* is a compendium of small stories, essays, musings on the nature of writing, reading, performing, criticizing, collaborating . . . "everything," the advertising copy says. Goulish pushes against and crosses all kinds of boundaries. He seems to delight in such trespassings, asking us to see and experience fluidity where we are inclined to certainty or fixity.

Criticism

Goulish's essay "Criticism" is an act of extended definition enriched through the auspices of three intriguing metaphors: glass, windows, and rain. You will look into the way these metaphors extend the meaning of *criticism* as Goulish understands it, how glass, windows, and rain add a tactile, visual, and auditory dimension to the act of defining.

2. Criticism

2.1 The example of glass
2.2 The example of windows
2.3 The example of rain

2.1 The Example of Glass

1 Each time we experience a work of performance, we start over almost from nothing. Despite recognizable trends, we face infinite differences—individual or cultural details, opposing traditions, idiosyncratic forms and settings, all kinds of aesthetic extremes.

Where do we begin, how do we begin, to engage a critical mind?

This question does not limit itself to performance. It relates to all art forms. In fact, it applies to all human endeavors and perceptions, from the humanities to the sciences to the practice of everyday life. Irreducible complexity seems to characterize the late twentieth century itself.

As a result, each field structures itself by propagating its own specialized vocabulary so that its practitioners might share some basic concepts. Yet each field necessarily interfaces and intersects any number of other fields, sometimes even spawning hybrid fields. Even the purist, in order to reach any depth of understanding on any given subject, must confront conflicting discourses. A serious student of performance thus might encounter the terminology of theatre, literature, music, psychology, architecture, anthropology, and biology, among other disciplines.

One might say that we face a landscape of vistas opening only onto more vistas. On the threshold of this landscape we might pause to recall the writer Isaac Babel who described his grandmother's sobering admonition when, as a child, he told her he wanted to grow up to be writer, and she replied, "To be a writer, you must know everything."

Faced with the impossibility of the task of knowing everything, we sometimes feel the desire to reject intellectuality altogether in favor of passionate expression. Such expression may take the form of the urgently political, the assertion of a solidified identity, or the following of individual inspiration wherever it may lead. And yet even these roads, if sincerely followed lead back to the discourse of complexity.

We have no choice but to accept this terrain, with the hope of discovering its exhilarating creative possibilities. Such acceptance requires a softening of the dividing lines between traditional differences: artist and critic, passion and intellect, accessible and hermetic, success and failure.

The softening of dividing lines does not however imply the disintegration of difference. Take for example the problem of glass. What is glass? Until recently, glass was considered a mostly transparent solid. It behaved like a solid; if struck, it shattered. But then, in the ancient cathedrals of Europe, it was observed that the tops of windows let in more light than the bottoms. A simple measurement proved that a window of once uniform thickness had grown thicker at the bottom and thinner at the top. Only one explanation exists for this phenomenon. Glass flows in the direction of the pull of gravity, exhibiting the behavior of a liquid. Thus one cannot conclusively define glass without the inclusion of time. At any given moment, glass is a solid, but over a period of one thousand years, it is a liquid. The problem of glass forces us to accept the inaccuracy of the traditional distinctions of solid or liquid. While the qualities of solidity and liquidity retain their difference, glass in fact is both, depending on the duration of observation, thus proving that these two states inextricably coexist.

We must ask not only how to engage the critical mind, but also why. Any act of critical thought finds its value through fulfilling one or both of two interrelated purposes:

1) to cause a change;
2) to understand how to understand.

As creative and critical thinkers, we may find it rewarding to attempt works of criticism, which, over time, reveal themselves as works of art, thus following the example of glass.

2.2 The Example of Windows

Most critics would not contest the idea that criticism exists to cause a change. But to cause a change in what?

Rarely has a work of critical thought successfully caused a change in the artwork it addresses. If a critic sees a film one day, and writes a review the next excoriating the weakness of the lead actor's performance, that same critic could return to the theater on the third day, and, despite the conviction of his argument, encounter the actor's performance unchanged. The same holds true for countless examples: condemned paintings, ridiculed concertos, buildings of reviled design, all survive, oblivious. Yet critics continue to offer their views. What are they trying to change?

Perhaps they attempt to change the future by effecting audience perceptions. If they can convince enough people, they believe they will achieve critical mass, causing an elimination of the despised, and an encouragement of the admired. But is this an accurate assessment of events? A critique may influence the thoughts of many audience members, but in the end they will make up their own minds. And those few powerful individuals who function in a producing capacity have the option of following the will of the majority, the minority, whatever sells the most tickets, or the advice of the critic. In this equation, the critic's power seems slight. If a critic believes in his or her own power to cause a change in audience thinking, that critic lives in delusion. Any changes of this kind are peripheral effects of a more central event.

Criticism only consistently changes the critic—whether further narrowing the views of the art policeman, or incrementally expanding the horizons of the open-minded thinker. If we accept this severe limitation—that in fact the first function of criticism is to cause a change in the critic—then we may begin to act accordingly.

We may agree on the premise that each work of art is at least in part perfect, while each critic is at least in part imperfect. We may then look to each work of art not for its faults and shortcomings, but for its moments of exhilaration, in an effort to bring our own imperfections into sympathetic vibration with these moments, and thus effect a creative change in ourselves. These moments will of course be somewhat subjective, and if we don't see one immediately, we will out of respect look again, because each work contains at least one, even if it occurs by accident. We may look at the totality of the work in the light of this moment—whether it be a moment of humor or sadness, an overarching structural element, a mood, a personal association, a distraction, an honest error, anything at all that speaks to us. In this way we will treat the work of art, in the words of South African composer Kevin Volans, not as an object in this world but as a window into another world. If we can articulate one window's particular exhilaration, we may open a way to inspire a change in ourselves, so that we may value and work from these recognitions.

15   What I advocate is not so unusual, because if we have been trained at all, we have probably been trained to spot the negatives, and to try to improve the work by eliminating them. Given, as we have established, that criticism always changes the critic, this approach means trouble. Whatever we fix our attention on seems to multiply before our eyes. If we look for problems, we will find them everywhere. Out of concern for ourselves and our psychic well-being, let us look instead for the aspects of wonder.

If others choose to change their own thinking as an inspired result of our critical articulations, or if they decide to dismiss us as idealists, that is their business, and we will leave it to them.

But can we recognize windows to other worlds without some formal, historical, or theoretical understanding of what we are looking at? If we deepen our understanding, might we increase our chances of locating these moments? How do we deepen our understanding?

We may think of critical thought itself as a process through which we deepen our understanding. This brings us to the second proposed function of criticism, to understand how to understand.

2.3   The Example of Rain

How do we understand something? We understand something by approaching it. How do we approach something? We approach it from any direction. We approach it using our eyes, our ears, our noses, our intellects, our imaginations. We approach it with silence. We approach it with childhood. We use pain or embarrassment. We use history. We take a safe route or a dangerous one. We discover our approach and we follow it.

20   In his 1968 essay 'Rain and the Rhinoceros', the American Trappist monk Thomas Merton attempted to understand Eugene Ionesco's play *Rhinoceros* by comparing it to the rain. Trappist monks take vows of

silence. They almost never speak. In keeping with their silent life, they live in a silent place. The sound of the rain on the tin roof of his isolated monastic cabin in the Kentucky woods must have given Merton the only inspiration he needed to approach Ionesco's rhinoceros. And when the rain stopped, he heard the sound of the military airplane overhead, leaving the nearby base, on its way to Vietnam. When the airplane passed, he heard the hiss of his lantern burning. The rain provided the window to the rhinoceros, and the rhinoceros the window to the rain. The essay's analysis balances the work of art, with the work of nature, with the work of war. Merton understood critical thought as an act of contemplation, not an act of production. At the same time, he understood it to be, like all human activity, absurd. And thus he liberated his critical mind to follow whatever might cross its path. As the zen saying goes, no matter where we go, we are never far from enlightenment.

How then can we understand the rain? We can understand it as a scientist might, by studying climatic conditions and learning the Latin names for clouds. Or we may understand the rain by looking at it and how it falls—straight down, or at an angle, or lashed by the wind. Is it a light drizzly rain, or is it only a mist and hardly rain at all? Is it the kind that falls when the sun is shining just down the street? We could understand rain by examining its effects—on plants, on people, on cities. Or we may catalogue the sounds it makes on glass, on water, on stone, on metal. We could even study the moods it evokes before it has started and after it has stopped. We could not look at it directly, but rather at what it reminds us of—childhood, violence, love, tears. Who could tell us that any of these approaches to rain is not valid? And yet we would be the first to admit their absurdity.

The modernists believed that each work of art somehow outstretches interpretation, that each criticism reduces the infinite possibilities of the work, that no critique is exhaustive. I agree to the extent that the opposite is also true—each artwork reduces its critique. Only when criticism can step a little away from the artwork that fostered it will it achieve a life of its own as a way of understanding. The way a critique discovers and explores becomes as personal, intellectual, and creative as any artwork; not to offer a comprehensive analysis of the rain, but instead one singular approach to it. Thus it might return us to our first purpose, that of causing a change. If our critique of rain allows us a different rain experience, then it has caused a change, if not in the rain, at least in the critic. And as our approaches to the rain increase, so too increases our understanding of the fleeting and fragile qualities of human life. And as our ways of understanding the rain multiply, so too will we begin to see the presence of rain in even the driest of subjects. We will realize at last that our objective all along was to understand that it is always raining.

Reading and Thinking

1. In the first section, "The Example of Glass," Goulish focuses on various kinds of performances, leading the reader to consider the intersections between performance and "theatre, literature, music, psychology, architecture, anthropology, and biology, among other disciplines." Goulish suggests that the critic's work comes down to a single phrase: *the discourse of complexity*. What does he mean by this term? What are its implications for the critic and for "readers" of performance or other art forms? How does the example of *glass* help clarify what Goulish means?

2. In the second section, "The Example of Windows," Goulish focuses on what we might call the function of criticism. He says that criticism should "cause a change." What does he mean by "cause a change"? Who or what undergoes change? What does the phrase "windows to other worlds" suggest about the function of criticism?

3. "The Example of Rain" has to do with how critics go about trying to understand whatever it is that they are criticizing. To understand what Goulish himself is doing with *rain*, we have to understand what he says the rain did for Thomas Merton. Study paragraph 20 to figure out what Goulish suggests that the rain did for Merton as he wrote about Eugene Ionesco's play *Rhinoceros*.

Thinking and Writing

1. Define *glass* in your own words, then expand your definition to include Goulish's suggestions about the nature of glass.

2. Define *window* in your own words. Provide at least two definitions of the word: 1) one that accounts for the physical object itself, and 2) one that points to its function. Modify one of those definitions to include Goulish's sense of the word in "windows to other worlds."

3. Define *rain* in your own words. Account for the way rain can come to the aid of a critic, according to Goulish. Does Goulish change your sense of the word itself? Does the word as he uses it change your understanding of criticism? Explain.

BOUNDARY CROSSINGS
AN OCCASION FOR DEFINITION

This Occasion will be as challenging as reading Goulish's playful piece "Criticism." You will consider two photographs that are so unusual they take on the characteristics of paintings. In the face of such polished realism, you may be compelled to blink, to re-think, or "doublethink." These two photographs call into question the definitions of things: *trees, houses, inside, outside, windows, glass,* and *perspective* itself.

JERRY N. UELSMANN

Jerry N. Uelsmann (b. 1934) is an influential experimental photographer, fascinated with the work of the darkroom, where he combines images, superimposes them, and recreates them to produce a series of interesting effects. Uelsmann seems to challenge the very meaning of *limitation*. The following two photographs were taken from *Uelsmann: Process and Perception*. The epigraph suggests that the book appeals "to the spirit of play in all of us."

PREPARING TO WRITE: UELSMANN PHOTOGRAPHS

1. Imagine that the image on the right is called *Tree-house*. Write a simple, comprehensive definition for *treehouse,* and then explain how you would have to change that definition to accommodate Uelsmann's photograph.

2. Imagine that the name of the photograph on page 428 is *Inside/Outside*. Explain how you would have to modify your sense of the meaning of *inside* and *outside* after looking at this photograph. Is the table inside or outside? Where is the person—outside the door or inside the house? Explain.

Occasion

MOVING TOWARD ESSAY: ANALYSIS AND REFLECTION

1. Compare the windows in the two photographs. What do they tell you about windows that you are not likely to find in a standard dictionary definition?

2. If you begin at the bottom of *Tree-house* and move up, what does that movement suggest about the connection between roots and sky?

3. What do these two photographs suggest about the nature of glass and the nature of nature? What about the scale of nature and the scale of human-made objects? How does Uelsmann define that scale with his photography?

WRITING THOUGHTFULLY: IDEA AND ESSAY

1. Compare Goulish's metaphor and Uelsmann's *Tree-house*. Write a short paper explaining how the tranformation in that photograph might help a reader better understand Goulish's sense of *complexity*.

2. Consider the windows in the two photographs and use them to help an interested reader understand how an act of criticism can open windows onto a larger world. Pay attention to the light and the dark in both photographs, and to the fuzziness of the windows in *Inside/Outside*. How do those characteristics of particular windows suggest something more complicated about Goulish's metaphor?

3. Using Goulish's critical method outlined in "Criticism," write your own critical essay about the two Uelsmann photographs. You can find other photographs of his to include in the essay. You may also refer to Burke's definition of criticism in "All Living Things Are Critics" (page 402) and ask yourself if that is also true of some inanimate things, such as photographs. Can photographs be critics?

CREATING OCCASIONS

1. Select a movie that both fascinates and puzzles you. Write a short essay about that movie under the influence of either Burke or Goulish, or both. In the essay be sure that you clearly develop your own critical vocabulary. If you borrow terms from Goulish or Burke, be sure that you let your readers know the meaning of those terms.

2. Select one of the essays from chapter 13 of this book that you have not read but that seems, on first glance, to interest you. Approach that essay under the influence of Goulish. Find within that essay one or two "moments of exhilaration" and explain to someone else why one of those moments is exhilarating and what the moment has to do with your understanding of the overall essay.

3. Create your own interactive Occasion on *Comp21* using the textual, visual, and video libraries, as well as the Explicator analysis tools. From the main menu, choose "Build Your Own Occasion for Writing."

Occasion

ARGUMENT

The United Nations is founded on the principle that healthy debate among nations can result in mutual understanding. Looking at this photograph of the Norway Room at the U.N., where such debate takes place, consider how the architectural setup of the room helps to make that argument.

Argument is an act of empathy.

The writer, having gone on a search for what she or he considers to be the truth about an issue, returns from that search to convince readers of the meaning and significance of the findings. The essay that results from this search shows as clearly as possible the relationship between the evidence and the findings that follow from it. Those findings, or conclusions, will almost never be self-evident, so the writer will have to make the reasoning process clear to the reader—the process that connects evidence and findings. That act of clarification must always be done with the readers' needs in mind.

Effective argument is seldom pugilistic. The writer does not come into the arena aggressively pursuing a knockout. Argument, if we liken it to a boxing match, might at the very most "sting like a bee," but even that should be a stinging into awareness. Argument never goes for the sucker punch. It aims for understanding, aims to turn resistance into consensus, deftness, and dexterity.

Empathy for readers ensures that the controversy—whether it be about politics, health care, an interpretation of an artistic performance, the cause of a particular war, the importance of preserving a vast tract of land, or the meaning of freedom—will be examined from several perspectives, that the reasoned conclusions reached by the writer aim to be fair and inclusive. Nothing gets left out just in the interest of winning; everything of relevance is considered in the interest of truth and honesty. Argument, in striving to win the readers' trust and confidence, leads to a reasoned consensus, a working agreement.

THE NATURE OF
ARGUMENT

To read more about Argument with interactive examples and opportunities to work with interactive texts, click on "The Rhetorical Patterns of Inquiry" from the main menu of *Comp21*.

Argument is always grounded in reason. It seeks to be logical and to avoid fallacious reasoning. It does so because to do otherwise is to be less than honest. Argument does not involve trickery. It aims to be inclusive, to consider the controversy from all sides, and to pay attention to those who might not agree with the point of view being presented. The writer knows that making certain concessions to those with other points of view is most often a matter of strength rather than weakness. Concession reveals the thoroughness with which the writer has considered the issues at stake. No long-term gain can result from hiding complications.

The tone of the written argument, the writer's attitude toward his or her material, must almost always be tempered. The most effective argument has about it an air of calmness that grows out of the writer's confidence about the issues and complications that are being written about. Equanimity, balance, and reasonableness are the watchwords. Aggressiveness, arch remarks, and sarcasm most often build up resistance and resentment. The argumentative essayist knows the subject, recognizes the pitfalls, understands the needs of the audience, and is skillful at leading the readers through the process that led to the findings in the first place.

. . . .

USING ARGUMENT
IN WRITING

Argument is the language of both the world of government and politics and the world of academe. It will be the discourse most commonly in demand as you move from class to class during your education. Whether your work is in the scientific laboratory, in the marketplace of contemporary culture, in the interpretive space of a humanities classroom, or later in your chosen profession, argument will be the pattern most often enacted by those trying to get the job done. Argument, implicitly conversational, leads to consensus, various courses of action, and new findings. But the work of argument is never final, never quite as definitive as some might think it ought to be. Like good ideas, the work of argument is always subject to further analysis.

Because argument is so important to the conduct of our daily lives, to our success in the marketplace, and in the halls of academe, our need to study it requires little more explanation than this: we cannot seem to get along without it. It is therefore necessary to learn how to work effectively and fairly within the pattern itself, seeking always the long-lasting consensus.

. . . .

LEADING
TO A CONCLUSION

Most everybody brings a practiced sense of the five-paragraph essay into the college classroom. You know that the beginning of that essay lays out a thesis, usually placed in the position of greatest emphasis: at the end of the first paragraph. The best of such introductions also include a plan, a brief suggestion about the essay's organization. The body of the essay then consists of three paragraphs, each devoted to the "proof" of a proposition that supports the thesis. The ending paragraph, or conclusion, restates the thesis and offers a closing generalization about the subject.

An opener—*Since the beginning of time we have been polluting the universe*—leads to a thesis—*We must therefore stop polluting Albany because pollution is destroying the air, the water, and the community*. The body of the essay devotes a paragraph each to problems related to *air, water*, and *community*. The conclusion restates the thesis—*We must stop destroying the air, the water, and the community of Albany*—and leads to a generalization about polluting the world—*because our actions in Albany are contributing to the pollution of the world*.

The three-part structure of this essay—its introduction, body, and conclusion—can serve you forever; that general structure is common to all forms of the essay. The essay's emphasis on logical relationships is also extremely important to all essays. The thesis and the propositions developed in the three paragraphs must be clearly related, just as the evidence in those paragraphs must be sound and its relationship to the proposition it supports must be made clear.

But it is easy to misunderstand how best to use this basic form of an argument. Instead of examining the evidence to see what it might reveal to you, it may be tempting to select only evidence that supports or substantiates what you have already discovered. Instead of letting your readers watch you figure something out as you work within the three-part structure, you may be tempted, without adequate practice, to

BOYS OF FREEDOM
AN OCCASION FOR ARGUMENT

Thomas Jefferson and our other founding fathers laid out in the "Declaration of Independence" a clear argument for proclaiming America's independence from England. This Occasion will give you an opportunity to think about independence in a more personal context. You will be thinking about independent citizens rather than independent nations. In the following photographs— one from the *New York Times* and one from *Time* magazine—you will see the effects of war and how the lives of children in America and in Iraq fall under war's spell.

PREPARING TO WRITE: TWO SOLDIERS AND A BOY

1. What are the soldiers, standing face to face, looking for in the boy's pockets? Do they have a right to search him? Explain.

2. How would you characterize the boy's clothing? Is his dress ironic?

3. How would you characterize the soldiers' dress? What is the most distinctive thing about the soldier with his back to you?

BOYS OF FREEDOM: AN OCCASION FOR ARGUMENT

At what point do national security

and common sense collide?

Join the conversation.

PREPARING TO WRITE: A BOY AND HIS FREEDOM

1. Consider the items that appear in red. What is their relationship? How does the advertisement play on the word *Time?* Name at least two ways.

2. What do the eyes in the advertisement tell you?

3. What questions do you have for the advertiser?

MOVING TOWARD ESSAY: ANALYSIS AND REFLECTION

1. Who is affected most profoundly in these two photographs? Using evidence from the photographs, defend your choice in a two-page argument.

2. Read the boys' posture in the two photographs. What does that reading tell you about the boys and their plight? Defend your reasonable conclusion in two paragraphs, one for each boy.

3. Which child do you think is in a better position to proclaim his independence? Confine your evidence to what you see in the photographs, thinking beyond the obvious fact of war.

WRITING THOUGHTFULLY: IDEA AND ESSAY

1. Write a letter to the editor of *Time* magazine or the *New York Times* expressing either your dissatisfaction or your approval of the decision to use the photograph as it has been used. Argue reasonably and succinctly.

2. Write an argumentative essay that responds thoughtfully and convincingly to the question that accompanies the *Time* magazine advertisement.

3. The Fourth Amendment to the Constitution (a part of the Bill of Rights) has this to say:

> The right of the people to be secure in their persons, houses, papers, and effects, against unreasonable searches and seizures, shall not be violated, and no Warrants shall issue, but upon probable cause, supported by Oath or affirmation, and particularly describing the place to be searched, and the persons or things to be seized.

Write a short memorandum for the U.S. attorney general that suggests what he should do to ensure that children like these two in the photographs are "secure" in their person. As you develop your memorandum, consider under what circumstances there is "probable cause" for such searches.

CREATING OCCASIONS

1. Imagine that you work in the public affairs office for the U.S. government. Write a short, two-page defense of the government's decision to curtail, during terrorist threats, certain liberties, including the right to buy certain types of firearms, the right of access to some government buildings, the right to travel in some foreign countries, and the right to criticize publicly the government's conduct of national security.

2. As a concerned private citizen, write a two-page letter to the attorney general of the United States, urging him to loosen the restrictions on the liberties enumerated in the previous question.

3. Create your own interactive Occasion on *Comp21* using the textual, visual, and video libraries, as well as the Explicator analysis tools. From the main menu, choose "Build Your Own Occasion for Writing."

MARTIN LUTHER KING, JR.

Martin Luther King, Jr. (1929–1968), who earned a Ph.D. from Boston University, was an ordained minister who worked tirelessly on behalf of civil rights. He rose up against unjust laws and encouraged other Americans to do the same. His tactic was nonviolent resistance, what he called *civil disobedience;* he staged and led protests all over the South. Many consider him the most influential civil rights leader in American history. The nation now honors Dr. King's efforts with a national holiday. By the time of his assassination in Memphis, Tennessee, many of King's dreams had been realized, but the struggle for civil rights had obviously not ended, nor had the hatred against minority groups.

Letter from Birmingham Jail

"Letter from Birmingham Jail" was written to a group of clergyman who had criticized Dr. King for leading sit-ins at lunch counters in and around Birmingham, Alabama. He and his followers had been subjected to violence and arrests for demonstrating against practices that violated their civil rights. During those days in the South, African Americans were not allowed to use the same rest-rooms as whites, could sit only in designated sections of some restaurants, were required to ride in the back of public busses, were unable to live in the best neighborhoods, could not rent rooms in most motels and hotels, and could not attend the best public schools. Segregation was the en-forced practice across much of the country.

April 16, 1963

1   My Dear Fellow Clergymen:

While confined here in the Birmingham city jail, I came across your recent statement calling my present activities "unwise and untimely." Seldom do I pause to answer criticism of my work and ideas. If I sought to answer all the criticisms that cross my desk, my secretaries would have little time for anything other than such correspondence in the course of the day, and I would have no time for constructive work. But since I feel that you are men of genuine good will and that your criticisms are sincerely set forth, I want to try to answer your statement in what I hope will be patient and reasonable terms.

I think I should indicate why I am here in Birmingham, since you have been influenced by the view which argues against "outsiders coming in." I have the honor of serving as president of the Southern Christian Lead-ership Conference, an organization operating in every southern state, with headquarters in Atlanta, Georgia. We have some eighty-five affiliated organizations across the South, and one of them is the Alabama Christian Movement for Human Rights. Frequently we share staff, educational, and financial resources with our affiliates. Several months ago the affiliate here in Birmingham asked us to be on call to engage in a nonviolent direct-action program if such were deemed necessary. We readily consented, and when the hour came we lived up to our promise. So I, along with several members of my staff, am here because I was invited here. I am here because I have organizational ties here.

But more basically, I am in Birmingham because in-justice is here. Just as the prophets of the eighth cen-tury B.C. left their villages and carried their "thus saith the Lord" far beyond the boundaries of their home towns, and just as the Apostle Paul left his village of

Tarsus and carried the gospel of Jesus Christ to the far corners of the GrecoRoman world, so am I compelled to carry the gospel of freedom beyond my own home town. Like Paul, I must constantly respond to the Macedonian call for aid.

5   Moreover, I am cognizant of the interrelatedness of all communities and states. I cannot sit idly by in Atlanta and not be concerned about what happens in Birmingham. Injustice anywhere is a threat to justice everywhere. We are caught in an inescapable network of mutuality, tied in a single garment of destiny. Whatever affects one directly, affects all indirectly. Never again can we afford to live with the narrow, provincial, "outside agitator" idea. Anyone who lives inside the United States can never be considered an outsider anywhere within its bounds.

You deplore the demonstrations taking place in Birmingham. But your statement, I am sorry to say, fails to express a similar concern for the conditions that brought about the demonstrations. I am sure that none of you would want to rest content with the superficial kind of social analysis that deals merely with effects and does not grapple with underlying causes. It is unfortunate that demonstrations are taking place in Birmingham, but it is even more unfortunate that the city's white power structure left the Negro community with no alternative.

In any nonviolent campaign there are four basic steps: collection of the facts to determine whether injustices exist; negotiation; self-purification; and direct action. We have gone through all these steps in Birmingham. There can be no gainsaying the fact that racial injustice engulfs this community. Birmingham is probably the most thoroughly segregated city in the United States. Its ugly record of brutality is widely known. Negroes have experienced grossly unjust treatment in courts. There have been more unsolved bombings of Negro homes and churches in Birmingham than in any other city in the nation. These are the hard, brutal facts of the case. On the basis of these conditions, Negro leaders sought to negotiate with the city fathers. But the latter consistently refused to engage in good-faith negotiation.

Then, last September, came the opportunity to talk with leaders of Birmingham's economic community. In the course of the negotiations, certain promises were made by the merchants—for example, to remove the stores' humiliating racial signs. On the basis of these promises, the Reverend Fred Shuttlesworth and the leaders of the Alabama Christian Movement for Human Rights agreed to a moratorium on all demonstrations. As the weeks and months went by, we realized that we were the victims of a broken promise. A few signs, briefly removed, returned; the others remained.

As in so many past experiences, our hopes had been blasted, and the shadow of deep disappointment settled upon us. We had no alternative except to prepare for direct action, whereby we would present our very bodies as means of laying our case before the conscience of the local and the national community. Mindful of the difficulties involved, we decided to undertake a process of self-purification. We began a series of workshops on nonviolence, and we repeatedly asked ourselves: "Are you able to accept blows without retaliating?" "Are you able to endure the ordeal of jail?" We decided to schedule our direct-action program for the Easter season, realizing that except for Christmas, this is the main shopping period of the year. Knowing that a strong economic-withdrawal program would be the by-product of direct action, we felt that this would be the best time to bring pressure to bear on the merchants for the needed change.

Then it occurred to us that Birmingham's mayoral election was coming up in March, and we speedily decided to postpone action until after election day. When we discovered that the Commissioner of Public Safety, Eugene "Bull" Connor, had piled up enough votes to be in the run-off, we decided again to postpone action until the day after the run-off so that the demonstrations could not be used to cloud the issues. Like many others, we waited to see Mr. Connor defeated, and to this end we endured postponement after postponement. Having aided in this community need, we felt that our direct-action program could be delayed no longer.

You may well ask, "Why direct action? Why sit-ins, marches, and so forth? Isn't negotiation a better path?" You are quite right in calling for negotiation. Indeed, this is the very purpose of direct action. Nonviolent direct action seeks to create such a crisis and foster such a tension that a community which has constantly re-

10

fused to negotiate is forced to confront the issue. It seeks so to dramatize the issue that it can no longer be ignored. My citing the creation of tension as part of the work of the nonviolent-resistor may sound rather shocking. But I must confess that I am not afraid of the word "tension." I have earnestly opposed violent tension, but there is a type of constructive, nonviolent tension which is necessary for growth. Just as Socrates felt that it was necessary to create a tension in the mind so that individuals could rise from the bondage of myths and half-truths to the unfettered realm of creative analysis and objective appraisal, so must we see the need for nonviolent gadflies to create the kind of tension in society that will help men rise from the dark depths of prejudice and racism to the majestic heights of understanding and brotherhood.

The purpose of our direct-action program is to create a situation so crisis-packed that it will inevitably open the door to negotiation. I therefore concur with you in your call for negotiation. Too long has our beloved Southland been bogged down in a tragic effort to live in monologue rather than dialogue.

One of the basic points in your statement is that the action that I and my associates have taken in Birmingham is untimely. Some have asked: "Why didn't you give the new city administration time to act?" The only answer that I can give to this query is that the new Birmingham administration must be prodded about as much as the outgoing one, before it will act. We are sadly mistaken if we feel that the election of Albert Boutwell as mayor will bring the millennium to Birmingham. While Mr. Boutwell is a much more gentle person than Mr. Connor, they are both segregationists, dedicated to maintenance of the status quo. I have hoped that Mr. Boutwell will be reasonable enough to see the futility of massive resistance to desegregation. But he will not see this without pressure from devotees of civil rights. My friends, I must say to you that we have not made a single gain in civil rights without determined legal and nonviolent pressure. Lamentably, it is an historical fact that privileged groups seldom give up their privileges voluntarily. Individuals may see the moral light and voluntarily give up their unjust posture; but, as Reinhold Niebuhr has reminded us, groups tend to be more immoral than individuals.

We know through painful experience that freedom is never voluntarily given by the oppressor; it must be demanded by the oppressed. Frankly, I have yet to engage in a direct-action campaign that was "well-timed" in the view of those who have not suffered unduly from the disease of segregation. For years now I have heard the word "Wait!" It rings in the ear of every Negro with piercing familiarity. This "Wait" has almost always meant "Never." We must come to see, with one of our distinguished jurists, that "justice too long delayed is justice denied."

We have waited for more than 340 years for our constitutional and God-given rights. The nations of Asia and Africa are moving with jetlike speed toward gaining political independence, but we still creep at horse-and-buggy pace toward gaining a cup of coffee at a lunch counter. Perhaps it is easy for those who have never felt the stinging darts of segregation to say, "Wait." But when you have seen vicious mobs lynch your mothers and fathers at will and drown your sisters and brothers at whim; when you have seen hate-filled policemen curse, kick, and even kill your black brothers and sisters; when you see the vast majority of your twenty million Negro brothers smothering in an airtight cage of poverty in the midst of an affluent society; when you suddenly find your tongue twisted and your speech stammering as you seek to explain to your six-year-old daughter why she can't go to the public amusement park that has just been advertised on television, and see tears welling up in her eyes when she is told that Funtown is closed to colored children, and see ominous clouds of inferiority beginning to form in her little mental sky, and see her beginning to distort her personality by developing an unconscious bitterness toward white people; when you have to concoct an answer for a five-year-old son who is asking, "Daddy, why do white people treat colored people so mean?"; when you take a cross-country drive and find it necessary to sleep night after night in the uncomfortable corners of your automobile because no motel will accept you; when you are humiliated day in and day out by nagging signs reading "white" and "colored"; when your first name becomes "nigger," your middle name becomes "boy" (however old you are) and your last name becomes "John," and your wife and

CONSIDERING LIBERTY
AN OCCASION FOR ARGUMENT

In "Letter from Birmingham Jail," Martin Luther King, Jr., argues that African Americans in the 1960s had a right to engage in civil disobedience so that they could gain access to the civil liberties they had long been denied. This Occasion allows you to discuss and consider a different threat to our national and individual freedoms.

We live in an interesting time in this the early part of the twenty-first century, a time when the so-called free world lives under the threat of a pervasive terrorism. But no one is quite sure where the terrorists are or just exactly how they are all connected. Since September 11, 2001, the United States has faced heightened security, fluctuating alerts, activation of the reserves and the national guard, a fear about homeland security, and a protracted war with Iraq, a country whose terrorist connections remain unclear. The insecurity that follows terrorism continues to threaten us, our freedoms, and our very way of life.

The following image by American photographer Keith Carter allows you to think about the longterm effects of terrorism and to consider how America's interests seem to have shifted in the last few decades from matters of civil disobedience on the national front to matters of threatened civil liberty and national security on both the local and international scene.

KEITH CARTER

Keith Carter (b. 1948) holds the Walles Chair of Art at Lamar University in Beaumont, Texas. His haunting photographs have been exhibited in Europe and North America and are included in permanent collections at the Art Institute of Chicago, the San Francisco Museum of Modern Art, and the George Eastman House. He has received grants from the National Endowment for the Arts and the Lange-Taylor Prize from the Center for Documentary Studies at Duke University. His photographs have been collected and published in eight different books, including *The Blue Man, Mojo, Keith Carter Photographs—Twenty-Five Years,* and *Holding Venus.*

PREPARING TO WRITE: BOY WITH WASHINGTON

1. What do you see in the child's eyes in Carter's photograph? In Washington's eyes?

2. Everyone knows that George Washington is considered the "Father of our Country." What else does he stand for in the nation's folklore?

3. Carter's photograph looks posed. Does that pose appeal to logos or pathos? Would the appeal have been different if the child had been photographed against a different backdrop, say an American flag?

4. What do you suppose this child's relationship is to the picture he is holding? Why do you imagine Carter deprives us of specific knowledge about that relationship by photographing the child and Washington in a relatively neutral context?

PREPARING TO WRITE: CHECK YOUR LIBERTIES

1. Consider the text in the cartoon. What do you suppose the security guard means by "civil liberties"? How can civil liberties be "removed" from our person?

2. What can you tell about Uncle Sam by his expression and his dress? Explain.

3. Who is Uncle Sam anyway? Conduct an Internet search to discover what he has stood for in America's history.

4. What does the cartoonist suggest that America has lost (other than some of its civil liberties) by depicting Uncle Sam under scrutiny by airport security?

5. Where do you suppose Uncle Sam is going?

MOVING TOWARD ESSAY: ANALYSIS AND REFLECTION

1. With your eye on Carter's photograph, imagine another child in need within America, a child you know more about. Whose portrait would he or she hold? What would that pair of faces tell us about the state of civil rights in America today? Defend your analysis in a 2-page response.

2. Consider the child in Carter's photograph along with Dr. King's comments about children in "Letter from Birmingham Jail." In a paragraph, explain how the child in the photograph seems either to underscore or contradict King's hopes for the future.

3. Considering the cartoon and the photograph together, speculate about the relationship that now exists in America between these two iconic figures: Uncle Sam (representative of the federal government's power) and George Washington ("Father of the Country," whose leadership led to the ratification of the Constitution and the Bill of Rights and also paved the way for the modern federal judiciary). Write a 2-page essay presenting your ideas.

WRITING THOUGHTFULLY: IDEA AND ESSAY

1. Consider the cartoon again, especially the way it depicts Uncle Sam. Compare that depiction with this World War I poster—one of the most popular posters ever printed in the United States. Using these two images of Uncle Sam as your primary evidence, write a 4- to 5-page argumentative essay in which you reveal the extent to which the country's collective mindset has changed in less than a century. You can also use evidence that you find on the Internet or that your own experience calls to mind.

2. Return to "Letter from Birmingham Jail" and reconsider King's case against the "white moderate" and the "white church" (paras. 23–32, 33–41). Make a three-column list with the headings logos, ethos, and pathos. As you read through the appropriate sections of the letter, put a checkmark under one heading or the other for each of King's paragraphs. At the end of your analysis, characterize King's argument in terms of those three aspects of persuasion. Defend your characterization with evidence from your analysis and from the text itself.

3. ***Comp21*** **Video Extension.** Extend this Occasion to include CNN® video footage using the Explicator video analysis tool on *Comp21*. From the main menu choose "Frames of Mind: Extending Occasions" and select "Considering Liberty: An Occasion for Argument" from the list.

CREATING OCCASIONS

1. Go to Keith Carter's Web site at http://keithcarterphotographs.com and find another photograph to replace the one that appears in this section. Justify your selection in a 3-page letter to the editors of this book. Attach the photograph to your letter.

2. Select a Carter photograph that helps you understand something crucial about "Letter from Birmingham Jail." The photograph need not suggest anything about race or civil disobedience. It might very well highlight other features of Dr. King's argument. Justify your selection in a 3-page letter to the editors of this book. Attach the photograph to your letter.

3. Create your own interactive Occasion on *Comp21* using the textual, visual, and video libraries, as well as the Explicator analysis tools. From the main menu, choose "Build Your Own Occasion for Writing."

Occasion

JONATHAN SWIFT

Jonathan Swift (1667–1745) was born in Dublin of English parents, and he received his education in Ireland. He is best known for his satirical attacks on various forms of injustice. Swift always wrote for the betterment of mankind, but his sometimes savage pen led to misunderstanding about his aims. His best-known works include *The Tale of a Tub, Gulliver's Travels,* and "A Modest Proposal."

A Modest Proposal

"A Modest Proposal" is a satirical attack on Ireland's failure to feed and care for its indigent population, the poor who could not fend for themselves. Satire blends humor and wit to instigate change. Swift is also ironic: he suggests one thing but really asks us to see and understand another. Writing tongue-in-cheek, he expects us to pay attention to double meaning. Swift's "Proposal" causes repulsion by the surface proposal (eating children), but we are moved to action by the cause that necessitates it (hunger).

For Preventing the Children of Poor People in Ireland from Being a Burden to Their Parents or Country, and for Making Them Beneficial to the Public

1 It is a melancholy object to those who walk through this great town or travel in the country, when they see the streets, the roads, and cabin doors, crowded with beggars of the female sex, followed by three, four, or six children, all in rags and importuning every passenger for an alms. These mothers, instead of being able to work for their honest livelihood, are forced to employ all their time in strolling to beg sustenance for their helpless infants, who, as they grow up, either turn thieves for want of work, or leave their dear native country to fight for the Pretender in Spain, or sell themselves to the Barbados.

I think it is agreed by all parties that this prodigious number of children in the arms, or on the backs, or at the heels of their mothers, and frequently of their fathers, is in the present deplorable state of the kingdom a very great additional grievance; and therefore whoever could find out a fair, cheap, and easy method of making these children sound, useful members of the commonwealth would deserve so well of the public as to have his statue set up for a preserver of the nation.

But my intention is very far from being confined to provide only for the children of professed beggars; it is of a much greater extent, and shall take in the whole number of infants at a certain age who are born of parents in effect as little able to support them as those who demand our charity in the streets.

As to my own part, having turned my thoughts for many years upon this important subject, and maturely weighed the several schemes of other projectors, I have always found them grossly mistaken in their computation. It is true, a child just dropped from its dam may be supported by her milk for a solar year, with little other nourishment; at most not above the value of two shillings, which the mother may certainly get, or the value in scraps, by her lawful occupation of begging; and it is exactly at one year that I propose to provide for them in such a manner as instead of being a charge upon their parents or the parish, or wanting food and raiment for the rest of their lives, they shall on the contrary contribute to the feeding, and partly to the clothing, of many thousands.

5 There is likewise another great advantage in my scheme, that it will prevent those voluntary abortions, and that horrid practice of women murdering their bastard children, alas, too frequent among us, sacrificing the poor innocent babes, I doubt, more to avoid the expense than the shame, which would

move tears and pity in the most savage and inhuman breast.

The number of souls in this kingdom being usually reckoned one million and a half, of these I calculate there may be about two hundred thousand couples whose wives are breeders; from which number I subtract thirty thousand couples who are able to maintain their own children, although I apprehend there cannot be so many under the present distress of the kingdom; but this being granted, there will remain an hundred and seventy thousand breeders. I again subtract fifty thousand for those women who miscarry, or whose children die by accident or disease within the year. There only remain an hundred and twenty thousand children of poor parents annually born. The question therefore is, how this number shall be reared and provided for, which, as I have already said, under the present situation of affairs, is utterly impossible by all the methods hitherto proposed. For we can neither employ them in handicraft or agriculture; we neither build houses (I mean in the country) nor cultivate land. They can very seldom pick up a livelihood stealing till they arrive at six years old, except where they are of towardly parts, although I confess they learn the rudiments much earlier, during which time they can however be looked upon only as probationers, as I have been informed by a principal gentleman in the country of Cavan, who protested to me that he never knew above one or two instances under the age of six, even in a part of the kingdom so renowned for the quickest proficiency in that art.

I am assured by our merchants that a boy or a girl before twelve years old is no salable commodity; and even when they come to this age they will not yield above three pounds, or three pounds and half a crown at most on the Exchange; which cannot turn to account either to the parents or the kingdom, the charge of nutriment and rags having been at least four times that value.

I shall now therefore humbly propose my own thoughts, which I hope will not be liable to the least objection.

I have been assured by a very knowing American of my acquaintance in London, that a young healthy child well nursed is at a year old a most delicious, nourishing, and wholesome food, whether stewed, roasted, baked, or boiled; and I make no doubt that it will equally serve in a fricassee or a ragout.

I do therefore humbly offer it to public consideration that of the hundred and twenty thousand children, already computed, twenty thousand may be reserved for breed, whereof only one fourth part to be males, which is more than we allow to sheep, black cattle, or swine; and my reason is that these children are seldom the fruits of marriage, a circumstance not much regarded by our savages, therefore one male will be sufficient to serve four females. That the remaining hundred thousand may at a year old be offered in sale to the persons of quality and fortune through the kingdom, always advising the mother to let them suck plentifully in the last month, so as to render them plump and fat for a good table. A child will make two dishes at an entertainment for friends; and when the family dines alone, the fore or hind quarter will make a reasonable dish, and seasoned with a little pepper or salt will be very good boiled on the fourth day, especially in winter.

I have reckoned upon a medium that a child just born will weigh twelve pounds, and in a solar year if tolerably nursed increaseth to twenty-eight pounds.

I grant this food will be somewhat dear, and therefore very proper for landlords, who, as they have already devoured most of the parents, seem to have the best title to the children.

Infant's flesh will be in season throughout the year, but more plentiful in March, and a little before and after. For we are told by a grave author, an eminent French physician, that fish being a prolific diet, there are more children born in Roman Catholic countries about nine months after Lent than at any other season; therefore, reckoning a year after Lent, the markets will be more glutted than usual, because the number of popish infants is at least three to one in this kingdom; and therefore it will have one other collateral advantage, by lessening the number of Papists among us.

I have already computed the charge of nursing a beggar's child (in which list I reckon all cottagers, laborers, and four-fifths of the farmers) to be about two shillings per annum, rags included; and I believe no gentleman would repine to give ten shillings for the carcass of a good fat child, which, as I have said, will make four dishes of excellent nutritive meat, when he hath only some particular friend or his own family to dine with him. Thus the squire will learn to be a good landlord, and grow people among the tenants; the mother will have eight shillings net profit, and be fit for work till she produces another child.

15   Those who are more thrifty (as I must confess the times require) may flay the carcass; the skin of which artificially dressed will make admirable gloves for ladies, and summer boots for fine gentlemen.

As to our city of Dublin, shambles may be appointed for this purpose in the most convenient parts of it, and butchers we may be assured will not be wanting; although I rather recommend buying the children alive, and dressing them hot from the knife as we do roasting pigs.

A very worthy person, a true lover of his country, and whose virtues I highly esteem, was lately pleased in discoursing on this matter to offer a refinement upon my scheme. He said that many gentlemen of his kingdom, having of late destroyed their deer, he conceived that the want of venison might be well supplied by the bodies of young lads and maidens, not exceeding fourteen years of age nor under twelve, so great a number of both sexes in every county being now ready to starve for want of work and service; and these to be disposed of by their parents, if alive, or otherwise by their nearest relations. But with due deference to so excellent a friend and so deserving a patriot, I cannot be altogether in his sentiments; for as to the males, my American acquaintance assured me from frequent experience that their flesh was generally tough and lean, like that of our schoolboys, by continual exercise, and their taste disagreeable; and to fatten them would not answer the charge. Then as to the females, it would, I think with humble submission, be a loss to the public, because they soon would become breeders themselves; and besides, it is not improbable that some scrupulous people might be apt to censure such a practice (although indeed very unjustly) as a little bordering upon cruelty; which, I confess, hath always been with me the strongest objection against any project, how well soever intended.

But in order to justify my friend, he confessed that this expedient was put into his head by the famous Psalmanazar, a native of the island Formosa, who came from thence to London above twenty years ago, and in conversation told my friend that in his country when any young person happened to be put to death, the executioner sold the carcass to persons of quality as a prime dainty; and that in his time the body of a plump girl of fifteen, who was crucified for an attempt to poison the emperor, was sold to his Imperial Majesty's prime minister of state, and other great mandarins of the court, in joints from the gibbet, at four hundred crowns. Neither indeed can I deny that if the same use were made of several plump young girls in this town, who without one single groat to their fortunes cannot stir abroad without a chair, and appear at the playhouse and assemblies in foreign fineries which they never will pay for, the kingdom would not be the worse.

Some persons of a desponding spirit are in great concern about that vast number of poor people who are aged, diseased, or maimed, and I have been desired to employ my thoughts what course may be taken to ease the nation of so grievous an encumbrance. But I am not in the least pain upon that matter, because it is very well known that they are every day dying and rotting by cold and famine, and filth and vermin, as fast as can be reasonably expected. And as to the younger laborers, they are now in almost as hopeful a condition. They cannot get work, and consequently pine away for want of nourishment to a degree that if any time they are accidentally hired to common labor, they have not strength to perform it; and thus the country and themselves are happily delivered from the evils to come.

20   I have too long digressed, and therefore shall return to my subject. I think the advantages by the proposal which I have made are obvious and many, as well as of the highest importance.

For first, as I have already observed, it would greatly lessen the number of Papists, with whom we are yearly overrun, being the principal breeders of the nation as well as our most dangerous enemies; and who stay at home on purpose to deliver the kingdom to the Pretender, hoping to take their advantage by the absence of so many good Protestants, who have chosen rather to leave their country than to stay at home and pay tithes against their conscience to an Episcopal curate.

Secondly, the poorer tenants will have something valuable of their own, which by law may be made liable to distress, and help to pay their landlord's rent, their corn and cattle being already seized and money a thing unknown.

Thirdly, whereas the maintenance of an hundred thousand children, from two years old and upwards, cannot be computed at less than ten shillings a piece per annum, the nation's stock will be thereby increased fifty thousand pounds per annum, besides the profit of a new dish introduced to the tables of all gentlemen of fortune in the kingdom who have any refinement in taste. And the money will circulate among ourselves, the goods being entirely of our own growth and manufacture.

Fourthly, the constant breeders, besides the gain of eight shillings sterling per annum by the sale of their children, will be rid of the charge of maintaining them after the first year.

Fifthly, this food would likewise bring great custom to taverns, where the vintners will certainly be so prudent as to procure the best recipes for dressing it to perfection, and consequently have their houses frequented by all the fine gentlemen, who justly value themselves upon their knowledge in good eating; and a skillful cook, who understands how to oblige his guests, will contrive to make it as expensive as they please.

Sixthly, this would be a great inducement to marriage, which all wise nations have either encouraged by rewards or enforced by laws and penalties. It would increase the care and tenderness of mothers toward their children, when they were sure of a settlement for life to the poor babes, provided in some sort by the public, to their annual profit instead of expense. We should see an honest emulation among the married women, which of them could bring the fattest child to the market. Men would become as fond of their wives during the time of their pregnancy as they are now of their mares in foal, their cows in calf, or sows when they are ready to farrow; nor offer to beat or kick them (as is too frequent a practice) for fear of a miscarriage.

Many other advantages might be enumerated. For instance, the addition of some thousand carcasses in our exportation of barreled beef, the propagation of swine's flesh, and improvements in the art of making good bacon, so much wanted among us by the great destruction of pigs, too frequent at our tables, which are no way comparable in taste or magnificence to a well-grown, fat, yearling child, which roasted whole will make a considerable figure at a lord mayor's feast or any other public entertainment. But this and many others I omit, being studious of brevity.

Supposing that one thousand families in this city would be constant customers for infants' flesh, besides others who might have it at merry meetings, particularly weddings and christenings, I compute that Dublin would take off annually about twenty thousand carcasses, and the rest of the kingdom (where probably they will be sold somewhat cheaper) the remaining eighty thousand.

I can think of no one objection that will possibly be raised against this proposal, unless it should be urged that the number of people will be thereby much lessened in the kingdom. This I freely own, and it was indeed one principal design in offering it to the world. I desire the reader will observe, that I calculate my remedy for this one individual kingdom of Ireland and for no other that ever was, is, or I think ever can be upon earth. Therefore let no man talk to me of other expedients: of taxing our absentees at five shillings a pound: of using neither clothes nor household furniture except what is of our own growth and manufacture: of utterly rejecting the materials and instruments that promote foreign luxury: of curing the expensiveness of pride, vanity, idleness, and gaming in our women: of introducing a vein of parsimony, prudence, and temperance: of learning to love our country, in the want of which we differ even from Laplanders and the inhabitants of Topinamboo: of quitting our animosities and factions, nor acting any longer like the Jews, who were murdering one another at the very moment their city was taken: of being a little cautious not to sell our country and conscience for nothing: of teaching landlords to have at least one degree of mercy toward their tenants: lastly, of putting a spirit of honesty, industry, and skill into our shopkeepers; who, if a resolution could now be taken to buy only our native goods, would immediately unite to cheat and exact upon us in the price, the measure, and the goodness, nor could ever yet be brought to make one fair proposal of just dealing, though often and earnestly invited to it.

Therefore I repeat, let no man talk to me of these and the like expedients, till he hath at least some

25

glimpse of hope that there will ever be some hearty and sincere attempt to put them in practice.

But as to myself, having been wearied out for many years with offering vain, idle, visionary thoughts, and at length utterly despairing of success, I fortunately fell upon this proposal, which, as it is wholly new, so it hath something solid and real, of no expense and little trouble, full in our own power, and whereby we can incur no danger in disobliging England. For this kind of commodity will not bear exportation, the flesh being of too tender a consistence to admit a long continuance in salt, although perhaps I could name a country which would be glad to eat up our whole nation without it.

After all, I am not so violently bent upon my own opinion as to reject any offer proposed by wise men, which shall be found equally innocent, cheap, easy, and effectual. But before something of that kind shall be advanced in contradiction to my scheme, and offering a better, I desire the author or authors will be pleased maturely to consider two points. First, as things now stand, how they will be able to find food and raiment for an hundred thousand useless mouths and backs. And secondly, there being a round million of creatures in human figure throughout this kingdom, whose sole subsistence put into a common stock would leave them in debt two millions of pounds sterling, adding those who are beggars by profession to the bulk of farmers, cottagers, and laborers, with their wives and children who are beggars in effect; I desire those politicians who dislike my overture, and may perhaps be so bold to attempt an answer, that they will first ask the parents of these mortals whether they would not at this day think it a great happiness to have been sold for food at a year old in this manner I prescribe, and thereby have avoided such a perpetual scene of misfortunes as they have since gone through by the oppression of landlords, the impossibility of paying rent without money or trade, the want of common sustenance, with neither house nor clothes to cover them from the inclemencies of the weather, and the most inevitable prospect of entailing the like or greater miseries upon their breed forever.

I profess, in the sincerity of my heart, that I have not the least personal interest in endeavoring to promote this necessary work, having no other motive than the public good of my country, by advancing our trade, providing for infants, relieving the poor, and giving some pleasure to the rich. I have no children by which I can propose to get a single penny; the youngest being nine years old, and my wife past childbearing.

Reading and Thinking

1. The first six paragraphs of this proposal identify a number of problems in Swift's Ireland. Make a list of these problems in the order that Swift identifies them.

2. What particular use does Swift make of the unnamed American in paragraph 9? Of the American in paragraph 17?

3. What is the effect of Swift's numerical calculations and his tone of voice? Do these aspects of his work appeal more to pathos, ethos, or logos?

Thinking and Writing

1. Return to paragraph 9 and recall your initial reaction to what Swift says. In a paragraph, explain how that paragraph influences your sense of the writer's character (ethos)?

2. Reread paragraph 4 and identify how Swift both disguises and foreshadows his proposal. Find two other examples of double meaning in the proposal.

3. Classify Swift's satire. Is it gentle, biting, or some combination of the two? Justify your claim with evidence from the proposal itself.

SIPRESS

"Let me be vague."

PREPARING TO WRITE: LET ME BE VAGUE

1. What are the three speakers doing? How do you know?

2. What do the words in this cartoon by David Sipress suggest about the nature of American politics and the voting public?

MOVING TOWARD ESSAY: ANALYSIS AND REFLECTION

1. In the first cartoon, how does cartoonist Gahan Wilson use image and language to reinforce one another? What do you have to know to get the joke?

2. How does David Sipress's use of language differ from Wilson's use of language? In what way do these two cartoonists seem to share a similar vision? Explain.

3. How do the two Sipress cartoons differ in their use of the written word? Are the images more significant in one cartoon than in the other? Explain.

4. Consider the religious and the political cartoon together. Each uses a simple, declarative sentence to achieve its effect. How do they differ in tone and in effect? Explain.

WRITING THOUGHTFULLY: IDEA AND ESSAY

1. In the political cartoon on the left, the speaker says exactly what he means, but the statement itself "Let me be vague," creates a double meaning. Swift also creates double meaning, but in a very different way. Compare this statement to Swift's appeal to the people of Ireland in "A Modest Proposal." Write a short essay that accounts for how Swift creates double meaning, drawing your evidence from his proposal. Use the cartoon to help you establish similarities and differences between Sipress's and Swift's methods.

2. These three cartoons create a rather dim view of the human condition in our time. To what extent does the language of reform (whether it be satirical, ironic, or earnest) depend on negative assumptions about the world we inhabit? Do these assumptions create an imprecise view of the world?

3. Is the language of satire or negativity an appropriate or inappropriate response to the actual situation in the world? Write a brief essay persuading others to see as you see.

4. Identify a serious problem in America that needs immediate attention. Attack that problem as Swift might attack it. Follow the structure of his argument, which identifies the problem, offers a proposal, and then reveals the benefits of the proposal. Use satire and irony to make your argument more effective.

CREATING OCCASIONS

1. Create a cartoon that combines images and words that make your audience think twice about some troubling or humorous aspect of American life. If you are not good at sketching, select a photograph or create a collage, then add words to create the double meaning.

2. Select two political cartoons from a magazine or newspaper that work in different but compelling ways. Write a short analysis of how the two cartoons work, then incorporate that analysis in an argument that assesses the two cartoons' relative effectiveness in instructing us about our human foibles.

3. Create your own interactive Occasion on *Comp21* using the textual, visual, and video libraries, as well as the Explicator analysis tools. From the main menu, choose "Build Your Own Occasion for Writing."

RAUSCHENBERG

chapter THIRTEEN

THE PATTERNS IN THEIR NATURAL HABITAT

In this chapter, unlike the previous ten chapters, we do not emphasize any one of the patterns of inquiry. As you have seen in the essays in previous chapters, good writing mixes and blends various patterns.

Some of the essays in this chapter emphasize one or another of the rhetorical strategies you learned about in previous chapters—narration, description, comparison and contrast, illustration, cause and effect, and so on. Other essays in this chapter have no one dominant pattern. In reading these essays, you will see how an author combines patterns. Your goal in reading is not primarily to identify these, but rather to follow the scent of idea a writer lays down and see not only what the writer is saying, but how he or she is saying it.

As in the previous chapters, each of the essays in this chapter on "blended essays" includes an introductory note on the author and a brief lead-in to the essay proper. The questions that follow each essay are similarly organized for your reading, thinking, and writing pleasure. Enjoy them.

. . . .

Robert Rauschenberg is known for his collages—works of art that use several media such as painting and photography together, rather than for creating art in only one media. This one is titled From the Seat of Authority. *How do all the elements work together to create meaning?*

JUDITH ORTIZ COFER

Judith Ortiz Cofer (b. 1952) is a poet, novelist, and essayist whose work has appeared in literary journals and magazines such as the *Georgia Review*, the *Kenyon Review*, and *Glamour*. Her work includes *Terms of Survival* and *Reaching for the Mainland*, poetry collections; *The Line of the Sun*, a novel; *Silent Dancing*, poems and essays; and *Woman in Front of the Sun: On Becoming a Writer*. Her work has been selected for *Best American Essays*, *The Pushcart Prize*, and the *O. Henry Short Stories*. She has received fellowships from the National Endowment for the Arts and the Witter Bynner Foundation for Poetry, and the Rockefeller Foundation awarded her a residency at Bellagio. She is a professor of English at the University of Georgia.

The Story of My Body

Cofer has told us that one of the goals in her life is to "replace the old pervasive stereotypes and myths about Latinas with a much more interesting set of realities." As you read "The Story of My Body," think about that more interesting set of realities. The title tells us that this piece of writing is a "story"; that story, as Cofer tells it, extends from childhood into adulthood. But instead of hearing just one story, we hear many—a series of stories arranged according to time and subject matter. Each story tells us something about Cofer's never-ending struggle to work her way through the difficulties that her body created for her as a young woman. Because she was a young Puerto Rican woman trying to make her way in what was largely a white world, she had to develop coping strategies. As you read, see if you can understand the relationship between her strategies and the new set of realities she discovers for herself.

1   I was born a white girl in Puerto Rico but became a brown girl when I came to live in the United States. My Puerto Rican relatives called me tall; at the American school, some of my rougher classmates called me Skinny Bones, and the Shrimp because I was the smallest member of my classes all through grammar school until high school, when the midget Gladys was given the honorary post of front row center for class pictures and scorekeeper, bench warmer, in P.E. I reached my full stature of five feet in sixth grade.

I started out life as a pretty baby and learned to be a pretty girl from a pretty mother. Then at ten years of age I suffered one of the worst cases of chicken pox I have ever heard of. My entire body, including the inside of my ears and in between my toes, was covered with pustules which in a fit of panic at my appearance I scratched off my face, leaving permanent scars. A cruel school nurse told me I would always have them—tiny cuts that looked as if a mad cat had plunged its claws deep into my skin. I grew my hair long and hid behind it for the first years of my adolescence. This was when I learned to be invisible.

COLOR

In the animal world it indicates danger: the most colorful creatures are often the most poisonous. Color is also a way to attract and seduce a mate. In the human world color triggers many more complex and often deadly reactions. As a Puerto Rican girl born of "white" parents, I spent the first years of my life hearing people refer to me as *blanca*, white. My mother insisted that I protect myself from the intense island sun because I was more prone to sunburn than some of my darker, *trigueño* playmates. People were always commenting within my hearing about how my black hair contrasted so nicely with my "pale" skin. I did not think of the color of my skin consciously except when I heard the adults talking about complexion. It seems to me that the subject is much more common in the conversation of mixed-race peoples than in mainstream United States society, where it is a touchy and sometimes even embarrassing topic to discuss, except in a political context. In Puerto Rico I heard many conversations about skin color. A pregnant woman could say, "I hope my baby doesn't turn out *prieto*" (slang for "dark" or "black") "like my husband's grandmother, although she was a good-looking *negra* in her time." I am a combination of both, being olive-skinned—lighter than my mother yet darker than my fairskinned father. In America, I am a person of color, obviously a Latina. On the Island I have been called everything from a *paloma blanca,* after the song (by a black suitor), to *la gringa.*

My first experience of color prejudice occurred in a supermarket in Paterson, New Jersey. It was Christmastime, and I was eight or nine years old. There was a display of toys in the store where I went two or three times a day to buy things for my mother, who never made lists but sent for milk, cigarettes, a can of this or that, as she remembered from hour to hour. I enjoyed being trusted with money and walking half a city block to the new, modern grocery store. It was owned by three good-looking Italian brothers. I liked the younger one with the crew-cut blond hair. The two older ones watched me and the other Puerto Rican kids as if they thought we were going to steal something. The oldest one would sometimes even try to hurry me with my purchases, although part of my pleasure in these expeditions came from looking at everything in the well-stocked aisles. I was also teaching myself to read English by sounding out the labels on packages: L&M cigarettes, Borden's homogenized milk, Red Devil potted ham, Nestle's chocolate mix, Quaker oats, Bustelo coffee, Wonder bread, Colgate toothpaste, Ivory soap, and Goya (makers of products used in Puerto Rican dishes) everything—these are some of the brand names that taught me nouns. Several times this man had come up to me, wearing his bloodstained butcher's apron, and towering over me had asked in a harsh voice whether there was something he

could help me find. On the way out I would glance at the younger brother who ran one of the registers and he would often smile and wink at me.

It was the mean brother who first referred to me as "colored." It was a few days before Christmas, and my parents had already told my brother and me that since we were in Los Estados now, we would get our presents on December 25 instead of Los Reyes, Three Kings Day, when gifts are exchanged in Puerto Rico. We were to give them a wish list that they would take to Santa Claus, who apparently lived in the Macy's store downtown—at least that's where we had caught a glimpse of him when we went shopping. Since my parents were timid about entering the fancy store, we did not approach the huge man in the red suit. I was not interested in sitting on a stranger's lap anyway. But I did covet Susie, the talking schoolteacher doll that was displayed in the center aisle of the Italian brothers' supermarket. She talked when you pulled a string on her back. Susie had a limited repertoire of three sentences: I think she could say: "Hello, I'm Susie Schoolteacher," "Two plus two is four," and one other thing I cannot remember. The day the older brother chased me away, I was reaching to touch Susie's blonde curls. I had been told many times, as most children have, not to touch anything in a store that I was not buying. But I had been looking at Susie for weeks. In my mind, she was my doll. After all, I had put her on my Christmas wish list. The moment is frozen in my mind as if there were a photograph of it on file. It was not a turning point, a disaster, or an earth-shaking revelation. It was simply the first time I considered—if naively—the meaning of skin color in human relations.

I reached to touch Susie's hair. It seems to me that I had to get on tiptoe, since the toys were stacked on a table and she sat like a princess on top of the fancy box she came in. Then I heard the booming "Hey, kid, what do you think you're doing!" spoken very loudly from the meat counter. I felt caught, although I knew I was not doing anything criminal. I remember not looking at the man, but standing there, feeling humiliated because I knew everyone in the store must have heard him yell at me. I felt him approach, and when I knew he was behind me, I turned around to face the bloody butcher's apron. His large chest was at my eye level. He blocked my way. I started to run out of the place, but even as I reached the door I heard him shout after me: "Don't come in here unless you gonna buy something. You PR kids put your dirty hands on stuff. You always look dirty. But maybe dirty brown is your natural color." I heard him laugh and someone else too in the back. Outside in the sunlight I looked at my hands. My nails needed a little cleaning as they always did, since I liked to paint with watercolors, but I took a bath every night. I thought the man was dirtier than I was in his stained apron. He was also always sweaty—it showed in big yellow circles under his shirt-sleeves. I sat on the front steps of the apartment building where we lived and looked closely at my hands, which showed the only skin I could see, since it was bitter cold and I was wearing my quilted play coat, dungarees, and a knitted navy cap of my father's. I was not pink like my friend Charlene and her sister Kathy, who had blue eyes and light brown hair. My skin is the color of the coffee my grandmother made, which was half milk, *leche con café* rather than *café con leche*. My mother is the opposite mix. She has a lot of *café* in her color. I could not understand how my skin looked like dirt to the supermarket man.

I went in and washed my hands thoroughly with soap and hot water, and borrowing my mother's nail file, I cleaned the crusted watercolors from underneath my nails. I was pleased with the results. My skin was the same color as before, but I knew I was clean. Clean enough to run my fingers through Susie's fine gold hair when she came home to me.

Size

My mother is barely four feet eleven inches in height, which is average for women in her family. When I grew to five feet by age twelve, she was amazed and began to use the word tall to describe me, as in "Since you are tall, this dress will look good on you." As with the color of my skin, I didn't consciously think about my height or size until other people made an issue of it. It is around the preadolescent years that in America the games children play for fun become fierce competitions where everyone is out to "prove" they are better than others. It was in the playground and sports fields that my size-related problems began. No matter how familiar the story is, every child who is the last chosen for a team knows the torment of waiting to be called up. At the Paterson, New Jersey, public schools that I attended, the volleyball or softball game was the metaphor for the battlefield of life to the inner city kids—the black kids versus the Puerto Rican kids, the whites versus the blacks versus the Puerto Rican kids; and I was 4F, skinny, short, bespectacled, and apparently impervious to the blood thirst that drove many of my classmates to play ball as if their lives depended on it. Perhaps they did. I would rather be reading a book than sweating, grunting, and running the risk of pain and injury. I simply did not see the point in competitive sports. My main form of exercise then was walking to the library, many city blocks away from my barrio.

Still, I wanted to be wanted. I wanted to be chosen for the teams. Physical education was compulsory, a class where you were actually given a grade. On my mainly all A report card, the C for compassion I always received from the P.E. teachers shamed me the same as a bad grade in a real class. Invariably, my father would say: "How can you make a low grade for *playing games?*" He did not understand. Even if I had managed to make a hit (it never happened) or get the ball over that ridiculously high net, I already had a reputation as a "shrimp," a hopeless nonathlete. It was an area where the girls who didn't like me for one reason or another—mainly because I did better than they in academic subjects—could lord it over me; the playing field was the place where even the smallest girl could make me feel powerless and inferior. I instinctively understood the politics even then; how the *not* choosing me until the teacher forced one of the team captains to call my name was a coup of sorts—there, you little show-off, tomorrow you can beat us in spelling and geography, but this afternoon you are the loser. Or perhaps those were only my own bitter thoughts as I sat or stood in the sidelines while the big girls were grabbed like fish and I, the little brown tadpole, was ignored until Teacher looked over in my general direction and shouted, "Call Ortiz," or, worse, "Somebody's *got* to take her."

No wonder I read Wonder Woman comics and had Legion of Super Heroes daydreams. Although I wanted to think of myself as "intellectual," my body was demanding that I notice it. I saw the little swelling around my once-flat nipples, the fine hairs growing in secret places; but my knees were still bigger than my thighs, and I always wore long- or half-sleeve blouses to hide my bony upper arms. I wanted flesh on my bones—a thick layer of it. I saw a new product advertised on TV. Wate-On. They showed skinny men and women before and after taking the stuff, and it was a transformation like the ninety-seven-pound-weakling-turned-into-Charles-Atlas ads that I saw on the back covers of my comic books. The Wate-On was very expensive. I tried to explain my need for it in Spanish to my mother, but it didn't translate very well, even to my ears—and she said with a tone of finality, eat more of my good food and you'll get fat—anybody can get fat. Right. Except me. I was going to have to join a circus someday as Skinny Bones, the woman without flesh.

Wonder Woman was stacked. She had a cleavage framed by the spread wings of a golden eagle and a muscular body that has become fashionable with women only recently. But since I wanted a body that would serve me in P.E., hers was my ideal. The breasts were an indulgence I allowed myself. Perhaps the daydreams of bigger girls were more glamorous, since our ambitions are filtered through our needs, but I wanted first a powerful body. I daydreamed of leaping up above the gray landscape of the city to where the sky was clear and blue, and in anger and self-pity, I fantasized about scooping my enemies up by their hair from the playing fields and dumping them on a barren asteroid. I would put the P.E. teachers each on their own rock in space too, where they would be the loneliest people in the universe, since I knew they had no "inner resources," no imagination, and in outer space, there would be no air for them to fill their deflated volleyballs with. In my mind all P.E. teachers have blended into one large spiky-haired woman with a whistle on a string around her neck and a volleyball under one arm. My Wonder Woman fantasies of revenge were a source of comfort to me in my early career as a shrimp.

I was saved from more years of P.E. torment by the fact that in my sophomore year of high school I transferred to a school where the midget, Gladys, was the focal point of interest for the people who must rank according to size. Because her height was considered a handicap, there was an unspoken rule about mentioning size around Gladys, but of course, there was no need to say anything. Gladys knew her place: front row center in class photographs. I gladly moved to the left or to the right of her, as far as I could without leaving the picture completely.

LOOKS

Many photographs were taken of me as a baby by my mother to send to my father, who was stationed overseas during the first two years of my life. With the army in Panama when I was born, he later traveled often on tours of duty with the navy. I was a healthy, pretty baby. Recently, I read that people are drawn to big-eyed round-faced creatures, like puppies, kittens, and certain other mammals and marsupials, koalas, for example, and, of course, infants. I was all eyes, since my head and body, even as I grew older, remained thin and small-boned. As a young child I got a lot of attention from my relatives and many other people we met in our barrio. My mother's beauty may have had something to do with how much attention we got from strangers in stores and on the street. I can imagine it. In the pictures I have seen of us together, she is a stunning young woman by Latino standards: long, curly black hair, and round curves in a compact frame. From her I learned how to move, smile, and talk like an attractive woman. I remember going into a bodega for our groceries and being given candy by the proprietor as a reward for being *bonita*, pretty.

I can see in the photographs, and I also remember, that I was dressed in the pretty clothes, the stiff, frilly dresses, with layers of crinolines underneath, the glossy patent leather shoes, and, on special occasions, the skull-hugging little hats and the white gloves that were popular in the late fifties and early sixties. My mother was proud of my looks, although I was a bit too thin. She could dress me up like a doll and take me by the hand to visit relatives, or go to the Spanish mass at the Catholic church, and show me off. How was I to know that she and the others who called me "pretty" were representatives of an aesthetic that would not apply when I went out into the mainstream world of school?

In my Paterson, New Jersey, public schools there were still quite a few white children, although the demographics of the city were changing rapidly. The original waves of Italian and Irish immigrants, silkmill

Reading

workers, and laborers in the cloth industries had been "assimilated." Their children were now the middle-class parents of my peers. Many of them moved their children to the Catholic schools that proliferated enough to have leagues of basketball teams. The names I recall hearing still ring in my ears: Don Bosco High versus St. Mary's High, St. Joseph's versus St. John's. Later I too would be transferred to the safer environment of a Catholic school. But I started school at Public School Number II. I came there from Puerto Rico, thinking myself a pretty girl, and found that the hierarchy for popularity was as follows: pretty white girl, pretty Jewish girl, pretty Puerto Rican girl, pretty black girl. Drop the last two categories; teachers were too busy to have more than one favorite per class, and it was simply understood that if there was a big part in the school play, or any competition where the main qualification was "presentability" (such as escorting a school visitor to or from the principal's office), the classroom's public address speaker would be requesting the pretty and/or nice-looking white boy or girl. By the time I was in the sixth grade, I was sometimes called by the principal to represent my class because I dressed neatly (I knew this from a progress report sent to my mother, which I translated for her) and because all the "presentable" white girls had moved to the Catholic schools (I later surmised this part). But I was still not one of the popular girls with the boys. I remember one incident where I stepped out into the playground in my baggy gym shorts and one Puerto Rican boy said to the other: "What do you think?" The other one answered: "Her face is OK, but look at the toothpick legs." The next best thing to a compliment I got was when my favorite male teacher, while handing out the class pictures, commented that with my long neck and delicate features I resembled the movie star Audrey Hepburn. But the Puerto Rican boys had learned to respond to a fuller figure: long necks and a perfect little nose were not what they looked for in a girl. That is when I decided I was a "brain." I did not settle into the role easily. I was nearly devastated by what the chicken pox episode had done to my self-image. But I looked into the mirror less often after I was told that I would always have scars on my face, and I hid behind my long black hair and my books.

After the problems at the public school got to the point where even nonconfrontational little me got beaten up several times, my parents enrolled me at St. Joseph's High School. I was then a minority of one among the Italian and Irish kids. But I found several good friends there—other girls who took their studies seriously. We did our homework together and talked about the Jackies. The Jackies were two popular girls, one blonde and the other red-haired, who had women's bodies. Their curves showed even in the blue jumper uniforms with straps that we all wore. The blonde Jackie would often let one of the straps fall off her shoulder, and although she, like all of us, wore a white blouse underneath, all the boys stared at her arm. My friends and I talked about this and practiced letting our straps fall off our shoulders. But it wasn't the same without breasts or hips.

My final two and a half years of high school were spent in Augusta, Georgia, where my parents moved our family in search of a more peaceful environment. There we became part of a little community of our army-connected relatives and friends. School was yet another matter. I was enrolled in a huge school of nearly two thousand students that had just that year been forced to integrate. There were two black girls and there was me. I did extremely well academically. As to my social life, it was, for the most part, uneventful—yet it is in my memory blighted by one incident. In my junior year, I became wildly infatuated with a pretty white boy. I'll call him Ted. Oh, he was pretty: yellow hair that fell over his forehead, a smile to die for—and he was a great dancer. I watched him at Teen Town, the youth center at the base where all the military brats gathered on Saturday nights. My father had retired from the navy, and we had all our base privileges—one other reason we had moved to Augusta. Ted looked like an angel to me. I worked on him for a year before he asked me out. This meant maneuvering to be within the periphery of his vision at every possible occasion. I took the long way to my classes in school just to pass by his locker, I went to football games, which I detested, and I danced (I too was a good dancer) in front of him at Teen Town—this took some fancy footwork, since it involved subtly moving my partner toward the right spot on the dance floor. When Ted finally approached me, "A Million to One" was playing on the jukebox, and when he took me into his arms, the odds suddenly turned in my favor. He asked me to go to a school dance the following Saturday. I said yes, breathlessly. I said yes, but there were obstacles to surmount at home. My father did not allow me to date casually. I was allowed to go to major events like a prom or a concert with a boy who had been properly screened. There was such a boy in my life, a neighbor who wanted to be a Baptist missionary and was practicing his anthropological skills on my family. If I was desperate to go somewhere and needed a date, I'd resort to Gary. This is the type of religious nut that Gary was: when the school bus did not show up one day, he put his hands over his face and prayed to Christ to get us a way to get to school. Within ten minutes a mother in a station wagon, on her way to town, stopped to ask why we weren't in school. Gary informed her that the Lord had sent her just in time to find us a way to get there in time for roll call. He assumed that I was impressed. Gary was even good-looking in a bland sort of way, but he kissed me with his lips tightly pressed together. I think Gary probably ended up marrying a native woman from wherever he may have gone to preach the Gospel according to Paul. She probably believes that all white men pray to God for transportation and kiss with their mouths closed. But it was Ted's mouth, his whole beautiful self, that concerned me in those days. I knew my father would say no to our date, but I planned to run away from home if necessary. I told my mother how important this date was. I cajoled and pleaded with her from Sunday to Wednesday. She listened to my arguments and must have heard the note of desperation in my voice. She said very gently to me: "You better be ready for disappointment." I did not ask what she meant. I did not want her fears for me to taint my happiness. I asked her to tell my father about my date. Thursday at breakfast my father looked at me across the table with his eyebrows together. My mother looked at him with her mouth set in a straight line. I looked down at my bowl of cereal. Nobody said anything. Friday I tried on every dress in my closet. Ted would be picking me up at six on Saturday: dinner and then the sock hop at school. Friday night I was in my room doing my nails or something else in preparation for Saturday (I know I groomed myself nonstop all week) when the telephone rang. I ran to get it. It was Ted. His voice sounded funny when he said my name, so funny that I felt compelled to ask: "Is something wrong?" Ted blurted it all out without a preamble. His father had asked who he was going out with. Ted had told him my name. "Ortiz? That's Spanish, isn't it?" the father had asked. Ted had told him yes, then shown him my picture in the yearbook. Ted's father had shaken his head. No. Ted would not be taking me out. Ted's father had known Puerto Ricans in the army. He had lived in New York City while studying architecture and had seen how the spics lived. Like rats. Ted repeated his father's words to me as if I should understand *his* predicament when I heard why he was breaking our date. I don't remember what I said before hanging up. I do recall the darkness of my room that sleepless night and the heaviness of my blanket in which I wrapped myself like a shroud. And I remember my parents' respect for my pain and their gentleness toward me that weekend. My mother did not say "I warned you," and I was grateful for her understanding silence.

In college, I suddenly became an "exotic" woman to the men who had survived the popularity wars in high school, who were now practicing to be worldly: they had to act liberal in their politics, in their lifestyles, and in the women they went out with. I dated heavily for a while, then married young. I had discovered that I needed stability more than social life. I had brains for sure and some talent in writing. These facts were a constant in my life. My skin color, my size, and my appearance were variables—things that were judged according to my current self-image, the aesthetic values of the times, the places I was in, and the people I met. My studies, later my writing, the respect of people who saw me as an individual person they cared about, these were the criteria for my sense of self-worth that I would concentrate on in my adult life.

LANGSTON HUGHES

Langston Hughes (1902–1967) was born in Missouri to a prominent African American family. He attended Columbia University as an engineering major but dropped out after his first year to pursue his literary aspirations, later graduating from Lincoln University. Spurred by the flourishing of black artists during the Harlem Renaissance, Hughes found a distinctive voice in the culture of African American experience. Best known for his poetry, Hughes also wrote fiction, essays, plays, children's books, and several volumes of autobiography.

Salvation

In "Salvation," Hughes describes an incident from his youth that had a decisive impact on his view of the world. In the span of just a few paragraphs, Hughes tells a story of faith and doubt, of belief and disbelief. The essay's paradoxical opening establishes a tension that culminates in an ironic reversal of expectations for the reader and a life-altering realization for Hughes.

1 I was saved from sin when I was going on thirteen. But not really saved. It happened like this. There was a big revival at my Auntie Reed's church. Every night for weeks there had been much preaching, singing, praying, and shouting, and some very hardened sinners had been brought to Christ, and the membership of the church had grown by leaps and bounds. Then just before the revival ended, they held a special meeting for children, "to bring the young lambs to the fold." My aunt spoke of it for days ahead. That night I was escorted to the front row and placed on the mourners' bench with all the other young sinners, who had not yet been brought to Jesus.

My aunt told me that when you were saved you saw a light, and something happened to you inside! And Jesus came into your life! And God was with you from then on! She said you could see and hear and feel Jesus in your soul. I believed her. I had heard a great many old people say the same thing and it seemed to me they ought to know. So I sat there calmly in the hot, crowded church, waiting for Jesus to come to me.

The preacher preached a wonderful rhythmical sermon, all moans and shouts and lonely cries and dire pictures of hell, and then he sang a song about the ninety and nine safe in the fold, but one little lamb was left out in the cold. Then he said: "Won't you come? Won't you come to Jesus? Young lambs, won't you come?" And he held out his arms to all us young sinners there on the mourners' bench. And the little girls cried. And some of them jumped up and went to Jesus right away. But most of us just sat there.

A great many old people came and knelt around us and prayed, old women with jet-black faces and braided hair, old men with work-gnarled hands. And the church sang a song about the lower lights are burning, some poor sinners to be saved. And the whole building rocked with prayer and song.

Still I kept waiting to *see* Jesus.

Finally all the young people had gone to the altar and were saved, but one boy and me. He was a rounder's son named Westley. Westley and I were surrounded by sisters and deacons praying. It was very hot in the church, and getting late now. Finally Westley said to me in a whisper: "God damn! I'm tired o' sitting here. Let's get up and be saved." So he got up and was saved.

Then I was left all alone on the mourners' bench. My aunt came and knelt at my knees and cried, while prayers and songs swirled all around me in the little church. The whole congregation prayed for me alone, in a mighty wail of moans and voices. And I kept waiting serenely for Jesus, waiting, waiting—but he didn't come. I wanted to see him, but nothing happened to me. Nothing! I wanted something to happen to me, but nothing happened.

I heard the songs and the minister saying: "Why don't you come? My dear child, why don't you come to Jesus? Jesus is waiting for you. He wants you. Why don't you come? Sister Reed, what is this child's name?"

"Langston," my aunt sobbed.

¹⁰ "Langston, why don't you come? Why don't you come and be saved? Oh, Lamb of God! Why don't you come?"

Now it was really getting late. I began to be ashamed of myself, holding everything up so long. I began to wonder what God thought about Westley, who certainly hadn't seen Jesus either, but who was now sitting proudly on the platform, swinging his knickerbockered legs and grinning down at me, surrounded by deacons and old women on their knees praying. God had not struck Westley dead for taking his name in vain or for lying in the temple. So I decided that maybe to save further trouble, I'd better lie, too, and say that Jesus had come, and get up and be saved.

So I got up.

Suddenly the whole room broke into a sea of shouting, as they saw me rise. Waves of rejoicing swept the place. Women leaped in the air. My aunt threw her arms around me. The minister took me by the hand and led me to the platform.

When things quieted down, in a hushed silence, punctuated by a few ecstatic "Amens," all the new young lambs were blessed in the name of God. Then joyous singing filled the room.

That night, for the last time in my life but one—for ¹⁵ I was a big boy twelve years old—I cried. I cried, in bed alone, and couldn't stop. I buried my head under the quilts, but my aunt heard me. She woke up and told my uncle I was crying because the Holy Ghost had come into my life, and because I had seen Jesus. But I was really crying because I couldn't bear to tell her that I had lied, that I had deceived everybody in the church, and I hadn't seen Jesus, and that now I didn't believe there was a Jesus any more, since he didn't come to help me.

Reading and Thinking

1. Why do you think Hughes entitles his essay "Salvation"? In what sense is the essay about and not about salvation—and salvation from what?

2. Why do you think Hughes begins the piece as he does, with three very short sentences? Explain the point and the effect of each of these sentences.

3. What do you think is Hughes's main idea in "Salvation"? Where is this idea conveyed most clearly and forcefully? Explain.

4. Besides narration, what other patterns does Hughes employ? Where, and to what effect?

Thinking and Writing

1. Write an analysis of Hughes's essay, focusing on how he uses descriptive details, including dialogue, to convey the feeling, flavor, and force of southern religious Protestant fundamentalism.

2. To what extent does Hughes's essay deal with issues of conformity and deception? How does Hughes link conformity and deception with religious belief? Explain.

3. Think about your own experience (or lack of experience) with religion. Write an essay that explores your religious background. You may wish to tell a story or two to convey an idea about this experience, or you may choose to explain why you are or are not religious.

Creating Occasions

Create your own interactive Occasion on *Comp21* using the textual, visual, and video libraries, as well as the Explicator analysis tools. From the main menu, choose "Build Your Own Occasion for Writing."

ZORA NEALE HURSTON

Zora Neale Hurston (1903–1960) was born in Eatonville, Florida, where she spent her early years. She attended Howard University and moved to New York City in 1925, becoming involved in cultural activities in Harlem. There she met Langston Hughes, who, like Hurston, was interested in the folk elements of African American culture, particularly as reflected in southern life. Hurston wrote books based on her study of folkways, including *Mules and Men* (1935). She also wrote novels, the best known of which is *Their Eyes Were Watching God* (1937). These and other works, including her essays, were rediscovered as a result of the women's movement and an upsurge in the study of African American literature.

How It Feels to Be Colored Me

In "How It Feels to Be Colored Me," Hurston discusses her blackness as an aspect of her cultural, social, and personal identity. The essay's tone is confident and upbeat as Hurston celebrates herself as a modern African American woman who knows her worth even when others do not.

1   I am colored but I offer nothing in the way of extenuating circumstances except the fact that I am the only Negro in the United States whose grandfather on the mother's side was *not* an Indian chief.

I remember the very day that I became colored. Up to my thirteenth year I lived in the little Negro town of Eatonville, Florida. It is exclusively a colored town. The only white people I knew passed through the town going to or coming from Orlando. The native whites rode dusty horses, the Northern tourists chugged down the sandy village road in automobiles. The town knew the Southerners and never stopped cane chewing when they passed. But the Northerners were something else again. They were peered at cautiously from behind curtains by the timid. The more venturesome would come out on the porch to watch them go past and got just as much pleasure out of the tourists as the tourists got out of the village.

The front porch might seem a daring place for the rest of the town, but it was a gallery seat for me. My favorite place was atop the gate-post. Proscenium box for a born first-nighter. Not only did I enjoy the show, but I didn't mind the actors knowing that I liked it. I usually spoke to them in passing. I'd wave at them and when they returned my salute, I would say something like this: "Howdy-do-well-I-thank-you-where-you-goin'?" Usually automobile or the horse paused at this, and after a queer exchange of compliments, I would probably "go a piece of the way" with them, as we say in farthest Florida. If one of my family happened to come to the front in time to see me, of course negotiations would be rudely broken off. But even so, it is clear that I was the first "welcome-to-our-state" Floridian, and I hope the Miami Chamber of Commerce will please take notice.

During this period, white people differed from colored to me only in that they rode through town and never lived there. They liked to hear me "speak pieces" and sing and wanted to see me dance the parse-me-la, and gave me generously of their small silver for doing these things, which seemed strange to me for I wanted to do them so much that I needed bribing to stop. Only they didn't know it. The colored people gave no dimes. They deplored any joyful tendencies in me, but I was their Zora nevertheless. I belonged to them, to the nearby hotels, to the country—everybody's Zora.

5   But changes came in the family when I was thirteen, and I was sent to school in Jacksonville. I left Eatonville, the town of the oleanders, as Zora. When I disembarked from the river-boat at Jacksonville, she

was no more. It seemed that I had suffered a sea change. I was not Zora of Orange County any more. I was now a little colored girl. I found it out in certain ways. In my heart as well as in the mirror, I became a fast brown—warranted not to rub nor run.

But I am not tragically colored. There is no great sorrow dammed up in my soul, nor lurking behind my eyes. I do not mind at all. I do not belong to the sobbing school of Negrohood who hold that nature somehow has given them a lowdown dirty deal and whose feelings are all hurt about it. Even in the helter-skelter skirmish that is my life, I have seen that the world is to the strong regardless of a little pigmentation more or less. No, I do not weep at the world—I am too busy sharpening my oyster knife.

Someone is always at my elbow reminding me that I am the granddaughter of slaves. It fails to register depression with me. Slavery is sixty years in the past. The operation was successful and the patient is doing well, thank you. The terrible struggle that made me an American out of a potential slave said "On the line!" The Reconstruction said "Get set!"; and the generation before said "Go!" I am off to a flying start and I must not halt in the stretch to look behind and weep. Slavery is the price I paid for civilization, and the choice was not with me. It is a bully adventure and worth all that I have paid through my ancestors for it. No one on earth ever had a greater chance for glory. The world to be won and nothing to be lost. It is thrilling to think—to know that for any act of mine, I shall get twice as much praise or twice as much blame. It is quite exciting to hold the center of the national stage, with the spectators not knowing whether to laugh or to weep.

The position of my white neighbor is much more difficult. No brown specter pulls up a chair beside me when I sit down to eat. No dark ghost thrusts its leg against mine in bed. The game of keeping what one has is never so exciting as the game of getting.

I do not always feel colored. Even now I often achieve the unconscious Zora of Eatonville before the Hegira. I feel most colored when I am thrown against a sharp white background.

For instance at Barnard. "Beside the waters of the Hudson" I feel my race. Among the thousand white persons, I am a dark rock surged upon, and overswept, but through it all, I remain myself. When covered by the waters, I am; and the ebb but reveals me again.

Sometimes it is the other way around. A white person is set down in our midst, but the contrast is just as sharp for me. For instance, when I sit in the drafty basement that is The New World Cabaret with a white person, my color comes. We enter chatting about any little nothing that we have in common and are seated by the jazz waiters. In the abrupt way that jazz orchestras have, this one plunges into a number. It loses no time in circumlocutions, but gets right down to business. It constricts the thorax and splits the heart with its tempo and narcotic harmonies. This orchestra grows rambunctious, rears on its hind legs and attacks the tonal veil with primitive fury, rending it, clawing it until it breaks through to the jungle beyond. I follow those heathen—follow them exultingly. I dance wildly inside myself; I yell within, I whoop; I shake my assegai above my head, I hurl it true to the mark *yeeeeooww!* I am in the jungle and living in the jungle way. My face is painted red and yellow and my body is painted blue. My pulse is throbbing like a war drum. I want to slaughter something—give pain, give death to what, I do not know. But the piece ends. The men of the orchestra wipe their lips and rest their fingers. I creep back slowly to the veneer we call civilization with the last tone and find the white friend sitting motionless in his seat, smoking calmly.

"Good music they have here," he remarks, drumming the table with his fingertips.

Music. The great blobs of purple and red emotion have not touched him. He has only heard what I felt. He is far away and I see him but dimly across the ocean and the continent that have fallen between us. He is so pale with his whiteness then and I am *so* colored.

At certain times I have no race, I am *me*. When I set my hat at a certain angle and saunter down Seventh Avenue, Harlem City, feeling as snooty as the lions in front of the Forty-Second Street Library, for instance. So far as my feelings are concerned, Peggy Hopkins Joyce on the Boule Mich with her gorgeous raiment, stately carriage, knees knocking together in a most

10

aristocratic manner, has nothing on me. The cosmic Zora emerges. I belong to no race nor time. I am the eternal feminine with its string of beads.

15   I have no separate feeling about being an American citizen and colored. I am merely a fragment of the Great Soul that surges within the boundaries. My country, right or wrong.

Sometimes, I feel discriminated against, but it does not make me angry. It merely astonishes me. How *can* any deny themselves the pleasure of my company? It's beyond me.

But in the main, I feel like a brown bag of miscellany propped against a wall. Against a wall in company with other bags, white, red and yellow. Pour out the contents, and there is discovered a jumble of small things priceless and worthless. A first-water diamond, an empty spool, bits of broken glass, lengths of string, a key to a door long since crumbled away, a rusty knife-blade, old shoes saved for a road that never was and never will be, a nail bent under the weight of things too heavy for any nail, a dried flower or two still a little fragrant. In your hand is the brown bag. On the ground before you is the jumble it held—so much like the jumble in the bags, could they be emptied, that all might be dumped in a single heap and the bags refilled without altering the content of any greatly. A bit of colored glass more or less would not matter. Perhaps that is how the Great Stuffer of Bags filled them in the first place—who knows?

Reading and Thinking

1. Do you think that Hurston's experience and her attitude toward her experience are characteristic of most people? Of most people of color? Why or why not?

2. How does Hurston organize her essay? Identify the focus and central point of each part. Explain how the four parts fit together to make a unified whole—the full essay. What does each part contribute toward the whole essay?

3. Identify two key images that Hurston uses to convey her feelings about herself. Explain how each image characterizes Hurston's perspective.

4. Identify at least three patterns that Hurston employs. Explain how she uses each strategy and the extent to which it is successful in enabling her to convey her feelings and ideas.

Thinking and Writing

1. What does Hurston see as the advantages of being black and a woman? To what extent can Hurston's celebration of herself as a black woman be applied by any reader regardless of race, ethnicity, or gender? Explain.

2. Write an essay in which you explore your identity in terms of gender, race, class, or ethnicity. Try to account for times when you feel this aspect of your identity most acutely and times when it seems invisible or less important.

3. Discuss Hurston's presentation of herself as a black woman in conjunction with the images she uses to convey her sense of herself. Analyze those images and connect them to explain how they yield a self portrait of Zora Neale Hurston.

4. Do some research on Hurston and on the Harlem Renaissance. Write a short piece putting Hurston's essay into the context of the Harlem Renaissance.

Creating Occasions

Create your own interactive Occasion on *Comp21* using the textual, visual, and video libraries, as well as the Explicator analysis tools. From the main menu, choose "Build Your Own Occasion for Writing."

PICO IYER

Pico Iyer (b. 1957) was born in England to Indian parents, grew up in California, attended Eton and Oxford, and has lived in suburban Japan. Iyer is the author of half a dozen books along with essays that have appeared in *Time, Harper's, The New Yorker, The New York Review of Books,* and many other publications around the world. He has described himself as a "multinational soul on a multicultural globe," and his writing frequently probes the meaning of personal identity in a global context. His most recent book is *Global Soul: Jet Lag, Shopping Malls, and the Search for Home.*

Why We Travel

The title, "Why We Travel," explains the main thrust of Iyer's essay. Indeed, the entire piece is a reflection on travel—its causes and its consequences. Iyer discusses how he interacts with the places that he travels, and how those places affect him as well. Notice as you read where Iyer uses the third person plural pronoun, "we," and where he speaks only of himself. Notice as well the construction of his essay—the order of the particular subjects he discusses.

1   We travel, initially, to lose ourselves; and we travel, next, to find ourselves. We travel to open our hearts and eyes and learn more about the world than our newspapers will accommodate. We travel to bring what little we can, in our ignorance and knowledge, to those parts of the globe whose riches are differently dispersed. And we travel, in essence, to become young fools again—to slow time down and get taken in, and fall in love once more. The beauty of this whole process was best described, perhaps, before people even took to frequent flying, by George Santayana in his lapidary essay "The Philosophy of Travel." We "need sometimes," the Harvard philosopher wrote, "to escape into open solitudes, into aimlessness, into the moral holiday of running some pure hazard, in order to sharpen the edge of life, to taste hardship, and to be compelled to work desperately for a moment at no matter what."

I like that stress on work, since never more than on the road are we shown how proportional our blessings are to the difficulty that precedes them; and I like the stress on a holiday that's "moral" since we fall into our ethical habits as easily as into our beds at night. Few of us ever forget the connection between "travel" and "travail," and I know that I travel in large part in search of hardship—both my own, which I want to feel, and others', which I need to see. Travel in that sense guides us toward a better balance of wisdom and compassion—of seeing the world clearly, and yet feeling it truly. For seeing without feeling can obviously be uncaring; while feeling without seeing can be blind.

Yet for me the first great joy of traveling is simply the luxury of leaving all my beliefs and certainties at home, and seeing everything I thought I knew in a different light, and from a crooked angle. In that regard, even a Kentucky Fried Chicken outlet (in Beijing) or a scratchy revival showing *Wild Orchids* (on the Champs-Elysées) can be both novelty and revelation: In China, after all, people will pay a whole week's wages to eat with Colonel Sanders, and in Paris, Mickey Rourke is regarded as the greatest actor since Jerry Lewis.

If a Mongolian restaurant seems exotic to us in Evanston, Illinois, it only follows that a McDonald's would seem equally exotic in Ulan Bator—or, at least, equally far from everything expected. Though it's fashionable nowadays to draw a distinction between those who leave their assumptions at home and those who don't: Among those who don't, a tourist is just someone who complains, "Nothing here is the way it is at home," while a traveler is one who grumbles, "Everything here is the same as it is in Cairo—or Cuzco or Kathmandu." It's all very much the same.

5   But for the rest of us, the sovereign freedom of traveling comes from the fact that it whirls you around and turns you upside down, and stands everything you took for granted on its head. If a diploma can famously be a passport (to a journey through hard realism), a passport can be a diploma (for a crash course in cultural relativism). And the first lesson we learn on the road, whether we like it or not, is how provisional and provincial are the things we imagine to be universal. When you go to North Korea, for example, you really do feel as if you've landed on a different planet—and the North Koreans doubtless feel that they're being visited by an extraterrestrial too (or else they simply assume that you, as they do, receive orders every morning from the Central Committee on what clothes to wear to what route to use when walking to work, and you, as they do, have loudspeakers in your bedroom broadcasting propaganda every morning at dawn, and you, as they do, have your radios fixed so as to receive only a single channel).

    We travel, then, in part just to shake up our complacencies by seeing all the moral and political urgencies, the life-and-death dilemmas, that we seldom have to face at home. And we travel to fill in the gaps left by tomorrow's headlines: When you drive down the streets of Port-au-Prince, for example, where there is almost no paving and women relieve themselves next to mountains of trash, your notions of the Internet and a "one world order" grow usefully revised. Travel is the best way we have of rescuing the humanity of places, and saving them from abstraction and ideology.

    And in the process, we also get saved from abstraction ourselves, and come to see how much we can bring to the places we visit, and how much we can become a kind of carrier pigeon—an anti-Federal Express, if you like—in transporting back and forth what every culture needs. I find that I always take Michael Jordan posters to Kyoto and bring woven ikebana baskets back to California; I invariably travel to Cuba with a suitcase piled high with bottles of Tylenol and bars of soap and come back with one piled high with salsa tapes, and hopes, and letters to long-lost brothers.

    But more significantly, we carry values and beliefs and news to the places we go, and in many parts of the world, we become walking video screens and living newspapers, the only channels that can take people out of the censored limits of their homelands. In closed or impoverished places, like Pagan or Lhasa or Havana, we are the eyes and ears of the people we meet, their only contact with the world outside and, very often, the closest, quite literally, they will ever come to Michael Jackson or Bill Clinton. Not the least of the challenges of travel, therefore, is learning how to import—and export—dreams with tenderness.

    By now all of us have heard (too often) the old Proust line about how the real voyage of discovery consists not in seeing new places but in seeing with new eyes. Yet one of the subtler beauties of travel is that it enables you to bring new eyes to the people you encounter. Thus even as holidays help you appreciate your own home more—not least by seeing it through a distant admirer's eyes—they help bring newly appreciative—distant—eyes to the places you visit. You can teach them what they have to celebrate as much as you celebrate what they have to teach. This, I think, is how tourism, which so obviously destroys cultures, can also resuscitate or revive them, how it has created new "traditional" dances in Bali, and caused craftsmen in India to pay new attention to their works. If the first thing we can bring the Cubans is a real and balanced sense of what contemporary America is like, the second—and perhaps more important—thing we can bring them is a fresh and renewed sense of how special are the warmth and beauty of their country, for those who can compare it with other places around the globe.

    Thus travel spins us round in two ways at once: It shows us the sights and values and issues that we might ordinarily ignore; but it also, and more deeply, shows us all the parts of ourselves that might otherwise grow rusty. For in traveling to a foreign place, we inevitably travel to moods and states of mind and hidden inward passages that we'd otherwise seldom have cause to visit.

On the most basic level, when I'm in Thailand, though a teetotaler who usually goes to bed at 9:00 P.M., I stay up till dawn in the local bars; and in Tibet, though not a real Buddhist, I spend days on end in temples, listening to the chants of sutras. I go to Iceland to visit the lunar spaces within me, and, in the uncanny quietude and emptiness of that vast and treeless world, to tap parts of myself generally obscured by chatter and routine.

We travel, then, in search of both self and anonymity—and, of course, in finding the one we apprehend the other. Abroad, we are wonderfully free of caste and job and standing; we are, as Hazlitt puts it, just the "gentlemen in the parlor," and people cannot put a name or tag to us. And precisely because we are clarified in this way, and freed of inessential labels, we have the opportunity to come into contact with more essential parts of ourselves (which may begin to explain why we may feel most alive when far from home).

Abroad is the place where we stay up late, follow impulse, and find ourselves as wide open as when we are in love. We live without a past or future, for a moment at least, and are ourselves up for grabs and open to interpretation. We even may become mysterious—to others, at first, and sometimes to ourselves—and, as no less a dignitary than Oliver Cromwell once noted, "A man never goes so far as when he doesn't know where he is going."

There are, of course, great dangers to this, as to every kind of freedom, but the great promise of it is that, traveling, we are born again, and able to return at moments to a younger and a more open kind of self. Traveling is a way to reverse time, to a small extent, and make a day last a year—or at least forty-five hours—and traveling is an easy way of surrounding ourselves, as in childhood, with what we cannot understand. Language facilitates this cracking open, for when we go to France, we often migrate to French and the more child-like self, simple and polite, that speaking a foreign language educes. Even when I'm not speaking pidgin English in Hanoi, I'm simplified in a positive way, and concerned not with expressing myself but simply making sense.

So, travel, for many of us, is a quest for not just the unknown but the unknowing; I, at least, travel in search of an innocent eye that can return me to a more innocent self. I tend to believe more abroad than I do at home (which, though treacherous again, can at least help me to extend my vision), and I tend to be more easily excited abroad, and even kinder. And since no one I meet can "place" me—no one can fix me in my résumé—I can remake myself for better, as well as, of course, for worse (if travel is notoriously a cradle for false identities, it can also, at its best, be a crucible for truer ones). In this way, travel can be a kind of monasticism on the move: On the road, we often live more simply (even when staying in a luxury hotel), with no more possessions than we can carry, and surrendering ourselves to chance.

And that is why many of us travel in search not of answers but of better questions. I, like many people, tend to ask questions of the places I visit, and relish most the ones that ask the most searching question back of me. In Paraguay, for example, where one car in every two is stolen, and two-thirds of the goods on sale are smuggled, I have to rethink my every Californian assumption. And in Thailand, where many young women give up their bodies in order to protect their families—to become better Buddhists—I have to question my own too-ready judgments.

"The ideal travel book," Christopher Isherwood once said, "should be perhaps a little like a crime story in which you're in search of something." And it's the best kind of something, I would add, if it's one that you can never quite find.

I remember, in fact, after my first trips to Southeast Asia, more than a decade ago, how I would come back to my apartment in New York and lie in my bed, kept up by something more than jet lag, playing back in my memory, over and over, all that I had experienced, and paging wistfully through my photographs and reading and rereading my diaries, as if to extract some mystery from them. Anyone witnessing this strange scene would have drawn the right conclusion: I was in love.

For if every true love affair can feel like a journey to a foreign country, when you can't quite speak the language and you don't know where you're going and you're pulled ever deeper into the inviting darkness, every trip to a foreign country can be a love affair, where you're left puzzling over who you are and whom you've fallen in love with. All the great travel books are love stories, by some reckoning—from the *Odyssey* and the *Aeneid* to the *Divine Comedy* and the New Testament—and all good trips are, like love, about being carried out of yourself and deposited in the midst of terror and wonder.

And what this metaphor also brings home to us is that all travel is a two-way transaction, as we too easily forget, and if warfare is one model of the meeting of nations, romance is another. For what we all too often ignore when we go abroad is that we are objects of scrutiny as much as the people we scrutinize, and we are being consumed by the cultures we consume, as much on the road as when we are at home. At the very least, we are objects of speculation (and even desire) who can seem as exotic to the people around us as they do to us.

We are the comic props in Japanese home movies, the oddities in Malian anecdotes, and the fall guys in Chinese jokes; we are the moving postcards or bizarre *objets trouvés* that villagers in Peru will later tell their friends about. If travel is about the meeting of realities, it is no less about the mating of illusions: You give me my dreamed-of vision of Tibet, and I'll give you your wished-for California. And in truth, many of us, even (or especially) the ones who are fleeing America abroad, will get taken, willy-nilly, as symbols of the American Dream.

That, in fact, is perhaps the most central and most wrenching of the questions travel proposes to us: how to respond to the dream that people tender to you? Do you encourage their notions of a Land of Milk and Honey across the horizon, even if it is the same land you've abandoned? Or do you try to dampen their enthusiasm for a place that exists only in the mind? To quicken their dreams may, after all, be to matchmake them with an illusion; yet to dash them may be to strip them of the one possession that sustains them in adversity.

That whole complex interaction—not unlike the dilemmas we face with those we love (how do we balance truthfulness and tact?)—is partly the reason why so many of the great travel writers, by nature, are enthusiasts: not just Pierre Loti, who famously, infamously, fell in love wherever he alighted (an archetypal sailor leaving offspring in the form of *Madame Butterfly* myths), but also Henry Miller, D. H. Lawrence, and Graham Greene, all of whom bore out of the hidden truth that we are optimists abroad as readily as pessimists at home. None of them was by any means blind to the deficiencies of the places around them, but all, having chosen to go there, chose to find something to admire.

All, in that sense, believed in "being moved" as one of the points of taking trips, and being "transported" by private as well as public means; all saw that "ecstasy" ("ex-stasis") tells us that our highest moments come when we're not stationary, and that epiphany can follow movement as much as it precipitates it. I remember once asking the great travel writer Norman Lewis if he'd ever be interested in writing on apartheid South Africa. He looked at me, astonished. "To write well about a thing," he said, "I've got to like it!"

At the same time, as all this is intrinsic to travel, from Ovid to O'Rourke, travel itself is changing as the world does, and with it, the mandate of the travel writer. It's not enough to go to the ends of the earth these days (not least because the ends of the earth are often coming to you); and where a writer like Jan Morris could, a few years ago, achieve something miraculous simply by voyaging to all the great cities of the globe, now anyone with a Visa card can do that. So where Morris, in effect, was chronicling the last days of the empire, a younger travel writer is in a better position to chart the first days of a new empire, postnational, global, mobile, and yet as diligent as the Raj in transporting its props and its values around the world.

In the mid-nineteenth century, the British famously sent the Bible and Shakespeare and cricket round the world; now a more international kind of empire is sending Madonna and the Simpsons and Brad Pitt. And the way in which each culture takes in this common pool of references tells you as much about them as their indigenous products might. Madonna in an Islamic country, after all, sounds radically different from Madonna in a Confucian one, and neither begins to mean the same as Madonna on East 14th Street. When you go to a McDonald's outlet in Kyoto, you will find Teriyaki McBurgers and Bacon Potato Pies. The place mats offer maps of the great temples of the city, and the posters all around broadcast the wonders of San Francisco. And—most crucial of all—the young people eating their Big Macs, with baseball caps worn backward and tight 501 jeans, are still utterly and inalienably Japanese in the way they move, they nod, they sip their oolong teas—and never to be mistaken for the patrons of a McDonald's outlet in Rio, Morocco, or Managua. These days a whole new realm of exotica arises out of the way one culture colors and appropriates the products of another.

The other factor complicating and exciting all of this is people, who are, more and more, themselves as many-tongued and mongrel as cities like Sydney or Toronto or Hong Kong. I am in many ways an increasingly typical specimen, if only because I was born, as the son of Indian parents, in England, moved to America at seven, and cannot really call myself an Indian, an American, or an Englishman. I was, in short, a traveler at birth, for whom even a visit to the candy store was a trip through a foreign world where no one I saw quite matched my parents' inheritance, or my own. And though some of this is involuntary and tragic—the number of refugees in the world, which came to just 2.5 million in 1970, is now at least 27.4 million—it does involve, for some of us, the chance to be transnational in a happier sense, able to adapt to anywhere, used to being outsiders everywhere, and forced to fashion our own rigorous sense of home. (And if nowhere is quite home, we can be optimists everywhere.)

Besides, even those who don't move around the world find the world moving more and more around them. Walk just six blocks in Queens or Berkeley, and you're traveling through several cultures in as many minutes; get into a cab outside the White House, and you're often in a piece of Addis Ababa. And technology too compounds this (sometimes deceptive) sense of availability, so that many people feel they can travel around the world without leaving the room—through cyberspace or CD-ROMs, videos and virtual travel. There are many challenges in this, of course, in what it says about essential notions of family and community and loyalty, and in the worry that air-conditioned, purely synthetic versions of places may replace the real thing—not to mention the fact that the world seems increasingly in flux, a moving target quicker than our

notions of it. But there is, for the traveler at least, the sense that learning about home and learning about a foreign world can be one and the same thing.

All of us feel this from the cradle, and know, in some sense, that all the significant movement we ever take is internal. We travel when we see a movie, strike up a new friendship, get held up. Novels are often journeys as much as travel books are fictions; and though this has been true since at least as long ago as Sir John Mandeville's colorful fourteenth-century accounts of a Far East he'd never visited, it's an even more shadowy distinction now, as genre distinctions join other borders in collapsing.

In Mary Morris's *House Arrest,* a thinly disguised account of Castro's Cuba, the novelist reiterates, on the copyright pages, "All dialogue is invented. Isabella, her family, the inhabitants, and even *la isla* itself are creations of the author's imagination." On page 172, however, we read, "*La isla,* of course does exist. Don't let anyone fool you about that. It just feels as if it doesn't. But it does." No wonder the travel-writer narrator—a fictional construct (or not)?—confesses to devoting her travel magazine column to places that never existed. "Erewhon," after all, the undiscovered land in Samuel Butler's great travel novel, is just "nowhere" rearranged.

Travel, then, is a voyage into that famously subjective zone, the imagination, and what the traveler brings back—and has to be—an ineffable compound of himself and the place, what's really there and what's only in him. Thus Bruce Chatwin's books seem to dance around the distinction between fact and fancy. V. S. Naipaul's recent book *A Way in the World* was published as a nonfictional "series" in England and a "novel" in the United States. And when some of the stories in Paul Theroux's half-invented memoir, *My Other Life,* were published in *The New Yorker,* they were slyly categorized as "Fact and Fiction."

And since travel is, in a sense, about the conspiracy of perception and imagination, the two great travel writers, for me, to whom I constantly return are Emerson and Thoreau (the one who famously advised that "traveling is a fool's paradise," and the other who "traveled a good deal in Concord"). Both of them insist on the fact that reality is our creation, and that we invent the places we see as much as we do the books that we read. What we find outside ourselves has to be inside ourselves for us to find it. Or, as Sir Thomas Browne sagely put it, "We carry within us the wonders we seek without us. There is Africa and her prodigies in us."

So, if more and more of us have to carry our sense of home inside us, we also—Emerson and Thoreau remind us—have to carry with us our sense of destination. The most valuable Pacifics we explore will always be the vast expanses within us, and the most important Northwest Crossings the thresholds we cross in the heart. The virtue of finding a gilded pavilion in Kyoto is that it allows you to take back a more lasting, private Golden Temple to your office in Rockefeller Center.

And even as the world seems to grow more exhausted, our travels do not, and some of the finest travel books in recent years have been those that undertake a parallel journey, matching the physical steps of a pilgrimage with the metaphysical steps of a questioning (as in Peter Matthiessen's great *The Snow Leopard*), or chronicling a trip to the farthest reaches of hu-man strangeness (as in Oliver Sack's *Island of the Colorblind,* which features a journey not just to a remote atoll in the Pacific but to a realm where people actually see light differently). The most distant shores, we are constantly reminded, lie within the person asleep at our side.

So travel, at heart, is just a quick way of keeping our minds mobile and awake. As Santayana, the heir to Emerson and Thoreau with whom I began, wrote, "There is wisdom in turning as often as possible from the familiar to the unfamiliar; it keeps the mind nimble; it kills prejudice, and it fosters humor." Romantic poets inaugurated an era of travel because they were the great apostles of open eyes. Buddhist monks are often vagabonds, in part because they believe in wakefulness. And if travel is like love, it is, in the end, mostly because it's a heightened state of awareness, in which we are mindful, receptive, undimmed by familiarity and ready to be transformed. That is why the best trips, like the best love affairs, never really end.

Reading and Thinking

1. Explain the paradox, or seeming contradiction, that opens Iyer's essay. What does it mean to say that we travel to "lose" ourselves? What does it mean to say that we travel to "find" ourselves? What do you think Iyer means by traveling to "slow time down"; to "get taken in"; to "fall in love again"?

2. Why does Iyer include a quotation from the American writer and philosopher, George Santayana? Explain each phrase of the Santayana quotation, but especially the notion of "sharpening the edge of life." How does Iyer himself play with and off the Santayana quotation?

3. What differences does Iyer identify between a "tourist" and a "traveler"? Why does he mention Kentucky Fried Chicken and the movie *Wild Orchids*?

4. What effects of travel does Iyer describe? Explain whether you agree with his ideas about the effects of travel on the traveler and the effects travelers have on the places they visit.

Thinking and Writing

1. Tell a story about an experience you have had while traveling. If you have not gone on a journey to an exciting, exotic, or distant location, you can write about a more local trip. Include something about the occasion, or background, of the trip, as well as its outcomes.

2. Write an essay about your attitude toward travel. Explain the reasons why you do or do not travel—or why you would prefer (or not prefer) to travel if it were up to you.

3. Write an essay in which you analyze the effects that travel has had on you—or the effects that you imagine it might have were you to begin traveling. Provide specific examples and details about particular places.

4. Use one of the following comments by Iyer as the starting point and basis for an essay on the value and values of travel:

   • "The first lesson we learn on the road . . . is how provisional and provincial are the things we imagine to be universal."

   • "Travel . . . shows us the parts of ourselves that might otherwise grow rusty."

   • "Every true love affair can feel like a journey to a foreign country."

   • "Many of us travel not in search of answers, but of better questions."

   • "Travel is, in a sense, about the conspiracy of perception and imagination."

Creating Occasions

Create your own interactive Occasion on *Comp21* using the textual, visual, and video libraries, as well as the Explicator analysis tools. From the main menu, choose "Build Your Own Occasion for Writing."

JAMAICA KINCAID

Jamaica Kincaid (b. 1949) grew up on the Caribbean island of Antigua, which was, at the time, a British colony. After graduating from high school, she was sent to New York to work as a nanny. After a series of odd jobs, Kincaid joined the staff of *Ingenue* magazine and went on to become a regular contributor to *The New Yorker*. Most of her book-length works, whether fiction or nonfiction, are largely autobiographical, often focusing on her childhood in Antigua. *Talk Stories*, her most recent book, collects profiles that originally appeared in *The New Yorker*.

On Seeing England for the First Time

In "On Seeing England for the First Time," Kincaid describes the influence England has had on her all her life. Kincaid contrasts England with Antigua, where she was born and grew up, by describing differences in food and clothes. Kincaid builds up her contrast and enlarges her theme of England's influence, invoking the names of the English kings in a paragraph that peaks powerfully with Kincaid's description of the pace of English life. Accumulating details that contrast the two countries' climates and topographies, she reveals just how different her Antiguan world is from that of England.

1   When I saw England for the first time, I was a child in school sitting at a desk. The England I was looking at was laid out on a map gently, beautifully, delicately, a very special jewel; it lay on a bed of sky blue—the background of the map—its yellow form mysterious, because though it looked like a leg of mutton, it could not really look like anything so familiar as a leg of mutton because it was England—with shadings of pink and green, unlike any shadings of pink and green I had seen before, squiggly veins of red running in every direction. England was a special jewel all right, and only special people got to wear it. The people who got to wear England were English people. They wore it well and they wore it everywhere: in jungles, in deserts, on plains, on top of the highest mountains, on all the oceans, on all the seas, in places where they were not welcome, in places they should not have been. When my teacher had pinned this map up on the blackboard, she said, "This is England"—and she said it with authority, seriousness, and adoration, and we all sat up. It was as if she had said, "This is Jerusalem, the place you will go to when you die but only if you have been good." We understood then—we were meant to understand then—that England was to be our source of myth and the source from which we got our sense of reality, our sense of what was meaningful, our sense of what was meaningless—and much about our own lives and much about the very idea of us headed that last list.

At the time I was a child sitting at my desk seeing England for the first time, I was already very familiar with the greatness of it. Each morning before I left for school, I ate a breakfast of half a grapefruit, and egg, bread and butter and a slice of cheese, and a cup of cocoa; or half a grapefruit, a bowl of oat porridge, bread and butter and a slice of cheese, and a cup of cocoa. The can of cocoa was often left on the table in front of me. It had written on it the name of the company, the year the company was established, and the words "Made in England." Those words, "Made in England," were written on the box the oats came in too. They would also have been written on the box the shoes I was wearing came in; a bolt of gray linen cloth lying on the shelf of a store from which my mother had bought three yards to make the uniform that I was wearing had written along its edge those three words. The shoes I wore were made in England; so were my socks and cotton undergarments and the satin ribbons I wore tied at the end of two plaits of my hair. My father, who might have sat next to me at breakfast, was a carpenter and cabinet maker. The shoes he wore to work would have been made in England, as were his khaki shirt and trousers, his underpants and undershirt, his socks and brown felt hat. Felt was not the proper material from which a hat that was expected to provide shade from the hot sun should be made, but my father must have seen and admired a picture of an Englishman wearing such a hat in England, and this picture that he saw must have been so compelling that it caused him to wear the wrong hat for a hot climate most of his long life. And this hat—a brown felt hat—became so central to his character that it was the first thing he put on in the morning as he stepped out of bed and the last thing he took off before he stepped back into bed at night. As we sat at breakfast a car might go by. The car, a Hillman or a Zephyr, was made in England. The very idea of the meal itself, breakfast, and its substantial quality and quantity was an idea from England; we somehow knew that in England they began the day with this meal called breakfast and a proper breakfast was a big breakfast. No one I knew liked eating so much food so early in the day; it made us feel sleepy, tired. But this breakfast business was Made in England like almost everything else that surrounded us, the exceptions being the sea, the sky, and the air we breathed.

At the time I saw this map—seeing England for the first time—I did not say to myself, "Ah, so that's what it looks like," because there was no longing in me to put a shape to those three words that ran through every part of my life, no matter how small; for me to have had such a longing would have meant that I lived in a certain atmosphere, an atmosphere in which those three words were felt as a burden. But I did not live in such an atmosphere. My father's brown felt hat would develop a hole in its crown, the lining would separate from the hat itself, and six weeks before he thought that he could not be seen wearing it—he was a very vain man—he would order another hat from England. And my mother taught me to eat my food in the English way: the knife in the right hand, the fork in the left, my elbows held still close to my side, the food carefully balanced on my fork and then brought up to my mouth. When I had finally mastered it, I overheard her saying to a friend, "Did you see how nicely she can eat?" But I knew then that I enjoyed my food more when I ate it with my bare hands, and I continued to do so when she wasn't looking. And when my teacher showed us the map, she asked us to study it carefully, because no test we would ever take would be complete without this statement: "Draw a map of England."

I did not know then that the statement "Draw a map of England" was something far worse than a declaration of war, for in fact a flat-out declaration of war would have put me on alert, and again in fact, there was no need for war—I had long ago been conquered. I did not know then that this statement was part of a process that would result in my erasure, not my physical erasure, but my erasure all the same. I did not know then that this statement was meant to make me feel in awe and small whenever I heard the word "England": awe at its existence, small because I was not from it. I did not know very much of anything then—certainly not what a blessing it was that I was unable to draw a map of England correctly.

After that there were many times of seeing England for the first time. I saw England in history. I knew the names of all the kings of England. I knew the names of their children, their wives, their disappointments, their triumphs, the names of people who betrayed them; I knew the dates on which they were born and the dates they died. I knew their conquests and was made to feel glad I figured in them; I knew their defeats. I knew the details of the year 1066 (the Battle of Hastings, the end of the reign of the Anglo-Saxon kings) before I knew the details of the year 1832 (the year slavery was abolished). It wasn't as bad as I make it sound now; it was worse. I did like so much hearing again and again how Alfred the Great, traveling in disguise, had been left to watch cakes, and because he wasn't used to this the cakes got burned, and Alfred burned his hands pulling them out of the fire, and the woman who had left him to watch the cakes screamed at him. I loved King Alfred. My grandfather was named after him; his son, my uncle, was named after King Alfred; my brother is named after King Alfred. And so there are three people in my family named after a man they have never met, a man who died over ten centuries ago. The first view I got of England then was not unlike the first view received by the person who named my grandfather.

This view, though—the naming of the kings, their deeds, their disappointments—was the vivid view, the forceful view. There were other views, subtler ones, softer, almost not there—but these were the ones that made the most lasting impression on me, these were the ones that made me really feel like nothing. "When morning touched the sky" was one phrase, for no morning touched the sky where I lived. The mornings where I lived came on abruptly, with a shock of heat and loud noises. "Evening approaches" was another, but the evenings where I lived did not approach; in fact, I had no evening—I had night and I had day and they came and went in a mechanical way: on, off; on, off. And then there were gentle mountains and low blue skies and moors over which people took walks for nothing but pleasure, when where I lived a walk was an act of labor, a burden, something only death or the automobile could relieve. And there were things that a small turn of a head could convey—entire worlds, whole lives would depend on this thing, a certain turn of a head. Everyday life could be quite tiring, more tiring than anything I was told not to do. I was told not to gossip, but they did that all the time. And they ate so much food, violating another of those rules they taught me: do not indulge in gluttony. And the foods they ate actually: if only sometime I could eat cold cuts after theater, cold cuts of lamb and mint sauce, and Yorkshire pudding and scones, and clotted cream, and sausages that came from up-country (imagine, "up-country"). And having troubling thoughts at twilight, a good time to have troubling thoughts, apparently; and servants who stole and left in the middle of a crisis, who were born with a limp or some other kind of deformity, not nourished properly in their mother's womb (that last part I figured out for myself; the point was, oh to have an untrustworthy servant); and wonderful cobbled streets onto which solid front doors opened; and people whose eyes were blue and who had fair skins and who smelled only of lavender, or sometimes sweet pea or primrose. And those flowers with

those names: delphiniums, foxgloves, tulips, daffodils, floribunda, peonies; in bloom, a striking display, being cut and placed in large glass bowls, crystal, decorating rooms so large twenty families the size of mine could fit in comfortably but used only for passing through. And the weather was so remarkable because the rain fell gently always, only occasionally in deep gusts, and it colored the air various shades of gray, each an appealing shade for a dress to be worn when a portrait was being painted; and when it rained at twilight, wonderful things happened: people bumped into each other unexpectedly and that would lead to all sorts of turns of events—a plot, the mere weather caused plots. I saw that people rushed: they rushed to catch trains, they rushed toward each other and away from each other; they rushed and rushed and rushed. That word: rushed! I did not know what it was to do that. It was too hot to do that, and so I came to envy people who would rush, even though it had no meaning to me to do such a thing. But there they are again. They loved their children; their children were sent to their own rooms as a punishment, rooms larger than my entire house. They were special, everything about them said so, even their clothes; their clothes rustled, swished, soothed. The world was theirs, not mine; everything told me so.

If now as I speak of all this I give the impression of someone on the outside looking in, nose pressed up against a glass window, that is wrong. My nose was pressed up against a glass window all right, but there was an iron vise at the back of my neck forcing my head to stay in place. To avert my gaze was to fall back into something from which I had been rescued, a hole filled with nothing, and that was the word for everything about me, nothing. The reality of my life was conquests, subjugation, humiliation, enforced amnesia. I was forced to forget. Just for instance, this: I lived in a part of St. John's, Antigua, called Ovals. Ovals was made up of five streets, each of them named after a famous English seaman—to be quite frank, an officially sanctioned criminal: Rodney Street (after George Rodney), Nelson Street (after Horatio Nelson), Drake Street (after Francis Drake), Hood Street, and Hawkins Street (after John Hawkins). But John Hawkins was knighted after a trip he made to Africa, opening up a new trade, the slave trade. He was then entitled to wear as his crest a Negro bound with a cord. Every single person living on Hawkins Street was descended from a slave. John Hawkins's ship, the one in which he transported the people he had bought and kidnapped, was called *The Jesus*. He later became the treasurer of the Royal Navy and rear admiral.

Again, the reality of my life, the life I led at the time I was being shown these views of England for the first time, for the second time, for the one-hundred-millionth time, was this: the sun shone with what sometimes seemed to be a deliberate cruelty; we must have done something to deserve that. My dresses did not rustle in the evening air as I strolled to the theater (I had no evening, I had no theater; my dresses were made of a cheap cotton, the weave of which would give way after not too many washings). I got up in the morning, I did my chores (fetched water from the public pipe for my mother, swept the yard), I washed myself, I went to a woman to have my hair combed freshly every day (because before we were allowed into our classroom our teachers would inspect us, and children who had not bathed that day, or had dirt under their fingernails, or whose hair had not been combed anew that day, might not be allowed to attend class). I ate that breakfast. I walked to school. At school we gathered in an auditorium and sang a hymn, "All Things Bright and Beautiful," and looking down on us as we sang were portraits of the Queen of England and her husband; they wore jewels and medals and they smiled. I was a Brownie. At each meeting we would form a little group around a flagpole, and after raising the Union Jack, we would say, "I promise to do my best, to do my duty to God and the Queen, to help other people every day and obey the scouts' law."

Who were these people and why had I never seen them, I mean really seen them, in the place where they lived? I had never been to England. No one I knew had ever been to England, or I should say, no one I knew had ever been and returned to tell me about it. All the people I knew who had gone to England had stayed there. Sometimes they left behind them their small children, never to see them again. England! I had seen England's representatives. I had seen the governor general at the public grounds at a ceremony celebrating the Queen's birthday. I had seen an old princess and I

had seen a young princess. They had both been extremely not beautiful, but who of us would have told them that? I had never seen England, really seen it, I had only met a representative, seen a picture, read books, memorized its history. I had never set foot, my own foot, in it.

The space between the idea of something and its reality is always wide and deep and dark. The longer they are kept apart—idea of thing, reality of thing—the wider the width, the deeper the depth, the thicker and darker the darkness. This space starts out empty, there is nothing in it, but it rapidly becomes filled up with obsession or desire or hatred or love—sometimes all of these things, sometimes some of these things, sometimes only one of these things. The existence of the world as I came to know it was a result of this: idea of thing over here, reality of thing way, way over there. There was Christopher Columbus, an unlikable man, an unpleasant man, a liar (and so, of course, a thief) surrounded by maps and schemes and plans, and there was the reality on the other side of that width, that depth, that darkness. He became obsessed, he became filled with desire, the hatred came later, love was never a part of it. Eventually, his idea met the longed-for reality. That the idea of something and its reality are often two completely different things is something no one ever remembers; and so when they meet and find that they are not compatible, the weaker of the two, idea or reality, dies. That idea Christopher Columbus had was more powerful than the reality he met, and so the reality he met died.

And so finally, when I was a grown-up woman, the mother of two children, the wife of someone, a person who resides in a powerful country that takes up more than its fair share of a continent, the owner of a house with many rooms in it and of two automobiles, with the desire and will (which I very much act upon) to take from the world more than I give back to it, more than I deserve, more than I need, finally then, I saw England, the real England, not a picture, not a painting, not through a story in a book, but England, for the first time. In me, the space between the idea of it and its reality had become filled with hatred, and so when at last I saw it I wanted to take it into my hands and tear it into little pieces and then crumble it up as if it were clay, child's clay. That was impossible, and so I could only indulge in not-favorable opinions.

There were monuments everywhere; they commemorated victories, battles fought between them and the people who lived across the sea from them, all vile people, fought over which of them would have dominion over the people who looked like me. The monuments were useless to them now, people sat on them and ate their lunch. They were like markers on an old useless trail, like a piece of old string tied to a finger to jog the memory, like old decoration in an old house, dirty, useless, in the way. Their skins were so pale, it made them look so fragile, so weak, so ugly. What if I had the power to simply banish them from their land, send boat after boatload of them on a voyage that in fact had no destination, force them to live in a place where the sun's presence was a constant? This would rid them of their pale complexion and make them look more like me, make them look more like the people I love and treasure and hold dear, and more like the people who occupy the near and far reaches of my imagination, my history, my geography, and reduce them and everything they have ever known to figurines as evidence that I was in divine favor, what if all this was in my power? Could I resist it? No one ever has.

And they were rude, they were rude to each other. They didn't like each other very much. They didn't like each other in the way they didn't like me, and it occurred to me that their dislike for me was one of the few things they agreed on.

I was on a train in England with a friend, an English woman. Before we were in England she liked me very much. In England she didn't like me at all. She didn't like the claim I said I had on England, she didn't like the views I had of England. I didn't like England, she didn't like England, but she didn't like me not liking it too. She said, "I want to show you my England, I want to show you the England that I know and love." I had told her many times before that I knew England and I didn't want to love it anyway. She no longer lived in England; it was her own country, but it had not been kind to her, so she left. On the train, the conductor was rude to her; she asked something, and he responded in a rude way. She became ashamed. She was ashamed at the way he treated her; she was ashamed at the way he

behaved. "This is the new England," she said. But I liked the conductor being rude; his behavior seemed quite appropriate. Earlier this had happened: we had gone to a store to buy a shirt for my husband; it was meant to be a special present, a special shirt to wear on special occasions. This was a store where the Prince of Wales has his shirts made, but the shirts sold in this store are beautiful all the same. I found a shirt I thought my husband would like and I wanted to buy him a tie to go with it. When I couldn't decide which one to choose, the salesman showed me a new set. He was very pleased with these, he said, because they bore the crest of the Prince of Wales, and the Prince of Wales had never allowed his crest to decorate an article of clothing before. There was something in the way he said it; his tone was slavish, reverential, awed. It made me feel angry; I wanted to hit him. I didn't do that. I said, my husband and I hate princes, my husband would never wear anything that had a prince's anything on it. My friend stiffened. The salesman stiffened. They both drew themselves in, away from me. My friend told me that the prince was a symbol of her Englishness, and I could see that I had caused offense. I looked at her. She was an English person, the sort of English person I used to know at home, the sort who was nobody in England but somebody when they came to live among the people like me. There were many people I could have seen England with; that I was seeing it with this particular person, a person who reminded me of the people who showed me England long ago as I sat in church or at my desk, made me feel silent and afraid, for I wondered if, all these years of our friendship, I had had a friend or had been in the thrall of a racial memory.

I went to Bath—we, my friend and I, did this, but though we were together, I was no longer with her. The landscape was almost as familiar as my own hand, but I had never been in this place before, so how could that be again? And the streets of Bath were familiar, too, but I had never walked on them before. It was all those years of reading, starting with Roman Britain. Why did I have to know about Roman Britain? It was of no real use to me, a person living on a hot, drought-ridden island, and it is of no use to me now, and yet my head is filled with this nonsense, Roman Britain. In Bath, I drank tea in a room I had read about in a novel written in the eighteenth century. In this very same room, young women wearing those dresses that rustled and so on danced and flirted and sometimes disgraced themselves with young men, soldiers, sailors, who were on their way to Bristol or someplace like that, so many places like that where so many adventures, the outcome of which was not good for me, began. Bristol, England. A sentence that began "That night the ship sailed from Bristol, England" would end not so good for me. And then I was driving through the countryside in an English motorcar, on narrow winding roads, and they were so familiar, though I had never been on them before; and through little villages the name of which I somehow knew so well though I had never been there before. And the countryside did have all those hedges and hedges, fields hedged in. I was marveling at all the toil of it, the planting of the hedges to begin with and then the care of it, all that clipping, year after year of clipping, and I wondered at the lives of the people who would have to do this, because wherever I see and feel the hands that hold up the world, I see and feel myself and all the people who look like me. And I said, "Those hedges" and my friend said that someone, a woman named Mrs. Rothchild, worried that the hedges weren't being taken care of properly; the farmers couldn't afford or find the help to keep up the hedges, and often they replaced them with wire fencing. I might have said to that, well if Mrs. Rothchild doesn't like the wire fencing, why doesn't she take care of the hedges herself, but I didn't. And then in those fields that were now hemmed in by wire fencing that a privileged woman didn't like was planted a vile yellow flowering bush that produced an oil, and my friend said that Mrs. Rothchild didn't like this either; it ruined the English countryside, it ruined the traditional look of the English countryside.

It was not at that moment that I wished every sentence, everything I knew, that began with England would end with "and then it all died; we don't know how, it just all died." At that moment, I was thinking, who are these people who forced me to think of them all the time, who forced me to think that the world I knew was incomplete, or without substance, or did not measure up because it was not England; that I was incomplete, or without substance, and did not measure up because I was not English. Who were these people? The person sitting next to me couldn't give me a clue;

no one person could. In any case, if I had said to her, I find England ugly, I hate England; the weather is like a jail sentence, the English are a very ugly people, the food in England is like a jail sentence, the hair of English people is so straight, so dead looking, the English have an unbearable smell so different from the smell of people I know, real people of course, she would have said that I was a person full of prejudice. Apart from the fact that it is I—that is, the people who look like me—who made her aware of the unpleasantness of such a thing, the idea of such a thing, prejudice, she would have been only partly right, sort of right: I may be capable of prejudice, but my prejudices have no weight to them, my prejudices have no force behind them, my prejudices remain opinions, my prejudices remain my personal opinion. And a great feeling of rage and disappointment came over me as I looked at England, my head full of personal opinions that could not have public, my public, approval. The people I come from are powerless to do evil on grand scale.

The moment I wished every sentence, everything I knew, that began with England would end with "and then it all died; we don't know how, it just all died" was when I saw the white cliffs of Dover. I had sung hymns and recited poems that were about a longing to see the white cliffs of Dover again. At the time I sang the hymns and recited the poems, I could really long to see them again because I had never seen them at all, nor had anyone around me at the time. But there we were, groups of people longing for something we had never seen. And so there they were, the white cliffs, but they were not that pearly majestic thing I used to sing about, that thing that created such a feeling in these people that when they died in the place where I lived they had themselves buried facing a direction that would allow them to see the white cliffs of Dover when they were resurrected, as surely they would be. The white cliffs of Dover, when finally I saw them, were cliffs, but they were not white; you would only call them that if the word "white" meant something special to you; they were dirty and they were steep; they were so steep, the correct height from which all my views of England, starting with the map before me in my classroom and ending with the trip I had just taken, should jump and die and disappear forever.

Reading and Thinking

1. What does England mean for Kincaid? To what extent is her view of England a product of her early education? To what extent is it affected by the world of cultural difference that she inhabits?

2. What does the phrase "Made in England" come to mean in the essay? With what does Kincaid contrast things "Made in England"? Toward what point and with what effect does she do this? Why does the command "Draw a map of England" resonate so powerfully in Kincaid's memory and imagination?

3. What ironies does Kincaid reveal in her discussion of street names in St. John's, Antigua? How does her discussion of Christopher Columbus tie in with her discussion of England?

Thinking and Writing

1. Kincaid sets up a number of contrasts between England and her Caribbean home. Identify two different types of these and explain what Kincaid conveys by emphasizing such differences.

2. Write an essay exploring the various views of England that Kincaid presents. Consider what she says about the white cliffs of Dover in her final paragraphs.

3. Write an essay in which you explore what Kincaid calls "the space between the idea of something and its reality." The subject may be a place, a situation, an anticipated experience, or a person. Whatever you write about, consider the extent to which the weaker of the two, the idea or the reality of the thing, diminishes when the two conflict.

Creating Occasions

Create your own interactive Occasion on *Comp21* using the textual, visual, and video libraries, as well as the Explicator analysis tools. From the main menu, choose "Build Your Own Occasion for Writing."

READING

MARTIN LUTHER KING, JR.

For a full biographical note on Martin Luther King, Jr., see page 457.

I Have a Dream

In "I Have a Dream," a speech Martin Luther King, Jr., gave at the March on Washington on August 28, 1963, King created a memorable moment of American oratory. Drawing upon his resources as a minister, an orator, and a political activist, King spoke eloquently and movingly of his vision for an American future in which racial equality was a living reality rather than a far-off ideal.

In presenting his vision, King uses his command of rhetorical resources to communicate not just the idea of his vision for the future but its spirit and feeling as well. King conveys, thus, more than information in his speech. He does more than make an appeal to the reasoning powers of his audience. Instead, he appeals to their emotions, their feelings, their sense of justice, their common sense, their human decency.

1   Five score years ago, a great American, in whose symbolic shadow we stand, signed the Emancipation Proclamation. This momentous decree came as a great beacon light of hope to millions of Negro slaves who had been seared in the flames of withering injustice. It came as a joyous daybreak to end the long night of captivity.

But one hundred years later, we must face the tragic fact that the Negro is still not free. One hundred years later, the life of the Negro is still sadly crippled by the manacles of segregation and the chains of discrimination. One hundred years later, the Negro lives on a lonely island of poverty in the midst of a vast ocean of material prosperity. One hundred years later, the Negro is still languished in the corners of American society and finds himself an exile in his own land. So we have come here today to dramatize an appalling condition.

In a sense we have come to our nation's Capital to cash a check. When the architects of our republic wrote the magnificent words of the Constitution and the Declaration of Independence, they were signing a promissory note to which every American was to fall heir. This note was a promise that all men would be guaranteed the unalienable rights of life, liberty, and the pursuit of happiness.

It is obvious today that America has defaulted on this promissory note insofar as her citizens of color are concerned. Instead of honoring this sacred obligation, America has given the Negro people a bad check; a check which has come back marked "insufficient funds." But we refuse to believe that the bank of justice is bankrupt. We refuse to believe that there are insufficient funds in the great vaults of opportunity of this nation. So we have come to cash this check—a check that will give us upon demand the riches of freedom and the security of justice. We have also come to this hallowed spot to remind America of the fierce urgency of *now*. This is no time to engage in the luxury of cooling off or to take the tranquilizing drug of gradualism. *Now* is the time to make real promises of Democracy. *Now* is the time to rise from the dark and desolate valley of segregation to the sunlit path of racial justice. *Now* is the time to open the doors of opportunity to all of God's children. *Now* is the time to lift our nation from the quicksands of racial injustice to the solid rock of brotherhood.

It would be fatal for the nation to overlook the urgency of the moment to underestimate the determination of the Negro. This sweltering summer of the Negro's legitimate discontent will not pass until there is an invigorating autumn of freedom and equality. 1963 is not an end, but a beginning. Those who hope that the Negro needed to blow off steam and will now be content will have a rude awakening if the nation returns to business as usual. There will be neither rest nor tranquility in America until the Negro is granted his citizenship rights. The whirlwinds of revolt will continue to shake the foundation of our nation until the bright day of justice emerges.

But there is something that I must say to my people who stand on the warm threshold which leads into the palace of justice. In the process of gaining our rightful place we must not be guilty of wrongful deeds. Let us not seek to satisfy our thirst for freedom by drinking from the cup of bitterness and hatred. We must forever conduct our struggle on the high plane of dignity and discipline. We must not allow our creative protest to degenerate into physical violence. Again and again we must rise to the majestic heights of meeting physical force with soul force. The marvelous new militancy which has engulfed the Negro community must not lead us to a distrust of all white people, for many of our white brothers, as evidenced by their presence here today, have come to realize that their destiny is tied up with our destiny and their freedom is inextricably bound to our freedom. We cannot walk alone.

And as we walk, we must make the pledge that we shall march ahead. We cannot turn back. There are those who are asking the devotees of civil rights, "When will you be satisfied?" We can never be satisfied as long as the Negro is the victim of the unspeakable horrors of police brutality. We can never be satisfied as long as our bodies, heavy with fatigue of travel, cannot gain lodging in the motels of the highways and the hotels of the cities. We cannot be satisfied as long as the Negro's basic mobility is from a smaller ghetto to a larger one. We can never be satisfied as long as a Negro in Mississippi cannot vote and a Negro is New York believes he has nothing for which to vote. No, no, we are not satisfied, and we will not be satisfied until justice rolls down like waters and righteousness like a mighty stream.

I am not unmindful that some of you have come here out of great trials and tribulations. Some of you have come fresh from narrow jail cells. Some of you have come from areas where your quest for freedom left you battered by the storms of persecution and staggered by the winds of police brutality. You have been the veterans of creative suffering. Continue to work with the faith that unearned suffering is redemptive.

Go back to Mississippi, go back to Alabama, go back to South Carolina, go back to Georgia, go back to Louisiana, go back to the slums and ghettos of our northern cities, knowing that somehow this situation can and will be changed. Let us not wallow in the valley of despair.

I say to you today, my friends, that in spite of the difficulties and frustrations of the moment I still have a dream. It is a dream deeply rooted in the American dream.

I have a dream that one day this nation will rise up and live out the true meaning of its creed: "We hold these truths to be self-evident; that all men are created equal."

I have a dream that one day on the red hills of Georgia the sons of former slaves and the sons of former slaveowners will be able to sit down together at the table of brotherhood.

I have a dream that one day even the state of Mississippi, a desert state sweltering with the heat of injustice and oppression, will be transformed into an oasis of freedom and justice.

I have a dream that my four little children will one day live in a nation where they will not be judged by the color of their skin but by the content of their character.

I have a dream today.

I have a dream that one day the state of Alabama, whose governor's lips are presently dripping with the words of interposition and nullification, will be transformed into a situation where little black boys and black girls will be able to join hands with little white boys and white girls and walk together as sisters and brothers.

I have a dream today.

I have a dream that one day every valley shall be exalted, every hill and mountain shall be made low, the rough places will be made plains, and the crooked places will be made straight, and the glory of the Lord shall be revealed, and all flesh shall see it together.

This is our hope. This is the faith with which I return to the South. With this faith we will be able to hew out of the mountain of despair a stone of hope. With this faith we will be able to transform the jangling discords of our nation into a beautiful symphony of brotherhood. With this faith we will be able to work together, to pray together, to struggle together, to go to jail together, to stand up for freedom together, knowing that we will be free one day.

This will be the day when all of God's children will be able to sing with new meaning

My country, 'tis of thee,
Sweet land of liberty,
Of thee I sing:
Land where my fathers died,
Land of the pilgrims' pride,
From every mountainside
Let freedom ring.

And if America is to be a great nation this must become true. So let freedom ring from the prodigious hilltops of New Hampshire. Let freedom ring from the mighty mountains of New York. Let freedom ring from the heightening Alleghenies of Pennsylvania!

Let freedom ring from the snowcapped Rockies of Colorado!

Let freedom ring from the curvacious peaks of California!

But not only that; let freedom ring from Stone Mountain of Georgia.

Let freedom ring from every hill and molehill of Mississippi. From every mountainside, let freedom ring.

When we let freedom ring, when we let it ring from every village and every hamlet, from every state and every city, we will be able to speed up that day when all of God's children, black men and white men, Jews and Gentiles, Protestants and Catholics, will be able to join hands and sing in the words of the old Negro spiritual, "Free at last! free at last! thank God almighty, we are free at last!"

Reading and Thinking

1. Consider the purpose of King's speech and consider how King responds to its occasion and its audience. Consider as well how King uses historical allusion to connect the circumstances of the speech with those of significant historical moments that preceded it.

2. Analyze the structure of the speech. Identify its introduction, body, and conclusion—or beginning, middle, and end. What does King provide and accomplish in each of these three major sections of the speech?

3. Analyze King's use of imagery and metaphor, including the extended metaphor in paragraphs 4 and 5. Consider also his use of repetition, both of these images and metaphors and of other key phrases.

Thinking and Writing

1. Use the notes you made for the first three questions to write an analysis of King's speech. Be sure to explain not only what King says, but also how he says what he does. That is, explain the rhetorical techniques of the speech and their effects on King's audience.

2. Compare King's speech to another important speech. For example, you can compare King's speech to one of Abraham Lincoln's—the Gettysburg Address, or the Second Inaugural Address. Be sure to analyze occasion and audience along with the speech's purpose, style, and effectiveness.

Creating Occasions

Create your own interactive Occasion on *Comp21* using the textual, visual, and video libraries, as well as the Explicator analysis tools. From the main menu, choose "Build Your Own Occasion for Writing."

15

MAYA LIN

Maya Lin (b. 1959) is a practicing architect and an artist, best known for designing the Vietnam Veterans Memorial, more commonly known as "The Vietnam Wall." Lin submitted her winning design for the memorial contest while an undergraduate student at Yale University. Against all odds, Lin won the contest as a 20-year-old undergraduate competing against professional architects with many years of experience. Although famous for her design of the Vietnam Veterans Memorial, Lin has created many kinds of architectural works, including houses, a garden, sculpture, landscapes, a library, a museum, a chapel, as well as lines of clothing and furniture. In designing her outstanding memorials, Lin has always attempted to fit the memorial into surrounding landscape.

Between Art and Architecture

This essay is taken from Lin's autobiography, *Boundaries*. In this selection, Lin describes the story of how she created the design for the Vietnam Veterans Memorial, how her design was selected as the winner of a competition, and the various consequences, both personal and political, that ensued from that choice. As you read, pay special attention to how Lin uses causal explanation to convey her experience and ideas.

It's taken me years to be able to discuss the making of the Vietnam Veterans Memorial, partly because I needed to move past it and partly because I had forgotten the process of getting it built. I would not discuss the controversy surrounding its construction and it wasn't until I saw the documentary, *Maya Lin: A Strong Clear Vision,* that I was able to remember that time in my life. But I wrote the essay just as the memorial was being completed—in the fall of 1982. Then I put it away...until now.

1   I think that the most important aspect of the design of the Vietnam Veterans Memorial was that I had originally designed it for a class I was taking at Yale and not for competition. In that sense, I had designed it for me—or, more exactly, for what I believed it should be. I never tried to second-guess a jury. And it wasn't until after I had completed the design that I decided to enter it in the competition.

The design emerged from an architectural seminar I was taking during my senior year. The initial idea of a memorial had come from a notice posted at the school announcing a competition for a Vietnam veterans memorial. The class, which was on funereal architecture, had spent the semester studying how people, through the built form, express their attitudes on death. As a class, we thought the memorial was an appropriate design idea for our program, so we adopted it as our final design project.

At that point, not much was known about the actual competition, so for the first half of the assignment we were left without concrete directions as to what "they" were looking for or even who "they" were. Instead, we had to determine for ourselves what a Vietnam memorial should be. Since a previous project had been to design a memorial for World War III, I had already begun to ask the simple questions: What exactly is a memorial? What should it do?

My design for a World War III memorial was a tomblike underground structure that I deliberately made to be a very futile and frustrating experience. I remember the professor of the class, Andrus Burr, coming up to me afterward, saying quite angrily, "If I had a brother who died in that war, I would never want

Reading and Thinking

1. What was Maya Lin's main goal in creating her design for what was to become the Vietnam Veterans Memorial? What was her concept of what a memorial should and should not do and of what it should and should not be?

2. How did the World War I memorial designed by Sir Edwin Lutyens in Thiepval, France, affect Lin, and how did it influence her own thinking about the memorial she herself was designing?

3. Lin talks about the importance of names. And she discusses the relationship of a memorial to nature. What does she say about names and about nature, and how are her ideas embodied in her design for the memorial.

Thinking and Writing

1. Summarize the reasons why Lin's proposed memorial design created problems for some individuals and for some groups. Explain how politics affected the response to her design, and how, later, other factors, including her age, gender, and race, affected people's perceptions of her ultimately winning design.

2. Write an essay in which you explain the rationale for something you designed or created, for some goal you achieved, some project you developed, or some plan you proposed and implemented. Explain what happened in the process of completing it and how you handled challenges, obstacles, or difficulties that interfered with your original intentions.

3. Read the poem on the following two pages, entitled "The Names," by the contemporary American poet and United States Poet Laureate, Billy Collins. Write a short piece in which you explain the link between Lin's memorial and Collins's poem, written in response to the events of September 11.

Creating Occasions

Create your own interactive Occasion on *Comp21* using the textual, visual, and video libraries, as well as the Explicator analysis tools. From the main menu, choose "Build Your Own Occasion for Writing."

The Names
Billy Collins

Yesterday, I lay awake in
the palm of the night.
A fine rain stole in,
unhelped by any breeze,
And when I saw the
silver gaze on the windows,
I started with A, with
Ackerman, as it happened,
Then with Baxter and Calabro,
Davis and Eberling,
names falling into place
As droplets fell through the dark.

Names printed on the
ceiling of the night.
Names slipping around a watery bend.
Twenty-six willows on
the banks of a stream.

In the morning, I walked out barefoot
Among thousands of flowers
Heavy with dew like the eyes of tears,
And each had name--
Fiori inscribed on a yellow petal
Then Gonzalez and Han,
Ishikawa and Jenkins.

Names written in the air
And stitched into the cloth of the day.
A name under a photograph
taped to a mailbox.
Monogram on a torn shirt,
I see you spelled out on
storefront windows
And on the bright unfurled
awnings of this city.
I say the syllables as
I turn a corner--
Kelly and Lee,
Medina, Nardella, and O'Connor.

When I peer into the woods,
I see a thick tangle where
letters are hidden

As in a puzzle concocted for children.
Parker and Quigley
in the twigs of an ash,
Rizzo, Schubert, Torres, and Upton,
Secrets in the bough
of an ancient maple.

Names written in the pale sky.
Names rising in the
updraft amid buildings.
Names silent in stone
Or cried out behind a door.
Names blown over the earth
and out to sea.

In the evening--weakening
light, the last swallows.
A boy on a lake lifts his oars.
A woman by a window puts
a match to a candle,
And the names are outlined
on the rose clouds--
Vanacore and Wallace,
(let X stand, if it can,
for the ones unfound)
Then Young and Ziminsky,
the final jolt of Z.

Names etched on the head of a pin.
One name spanning a bridge,
another undergoing a tunnel.
A blue name needled into the skin.
Names of citizens, workers,
mothers and fathers,
The bright-eyed daughter,
the quick son.
Alphabet of names in
green rows in a field.
Names in the small tracks of birds.
Names lifted from a hat
Or balanced on the tip of a tongue.
Names wheeled into the dim warehouse
of memory.
So many names, there is barely room
on the walls of the heart.

N. SCOTT MOMADAY

N. Scott Momaday (b. 1934), who is of Kiowa ancestry, grew up on a reservation in New Mexico. His first novel, *House Made of Dawn* (1968), won a Pulitzer Prize. In addition to fiction, Momaday has also published books of poetry, including *The Gourd Dancer* (1976), and the memoirs *The Way to Rainy Mountain* (1969) and *The Names* (1976). He has also written children's books, plays, and essays, including the collection *The Man Made of Words* (1997).

The Way to Rainy Mountain

The following selection is excerpted from Momaday's memoir *The Way to Rainy Mountain,* in which he celebrates his Kiowa heritage. He memorializes both a place sacred in Kiowa tradition and a person, his grandmother, herself a repository of Kiowa history and culture. Momaday's carefully articulated description of both place and person conveys a vanished world with respect and reverence.

1   A single knoll rises out of the plain in Oklahoma, north and west of the Wichita Range. For my people, the Kiowas, it is an old landmark, and they gave it the name Rainy Mountain. The hardest weather in the world is there. Winter brings blizzards, hot tornadic winds arise in the spring, and in summer the prairie is an anvil's edge. The grass turns brittle and brown, and it cracks beneath your feet. There are green belts along the rivers and creeks, linear groves of hickory and pecan, willow and witch hazel. At a distance in July or August the steaming foliage seems almost to writhe in fire. Great green-and-yellow grasshoppers are everywhere in the tall grass, popping up like corn to sting the flesh, and tortoises crawl about on the red earth, going nowhere in the plenty of time. Loneliness is an aspect of the land. All things in the plain are isolate; there is no confusion of objects in the eye, but *one* hill or *one* tree or *one* man. To look upon that landscape in the early morning, with the sun at your back, is to lose the sense of proportion. Your imagination comes to life, and this, you think, is where Creation was begun.

I returned to Rainy Mountain in July. My grandmother had died in the spring, and I wanted to be at her grave. She had lived to be very old and at last infirm. Her only living daughter was with her when she died, and I was told that in death her face was that of a child.

I like to think of her as a child. When she was born, the Kiowas were living that last great moment of their history. For more than a hundred years they had controlled the open range from the Smoky Hill River to the Red, from the headwaters of the Canadian to the fork of the Arkansas and Cimarron. In alliance with the Comanches, they had ruled the whole of the southern Plains. War was their sacred business, and they were among the finest horsemen the world has ever known. But warfare for the Kiowas was preeminently a matter of disposition rather than of survival, and they never understood the grim, unrelenting advance of the U.S. Cavalry. When at last, divided and ill-provisioned, they were driven onto the Staked Plains in the cold rains of autumn, they fell into panic. In Palo Duro Canyon they abandoned their crucial stores to pillage and had nothing then but their lives. In order to save themselves, they surrendered to the soldiers at Fort Sill and were imprisoned in the old stone corral that now stands as a military museum. My grandmother was spared the humiliation of those high gray walls by eight or ten years, but she must have known from birth the affliction of defeat, the dark brooding of old warriors.

Her name was Aho, and she belonged to the last culture to evolve in North America. Her forebears came down from the high country in western Montana nearly three centuries ago. They were a mountain people, a mysterious tribe of hunters whose language has never been positively classified in any major group. In the late seventeenth century they began a long migration to the south and east. It was a long journey toward the dawn, and it led to a golden age. Along the way the Kiowas were befriended by the Crows, who gave them the culture and religion of the Plains. They acquired horses, and their ancient nomadic spirit was suddenly free of the ground. They acquired Tai-me, the sacred Sun Dance doll, from that moment the object and symbol of their worship, and so shared in the divinity of the sun. Not least, they acquired the sense of destiny, therefore courage and pride. When they entered upon the southern Plains, they had been transformed. No longer were they slaves to the simple necessity of survival; they were a lordly and dangerous society of fighters and thieves, hunters and priests of the sun. According to their origin myth, they entered the world through a hollow log. From one point of view, their migration was the fruit of an old prophecy, for indeed they emerged from a sunless world.

5   Although my grandmother lived out her long life in the shadow of Rainy Mountain, the immense landscape of the continental interior lay like memory in her blood. She could tell of the Crows, whom she had never seen, and of the Black Hills, where she had never been. I wanted to see in reality what she had seen more perfectly in the mind's eye, and traveled fifteen hundred miles to begin my pilgrimage.

Yellowstone, it seemed to me, was the top of the world, a region of deep lakes and dark timber, canyons and waterfalls. But, beautiful as it is, one might have the sense of confinement there. The skyline in all directions is close at hand, the high wall of the woods and deep cleavages of shade. There is a perfect freedom in the mountains, but it belongs to the eagle and the elk, the badger and the bear. The Kiowas reckoned their stature by the distance they could see, and they were bent and blind in the wilderness.

Descending eastward, the highland meadows are a stairway to the plain. In July the inland slope of the Rockies is luxuriant with flax and buckwheat, stonecrop and larkspur. The earth unfolds and the limit of the land recedes. Clusters of trees and animals grazing far in the distance cause the vision to reach away and wonder to build upon the mind. The sun follows a longer course in the day, and the sky is immense beyond all comparison. The great billowing clouds that sail upon it are shadows that move upon the grain like water, dividing light. Farther down, in the land of the Crows and Blackfeet, the plain is yellow. Sweet clover takes hold of the hills and bends upon itself to cover and seal the soil. There the Kiowas paused on their way; they had come to the place where they must change their lives. The sun is at home in the plains. Precisely there does it have the certain character of a god. When the Kiowas came to the land of the Crows, they could see the dark lees of the hills at dawn across the Bighorn River, the profusion of light on the grain shelves, the oldest deity ranging after the solstices. Not yet would they veer southward to the caldron of the land that lay below; they must wean their blood from the northern winter and hold the mountains a while longer in their view. They bore Tai-me in procession to the east.

A dark mist lay over the Black Hills, and the land was like iron. At the top of a ridge I caught sight of Devil's Tower upthrust against the gray sky as if in the birth of time the core of the earth had broken through its crust and the motion of the world was begun. There are things in nature that engender an awful quiet in the heart of man; Devil's Tower is one of them. Two centuries ago, because they could not do otherwise, the Kiowas made a legend at the base of the rock. My grandmother said:

"Eight children were there at play, seven sisters and their brother. Suddenly the boy was struck dumb; he trembled and began to run upon his hands and feet. His fingers became claws, and his body was covered with fur. Directly there was a bear where the boy had been. The sisters were terrified; they ran, and the bear after them. They came to the stump of a great tree, and the tree spoke to them. It bade them climb upon it, and as they did so, it began to rise into the air. The bear came to kill them, but they were just beyond its reach. It reared against the tree and scored the bark all around with its claws. The seven sisters were borne into the sky, and they became the stars of the Big Dipper."

From that moment, and so long as the legend lives, the Kiowas have kinsmen in the night sky. Whatever they were in the mountains, they could be no more. However tenuous their well-being, however much they had suffered and would suffer again, they had found a way out of the wilderness.

My grandmother had a reverence for the sun, a holy regard that now is all but gone out of mankind. There was a wariness in her, and an ancient awe. She was a Christian in her later years, but she had come a long way about, and she never forgot her birthright. As a child she had been to the Sun Dances; she had taken part in those annual rites, and by them she had learned the restoration of her people in the presence of Tai-me. She was about seven when the last Kiowa Sun Dance was held in 1887 on the Washita River above Rainy Mountain Creek. The buffalo were gone. In order to consummate the ancient sacrifice — to impale the head of a buffalo bull upon the medicine tree — a delegation of old men journeyed into Texas, there to beg and barter for an animal from the Goodnight herd. She was ten when the Kiowas came together for the last time as a living Sun Dance culture. They could find no buffalo; they had to hang an old hide from the sacred tree. Before the dance could begin, a company of soldiers rode out from Fort Sill under orders to disperse the tribe. Forbidden without cause the essential act of their faith, having seen the wild herds slaughtered and left to rot upon the ground, the Kiowas backed away forever from the medicine tree. That was July 20, 1890, at the great bend of the Washita. My grandmother was there. Without bitterness, and for as long as she lived, she bore a vision of deicide.

Now that I can have her only in memory, I see my grandmother in the several postures that were peculiar to her: standing at the wood stove on a winter morning and turning meat in a great iron skillet; sitting at the south window, bent above her beadwork, and afterwards, when her vision had failed, looking down for a long time into the fold of her hands; going out upon a cane, very slowly as she did when the weight of age came upon her; praying. I remember her most often at prayer. She made long, rambling prayers out of suffering and hope, having seen many things. I was never sure that I had the right to hear, so exclusive were they of all mere custom and company. The last time I saw her she prayed standing by the side of her bed at night, naked to the waist, the light of a kerosene lamp moving upon her dark skin. Her long, black hair, always drawn and braided in the day, lay upon her shoulders and against her breasts like a shawl. I do not speak Kiowa, and I never understood her prayers, but there was something inherently sad in the sound, some merest hesitation upon the syllables of sorrow. She began in a high and descending pitch, exhausting her breath to silence; then again and again — and always the same intensity of effort, of something that is, and is not, like urgency in the human voice. Transported so in the dancing light among the shadows of her room, she seemed beyond the reach of time. But that was illusion; I think I knew that I should not see her again.

Reading and Thinking

1. What details of Momaday's description best convey his sense of Rainy Mountain? What details convey his attitude toward his grandmother? Explain.

2. Why do you think that Momaday includes a quotation from his grandmother? What is conveyed through her words? How does Momaday evoke the world of his grandmother's youth? What is the writer's attitude toward the vanished world that his grandmother represents? Explain.

3. Besides description, which Momaday employs heavily, what other patterns does Momaday use? Identify specific examples and his purpose in using them.

Thinking and Writing

1. Write an analysis of how Momaday conveys a sense of his grandmother and of Rainy Mountain. Discuss his use of language, selection of detail, and the organization of the piece.

2. Describe a person and place from your past. Use specific details to convey an impression of the person and place you describe. Provide aural as well as visual images, perhaps including some words spoken by the person you describe. Before writing, decide on an overall impression you want to create.

3. Explore your own relation to your heritage by describing scenes, narrating stories, or explaining circumstances from your past. You may wish to focus on family stories, or you may choose to write specifically about your parents or other relatives.

Creating Occasions

Create your own interactive Occasion on *Comp21* using the textual, visual, and video libraries, as well as the Explicator analysis tools. From the main menu, choose "Build Your Own Occasion for Writing."

GEORGE ORWELL

Best known for his fictional allegories *Animal Farm* and *1984*, George Orwell (1903–1950) has also written a considerable amount of nonfiction, such as *Homage to Catalonia,* an eyewitness account of the Spanish Civil War, and numerous essays. Read more about Orwell on page 440.

Marrakech

In "Marrakech," Orwell presents an account of a visit to the north African city in Morocco. He organizes his essay as a series of vignettes—brief descriptions of different places around the city, each of which conveys, through carefully selected details and artfully constructed incidents, an idea about the people who inhabit Marrakech.

1   As the corpse went past the flies left the restaurant table in a cloud and rushed after it, but they came back a few minutes later.

The little crowd of mourners—all men and boys, no women—threaded their way across the market-place between the piles of pomegranates and the taxis and the camels, wailing a short chant over and over again. What really appeals to the flies is that the corpses here are never put into coffins, they are merely wrapped in a piece of rag and carried on a rough wooden bier on the shoulders of four friends. When the friends get to the burying-ground they hack an oblong hole a foot or two deep, dump the body in it and fling over it a little of the dried-up, lumpy earth, which is like broken brick. No gravestone, no name, no identifying mark of any kind. The burying-ground is merely a huge waste of hummocky earth, like a derelict building-lot. After a month or two no one can even be certain where his own relatives are buried.

When you walk through a town like this—two hundred thousand inhabitants, of whom at least twenty thousand own literally nothing except the rags they stand up in—when you see how the people live, and still more how easily they die, it is always difficult to believe that you are walking among human beings. All colonial empires are in reality founded upon that fact. The people have brown faces—besides, there are so many of them! Are they really the same flesh as yourself? Do they even have names? Or are they merely a kind of undifferentiated brown stuff, about as individual as bees or coral insects? They rise out of the earth, they sweat and starve for a few years, and then they sink back into the nameless mounds of the graveyard and nobody notices that they are gone. And even the graves themselves soon fade back into the soil. Sometimes, out for a walk, as you break your way through the prickly pear, you notice that it is rather bumpy underfoot, and only a certain regularity in the bumps tells you that you are walking over skeletons.

I was feeding one of the gazelles in the public gardens.

5   Gazelles are almost the only animals that look good to eat when they are still alive, in fact, one can hardly look at their hindquarters without thinking of mint sauce. The gazelle I was feeding seemed to know that this thought was in my mind, for though it took the piece of bread I was holding out it obviously did not like me. It nibbled rapidly at the bread, then lowered its head and tried to butt me, then took another nibble and then butted again. Probably its idea was that if it could drive me away the bread would somehow remain hanging in mid-air.

An Arab navvy working on the path nearby lowered his heavy hoe and sidled towards us. He looked from the gazelle to the bread and from the bread to the gazelle, with a sort of quiet amazement, as though he had never seen anything quite like this before. Finally he said shyly in French:

"I could eat some of that bread."

I tore off a piece and he stowed it gratefully in some secret place under his rags. This man is an employee of the Municipality.

When you go through the Jewish quarters you gather some idea of what the medieval ghettoes were probably like. Under their Moorish rulers the Jews were only allowed to own land in certain restricted areas, and after centuries of this kind of treatment they have ceased to bother about overcrowding. Many of the streets are a good deal less than six feet wide, the houses are completely windowless, and sore-eyed children cluster everywhere in unbelievable numbers, like clouds of flies. Down the centre of the street there is generally running a little river of urine.

In the bazaar huge families of Jews, all dressed in the long black robe and little black skull-cap, are working in dark fly-infested booths that look like caves. A carpenter sits cross-legged at a prehistoric lathe, turning chair-legs at lightning speed. He works the lathe with a bow in his right hand and guides the chisel with his left foot, and thanks to a lifetime of sitting in this position his left leg is warped out of shape. At his side his grandson, aged six, is already starting on the simpler parts of the job.

I was just passing the coppersmiths' booths when somebody noticed that I was lighting a cigarette. Instantly, from the dark holes all round, there was a frenzied rush of Jews, many of them old grandfathers with flowing grey beards, all clamouring for a cigarette. Even a blind man somewhere at the back of one of the booths heard a rumour of cigarettes and came crawling out, groping in the air with his hand. In about a minute I had used up the whole packet. None of these people, I suppose, works less than twelve hours a day, and every one of them looks on a cigarette as a more or less impossible luxury.

As the Jews live in self-contained communities they follow the same trades as the Arabs, except for agriculture. Fruit-sellers, potters, silversmiths, blacksmiths, butchers, leather-workers, tailors, water-carriers, beggars, porters—whichever way you look you see nothing but Jews. As a matter of fact there are thirteen thousand of them, all living in the space of a few acres. A good job Hitler isn't here. Perhaps he is on his way, however. You hear the usual dark rumours about the Jews, not only from the Arabs but from the poorer Europeans.

"Yes, *mon vieux,* they took my job away from me and gave it to a Jew. The Jews! They're the real rulers of this country, you know. They've got all the money. They control the banks, finance—everything."

"But," I said, "isn't it a fact that the average Jew is a labourer working for about a penny an hour?"

"Ah, that's only for show! They're all moneylenders really. They're cunning, the Jews."

In just the same way, a couple of hundred years ago, poor old women used to be burned for witchcraft when they could not even work enough magic to get themselves a square meal.

All people who work with their hands are partly invisible, and the more important the work they do, the less visible they are. Still, a white skin is always fairly conspicuous. In northern Europe, when you see a labourer ploughing a field, you probably give him a second glance. In a hot country, anywhere south of Gibraltar or east of Suez, the chances are that you don't even see him. I have noticed this again and again. In a tropical landscape one's eye takes in everything except the human beings. It takes in the dried-up soil, the prickly pear, the palm-tree and the distant mountain, but it always misses the peasant hoeing at his patch. He is the same colour as the earth, and a great deal less interesting to look at.

It is only because of this that the starved countries of Asia and Africa are accepted as tourist resorts. No one would think of running cheap trips to the Distressed Areas. But where the human beings have brown skins their poverty is simply not noticed. What does Morocco mean to a Frenchman? An orange-grove or a job in government service. Or to an Englishman? Camels, castles, palm-trees, Foreign Legionnaires, brass trays and bandits. One could probably live here for years without noticing that for nine-tenths of the people the reality of life is an endless, back-breaking struggle to wring a little food out of an eroded soil.

Most of Morocco is so desolate that no wild animal bigger than a hare can live on it. Huge areas which were once covered with forest have turned into a treeless waste where the soil is exactly like broken-up brick. Nevertheless a good deal of it is cultivated, with frightful labour. Everything is done by hand. Long lines of women, bent double like inverted capital Ls, work their way slowly across the field, tearing up the prickly weeds with their hands, and the peasant gathering lucerne for fodder pulls it up stalk by stalk instead of reaping it, thus saving an inch or two on each stalk. The plough is a wretched wooden thing, so frail that one can easily carry it on one's shoulder, and fitted underneath with a rough iron spike which stirs the soil to a depth of about four inches. This is as much as the strength of the animals is equal to. It is usual to plough with a cow and a donkey yoked together. Two donkeys would not be quite strong enough, but on the other hand two cows would cost a little more to feed. The peasants possess no harrows, they merely plough the soil several times over in different directions, finally leaving it in rough furrows, after which the whole field has to be shaped with hoes into small oblong patches, to conserve water. Except for a day or two after the rare rainstorms there is never enough water. Along the edges of the fields channels are hacked out to a depth of thirty or forty feet to get at the tiny trickles which run through the subsoil.

Every afternoon a file of very old women passes down the road outside my house, each carrying a load of firewood. All of them are mummified with age and the sun, and all of them are tiny. It seems to be generally the case in primitive communities that the women, when they get beyond a certain age, shrink to the size of children. One day a poor old creature who could not have been more than four feet tall crept past me under a vast load of wood. I stopped her and put a five-sou piece (a little more than a farthing) into her hand. She answered with a shrill wail, almost a scream, which was partly gratitude but mainly surprise. I suppose that from her point of view, by taking any notice of her, I seemed almost to be violating a law of nature. She accepted her status as an old woman, that is to say as a

beast of burden. When a family is travelling it is quite usual to see a father and a grown-up son riding ahead on donkeys, and an old woman following on foot, carrying the baggage.

But what is strange about these people is their invisibility. For several weeks, always at about the same time of day, the file of old women had hobbled past the house with their firewood, and though they had registered themselves on my eyeballs I cannot truly say that I had seen them. Firewood was passing—that was how I saw it. It was only that one day I happened to be walking behind them, and the curious up-and-down motion of a load of wood drew my attention to the human being underneath it. Then for the first time I noticed the poor old earth-coloured bodies, bodies reduced to bones and leathery skin, bent double under the crushing weight. Yet I suppose I had not been five minutes on Moroccan soil before I noticed the overloading of the donkeys and was infuriated by it. There is no question that the donkeys are damnably treated. The Moroccan donkey is hardly bigger than a St. Bernard dog, it carries a load which in the British army would be considered too much for a fifteen-hands mule, and very often its pack-saddle is not taken off its back for weeks together. But what is peculiarly pitiful is that it is the most willing creature on earth, it follows its master like a dog and does not need either bridle or halter. After a dozen years of devoted work it suddenly drops dead, whereupon its master tips it into the ditch and the village dogs have torn its guts out before it is cold.

This kind of thing makes one's blood boil, whereas—on the whole—the plight of the human beings does not. I am not commenting, merely pointing to a fact. People with brown skins are next door to invisible. Anyone can be sorry for the donkey with its galled back, but it is generally owing to some kind of accident if one even notices the old woman under her load of sticks.

As the storks flew northward the Negroes were marching southward—a long, dusty column, infantry, screw-gun batteries and then more infantry, four or five thousand men in all, winding up the road with a clumping of boots and a clatter of iron wheels.

They were Senegalese, the blackest Negroes in Africa, so black that sometimes it is difficult to see whereabouts on their necks the hair begins. Their splendid bodies were hidden in reach-me-down khaki uniforms, their feet squashed into boots that looked like blocks of wood, and every tin hat seemed to be a couple of sizes too small. It was very hot and the men had marched a long way. They slumped under the weight of their packs and the curiously sensitive black faces were glistening with sweat.

25   As they went past a tall, very young Negro turned and caught my eye. But the look he gave me was not in the least the kind of look you might expect. Not hostile, not contemptuous, not sullen, not even inquisitive. It was the shy, wide-eyed Negro look, which actually is a look of profound respect. I saw how it was. This wretched boy, who is a French citizen and has therefore been dragged from the forest to scrub floors and catch syphilis in garrison towns, actually has feelings of reverence before a white skin. He has been taught that the white race are his masters, and he still believes it.

But there is one thought which every white man (and in this connection it doesn't matter twopence if he calls himself a Socialist) thinks when he sees a black army marching past. "How much longer can we go on kidding these people? How long before they turn their guns in the other direction?"

It was curious, really. Every white man there has this thought stowed somewhere or other in his mind. I had it, so had the other onlookers, so had the officers on their sweating chargers and the white NCOs marching in the ranks. It was a kind of secret which we all knew and were too clever to tell; only the Negroes didn't know it. And really it was almost like watching a flock of cattle to see the long column, a mile or two miles of armed men, flowing peacefully up the road, while the great white birds drifted over them in the opposite direction, glittering like scraps of paper.

Reading and Thinking

1. Orwell's essay says something about Marrakech and about its people. What political point does Orwell make in describing both the place and the people?

2. To make his point, Orwell relies on incident, illustration, and analogy. In the gazelle episode, for example, a brief scenario is described and a bit of conversation is included. What is implied by the man's remark, "I could eat some of that bread"? What is implied by his act of putting the bread in his clothes?

3. You might think of the section that begins, "When you go through the Jewish quarters" as a miniature version of the essay as a whole. This section contains a series of vignettes, all of which suggests an idea. Identify the scenes and explain what they have in common.

Thinking and Writing

1. In the essay, Orwell presents a series of scenes—the burial ground, the zoo, the ghetto, the women carrying firewood, and the Senegalese troops—all to convey his view of Marrakech and its people. What does each scene imply individually, and how are the scenes related?

2. Describe your neighborhood or campus by selecting a series of locations for brief descriptive vignettes. Try to suggest, rather than explicitly state, your overall view of the place that the vignettes describe together.

3. Write an advertisement or travel poster inviting Americans to vacation in Marrakech, either Orwell's Marrakech or the Marrakech of today. You might think of yourself as a representative for public relations for the Moroccan government. Or you might write as a member of a committee on world brotherhood.

Creating Occasions

Create your own interactive Occasion on *Comp21* using the textual, visual, and video libraries, as well as the Explicator analysis tools. From the main menu, choose "Build Your Own Occasion for Writing."

WALKER PERCY

Walker Percy (1916-1990) was a physician before he became a writer. His first novel, *The Moviegoer,* won the National Book Award for fiction in 1962. His other novels include *Love in the Ruins* and *The Thanatos Syndrome.* He also published two books of essays. "The Loss of the Creature" comes from the first of those books, *The Message in the Bottle: How Queer Man Is, How Queer Language Is, and What One Has to Do with the Other.* The title suggests Percy's lingering preoccupation with language.

The Loss of the Creature

In "The Loss of the Creature," Walker Percy's discussion of language is often intertwined with his discussion of perception. As you read the essay, try to keep separate the places where he discusses language, *per se,* and those places where he discusses the role of language in perception. A subtle essay, "The Loss of the Creature" is lengthy as well, but rewarding in its insights. After you have read the essay, you may find yourself encountering creatures lost and found in your everyday life.

1   Every explorer names his island Formosa, beautiful. To him it is beautiful because, being first, he has access to it and can see it for what it is. But to no one else is it ever as beautiful—except the rare man who manages to recover it, who knows that it has to be recovered.

Garcia López de Cárdenas discovered the Grand Canyon and was amazed at the sight. It can be imagined: One crosses miles of desert, breaks through the mesquite, and there it is at one's feet. Later the government set the place aside as a national park, hoping to pass along to millions the experience of Cárdenas. Does not one see the same sight from the Bright Angel Lodge that Cárdenas saw?

The assumption is that the Grand Canyon is a remarkably interesting and beautiful place and that if it had a certain value *P* for Cárdenas, the same value *P* may be transmitted to any number of sightseers—just as Banting's discovery of insulin can be transmitted to any number of diabetics. A counterinfluence is at work, however, and it would be nearer the truth to say that if the place is seen by a million sightseers, a single sightseer does not receive the value *P* but a millionth part of value *P*.

It is assumed that since the Grand Canyon has the fixed interest value *P*, tours can be organized for any number of people. A man in Boston decides to spend his vacation at the Grand Canyon. He visits his travel bureau, looks at the folder, signs up for a two-week tour. He and his family take the tour, see the Grand Canyon, and return to Boston. May we say that this man has seen the Grand Canyon? Possibly he has. But it is more likely that what he has done is the one sure way not to see the canyon.

Why is it almost impossible to gaze directly at the Grand Canyon under these circumstances and see it for what it is—as one picks up a strange object from one's back yard and gazes directly at it? It is almost impossible because the Grand Canyon, the thing as it is, has been appropriated by the symbolic complex which has already been formed in the sightseer's mind. Seeing the canyon under approved circumstances is seeing the symbolic complex head on. The thing is no longer the thing as it confronted the Spaniard; it is rather that which has already been formulated—by picture postcard, geography book, tourist folders, and the words *Grand Canyon.* As a result of this preformulation, the

5

source of the sightseer's pleasure undergoes a shift. Where the wonder and delight of the Spaniard arose from his penetration of the thing itself, from a progressive discovery of depths, patterns, colors, shadows, etc., now the sightseer measures his satisfaction *by the degree to which the canyon conforms to the preformed complex.* If it does so, if it looks just like the postcard, he is pleased; he might even say, "Why it is every bit as beautiful as a picture postcard!" He feels he has not been cheated. But if it does not conform, if the colors are somber, he will not be able to see it directly; he will only be conscious of the disparity between what it is and what it is supposed to be. He will say later that he was unlucky in not being there at the right time. The highest point, the term of the sightseer's satisfaction, is not the sovereign discovery of the thing before him; it is rather the measuring up of the thing to the criterion of the preformed symbolic complex.

Seeing the canyon is made even more difficult by what the sightseer does when the moment arrives, when sovereign knower confronts the thing to be known. Instead of looking at it, he photographs it. There is no confrontation at all. At the end of forty years of preformulation and with the Grand Canyon yawning at his feet, what does he do? He waives his right of seeing and knowing and records symbols for the next forty years. For him there is no present; there is only the past of what has been formulated and seen and the future of what has been formulated and not seen. The present is surrendered to the past and the future.

The sightseer may be aware that something is wrong. He may simply be bored; or he may be conscious of the difficulty: that the great thing yawning at his feet somehow eludes him. The harder he looks at it, the less he can see. It eludes everybody. The tourist cannot see it; the bellboy at the Bright Angel Lodge cannot see it: for him it is only one side of the space he lives in, like one wall of a room; to the ranger it is a tissue of everyday signs relevant to his own prospects — the blue haze down there means that he will probably get rained on during the donkey ride.

How can the sightseer recover the Grand Canyon? He can recover it in any number of ways, all sharing in common the stratagem of avoiding the approved confrontation of the tour and the Park Service.

It may be recovered by leaving the beaten track. The tourist leaves the tour, camps in the back country. He arises before dawn and approaches the South Rim through a wild terrain where there are no trails and no railed-in lookout points. In other words, he sees the canyon by avoiding all the facilities for seeing the canyon. If the benevolent Park Service hears about this fellow and thinks he has a good idea and places the following notice in the Bright Angel Lodge: *Consult ranger for information on getting off the beaten track* — the end result will only be the closing of another access to the canyon.

It may be recovered by a dialectical movement which brings one back to the beaten track but at a level above it. For example, after a lifetime of avoiding the beaten track and guided tours, a man may deliberately seek out the most beaten track of all, the most commonplace tour imaginable: he may visit the canyon by a Greyhound tour in the company of a party from Terre Haute — just as a man who has lived in New York all his life may visit the Statue of Liberty. (Such dialectical savorings of the familiar as the familiar are, of course, a favorite stratagem of *The New Yorker* magazine.) The thing is recovered from familiarity by means of an exercise in familiarity. Our complex friend stands behind his fellow tourists at the Bright Angel Lodge and sees the canyon through them and their predicament, their picture taking and busy disregard. In a sense, he exploits his fellow tourists; he stands on their shoulders to see the canyon.

Such a man is far more advanced in the dialectic that the sightseer who is trying to get off the beaten track — getting up at dawn and approaching the canyon through the mesquite. This stratagem is, in fact, for our complex man the weariest, most beaten track of all.

It may be recovered as a consequence of a breakdown of the symbolic machinery by which the experts present the experience to the consumer. A family visits the canyon in the usual way. But shortly after their arrival, the park is closed by an outbreak of typhus in the south. They have the canyon to themselves. What do they mean when they tell the home folks of their good luck: "We had the whole place to ourselves"? How does one see the thing better when the others are absent? Is looking like sucking: the more lookers, the less there is to see? They could hardly answer, but by saying this they testify to a state of affairs which is considerably more complex than the simple statement of the schoolbook about the Spaniard and the millions who followed him. It is a state in which there is a complex distribution of sovereignty, of zoning.

It may be recovered in a time of national disaster. The Bright Angel Lodge is converted into a rest home, a function that has nothing to do with the canyon a few yards away. A wounded man is brought in. He regains consciousness; there outside his window is the canyon.

The most extreme case of access by privilege conferred by disaster is the Huxleyan novel of the adventures of the surviving remnant after the great wars of the twentieth century. An expedition from Australia lands in Southern California and heads east. They stumble across the Bright Angel Lodge, now fallen into ruins. The trails are grown over, the guard rails fallen away, the dime telescope at Battleship Point rusted. But there is the canyon, exposed at last. Exposed by what? By the decay of those facilities which were designed to help the sightseer.

This dialectic of sightseeing cannot be taken into account by planners, for the object of the dialectic is nothing other than the subversion of the efforts of the planners.

The dialectic is not known to objective theorists, psychologists, and the like. Yet it is quite well known in the fantasy-consciousness of the popular arts. The devices by which the museum exhibit, the Grand Canyon, the ordinary thing, is recovered have long since been stumbled upon. A movie shows a man visiting the Grand Canyon. But the movie maker knows something the planner does not know. He knows that one cannot take the sight frontally. The canyon must be approached by the stratagems we have mentioned: the Inside Track, the Familiar Revisited, the Accidental Encounter. Who is the stranger at the Bright Angel Lodge? Is he the ordinary tourist from Terre Haute that he makes himself out to be? He is not. He has another objective in mind, to revenge his wronged brother, counterespionage, etc. By virtue of the fact that he has other fish to fry, he may take a stroll along the rim after supper and then we can see the canyon

through him. The movie accomplishes its purpose by concealing it. Overtly the characters (the American family marooned by typhus) and we the onlookers experience pity for the sufferers, and the family experience anxiety for themselves; covertly and in truth they are the happiest of people and we are happy for them through them, for we have the canyon to ourselves. The movie cashes in on the recovery of sovereignty through disaster. Not only is the canyon now accessible to the remnant: the members of the remnant are now accessible to each other, a whole new ensemble of relations becomes possible—friendship, love, hatred, clandestine sexual adventures. In a movie when a man sits next to a woman on a bus, it is necessary either that the bus break down or that the woman lose her memory. (The question occurs to one: Do you imagine there are sightseers who see sights just as they are supposed to? a family who live in Terre Haute, who decide to take the canyon tour, who go there, see it, enjoy it immensely, and go home content? a family who are entirely innocent of all the barriers, zones, losses of sovereignty I have been talking about? Wouldn't most people be sorry if Battleship Point fell into the canyon, carrying all one's fellow passengers to their death, leaving one alone on the South Rim? I cannot answer this. Perhaps there are such people. Certainly a great many American families would swear they had no such problems, that they came, saw, and went away happy. Yet it is just these families who would be happiest if they had gotten the Inside Track and been among the surviving remnant.)

It is now apparent that as between the many measures which may be taken to overcome the opacity, the boredom, of the direct confrontation of the thing or creature in its citadel of symbolic investiture, some are less authentic than others. That is to say, some stratagems obviously serve other purposes than that of providing access to being—for example, various unconscious motivations which it is not necessary to go into here.

Let us take an example in which the recovery of being is ambiguous, where it may under the same circumstances contain both authentic and unauthentic components. An American couple, we will say, drives down into Mexico. They see the usual sights and have a fair

Reading

time of it. Yet they are never without the sense of missing something. Although Taxco and Cuernavaca are interesting and picturesque as advertised, they fall short of "it." What do they couple have in mind by "it"? What do they really hope for? What sort of experience could they have in Mexico so that upon their return, they would feel that "it" had happened? We have a clue: Their hope has something to do with their own role as tourists in a foreign country and the way in which they conceive this role. It has something to do with other American tourists. Certainly they feel that they are very far from "it" when, after traveling five thousand miles, they arrive at the plaza in Guanajuato only to find themselves surrounded by a dozen other couples from the Midwest.

Already we may distinguish authentic and unauthentic elements. First, we see the problem the couple faces and we understand their efforts to surmount it. The problem is to find an "unspoiled" place. "Unspoiled" does not mean only that a place is left physically intact; it means also that it is not encrusted by renown and by the familiar (as in Taxco), that it has not been discovered by others. We understand that the couple really want to get at the place and enjoy it. Yet at the same time we wonder if there is not something wrong in their dislike of their compatriots. Does access to the place require the exclusion of others?

Let us see what happens.

The couple decide to drive from Guanajuato to Mexico City. On the way they get lost. After hours on a rocky mountain road, they find themselves in a tiny valley not even marked on the map. There they discover an Indian village. Some sort of religious festival is going on. It is apparently a corn dance in supplication of the rain god.

The couple know at once that this is "it." They are entranced. They spend several days in the village, observing the Indians and being themselves observed with friendly curiosity.

Now may we not say that the sightseers have at last come face to face with an authentic sight, a sight which is charming, quaint, picturesque, unspoiled, and that they see the sight and come away rewarded? Possibly this may occur. Yet it is more likely that what happens is a far cry indeed from an immediate encounter with

being, that the experience, while masquerading as such, is in truth a rather desperate impersonation. I use the word *desperate* advisedly to signify an actual loss of hope.

The clue to the spuriousness of their enjoyment of the village and the festival is a certain restiveness in the sightseers themselves. It is given expression by their repeated exclamations that "this is too good to be true," and by their anxiety that it may not prove to be so perfect, and finally by their downright relief at leaving the valley and having the experience in the bag, so to speak—that is, safely embalmed in memory and movie film.

What is the source of their anxiety during the visit? Does it not mean that the couple are looking at the place with a certain standard of performance in mind? Are they like Fabre, who gazed at the world about him with wonder, letting it be what it is; or are they not like the overanxious mother who sees her child as one performing, now doing badly, now doing well? The village is their child and their love for it is an anxious love because they are afraid that at any moment it might fail them.

We have another clue in their subsequent remark to an ethnologist friend. "How we wished you had been there with us! What a perfect goldmine of folkways! Every minute we would say to each other, if only you were here! You must return with us." This surely testifies to a generosity of spirit, a willingness to share their experience with others, not at all like their feelings toward their fellow Iowans on the plaza at Guanajuato!

I am afraid this is not the case at all. It is true that they longed for their ethnologist friend, but it was for an entirely different reason. They wanted him, not to share the experience, but to certify their experience as genuine.

"This is it" and "Now we are really living" do not necessarily refer to the sovereign encounter of the person with the sight that enlivens the mind and gladdens the heart. It means that now at last we are having the acceptable experience. The present experience is always measured by a prototype, the "it" of their dreams. "Now I am really living" means that now I am filling the role of sightseer and the sight is living up to the prototype of sights. The quaint and picturesque village

20

is measured by a Platonic ideal of the Quaint and Picturesque.

Hence their anxiety during the encounter. For at any minute something could go wrong. A fellow Iowan might emerge from a 'dobe hut; the chief might show them his Sears catalog. (If the failures are "wrong" enough, as these are, they might still be turned to account as rueful conversation pieces. "There we were expecting the chief to bring us a churinga and he shows up with a Sears catalog!") They have snatched victory from disaster, but their experience always runs the danger of failure.

They need the ethnologist to certify their experience as genuine. This is borne out by their behavior when the three of them return for the next corn dance. During the dance, the couple do not watch the goings-on; instead they watch the ethnologist! Their highest hope is that their friend should find the dance interesting. And if he should show signs of true absorption, an interest in the goings-on so powerful that he becomes oblivious to his friends—then their cup is full. "Didn't we tell you?" they say at last. What they want from him is not ethnological explanations; all they want is his approval.

What has taken place is a radical loss of sovereignty over that which is as much theirs as it is the ethnologist's. The fault does not lie with the ethnologist. He has no wish to stake a claim to the village; in fact, he desires the opposite: he will bore his friends to death by telling them about the village and the meaning of the folkways. A degree of sovereignty has been surrendered by the couple. It is the nature of the loss, moreover, that they are not aware of the loss, beyond a certain uneasiness. (Even if they read this and admitted it, it would be very difficult for them to bridge the gap in their confrontation of the world. Their consciousness, so that with the onset of the first direct enjoyment, their higher consciousness pounces and certifies: "Now you are doing it! Now you are really living!" and, in certifying the experience, sets it at nought.)

Their basic placement in the world is such that they recognize a priority of title of the expert over his particular department of being. The whole horizon of being staked out by "them," the experts. The highest satisfaction of the sightseer (not merely the tourist but any layman seer of sights) is that his sight should be certified as genuine. The worst of this impoverishment is that there is no sense of impoverishment. The surrender of title is so complete that it never even occurs to one to reassert title. A poor man may envy the rich man, but the sightseer does not envy the expert. It is due altogether to the eager surrender of sovereignty by the layman so that he may take up the role not of the person but of the consumer.

I do not refer only to the special relation of layman to theorist. I refer to the general situation in which sovereignty is surrendered to a class of privileged knowers, whether these be theorists or artists. A reader may surrender sovereignty over that which has been written about, just as a consumer may surrender sovereignty over a thing which has been theorized about. The consumer is content to receive an experience just as it has been presented to him by theorists and planners. The reader may also be content to judge life by whether it has or has not been formulated by those who know and write about life. A young man goes to France. He too has a fair time of it, sees the sights, enjoys the food. On his last day, in fact as he sits in a restaurant in Le Havre waiting for his boat, something happens. A group of French students in the restaurant get into an impassioned argument over a recent play. A riot takes place. Madame le concierge joins in, swinging her mop at the rioters. Our young American is transported. This is "it." And he had almost left France without seeing "it"!

But the young man's delight is ambiguous. On the one hand, it is a pleasure for him to encounter the same Gallic temperament he had heard about from Puccini and Rolland. But on the other hand, the source of his pleasure testifies to a certain alienation. For the young man is actually barred from a direct encounter with anything French excepting only that which has been set forth, authenticated by Puccini and Rolland—those who know. If he had encountered the restaurant scene without reading Hemingway, without knowing that the performance was so typically, charmingly French, he would not have been delighted. He would only have been anxious at seeing those things get so out of hand. The source of his delight is the sanction of those who know.

This loss of sovereignty is not a marginal process, as might appear from my example of estranged sightseers. It is a generalized surrender of the horizon to those experts within whose competence a particular segment of the horizon is thought to lie. Kwakuitls are surrendered to Franz Boas; decaying Southern mansions are surrendered to Faulkner and Tennessee Williams. So that, although it is by no means the intention of the expert to expropriate sovereignty—in fact he would not even know what sovereignty meant in this context—the danger of theory and consumption is a seduction and deprivation of the consumer.

In the New Mexico desert, natives occasionally come across strange-looking artifacts which have fallen from the skies and which are stenciled: *Return to U.S. Experimental Project, Alamogordo. Reward.* The finder returns the object and is rewarded. He knows nothing of the nature of the object he has found and does not care to know. The sole role of the native, the highest role he can play, is that of finder and returner of the mysterious equipment.

The same is true of the laymen's relation to *natural* objects in the modern technical society. No matter what the object or event is, whether it is a star, a swallow, a Kwakuitl, a "psychological phenomenon," the layman who confronts it does not confront it as a sovereign person, as Crusoe confronts a seashell he finds on the beach. The highest role he can conceive himself as playing is to be able to recognize the title of the object, to return it to the appropriate expert and have it certified as a genuine find. He does not even permit himself to see the thing—as Gerard Hopkins could see a rock or a cloud or a field. If anyone asks him why he doesn't look, he may reply that he didn't take that subject in college (or he hasn't read Faulkner).

This loss of sovereignty extends even to oneself. There is the neurotic who asks nothing more of his doctor than that his symptoms should prove interesting. When all else fails, the poor fellow has nothing to offer but his own neurosis. But even this is sufficient if only the doctor will show interest when he says, "Last night I had a curious sort of dream; perhaps it will be significant to one who knows about such things. It seems I was standing in a sort of alley—" (I have nothing else to offer you but my own unhappiness. Please say that it, at least, measures up, that it is a *proper* sort of unhappiness.)

II

A young Falkland Islander walking along a beach and spying a dead dogfish and going to work on it with his jackknife has, in a fashion wholly unprovided in modern educational theory, a great advantage over the Scarsdale high-school pupil who finds the dogfish on his laboratory desk. Similarly the citizen of Huxley's *Brave New World* who stumbles across a volume of Shakespeare in some vine-grown ruins and squats on a potsherd to read it is in a fairer way of getting at a sonnet than the Harvard sophomore taking English Poetry II.

The educator whose business it is to teach students biology or poetry is unaware of a whole ensemble of relations which exist between the student and the dogfish and between the student and the Shakespeare sonnet. To put it bluntly: A student who has the desire to get at a dogfish or a Shakespeare sonnet may have the greatest difficulty in salvaging the creature itself from the educational package in which it is presented. The great difficulty is that he is not aware that there is a difficulty; surely, he thinks, in such a fine classroom, with such a fine textbook, the sonnet must come across! What's wrong with me?

The sonnet and the dogfish are obscured by the two different processes. The sonnet is obscured by the symbolic package which is formulated not by the sonnet itself but by the media through which the sonnet is transmitted, the media which the educators believe for some reason to be transparent. The new textbook, the type, the smell of the page, the classroom, the aluminum windows and the winter sky, the personality of Miss Hawkins—these media which are supposed to transmit the sonnet may only succeed in transmitting themselves. It is only the hardiest and cleverest of students who can salvage the sonnet from this many-tissued package. It is only the rarest student who knows that the sonnet must be salvaged from the package. (The educator is well aware that something is wrong, that there is a fatal gap between the student's learning and the student's life: the student reads the poem, appears to understand it, and gives all the answers. But what does he recall if he should happen to read a Shakespeare sonnet twenty years later? Does he recall the poem or does he recall the smell of the page and the smell of Miss Hawkins?)

One might object, pointing out that Huxley's citizen reading his sonnet in the ruins and the Falkland Islander looking at his dogfish on the beach also receive them in a certain package. Yes, but the difference lies in the fundamental placement of the student in the world, a placement which makes it possible to extract the thing from the package. The pupil at Scarsdale High sees himself placed as a consumer receiving an experience-package; but the Falkland Islander exploring his dogfish is a person exercising the sovereign right of a person in his lordship and mastery of creation. He too could use an instructor and a book and a technique, but he would use them as his subordinates, just as he uses his jackknife. The biology student does not use his scalpel as an instrument, he uses it as a magic wand! Since it is a "scientific instrument," it should do "scientific things."

The dogfish is concealed in the same symbolic package as the sonnet. But the dogfish suffers an additional loss. As a consequence of this double deprivation, the Sarah Lawrence student who scores A in zoology is apt to know very little about a dogfish. She is twice removed from the dogfish, once by the symbolic complex by which the dogfish is concealed, once again by the spoliation of the dogfish by theory which renders it invisible. Through no fault of zoology instructors, it is nevertheless a fact that the zoology laboratory at Sarah Lawrence College is one of the few places in the world where it is all but impossible to see a dogfish.

The dogfish, the tree, the seashell, the American Negro, the dream, are rendered invisible by a shift of reality from concrete thing to theory which Whitehead has called the fallacy of misplaced concreteness. It is the mistaking of an idea, a principle, an abstraction, for the real. As a consequence of the shift, the "specimen" is seen as less real than the theory of the specimen. As Kierkegaard said, once a person is seen as a specimen of a race or a species, at that very moment he ceases to be an individual. Then there are no more individuals but only specimens.

To illustrate: A student enters a laboratory which, in the pragmatic view, offers the students the optimum conditions under which an educational experience may be had. In the existential view, however—that view of the student in which he is regarded not as a receptacle of experience but as a knowing being whose peculiar property it is to see himself as being in a certain situation—the modern laboratory could not have been more effectively designed to conceal the dogfish forever.

The student comes to his desk. On it, neatly arranged by his instructor, he finds his laboratory manual, a dissecting board, instruments, and a mimeographed list:

Exercise 22: Materials
  1 dissecting board
  1 scalpel
  1 forceps
  1 probe
  1 bottle india ink and syringe
  1 specimen of *Squalus acanthias*

The clue of the situation in which the student finds himself is to be found in the last item: 1 specimen of *Squalus acanthias.*

The phrase *specimen of* expresses in the most succinct way imaginable the radical character of the loss of being which has occurred under his very nose. To refer to the dogfish, the unique concrete existence before him, as a "specimen of *Squalus acanthias*" reveals by its grammar the spoliation of the dogfish by the theoretical method. This phrase, *specimen of,* example of, instance of, indicates the ontological status of the individual creature in the eyes of the theorist. The dogfish itself is seen as a rather shabby expression on an ideal reality, the species *Squalus acanthias.* The result is the radical devaluation of the individual dogfish. (The *reductio ad absurdum* of Whitehead's shift is Toynbee's employment of it in his historical method. If a gram of NaCl is referred to by the chemist as a "sample of" NaCl, one may think of it as such and not much is missed by the oversight of the act of being of this particular pinch of salt, but when the Jews and the Jewish religion are understood as—in Toynbee's favorite phrase—a "classical example of" such and such a kind of *Voelkerwanderung,* we begin to suspect that something is being left out.)

If we look into the ways in which the student can recover the dogfish (or the sonnet), we will see that they have in common the stratagem of avoiding the educator's direct presentation of the object as a lesson to be learned and restoring access to sonnet and dogfish as being to be known, reasserting the sovereignty of knower over known.

50 In truth, the biography of scientists and poets is usually the story of the discovery of the indirect approach, the circumvention of the educator's presentation—the young man who was sent to the *Technikum* and on his way fell into the habit of loitering in book stores and reading poetry; or the young man dutifully attending law school who on the way became curious about the comings and goings of ants. One remembers the scene in *The Heart Is a Lonely Hunter* where the girl hides in the bushes to hear the Capehart in the big house play Beethoven. Perhaps she was the lucky one after all. Think of the unhappy souls inside, who see the record, worry about scratches, and most of all worry about whether they are *getting it,* whether they are bona fide music lovers. What is the best way to hear Beethoven: sitting in a proper silence around the Capehart or eavesdropping from an azalea bush?

However it may come about, we notice two traits of the second situation: (1) an openness of the thing before one—instead of being an exercise to be learned according to an approved mode, it is a garden of delights which beckons to one; (2) a sovereignty of the knower—instead of being a consumer of a prepared experience, I am a sovereign wayfarer, a wanderer in the neighborhood of being who stumbles into the garden.

One can think of two sorts of circumstances through which the thing may be restored to the person. (There is always, of course, the direct recovery: A student may simply be strong enough, brave enough, clever enough to take the dogfish and the sonnet by storm, to wrest control of it from the educators and the educational package.) First by ordeal: The Bomb falls; when the young man recovers consciousness in the shambles of the biology laboratory, there not ten

inches from his nose lies the dogfish. Now all at once he can see it directly without let, just as the exile or the prisoner or the sick man sees the sparrow at his window in all its inexhaustibility; just as the commuter who has had a heart attack sees his own hand for the first time. In these cases, the simulacrum of everydayness and of consumption has been destroyed by disaster; in the case of the bomb, literally destroyed. Secondly, by apprenticeship to a great man: one day a great biologist walks into the laboratory; he stops in front of our student's desk; he leans over, picks up the dogfish, and, ignoring instruments and procedure, probes with a broken fingernail into the little carcass. "Now here is a curious business," he says, ignoring also the proper jargon of the speciality. "Look here how this little duct reverses its direction and drops into the pelvis. Now if you would look into a coelacanth, you would see that it—"And all at once the student can see. The technician and the sophomore who loves his textbooks are always offended by the genuine research man because the latter is usually a little vague and always humble before the thing; he doesn't have much use for the equipment or the jargon. Whereas the technician is never vague and never humble before the thing; he holds the thing disposed of by the principle, the formula, the textbook outline; and he thinks a great deal of equipment and jargon.

But since neither of these methods of recovering the dogfish is pedagogically feasible—perhaps the great man even less so than the Bomb—I wish to propose the following educational technique which should prove equally effective for Harvard and Shreveport High School. I propose that English poetry and biology should be taught as usual, but that at irregular intervals, poetry students should find dogfishes on their desks and biology students should find Shakespeare sonnets on their dissection boards. I am serious in declaring that a Sarah Lawrence English major who began poking about in a dogfish with a bobby pin would learn more in thirty minutes than a biology major in a whole semester; and that the latter upon reading on her dissecting board

That time of year Thou may'st in me behold
When yellow leaves, or none, or few, do hang

Upon those boughs which shake against the cold—
Bare ruin'd choirs where late the sweet birds sang

might catch fire at the beauty of it.

The situation of the tourist at the Grand Canyon and the biology student are special cases of a predicament in which everyone finds himself in a modern technical society—a society, that is, in which there is a division between expert and layman, planner and consumer, in which experts and planners take special measures to teach and edify the consumer. The measures taken are measures appropriate to the consumer: the expert and the planner *know* and *plan,* but the consumer *needs* and *experiences.*

There is a double deprivation. First, the thing is lost through its packaging. The very means by which the things is presented for consumption, the very techniques by which the thing is made available as an item of need-satisfaction, these very means operate to remove the thing from the sovereignty of the knower. A loss of title occurs. The measures which the museum curator takes the present the thing to the public are self-liquidating. The upshot of the curator's efforts are not that everyone can see the exhibit but that no one can see it. The curator protests: why are they so different? Why do they even deface the exhibit? Don't they know it is theirs? But it is not theirs. It is his, the curator's. By the most exclusive sort of zoning, the museum exhibit, the park oak tree, is part of an ensemble, a package, which is almost impenetrable to them. The archaeologist who puts his find in a museum so that everyone can see it accomplishes the reverse of his expectations. The result of his action is that no one can see it now but the archaeologist. He would have done better to keep it in his pocket and show it now and then to strangers.

The tourist who carves his initials in a public place, which is theoretically "his" in the first place, has good reasons for doing so, reasons which the exhibitor and planner know nothing about. He does so because in his role of consumer of an experience (a "recreational experience" to satisfy a "recreational need") he knows that he is disinherited. He is deprived of his title over being. He knows very well that he is in a very special sort of zone in which his only rights are the rights of a consumer. He moves like a ghost through schoolroom, city streets, trains, parks, movies. He carves his initials as a last desperate measure to escape his ghostly role of consumer. He is saying in effect: I am not a ghost after all; I am a sovereign person. And he establishes title the only way remaining to him, by staking his claim over one square inch of wood or stone.

Does this mean that we should get rid of museums? No, but it means that the sightseer should be prepared to enter into a struggle to recover sight from a museum.

The second loss is the spoliation of the thing, the tree, the rock, the swallow, by the layman's misunderstanding of scientific theory. He believes that the thing is *disposed of* by theory, that it stands in the Platonic relation of being a *specimen* of such and such an underlying principle. In the transmission of scientific theory from theorist to layman, the expectation of the theorist is reversed. Instead of marvels of the universe being made available to the public, the universe is disposed of by theory. The loss of sovereignty takes this form: as a result of the science of botany, trees are not made available to every man. On the contrary. The tree loses its proper density and mystery as a concrete existent and, as merely another *specimen* of a species, becomes itself nugatory.

Does this mean that there is no use in taking biology at Harvard and Shreveport High? No, but it means that the student should know what a fight he has on his hands to rescue the specimen from the educational package. The educator is only partly to blame. For there is nothing the educator can do to provide for this need of the student. Everything the educator does only succeeds in becoming, for the student, part of the educational package. The highest role of the educator is the maieutic role of Socrates: to help the student come to himself not as a consumer of experience but as a sovereign individual.

The thing is twice lost to the consumer. First, sovereignty is lost: it is theirs, not his. Second, it is radically devalued by theory. This is a loss which has been brought about by science but through no fault of the scientist and through no fault of scientific theory. The loss has come about as a consequence of the seduction of the layman by science. The layman will be seduced as

55

60

long as he regards beings as consumer items to be experienced rather than prizes to be won, and as long as he waives his sovereign rights as a person and accepts his role of consumer as the highest estate to which the layman can aspire.

As Mounier said, the person is not something one can study and provide for; he is something one struggles for. But unless he also struggles for himself, unless he knows that there is a struggle, he is going to be just what the planners think he is.

Reading and Thinking

1. Percy devotes some seventeen paragraphs to the story of the Grand Canyon. Through careful analysis (with pencil in hand), break that story down into its component parts. Mark the breaks. Note in the margin what develops in each section.

2. As you analyze the logical ordering of those early paragraphs, consider what Percy means by these terms: *preformed symbolic complex, sovereignty, seeing and knowing, recovery, authenticity*. Trace their importance throughout the essay.

3. Are you willing to concede that you are one of those who has unknowingly given up your sovereignty, a victim, if you will, of your *loss of sovereignty*? Explain to yourself why or why not.

4. In part II of the essay, Percy moves directly into the domain of education—presumably the source of our blighted perceptions. How effective do you find Percy's examples of the dogfish and the sonnet? Do those examples ring true of your own experiences in college?

5. What does Percy mean about extracting the thing itself (the dogfish, the poem, the Grand Canyon) from the "symbolic package"? What is the fundamental requirement of a proper education: to create the package or to nullify its effect—or is there another way to think about this complex matter?

Thinking and Writing

1. Throughout the essay, Percy makes a number of assumptions about the way we see, the way we are constrained by what we know and have learned. Select one of those assumptions and question it, analyze it in terms of your own experience, and make some informed judgment about the assumption itself.

2. In one or two succinct paragraphs identify what Percy believes that we perceivers have *lost*. In two additional paragraphs outline Percy's plan for *recovery*. Finally, respond to Percy in an essay that develops your own ideas about seeing and knowing, loss and recovery. Let the essay reveal what you consider to be a proper education, an antidote to the loss of sovereignty.

Creating Occasions

Create your own interactive Occasion on *Comp21* using the textual, visual, and video libraries, as well as the Explicator analysis tools. From the main menu, choose "Build Your Own Occasion for Writing."

EDGAR ALLAN POE

Edgar Allan Poe (1809–1849) led a brief and tormented life, its end tragically hastened by alcohol and drug abuse. In addition to being a masterful storyteller, Poe was a poet, journalist, magazine editor, and literary critic. He is the inventor of the detective story and a pioneer in the development of the horror story. His influence on contemporary detective and horror writers continues unabated, and his popularity has hardly waned in more than a century and a half.

The Tell-Tale Heart

His short story, "The Tell-Tale Heart," is one of his best known and most masterful. It reveals Poe not just as a writer of stories of madness, murder, and mayhem, but as a consummate psychologist as well.

1   True!—nervous—very, very dreadfully nervous I had been and am; but why *will* you say that I am mad? The disease had sharpened my senses—not destroyed—not dulled them. Above all was the sense of hearing acute. I heard all things in the heaven and in the earth. I heard many things in hell. How, then, am I mad? Hearken! and observe how healthily—how calmly I can tell you the whole story.

It is impossible to say how first the idea entered my brain; but once conceived, it haunted me day and night. Object there was none. Passion there was none. I loved the old man. He had never wronged me. He had never given me insult. For his gold I had no desire. I think it was his eye! yes, it was this! One of his eyes resembled that of a vulture—a pale blue eye, with a film over it. Whenever it fell upon me, my blood ran cold; and so by degrees—very gradually—I made up my mind to take the life of the old man, and thus rid myself of the eye for ever.

Now this is the point. You fancy me mad. Madmen know nothing. But you should have seen *me*. You should have seen how wisely I proceeded—with what caution—with what foresight—with what dissimulation I went to work! I was never kinder to the old man than during the whole week before I killed him. And every night, about midnight, I turned the latch of his door and opened it—oh, so gently! And then, when I had made an opening sufficient for my head, I put in a dark lantern, all closed, closed, so that no light shone out, and then I thrust in my head. Oh, you would have laughed to see how cunningly I thrust it in! I moved it slowly—very, very slowly, so that I might not disturb the old man's sleep. It took me an hour to place my whole head within the opening so far that I could see him as he lay upon his bed. Ha—would a madman have been so wise as this? And then, when my head was well in the room, I undid the lantern cautiously—oh, so cautiously—cautiously (for the hinges creaked)—I undid it just so much that a single thin ray fell upon the vulture eye. And this I did for seven long nights—every night just after midnight—but I found the eye always closed; and so it was impossible to do the work; for it was not the old man who vexed me, but his Evil Eye. And every morning, when the day broke, I went boldly into the chamber, and spoke courageously to him, calling him by name in a hearty tone, and inquiring how he had passed the night. So you see he would have been a very profound old man, indeed, to suspect that every night, just at twelve, I looked in upon him while he slept.

Upon the eighth night I was more than usually cautious in opening the door. A watch's minute hand moves more quickly than did mine. Never before that night had I *felt* the extent of my own powers—of my sagacity. I could scarcely contain my feelings of triumph. To think that there I was, opening the door, little by little, and he not even to dream of my secret deeds or thoughts. I fairly chuckled at the idea; and perhaps he heard me; for he moved on the bed suddenly, as if startled. Now you may think that I drew back—but no. His room was as black as pitch with the thick darkness (for the shutters were close fastened, through fear of robbers), and so I knew that he could not see the opening of the door, and I kept pushing it on steadily, steadily.

5   I had my head in, and was about to open the lantern, when my thumb slipped upon the tin fastening, and the old man sprang up in the bed, crying out—"Who's there?"

I kept quite still and said nothing. For a whole hour I did not move a muscle, and in the meantime I did not hear him lie down. He was still sitting up in the bed listening;—just as I have done, night after night, hearkening to the death watches in the wall.

Presently I heard a slight groan, and I knew it was the groan of mortal terror. It was not a groan of pain or of grief—oh, no!—it was the low stifled sound that arises from the bottom of the soul when overcharged with awe. I knew the sound well. Many a night, just at midnight, when all the world slept, it has welled up from my own bosom, deepening with its dreadful echo, the terrors that distracted me. I say I knew it well. I knew what the old man felt, and pitied him, although I chuckled at heart. I knew that he had been lying awake ever since the first slight noise, when he had turned in the bed. His fears had been ever since growing upon him. He had been trying to fancy them causeless, but could not. He had been saying to himself— "It is nothing but the wind in the chimney—it is only a mouse crossing the floor," or "it is merely a cricket which has made a single chirp." Yes, he has been trying to comfort himself with these suppositions; but he had found all in vain. *All in vain;* because Death, in approaching him, had stalked with his black shadow before him, and enveloped the victim. And it was the mournful influence of the unperceived shadow that caused him to feel—although he neither saw nor heard—to *feel* the presence of my head within the room.

When I had waited a long time, very patiently, without hearing him lie down, I resolved to open a little—a very, very little crevice in the lantern. So I opened it—you cannot imagine how stealthily, stealthily—until, at length, a single dim ray, like the thread of the spider, shot from out the crevice and full upon the vulture eye.

It was open—wide, wide open—and I grew furious as I gazed upon it. I saw it with perfect distinctness—all a dull blue, with a hideous veil over it that chilled the very marrow in my bones, but I could see nothing else of the old man's face or person: for I had directed the ray as if by instinct, precisely upon the damned spot.

And now have I not told you that what you mistake for madness is but over-acuteness of the senses?—now, I say, there came to my ears a low, dull, quick sound, such as a watch makes when enveloped in cotton. I knew *that* sound well too. It was the beating of the old man's heart. It increased my fury, as the beating of a drum stimulates the soldier into courage.

But even yet I refrained and kept still. I scarcely breathed. I held the lantern motionless. I tried how steadily I could maintain the ray upon the eye. Meantime the hellish tattoo of the heart increased. It grew quicker and quicker, and louder and louder every instant. The old man's terror *must* have been extreme! It grew louder, I say, louder every moment!—do you mark me well? I have told you that I am nervous: so I am. And now at the dead hour of the night, amid the dreadful silence of that old house, so strange a noise as this excited me to uncontrollable terror. Yet, for some minutes longer I refrained and stood still. But the beating grew louder, louder! I thought the heart must burst. And now a new anxiety seized me—the sound would be heard by a neighbor! The old man's hour had come! With a loud yell, I threw open the lantern and leaped into the room. He shrieked once— once only. In an instant I dragged him to the floor, and pulled the heavy bed over him. I then smiled gaily, to find the deed so far done. But, for many minutes, the heart beat on with a muffled sound. This, however, did not vex me; it would not be heard through the wall. At length it ceased. The old man was dead. I removed the bed and examined the corpse. Yes, he was stone, stone dead. I placed my hand upon the heart and held it there many minutes. There was no pulsation. He was stone dead. His eye would trouble me no more.

If still you think me mad, you will think so no longer when I describe the wise precautions I took for the concealment of the body. The night waned, and I worked hastily, but in silence. First of all I dismembered the corpse. I cut off the head and the arms and the legs.

I then took up three planks from the flooring of the chamber, and deposited all between the scantlings. I then replaced the boards so cleverly, so cunningly, that no human eye—not even *his*—could have detected anything wrong. There was nothing to wash out—no stain of any kind—no blood-spot whatever. I had been too wary for that. A tub had caught all—ha! ha!

When I had made an end of these labors, it was four o'clock—still dark as midnight. As the bell sounded the hour, there came a knocking at the street door. I went down to open it with a light heart—for what had I *now* to fear? There entered three men, who introduced themselves, with perfect suavity, as officers of the police. A shriek had been heard by a neighbor during the night; suspicion of foul play had been aroused; information had been lodged at the police office, and they (the officers) had been deputed to search the premises.

I smiled—for *what* had I to fear? I bade the gentlemen welcome. The shriek, I said, was my own in a dream. The old man, I mentioned, was absent in the country. I took my visitors all over the house. I bade them search—search well. I led them, at length, to *his* chamber. I showed them his treasures, secure, undisturbed. In the enthusiasm of my confidence, I brought chairs into the room, and desired them *here* to rest from their fatigues, while I myself, in the wild audacity of my perfect triumph, placed my own seat upon the very spot beneath which reposed the corpse of the victim.

The officers were satisfied. My *manner* had convinced them. I was singularly at ease. They sat, and while I answered cheerily, they chatted familiar things. But, ere long, I felt myself getting pale and wished them gone. My head ached, and I fancied a ringing in my ears: but still they sat and still chatted. The ringing became more distinct:—it continued and became more distinct: I talked more freely to get rid of the feeling: but it continued and gained definitiveness—until, at length, I found that the noise was *not* within my ears.

No doubt I now grew *very* pale;—but I talked more fluently, and with a heightened voice. Yet the sound increased—and what could I do? It was *a low, dull, quick sound—much such a sound as a watch makes when enveloped in cotton.* I gasped for breath—and yet the officers heard it not. I talked more quickly—more vehemently; but the noise steadily increased. I arose and argued about trifles, in a high key and with violent gesticulations, but the noise steadily increased. Why *would* they not be gone? I paced the floor to and fro with heavy strides, as if excited to fury by the observation of the men—but the noise steadily increased. Oh God! what *could* I do? I foamed—I raved—I swore! I swung the chair upon which I had been sitting, and grated it upon the boards, but the noise arose over all and continually increased. It grew louder—louder—*louder!* And still the men chatted pleasantly, and smiled. Was it possible they heard not? Almighty God!—no, no! They heard!—they suspected!—they *knew!*—they were making a mockery of my horror!—this I thought, and this I think. But any thing was better than this agony! Any thing was more tolerable than this derision! I could bear those hypocritical smiles no longer! I felt that I must scream or die!—and now—again!—hark! louder! louder! louder! *louder!*—

"Villains!" I shrieked, "dissemble no more! I admit the deed!—tear up the planks!—here, here!—it is the beating of his hideous heart!"

15

Reading

Reading and Thinking

1. What is your impression of the narrator of "The Tell-Tale Heart"? What details led you to that impression? Did you find yourself changing your view of the narrator at any point in the story? Why or why not?

2. Identify one passage of description in the story that you find especially interesting. Explain what interests you about the passage and why you think it is important.

3. Why do you think the narrator is obsessed with the old man's eye? What possible symbolic significance might the eye have? Explain.

4. Do you think that the story is appropriately titled? Why or why not? Explain.

Thinking and Writing

1. Write an analysis of "The Tell-Tale Heart," focusing on the narrator and his relationship with the old man.

2. Provide an explanation of what happens at the end of the story. What influences the narrator to talk the way he does with the police? What is the reaction of the police to his manner of talking and to his behavior?

3. Write an essay about a time you felt guilty for something you had done. Explain how you may have tried to hide your guilt, if and how you were found out, and how you felt about it all.

4. Read another of Poe's stories—"The Black Cat," "The Cask of Amontillado," or "The Pit and the Pendulum," for example—and compare that story with "The Tell-Tale Heart."

Creating Occasions

Create your own interactive Occasion on *Comp21* using the textual, visual, and video libraries, as well as the Explicator analysis tools. From the main menu, choose "Build Your Own Occasion for Writing."

OLIVER SACKS

Born in London in 1933 to two physicians, Oliver Sacks received his medical degree at Oxford University before moving to the United States to practice neurology, as an intern in San Francisco, at the University of California in Los Angeles, and at the Albert Einstein College of Medicine in the Bronx. Best known for his down-to-earth writings on neurology, Sacks's 1974 book *Awakenings,* about patients recovering from comas, was made into a movie starring Robin Williams. Besides *Awakenings,* Sacks is the author of several other books and essays. According to his own Web site at http://www.oliversacks.com, he is "concerned above all with the ways in which individuals survive and adapt to different neurological diseases and conditions, and what this experience can tell us about the human brain and mind."

The Man Who Mistook His Wife for a Hat

This essay, taken from *Awakenings,* tells the story of a patient who has difficulty understanding what he perceives. As you read the essay, take particular note of the ways Sacks uses the various patterns of inquiry to make his point. In particular, pay attention to how Sacks's essay—while scientific in nature—transcends scientific writing and is approachable to audiences who may not share medical training.

1   Dr. P. was a musician of distinction, well-known for many years as a singer, and then, at the local School of Music, as a teacher. It was here, in relation to his students, that certain strange problems were first observed. Sometimes a student would present himself, and Dr. P. would not recognise him; or, specifically, would not recognise his face. The moment the student spoke, he would be recognised by his voice. Such incidents multiplied, causing embarrassment, perplexity, fear—and, sometimes, comedy. For not only did Dr. P. increasingly fail to see faces, but he saw faces when there were no faces to see: genially, Magoo-like, when in the street he might pat the heads of water hydrants and parking meters, taking these to be the heads of children; he would amiably address carved knobs on the furniture and be astounded when they did not reply. At first these odd mistakes were laughed off as jokes, not least by Dr. P. himself. Had he not always had a quirky sense of humour and been given to Zen-like paradoxes and jests? His musical powers were as dazzling as ever; he did not feel ill—he had never felt better; and the mistakes were so ludicrous—and so ingenious—that they could hardly be serious or betoken anything serious. The notion of there being "something the matter" did not emerge until some three years later, when diabetes developed. Well aware that diabetes could affect his eyes, Dr. P. consulted an ophthalmologist, who took a careful history and examined his eyes closely. "There's nothing the matter with your eyes," the doctor concluded. "But there is trouble with the visual parts of your brain. You don't need my help, you must see a neurologist." And so, as a result of this referral, Dr. P. came to me.

It was obvious within a few seconds of meeting him that there was no trace of dementia in the ordinary sense. He was a man of great cultivation and charm who talked well and fluently, with imagination and humour. I couldn't think why he had been referred to our clinic.

And yet there *was* something a bit odd. He faced me as he spoke, was oriented towards me, and yet there was something the matter—it was difficult to formulate. He faced me with his *ears,* I came to think, but not with his eyes. These, instead of looking, gazing, at me, "taking me in," in the normal way, made sudden strange fixations—on my nose, on my right ear, down to my chin, up to my right eye—as if noting (even studying) these individual features, but not seeing my whole face, its changing expressions, "me," as a whole. I am not sure that I fully realised this at the time—there was just a teasing strangeness, some failure in the normal interplay of gaze and expression. He saw me, he *scanned* me, and yet . . .

"What seems to be the matter?" I asked him at length.

5 "Nothing that I know of," he replied with a smile, "but people seem to think there's something wrong with my eyes."

"But *you* don't recognise any visual problems?"

"No, not directly, but I occasionally make mistakes."

I left the room briefly to talk with his wife. When I came back, Dr. P. was sitting placidly by the window, attentive, listening rather than looking out. "Traffic," he said, "street sounds, distant trains—they make a sort of symphony, do they not? You know Honegger's *Pacific 234?*"

What a lovely man, I thought to myself. How can there be anything seriously the matter? Would he permit me to examine him?

10 "Yes, of course, Dr. Sacks."

I stilled my disquiet, his perhaps, too, in the soothing routine of a neurological exam—muscle strength, coordination, reflexes, tone. . . . It was while examining his reflexes—a trifle abnormal on the left side—that the first bizarre experience occurred. I had taken off his left shoe and scratched the sole of his foot with a key—a frivolous-seeming but essential test of a reflex—and then, excusing myself to screw my ophthalmoscope together, left him to put on the shoe himself. To my surprise, a minute later, he had not done this.

"Can I help?" I asked.

"Help what? Help whom?"

"Help you put on your shoe."

15 "Ach," he said, "I had forgotten the shoe," adding, *sotto voce,* "The shoe? The shoe?" He seemed baffled.

"Your shoe," I repeated. "Perhaps you'd put it on."

He continued to look downwards, though not at the shoe, with an intense but misplaced concentration. Finally his gaze settled on his foot: "That is my shoe, yes?"

Did I mis-hear? Did he mis-see?

"My eyes," he explained, and put a hand to his foot. "*This* is my shoe, no?"

"No, it is not. That is your foot. *There* is your shoe."

"Ah! I thought that was my foot."

Was he joking? Was he mad? Was he blind? If this was one of his "strange mistakes," it was the strangest mistake I had ever come across.

I helped him on with his shoe (his foot), to avoid further complication. Dr. P. himself seemed untroubled, indifferent, maybe amused. I resumed my examination. His visual acuity was good: he had no difficulty seeing a pin on the floor, though sometimes he missed it if it was placed to his left.

He saw all right, but what did he see? I opened out a copy of the *National Geographic Magazine* and asked him to describe some pictures in it.

His responses here were very curious. His eyes would dart from one thing to another, picking up tiny features, individual features, as they had done with my face. A striking brightness, a colour, a shape would arrest his attention and elicit comment—but in no case did he get the scene-as-a-whole. He failed to see the whole, seeing only details, which he spotted like blips on a radar screen. He never entered into relation with the picture as a whole—never faced, so to speak, *its* physiognomy. He had no sense whatever of a landscape or scene.

I showed him the cover, an unbroken expanse of Sahara dunes.

"What do you see here?" I asked.

"I see a river," he said. "And a little guest-house with its terrace on the water. People are dining out on the terrace. I see coloured parasols here and there." He was looking, if it was "looking," right off the cover into mid-air and confabulating nonexistent features, as if the absence of features in the actual picture had driven him to imagine the river and the terrace and the coloured parasols.

I must have looked aghast, but he seemed to think he had done rather well. There was a hint of a smile on his face. He also appeared to have decided that the examination was over and started to look around for his hat. He reached out his hand and took hold of his wife's head, tried to lift it off, to put it on. He had apparently mistaken his wife for a hat! His wife looked as if she was used to such things.

I could make no sense of what had occurred in terms of conventional neurology (or neuropsychology). In some ways he seemed perfectly preserved, and in others absolutely, incomprehensibly devastated. How could he, on the one hand, mistake his wife for a hat and, on the other, function, as apparently he still did, as a teacher at the Music School?

I had to think, to see him again—and to see him in his own familiar habitat, at home.

A few days later I called on Dr. P. and his wife at home, with the score of the *Dichterliebe* in my briefcase (I knew he liked Schumann), and a variety of odd objects for the testing of perception. Mrs. P. showed me into a lofty apartment, which recalled fin-de-siècle Berlin. A magnificent old Bösendorfer stood in state in the centre of the room, and all around it were music stands, instruments, scores. . . . There were books, there were paintings, but the music was central. Dr. P. came in, a little bowed, and, distracted, advanced with outstretched hands to the grandfather clock, but, hearing my voice, corrected himself, and shook hands with me. We exchanged greetings and chatted a little of current concerts and performances. Diffidently, I asked him if he would sing.

"The *Dichterliebe!*" he exclaimed. "But I can no longer read music. You will play them, yes?"

I said I would try. On that wonderful old piano even my playing sounded right, and Dr. P. was an aged but infinitely mellow Fischer-Dieskau, combining a perfect ear and voice with the most incisive musical intelligence. It was clear that the Music School was not keeping him on out of charity.

Dr. P.'s temporal lobes were obviously intact: he had a wonderful musical cortex. What, I wondered, was going on in his parietal and occipital lobes, especially in those areas where visual processing occurred? I carry the Platonic solids in my neurological kit and decided to start with these.

"What is this?" I asked, drawing out the first one.

"A cube, of course."

"Now this?" I asked, brandishing another.

He asked if he might examine it, which he did swiftly and systematically: "A dodecahedron, of course. And don't bother with the others—I'll get the icosahedron, too."

Abstract shapes clearly presented no problems. What about faces? I took out a pack of cards. All of these he identified instantly, including the jacks, queens, kings, and the joker. But these, after all, are stylised designs, and it was impossible to tell whether he saw faces or merely patterns. I decided I would show him a volume of cartoons which I had in my briefcase. Here, again, for the most part, he did well. Churchill's cigar, Schnozzle's nose: as soon as he had picked out a key feature he could identify the face. But cartoons, again, are formal and schematic. It remained to be seen how he would do with real faces, realistically represented.

I turned on the television, keeping the sound off, and found an early Bette Davis film. A love scene was in progress. Dr. P. failed to identify the actress—but this could have been because she had never entered his world. What was more striking was that he failed to identify the expressions on her face or her partner's, though in the course of a single torrid scene these passed from sultry yearning through passion, surprise, disgust, and fury to a melting reconciliation. Dr. P. could make nothing of any of this. He was very unclear as to what was going on, or who was who or even what sex they were. His comments on the scene were positively Martian.

It was just possible that some of his difficulties were associated with the unreality of a celluloid, Hollywood world; and it occurred to me that he might be more successful in identifying faces from his own life. On the walls of the apartment there were photographs of his family, his colleagues, his pupils, himself. I gathered a pile of these together and, with some misgivings, presented them to him. What had been funny, or farcical, in relation to the movie, was tragic in relation to real life. By and large, he recognised nobody: neither his family, nor his colleagues, nor his pupils, nor himself. He recognised a portrait of Einstein because he picked up the characteristic hair and moustache; and the same thing happened with one or two other people. "Ach, Paul!" he said, when shown a portrait of his brother.

"That square jaw, those big teeth—I would know Paul anywhere!" But was it Paul he recognised, or one or two of his features, on the basis of which he could make a reasonable guess as to the subject's identity? In the absence of obvious "markers," he was utterly lost. But it was not merely the cognition, the *gnosis,* at fault; there was something radically wrong with the whole way he proceeded. For he approached these faces—even of those near and dear—as if they were abstract puzzles or tests. He did not relate to them, he did not behold. No face was familiar to him, seen as a "thou," being just identified as a set of features, an "it." Thus, there was formal, but no trace of personal, gnosis. And with this went his indifference, or blindness, to expression. A face, to us, is a person looking out—we see, as it were, the person through his *persona,* his face. But for Dr. P. there was no *persona* in this sense—no outward *persona,* and no person within.

I had stopped at a florist on my way to his apartment and bought myself an extravagant red rose for my buttonhole. Now I removed this and handed it to him. He took it like a botanist or morphologist given a specimen, not like a person given a flower.

"About six inches in length," he commented. "A convoluted red form with a linear green attachment."

"Yes," I said encouragingly, "and what do you think it *is,* Dr. P.?"

"Not easy to say." He seemed perplexed. "It lacks the simple symmetry of the Platonic solids, although it may have a higher symmetry of its own. . . . I think this could be an inflorescence or flower."

"Could be?" I queried.

"Could be," he confirmed.

"Smell it," I suggested, and he again looked somewhat puzzled, as if I had asked him to smell a higher symmetry. But he complied courteously, and took it to his nose. Now, suddenly, he came to life.

"Beautiful!" he exclaimed. "An early rose. What a heavenly smell!" He started to hum "*Die Rose, die Lillie . . .* " Reality, it seemed, might be conveyed by smell, not by sight.

I tried one final test. It was still a cold day, in early spring, and I had thrown my coat and gloves on the sofa.

"What is this?" I asked, holding up a glove.

"May I examine it?" he asked, and, taking it from me, he proceeded to examine it as he had examined the geometrical shapes.

"A continuous surface," he announced at last, "infolded on itself. It appears to have"—he hesitated—"five outpouchings, if this is the word."

"Yes," I said cautiously. "You have given me a description. Now tell me what it is."

"A container of some sort?"

"Yes," I said, "and what would it contain?"

"It would contain its contents!" said Dr. P., with a laugh. "There are many possibilities. It could be a change purse, for example, for coins of five sizes. It could . . ."

I interrupted the barmy flow. "Does it not look familiar? Do you think it might contain, might fit, a part of your body?"

No light of recognition dawned on his face.

No child would have the power to see and speak of "a continuous surface . . . infolded on itself," but any child, any infant, would immediately know a glove as a glove, see it as familiar, as going with a hand. Dr. P. didn't. He saw nothing as familiar. Visually, he was lost in a world of lifeless abstractions. Indeed, he did not have a real visual world, as he did not have a real visual self. He could speak about things, but did not see them face-to-face. Hughlings Jackson, discussing patients with aphasia and left-hemisphere lesions, says they have lost "abstract" and "propositional" thought—and compares them with dogs (or, rather, he compares dogs to patients with aphasia). Dr. P., on the other hand, functioned precisely as a machine functions. It wasn't merely that he displayed the same indifference to the visual world as a computer but—even more strikingly—he construed the world as a computer construes it, by means of key features and schematic relationships. The scheme might be identified—in an "identi-kit" way—without the reality being grasped at all.

The testing I had done so far told me nothing about Dr. P.'s inner world. Was it possible that his visual memory and imagination were still intact? I asked him to imagine entering one of our local squares from the north side, to walk through it, in imagination or in memory, and tell me the buildings he might pass as he walked. He listed the buildings on his right side, but none of those on his left. I then asked him to imagine entering the square from the south. Again he mentioned only those buildings that were on the right side, although these were the very buildings he had omitted before. Those he had "seen" internally before were not mentioned now; presumably, they were no longer "seen." It was evident that his difficulties with leftness, his visual field deficits, were as much internal as external, bisecting his visual memory and imagination.

What, at a higher level, of his internal visualisation? Thinking of the almost hallucinatory intensity with which Tolstoy visualises and animates his characters, I questioned Dr. P. about *Anna Karenina*. He could remember incidents without difficulty, had an undiminished grasp of the plot, but completely omitted visual characteristics, visual narrative, and scenes. He remembered the words of the characters but not their faces; and though, when asked, he could quote, with his remarkable and almost verbatim memory, the original visual descriptions, these were, it became apparent, quite empty for him and lacked sensorial, imaginal, or emotional reality. Thus, there was an internal agnosia as well.

But this was only the case, it became clear, with certain sorts of visualisation. The visualisation of faces and scenes, of visual narrative and drama—this was profoundly impaired, almost absent. But the visualisation of *schemata* was preserved, perhaps enhanced. Thus, when I engaged him in a game of mental chess, he had no difficulty visualising the chessboard or the moves—indeed, no difficulty in beating me soundly.

Luria said of Zazetsky that he had entirely lost his capacity to play games but that his "vivid imagination" was unimpaired. Zazetsky and Dr. P. lived in worlds which were mirror images of each other. But the saddest difference between them was that Zazetsky, as Luria said, "fought to regain his lost faculties with the indomitable tenacity of the damned," whereas Dr. P. was not fighting, did not know what was lost, did not indeed know that anything was lost. But who was more tragic, or who was more damned—the man who knew it, or the man who did not?

When the examination was over, Mrs. P. called us to the table, where there was coffee and a delicious spread of little cakes. Hungrily, hummingly, Dr. P. started on the cakes. Swiftly, fluently, unthinkingly, melodiously,

he pulled the plates towards him and took this and that in a great gurgling stream, an edible song of food, until, suddenly, there came an interruption: a loud, peremptory rat-tat-tat at the door. Startled, taken aback, arrested by the interruption, Dr. P. stopped eating and sat frozen, motionless, at the table, with an indifferent, blind bewilderment on his face. He saw, but no longer saw, the table; no longer perceived it as a table laden with cakes. His wife poured him some coffee: the smell titillated his nose and brought him back to reality. The melody of eating resumed.

How does he do anything? I wondered to myself. What happens when he's dressing, goes to the lavatory, has a bath? I followed his wife into the kitchen and asked her how, for instance, he managed to dress himself. "It's just like the eating," she explained. "I put his usual clothes out, in all the usual places, and he dresses without difficulty, singing to himself. He does everything singing to himself. But if he is interrupted and loses the thread, he comes to a complete stop, doesn't know his clothes—or his own body. He sings all the time—eating songs, dressing songs, bathing songs, everything. He can't do anything unless he makes it a song."

While we were talking my attention was caught by the pictures on the walls.

"Yes," Mrs. P. said, "he was a gifted painter as well as a singer. The School exhibited his pictures every year."

I strolled past them curiously—they were in chronological order. All his earlier work was naturalistic and realistic, with vivid mood and atmosphere, but finely detailed and concrete. Then, years later, they became less vivid, less concrete, less realistic and naturalistic, but far more abstract, even geometrical and cubist. Finally, in the last paintings, the canvasses became nonsense, or nonsense to me—mere chaotic lines and blotches of paint. I commented on this to Mrs. P.

"Ach, you doctors, you're such Philistines!" she exclaimed. "Can you not see *artistic development*—how he renounced the realism of his earlier years, and advanced into abstract, nonrepresentational art?"

"No, that's not it," I said to myself (but forbore to say it to poor Mrs. P.). He had indeed moved from realism to nonrepresentation to the abstract, yet this was not the artist, but the pathology, advancing—advancing towards a profound visual agnosia, in which all powers of representation and imagery, all sense of the concrete, all sense of reality, were being destroyed. This wall of paintings was a tragic pathological exhibit, which belonged to neurology, not art.

And yet, I wondered, was she not partly right? For there is often a struggle, and sometimes, even more interestingly, a collusion between the powers of pathology and creation. Perhaps, in his cubist period, there might have been both artistic and pathological development, colluding to engender an original form; for as he lost the concrete, so he might have gained in the abstract, developing a greater sensitivity to all the structural elements of line, boundary, contour—an almost Picasso-like power to see, and equally depict, those abstract organisations embedded in, and normally lost in, the concrete. . . . Though in the final pictures, I feared, there was only chaos and agnosia.

We returned to the great music room, with the Bösendorfer in the centre, and Dr. P. humming the last torte.

"Well, Dr. Sacks," he said to me. "You find me an interesting case, I perceive. Can you tell me what you find wrong, make recommendations?"

"I can't tell you what I find wrong," I replied, "but I'll say what I find right. You are a wonderful musician, and music is your life. What I would prescribe, in a case such as yours, is a life which consists entirely of music. Music has been the centre, now make it the whole, of your life."

This was four years ago—I never saw him again, but I often wondered about how he apprehended the world, given his strange loss of image, visuality, and the perfect preservation of a great musicality. I think that music, for him, had taken the place of image. He had no body-image, he had body-music: this is why he could move and act as fluently as he did, but came to a total confused stop if the "inner music" stopped. And equally with the outside, the world . . .

In *The World as Will and Representation*, Schopenhauer speaks of music as "pure will." How fascinated he would have been by Dr. P., a man who had wholly lost the world as representation, but wholly preserved it as music or will.

And this, mercifully, held to the end—for despite the gradual advance of his disease (a massive tumor or degenerative process in the visual parts of his brain) Dr. P. lived and taught music to the last days of his life.

Reading

Reading and Thinking

1. What else, other than an effective diagnosis, can you identify in this piece of writing? Is it an essay? Work out in your mind your defense of that judgment.

2. Take the first sentence of the piece: "Dr. P. was a musician of distinction, well-known for many years as a singer, and then, at the local School of Music, as a teacher." Trace the ramifications throughout the piece of that simple declarative sentence.

3. Identify two of your favorite stories from this piece and figure out how Sacks weaves them into the longer narrative. How does he get from one story to the next? Name for yourself what each of these stories accomplishes.

4. The stories are told in a particular chronological order. Can you detect an alternate order at work in the arrangement?

5. Identify the most interesting words in the essay. Account for why they are interesting to you and what they have to do with Sacks's idea about Dr. P.

Thinking and Writing

1. Study Sacks's first paragraph. Figure out how much of the entire piece is contained in microcosm in that paragraph. Write an analytical paragraph explaining your findings.

2. Write a short account of the part the wife plays in the piece. Instead of thinking about her part as an actual wife, think of her as a character in Sacks's longer story. How does he use her rhetorically?

3. Select your favorite character from real life. Bring that person to life for us the way Sacks brings Dr. P. to life, using lively stories, a sense of humor, and a group of telling anecdotes within a longer story.

Creating Occasions

Create your own interactive Occasion on *Comp21* using the textual, visual, and video libraries, as well as the Explicator analysis tools. From the main menu, choose "Build Your Own Occasion for Writing."

READING

HENRY DAVID THOREAU

Henry David Thoreau (1817-1862) was born in Concord, Massachusetts, where he spent most of his life. A graduate of Harvard, he was an early follower of Ralph Waldo Emerson, who ideas about nature Thoreau exemplified in his life and his writings. For two years Thoreau retreated from society to live alone at Walden Pond, where he built himself a simple wooden cabin, grew much of his own food, and spent his time reading, thinking, and observing nature. Out of this experience came his book *Walden,* a classic of American nonfiction. Aside from *Walden*, Thoreau is best known for his essay "On Civil Disobedience," which had a profound influence on subsequent political movements, particularly those of Mahatma Ghandi in India and the Reverend Dr. Martin Luther King, Jr., in the United States.

Why I Went to the Woods

In this excerpt from the second chapter of *Walden,* Thoreau explains why he "went to the woods," that is, why he took a sabbatical from civilization to get away from it all for a while. Essentially, Thoreau wanted time to read, write, and think. He wanted to make time for nature. And he wanted to test himself, to see just how much he could simplify his life, to determine how much time he could save to do what he really wanted to do every minute of every day.

The appeal of Thoreau's central idea and fundamental ideal is especially acute for twenty-first century America, where people strive to accomplish as much as they can as fast as they can so as to accumulate everything they think they need. Thoreau postulates an opposite alternative idea: to see how little we really require to live our lives, with an appreciation for what is truly essential and a respect for the rhythms of the natural world.

1   I went to the woods because I wished to live deliberately, to front only the essential facts of life, and see if I could not learn what it had to teach, and not, when I came to die, discover that I had not lived. I did not wish to live what was not life, living is so dear; nor did I wish to practice resignation, unless it was necessary. I wanted to live deep and suck out all the marrow of life to live so sturdily and Spartan-like as to put out all that was not life, to cut a broad swath and shave close, to drive life into a corner, and reduce it to its lowest terms, and, if it proved to be mean, why then to get the whole and genuine meanness of it, and publish its meanness to the world; or if it were sublime, to know it by experience, and be able to give a true account of it in my next excursion. For most men, it appears to me, are in a strange uncertainty about it, whether it is of the devil or of God, and have *somewhat hastily* concluded that it is the chief end of man here to "glorify God and enjoy him forever."

Still we live meanly, like ants; though the fable tells us that we were long ago changed into men; like pygmies we fight with cranes; it is error upon error, and clout upon clout, and our best virtue has for its occasion a superfluous and evitable wretchedness. Our life is frittered away by detail. An honest man has hardly need to count more than his ten fingers, or in extreme cases he may add his ten toes, and lump the rest. Simplicity, simplicity, simplicity! I say, let your affairs be as two or three, and not a hundred or a thousand; instead of a million count half a dozen, and keep your accounts on your thumbnail. In the midst of this chopping sea of civilized life, such are the clouds and storms and quicksands and thousand-and-one items to be allowed for, that a man had to live, if he would not founder and go to the bottom and not make his port at all, by dead reckoning and he must be a great calculator indeed who succeeds. Simplify, simplify. Instead of three meals a day, if it be necessary to eat but one; instead of a hundred dishes, five; and reduce other things in proportion. Our life is like a German Confederacy, made up of petty states, with its boundary forever fluctuating, so that even a German cannot tell you how it is bounded at any moment. The nation itself, with all its so-called internal improvements, which by the way are all external and superficial, is just such an unwieldy and overgrown establishment, cluttered with furniture and tripped up by its own traps, ruined by luxury and heedless expense, by want of calculation and a worthy aim, as the million households in the lands; and the only cure for it, as for them, is in a rigid economy, a stern and more than Spartan simplicity of life and elevation of purpose. It lives too fast. Men think that it is essential that the *Nation* have commerce, and export ice, and talk through a telegraph, and ride thirty miles an hour, without a doubt, whether *they* do or not; but whether we should live like baboons or like men, is a little uncertain. If we do not get our sleepers, and forge rails, and devote days and nights to the work, but go to tinkering upon our *lives* to improve *them,* who will build railroads? And if railroads are not built, how shall we get to heaven in season? But if we stay at home and mind our business, who will want railroads? We do not ride on the railroad; it rides upon us. Did you ever think what those sleepers are that underlie the railroad? Each one is a man, an Irishman, or a Yankee man. The rails are laid on them, and they are covered with sand, and the cars run smoothly over them. They are sound sleepers, I assure you. And every few years a new lot is laid down and run over; so that, if some have the pleasure of riding on a rail, others have the misfortune to be ridden upon. And when they run over a man that is walking in his sleep, a supernumerary sleeper in the wrong position, and wake him up, they suddenly stop the cars, and make a hue and cry about it, as if this were an exception. I am glad to know that it takes a gang of men for every five miles to keep the sleepers down and level in their beds as it is, for this is a sign that they may sometimes get up again.

Why should we live with such hurry and waste of life? We are determined to be starved before we are hungry. Men say that a stitch in time saves nine, and so they take a thousand stitches to-day to save nine to-morrow. As for *work,* we haven't any of any consequence. We have the Saint Vitus' dance, and cannot possibly keep our heads still. If I should only give a few pulls at the parish bell-rope, as for a fire, that is, without setting the bell, there is hardly a man on his farm in the outskirts of Concord, notwithstanding that press of engagements which was his excuse so many times this morning, nor a boy, nor a woman, I might almost say, but would forsake all and follow that sound, not mainly to save property from the flames, but if we will confess the truth, much more to see it burn, since burn it must, and we, be it known, did not set it on fire—or to see it put out, and have a hand in it, if that is done as handsomely; yes, even if it were the parish church itself. Hardly a man takes a half-hour's nap after dinner, but when he wakes he holds up his head and asks, "What's the news?" as if the rest of mankind had stood his sentinels. Some give directions to be waked every half-hour, doubtless for no other purpose; and then, to pay for it, they tell what they have dreamed. After a night's sleep the news is as indispensable as the breakfast. "Pray tell me anything new that has happened to a man anywhere on this globe"—and he reads it over his coffee and rolls, that a man has had his eyes gouged out this morning on the Wachito River; never dreaming the while that he lives in the dark unfathomed mammoth cave of this world, and has but the rudiment of an eye himself.

For my part, I could easily do without the post-office. I think that there are very few important communications made through it. To speak critically, I never received more than one or two letters in my life—I wrote this some years ago—that were worth the postage. The penny-post is, commonly, an institution through which you seriously offer a man that penny for his thoughts which is so often safely offered in jest. And I am sure that I never read any memorable news in a newspaper. If we read of one man robbed, or murdered, or killed by accident, or one house burned, or one vessel wrecked, or one steamboat blown up, or one cow run over on the Western Railroad, or one mad dog killed, or one lot of grasshoppers in the winter—we never need

Reading

read of another. One is enough. If you are acquainted with the principle, what do you care for a myriad instances and applications? To a philosopher all *news,* as it is called, is gossip, and they who edit and read it are old women over their tea. Yet not a few are greedy after this gossip. There was such a rush, as I hear, the other day at one of the offices to learn the foreign news by the last arrival, that several large squares of plate glass belonging to the establishment were broken by the pressure—news which I seriously think a ready wit might write a twelvemonth, or twelve years, beforehand with sufficient accuracy. As for Spain, for instance, if you know how to throw in Don Carlos and the Infanta, and Don Pedro and Seville and Granada, from time to time in the right proportions—they may have changed the names a little since I saw the papers—and serve up a bullfight when other entertainments fail, it will be true to the letter, and give us as good an idea of the exact state or ruin of things in Spain as the most succinct and lucid reports under this head in the newspapers; and as for England, almost the last significant scrap of news from that quarter was the revolution of 1649; and if you have learned the history of her crops for an average year, you never need attend to that thing again, unless your speculations are of a merely pecuniary character. If one may judge who rarely looks into the newspapers, nothing new does ever happen in foreign parts, a French revolution not excepted.

5   What news! how much more important to know what that is which was never old! "Kieou-he-yu (great dignitary of the state of Wei) sent a man to Khoung-tseu to know his news. Khoung-tseu caused the messenger to be seated near him, and questioned him in these terms: What is your master doing? The messenger answered with respect: My master desires to diminish the number of his faults, but he cannot come to the end of them. The messenger being gone, the philosopher remarked: What a worthy messenger! What a worthy messenger!" The preacher, instead of vexing the ears of drowsy farmers on their day of rest at the end of the week—for Sunday is the fit conclusion of an ill-spent week, and not the fresh and brave beginning of a new one—with this one other draggle-tail of a sermon, should shout with thundering voice, "Pause! Avast! Why so seeming fast, but deadly slow?"

Shams and delusions are esteemed for soundless truths, while reality is fabulous. If men would steadily observe realities only, and not allow themselves to be deluded, life, to compare it with such things as we know, would be like a fairy tale and the Arabian Nights' Entertainments. If we respected only what is inevitable and has a right to be, music and poetry would resound along the streets. When we are unhurried and wise, we perceive that only great and worthy things have any permanent and absolute existence, that petty fears and petty pleasures are but the shadow of the reality. This is always exhilarating and sublime. By closing the eyes and slumbering, and consenting to be deceived by shows, men establish and confirm their daily life of routine and habit everywhere, which still is built on purely illusory foundations. Children, who play life, discern its true law and relations more clearly than men, who fail to live it worthily, but who think that they are wiser by experience, that is, by failure. I have read in a Hindoo book, that "there was a king's son, who, being expelled in infancy from his native city, was brought up by a forester, and, growing up to maturity in that state, imagined himself to belong to the barbarous race with which he lived. One of his father's ministers having discovered him, revealed to him what he was, and the misconception of his character was removed, and he knew himself to be a prince. So soul," continues the Hindoo philosopher, "from the circumstances in which it is placed, mistakes its own character, until the truth is revealed to it by some holy teacher and then it knows itself to be *Brahme.*" I perceive that we inhabitants of New England live this mean life that we do because our vision does not penetrate the surface of things. We think that that *is* which *appears* to be. If a man should walk through this town and see only the reality, where, think you, would the "Milldam" go to? If he should give us an account of the realities he beheld there, we should not recognize the place in his description. Look at the meetinghouse, or a courthouse, or a jail, or a shop, or a dwelling-house, and say what that thing really is before a true gaze, and they would all go to pieces in your account of them. Men esteem truth remote, in the outskirts of the system, behind the farthest star, before Adam and after the last man. In eternity there is indeed something true and sublime. But

Reading

all these times and places and occasions are now and here. God himself culminates in the present moment, and will never be more divine in the lapse of all the ages. And we are enabled to apprehend at all what is sublime and noble only by the perpetual instilling and drenching of the reality that surrounds us. The universe constantly and obediently answers to our conceptions; whether we travel fast or slow, the track is laid for us. Let us spend our lives in conceiving then. The poet or the artist never yet had so fair and noble a design but some of his posterity at least could accomplish it.

Let us spend one day as deliberately as Nature, and not be thrown off the track by every nutshell and mosquito's wing that falls on the rails. Let us rise early and fast, or breakfast, gently, and without perturbation; let company come and let company go, let the bells ring and the children cry—determined to make a day of it. Why should we knock under and go with the stream? Let us not be upset and overwhelmed in that terrible rapid and whirlpool called a dinner, situated in the meridian shallows. Weather this danger and you are safe, for the rest of the way is downhill. With unrelaxed nerves, with morning vigor, sail by it, looking another way, tied to the mast like Ulysses. If the engine whistles, let it whistle till it is hoarse for its pains. If the bell rings, why should we run? We will consider what kind of music they are like. Let us settle ourselves and work and wedge our feet downward through the mud and slush of opinion, and prejudice, and tradition, and delusion, and appearance, that alluvion which covers the globe, through Paris and London, through New York and Boston and Concord, through Church and State, through poetry and philosophy and religion, till

we come to a hard bottom and rocks in place, which we can call *reality,* and say, This is, and no mistake; and then begin, having a *point d'appui,* below freshet and frost and fire, a place where you might found a wall or a state, or set a lamppost safely, or perhaps a gauge, not a Nilometer, but a Realometer, that future ages might know how deep a freshet of shams and appearances had gathered from time to time. If you stand right fronting and face to face to a fact, you will see the sun glimmer on both its surfaces, as if it were a cimeter, and feel its sweet edge dividing you through the heart and marrow, and so you will happily conclude your mortal career. Be it life or death, we crave only reality. If we are really dying, let us hear the rattle in our throats and feel cold in the extremities; if we are alive, let us go about our business.

Time is but the stream I go afishing in. I drink at it; but while I drink I see the sandy bottom and detect how shallow it is. Its thin current slides away but eternity remains. I would drink deeper; fish in the sky, whose bottom is pebbly with stars. I cannot count one. I know not the first letter of the alphabet. I have always been regretting that I was not as wise as the day I was born. The intellect is a cleaver; it discerns and rifts its way into the secret of things. I do not wish to be any more busy with my hands than is necessary. My head is hands and feet. I feel all my best faculties concentrated in it. My instinct tells me that my head is an organ for burrowing, as some creatures use their snout and fore paws, and with it I would mine and burrow my way through these hills. I think that the richest vein is somewhere hereabouts; so by the divining-rod and thin rising vapors, I judge; and here I will begin to mine.

Reading and Thinking

1. What do you think was Thoreau's purpose in this essay? Where is this purpose clearest and most explicit? What is Thoreau's central idea, and where is it expressed most strongly?

2. Identify three key images and/or metaphors Thoreau uses to explain his thinking here. How do those metaphors work to convey his meaning and his feeling?

3. Analyze Thoreau's tone in this piece. How would you characterize his tone? Does the tone change at any point? If so, where and to what effect?

Thinking and Writing

1. Use the notes you made for the first three questions to write an analysis of "Why I Went to the Woods." Be sure to explain not only what Thoreau says in the piece, but his manner of saying it—his rhetorical strategies—as well.

2. Write a response to Thoreau's ideas about how we should live our lives. Consider the extent to which his ideas can be adapted to life in the twenty-first century.

3. Select a few advertisements that use nature as part of their selling strategy. Identify the selling pitch and the way nature is used to help make that pitch either directly or indirectly.

Creating Occasions

Create your own interactive Occasion on *Comp21* using the textual, visual, and video libraries, as well as the Explicator analysis tools. From the main menu, choose "Build Your Own Occasion for Writing."

MARK TWAIN

Mark Twain (1835-1910) was born Samuel L. Clemens in Missouri, where he grew up, spending most of his time in the river town of Hannibal. Like Ben Franklin a century earlier, Twain held a variety of jobs, including working as a printer and a journalist. His most distinctive and memorable job, however, was that of a Mississippi steamboat pilot, the experience of which he turned into a pair of books, *Old Times on the Mississippi* and *Life on the Mississippi*. In addition to this work based on his boyhood memories and his own working experience, Twain is best known for his two novels, *The Adventures of Tom Sawyer* and *The Adventures of Huckleberry Finn*. Twain was also a popular lecturer both in the United States and in Europe. He mined his experience traveling the United States and the European continent and wrote other books, *Roughing It,* about the American west, and *A Tramp Abroad,* about his European travels.

Reading the River

In the following excerpt from *Life on the Mississippi,* Twain describes his experience as an apprentice steamboat pilot, particularly his attempt to learn to "read" the Mississippi River to ensure the safety of his boat, his crew, and his passengers. Twain compares the river to a book that requires interpretation if it is to be understood. By using analogies, Twain conveys the extent of the knowledge necessary for piloting a steamboat on the Mississippi River and the ever present dangers associated with that work. Twain also deepens the import and the impact of his writing through his use of analogy, so that the pilot's reading of the river becomes a metaphor for other aspects of life and knowledge.

1   It turned out to be true. The face of the water in time became a wonderful book—a book that was a dead language to the uneducated passenger but which told its mind to me without reserve, delivering its most cherished secrets as clearly as if it uttered them with a voice. And it was not a book to be read once and thrown aside, for it had a new story to tell every day. Throughout the long twelve hundred miles there was never a page that was void of interest, never one that you could leave unread without loss, never one that you would want to skip, thinking you could find higher enjoyment in some other thing. There never was so wonderful a book written by man, never one whose interest was so absorbing, so unflagging, so sparklingly renewed with every reperusal. The passenger who could not read it was charmed with a peculiar sort of faint dimple on its surface (on the rare occasions when he did not overlook it altogether) but to the pilot, that was an italicized passage; indeed it was more than that, it was a legend of the largest capitals with a string of shouting exclamation-points at the end of it, for it meant that a wreck or a rock was buried there that could tear the life out of the strongest vessel that ever floated. It is the faintest and simplest expression the water ever makes, and the most hideous to a pilot's eye. In truth, the passenger who could not read this book saw nothing but all manner of pretty pictures in it, painted by the sun and shaded by the clouds, whereas to the trained eye these were not pictures at all, but the grimmest and most dead-earnest of reading matter.

Now when I had mastered the language of this water and had come to know every trifling feature that bordered the great river as familiarly as I knew the letters of the alphabet, I had made a valuable acquisition.

But I had lost something, too. I had lost something which could never be restored to me while I lived. All the grace, the beauty, the poetry, had gone out of the majestic river! I still kept in mind a certain wonderful sunset which I witnessed when steamboating was new to me. A broad expanse of the river was turned to blood; in the middle distance the red hue brightened into gold, through which a solitary log came floating, black and conspicuous; in one place a long, slanting mark was broken by boiling, tumbling rings, that were as many-tinted as an opal; where the ruddy flush was faintest, was a smooth spot that was covered with graceful circles and radiating lines, ever so delicately traced; the shore on our left was densely wooded and the somber shadow that fell from this forest was broken in one place by a long, ruffled trail that shone like silver; and high above the forest wall a clean-stemmed dead tree waved a single leafy bough that glowed like a flame in the unobstructed splendor that was flowing from the sun. There were graceful curves, reflected images, woody heights, soft distances, and over the whole scene, far and near, the dissolving lights drifted steadily, enriching it every passing moment with new marvels of coloring.

I stood like one bewitched. I drank it in, in a speechless rapture. The world was new to me and I had never seen anything like this at home. But as I have said, a day came when I began to cease from noting the glories and the charms which the moon and the sun and the twilight wrought upon the river's face; another day came when I ceased altogether to note them. Then, if that sunset scene had been repeated, I should have looked upon it without rapture, and should have commented upon it inwardly after this fashion: "This sun means that we are going to have wind to-morrow; that floating log means that the river is rising, small thanks to it; that slanting mark on the water refers to a bluff reef which is going to kill someone's steamboat one of these nights, if it keeps on stretching out like that; those tumbling 'boils' show a dissolving bar and a changing channel there; the lines and circles in the slick water over yonder are a warning that that troublesome place is shoaling up dangerously; that silver streak in the shadow of the forest is the 'break' from a new snag and he has located himself in the very place he could have found to fish for steamboats; that tall dead tree, with a single living branch, is not going to last long, and then how is a body ever going to get through this blind place at night without the friendly old landmark?"

No, the romance and beauty were all gone from the river. All the value any feature of it had for me now was the amount of usefulness it could furnish toward compassing the safe piloting of a steamboat. Since those days, I have pitied doctors from my heart. What does the lovely flush in a beauty's cheek mean to a doctor but a "break" that ripples above some deadly disease? Are not all her visible charms sown thick with what are to him the signs and symbols of hidden decay? Does he ever see her beauty at all, or doesn't he simply view her professionally and comment upon her unwholesome condition all to himself? And doesn't he sometimes wonder whether he has gained most or lost most by learning his trade?

Reading and Thinking

1. Analyze the structure of "Reading the River." How is the piece organized? How does it develop? Explain the relationship among its paragraphs.

2. Identify and explain the analogies Twain uses to describe the river and the work of the steamboat pilot. What idea and what impression are conveyed through these analogies?

3. Analyze Twain's sentences—his use of long and short sentences, for example, and his use of questions. Identify three sentences you find particularly effective, and explain how they work and why they are effective.

Thinking and Writing

1. Use the notes you made in answering the first three questions to write an analysis of "Reading the River." Explain what Twain says and suggests in this piece. And explain how his use of language—diction, imagery, syntax, analogy—and his use of organizational structure convey his meaning.

2. Using one of Twain's analogies as a model, write a paragraph in which you use analogy to explain an idea or convey what it is like to do or experience something.

3. Write an autobiographical sketch of yourself as you were learning how to do a particular job or kind of work. Try to convey what the experience was like for you and capture something of what those who were teaching you were themselves able to do.

Creating Occasions

Create your own interactive Occasion on *Comp21* using the textual, visual, and video libraries, as well as the Explicator analysis tools. From the main menu, choose "Build Your Own Occasion for Writing."

READING

E. B. WHITE

One of the most widely read (and widely reprinted) essayists in America, E. B. White is known for his ability to render his subjects simply—sometimes humorously—and with a light touch, but always with a complex depth residing just below the surface. Born Elwyn Brooks White in 1899, White was a regular writer for *The New Yorker* for nearly fifty years. Read more about White on page 124.

Once More to the Lake

"Once More to the Lake" first appeared in *The New Yorker* in 1941. In the essay, White tells the story of a vacation he takes with his son to his own boyhood vacation resort. As you read the essay, notice the narrative drive, the descriptive detail, and the analytical undercurrent coursing through the entire essay. Notice as well the symbolism of numbers (often three), and relationships between fathers, sons, and memory. Ask yourself what these symbols represent.

1   One summer, along about 1904, my father rented a camp on a lake in Maine and took us all there for the month of August. We all got ringworm from some kittens and had to rub Pond's Extract on our arms and legs night and morning, and my father rolled over in a canoe with all his clothes on; but outside of that the vacation was a success and from then on none of us ever thought there was any place in the world like that lake in Maine. We returned summer after summer—always on August 1st for one month. I have since become a salt-water man, but sometimes in summer there are days when the restlessness of the tides and the fearful cold of the sea water and the incessant wind which blows across the afternoon and into the evening make me wish for the placidity of a lake in the woods. A few weeks ago this feeling got so strong I bought myself a couple of bass hooks and a spinner and returned to the lake where we used to go, for a week's fishing and to revisit old haunts.

I took along my son, who had never had any fresh water up his nose and who had seen lily pads only from train windows. On the journey over to the lake I began to wonder what it would be like. I wondered how time would have marred this unique, this holy spot—the coves and streams, the hills that the sun set behind, the camps and the paths behind the camps. I was sure that the tarred road would have found it out and I wondered in what other ways it would be desolated. It is strange how much you can remember about places like that once you allow your mind to return into the grooves which lead back. You remember one thing, and that suddenly reminds you of another thing. I guess I remembered clearest of all the early mornings, when the lake was cool and motionless, remembered how the bedroom smelled of the lumber it was made of and the wet woods whose scent entered through the screen. The partitions in the camp were thin and did not extend clear to the top of the rooms, and as I was always the first up I would dress softly so as not to wake the others, and sneak out into the sweet outdoors and start out in the canoe, keeping close along the shore in the long shadows of the pines. I remembered being very careful never to rub my paddle against the gunwale for fear of disturbing the stillness of the cathedral.

The lake had never been what you would call a wild lake. There were cottages sprinkled around the shores, and it was in farming country although the shores of the lake were quite heavily wooded. Some of the cottages were owned by nearby farmers, and you would live at the shore and eat your meals at the farmhouse.

That's what our family did. But although it wasn't wild, it was a fairly large and undisturbed lake and there were places in it which, to a child at least, seemed infinitely remote and primeval.

I was right about the tar: it led to within half a mile of the shore. But when I got back there, with my boy, and we settled into a camp near a farmhouse and into the kind of summertime I had known, I could tell that it was going to be pretty much the same as it had been before—I knew it, lying in bed the first morning, smelling the bedroom, and hearing the boy sneak quietly out and go off along the shore in a boat. I began to sustain the illusion that he was I, and therefore, by simple transposition, that I was my father. This sensation persisted, kept cropping up all the time we were there. It was not an entirely new feeling, but in this setting it grew much stronger. I seemed to be living a dual existence. I would be in the middle of some simple act, I would be picking up a bait box or laying down a table fork, or I would be saying something, and suddenly it would be not I but my father who was saying the words or making the gesture. It gave me a creepy sensation.

5   We went fishing the first morning. I felt the same damp moss covering the worms in the bait can, and saw the dragonfly alight on the tip of my rod as it hovered a few inches from the surface of the water. It was the arrival of this fly that convinced me beyond any doubt that everything was as it always had been, that the years were a mirage and there had been no years. The small waves were the same, chucking the rowboat under the chin as we fished at anchor, and the boat was the same boat, the same color green and the ribs broken in the same places, and under the floor-boards the same freshwater leavings and débris—the dead helgramite, the wisps of moss, the rusty discarded fishhook, the dried blood from yesterday's catch. We stared silently at the tips of our rods, at the dragonflies that came and went. I lowered the tip of mine into the water, tentatively, pensively dislodging the fly, which darted two feet away, poised, darted two feet back, and came to rest again a little farther up the rod. There had been no years between the ducking of this dragonfly and the other one—the one that was part of memory. I looked at the boy, who was silently watching his fly, and it was my hands that held his rod, my eyes watching. I

felt dizzy and didn't know which rod I was at the end of.

We caught two bass, hauling them in briskly as though they were mackerel, pulling them over the side of the boat in a businesslike manner without any landing net, and stunning them with a blow on the back of the head. When we got back for a swim before lunch, the lake was exactly where we had left it, the same number of inches from the dock, and there was only the merest suggestion of a breeze. This seemed an utterly enchanted sea, this lake you could leave to its own devices for a few hours and come back to, and find that it had not stirred, this constant and trustworthy body of water. In the shallows, the dark, water-soaked sticks and twigs, smooth and old, were undulating in clusters on the bottom against the clean ribbed sand, and the track of the mussel was plain. A school of minnows swam by, each minnow with its small individual shadow, doubling the attendance, so clear and sharp in the sunlight. Some of the other campers were in swimming, along the shore, one of them with a cake of soap, and the water felt thin and clear and unsubstantial. Over the years there had been this person with the cake of soap, this cultist, and here he was. There had been no years.

Up to the farmhouse to dinner through the teeming, dusty field, the road under our sneakers was only a two-track road. The middle track was missing, the one with the marks of the hooves and the splotches of dried, flaky manure. There had always been three tracks to choose from in choosing which track to walk in; now the choice was narrowed down to two. For a moment I missed terribly the middle alternative. But the way led past the tennis court, and something about the way it lay there in the sun reassured me; the tape had loosened along the backline, the alleys were green with plantains and other weeds, and the net (installed in June and removed in September) sagged in the dry noon, and the whole place steamed with midday heat and hunger and emptiness. There was a choice of pie for dessert, and one was blueberry and one was apple, and the waitresses were the same country girls, there having been no passage of time, only the illusion of it as in a dropped curtain—the waitresses were still fifteen; their hair had been washed, that was the only differ-

Yet, because he was so small, and so simple a form of the energy that was rolling in at the open window and driving its way through so many narrow and intricate corridors in my own brain and in those of other human beings, there was something marvelous as well as pathetic about him. It was as if someone had taken a tiny bead of pure life and decking it as lightly as possible with down and feathers, had set it dancing and zigzagging to show us the true nature of life. Thus displayed one could not get over the strangeness of it. One is apt to forget all about life, seeing it humped and bossed and garnished and cumbered so that it has to move with the greatest circumspection and dignity. Again, the thought of all that life might have been had he been born in any other shape caused one to view his simple activities with a kind of pity.

After a time, tired by his dancing apparently, he settled on the window ledge in the sun, and, the queer spectacle being at an end, I forgot about him. Then, looking up, my eye was caught by him. He was trying to resume his dancing, but seemed either so stiff or so awkward that he could only flutter to the bottom of the windowpane; and when he tried to fly across it he failed. Being intent on other matters I watched these futile attempts for a time without thinking, unconsciously waiting for him to resume his flight, as one waits for a machine, that has stopped momentarily, to start again without considering the reason of its failure. After perhaps a seventh attempt he slipped from the wooden ledge and fell, fluttering his wings, on to his back on the windowsill. The helplessness of his attitude roused me. It flashed upon me that he was in difficulties; he could no longer raise himself; his legs struggled vainly. But, as I stretched out a pencil, meaning to help him to right himself, it came over me that the failure and awkwardness were the approach of death. I laid the pencil down again.

The legs agitated themselves once more. I looked as if for the enemy against which he struggled. I looked out of doors. What had happened there? Presumably it was midday, and work in the fields had stopped. Stillness and quiet had replaced the previous animation. The birds had taken themselves off to feed in the brooks. The horse stood still. Yet the power was there all the same, massed outside, indifferent, impersonal, not attending to anything in particular. Somehow it was opposed to the little hay-colored moth. It was useless to try to do anything. One could only watch the extraordinary efforts made by those tiny legs against an oncoming doom which would, had it chosen, have submerged an entire city, not merely a city, but masses of human beings; nothing, I knew had any chance against death. Nevertheless after a pause of exhaustion the legs fluttered again. It was superb this last protest, and so frantic that he succeeded at last in righting himself. One's sympathies, of course, were all on the side of life. Also, when there was nobody to care or to know, this gigantic effort on the part of an insignificant little moth, against a power of such magnitude, to retain what no one else valued or desired to keep, moved one strangely. Again, somehow, one saw life, a pure bead. I lifted the pencil again, useless though I knew it to be. But even as I did so, the unmistakable tokens of death showed themselves. The body relaxed, and instantly grew stiff. The struggle was over. The insignificant little creature now knew death. As I looked over at the dead moth, this minute wayside triumph of so great a force over so mean an antagonist filled me with wonder. Just as life had been strange a few minutes before, so death was now as strange. The moth having righted himself now lay most decently and uncomplainingly composed. O yes, he seemed to say, death is stronger than I am.

Reading and Thinking

1. Look carefully at the first paragraph of the essay and list the ways that Woolf invokes life and what she calls *vigor*. Which do you consider the most effective?

2. Where does Woolf first put us on the scent of death? Is it with the image of the birds in the first paragraph, the introduction of the word *pity* in the second paragraph, or elsewhere? Explain.

3. How does Woolf make the moth represent all of us?

4. Trace the appearance of the pencil throughout the essay and begin to figure out why Woolf introduces it.

Thinking and Writing

1. Make a list of all the words associated with life and another of the words associated with death. From these lists, what can you infer about the relationship between life and death in Woolf's imagination? Explain in one paragraph.

2. What do the moth and Woolf have to do with one another? Consider her attitude towards the moth and its struggle; consider as well the words *right* and *righted*. Explain why she might be punning with those words.

3. Select three of your favorite instances of description. What do those instances tell us about Woolf's idea? Explain in a paragraph or two.

4. What is the importance of the moth's size and its seeming insignificance? In terms of what Woolf shows us, how does the moth's smallness make us (and Woolf) akin to it?

5. In a short essay account for Woolf's attitude toward death, as she develops it in this essay.

Creating Occasions

Create your own interactive Occasion on *Comp21* using the textual, visual, and video libraries, as well as the Explicator analysis tools. From the main menu, choose "Build Your Own Occasion for Writing."

FINDING EVIDENCE
AND DOCUMENTING SOURCES

TYPES OF EVIDENCE

Good writing not only uses the English language effectively, but also incorporates evidence appropriately. Consider your everyday conversations with friends, family, or other students. Even in these informal situations, most of us use a variety of techniques to support our assertions. If you want to convince your friends to try a new restaurant, you might tell them that the restaurant was positively reviewed by the local newspaper. You might also point to the ways in which the testimony of others or personal experience corroborates your claim. Similarly, a strong written argument is comprised of both claims and evidence.

WHAT IS EVIDENCE?

Any outside source that enables you to write more critically and thoroughly about your topic of research, and assists you in persuading your audience of your argument, can be considered evidence. Evidence includes a wide range of materials; it can be either written or visual. Remember that you can find evidence from your reading, your observation, and your own experiences. As you develop your idea, or account for your evidence, you may look to traditional forms of evidence, such as books, journals, magazines, newspapers, and electronic sources (such as Web sites, discussion forums, and online books and magazines). You might also, however, turn to nontraditional items as sources. Billboards and signs, even song lyrics and video games, can be used as evidence. The controversies that shape the world around us are reflected not only in

A painting, sculpture, or photograph

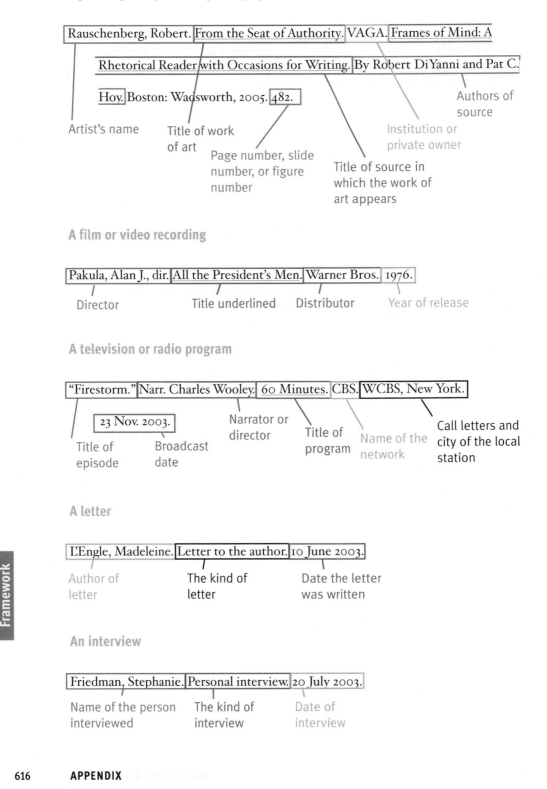

Rauschenberg, Robert. From the Seat of Authority. VAGA. Frames of Mind: A Rhetorical Reader with Occasions for Writing. By Robert DiYanni and Pat C. Hoy. Boston: Wadsworth, 2005. 482.

- Artist's name
- Title of work of art
- Page number, slide number, or figure number
- Title of source in which the work of art appears
- Institution or private owner
- Authors of source

A film or video recording

Pakula, Alan J., dir. All the President's Men. Warner Bros. 1976.

- Director
- Title underlined
- Distributor
- Year of release

A television or radio program

"Firestorm." Narr. Charles Wooley. 60 Minutes. CBS. WCBS, New York. 23 Nov. 2003.

- Title of episode
- Broadcast date
- Narrator or director
- Title of program
- Name of the network
- Call letters and city of the local station

A letter

L'Engle, Madeleine. Letter to the author. 10 June 2003.

- Author of letter
- The kind of letter
- Date the letter was written

An interview

Friedman, Stephanie. Personal interview. 20 July 2003.

- Name of the person interviewed
- The kind of interview
- Date of interview

SAMPLE WORKS CITED PAGE

Works Cited

Bowman, Darcia Harris. "States Target School Vending Machines to Curb Child

  Obesity." <u>Education Week</u> 1 Oct. 2003: 1. <u>Academic Search Premier</u>. EBSCO.

  U of Texas at Austin, Perry-Castaneda Lib. 3 Mar. 2004

  <http://www.epnet.com>.

Chen, Chunming and William H. Dietz, ed. <u>Obesity in Childhood and Adolescence</u>.

  Philadelphia: Lippincott, 2002.

Drummond, Jon W. "Man vs. Machine: School Vending Machines Are in the

  Crosshairs of the Obesity Debate." <u>Restaurants and Institutions</u> 113.25 (2003):

  63–66.

Fairburn, Christopher G. and Kelly D. Brownell, ed. <u>Eating Disorders and Obesity: A</u>

  <u>Comprehensive Handbook</u>. 2nd ed. New York: Guilford, 2002.

Goode, Erica. "The Gorge-Yourself Environment." <u>New York Times</u> 22 July 2003: F1.

  <u>InfoTrac College Edition</u>. University of Texas at Austin, Perry-Castaneda Lib.

  22 Dec. 2003 <http://www.infotrac.thomsonlearning.com/>.

Goodnough, Abby. "Schools Cut Down on Fat and Sweets in Menus." <u>New York</u>

  <u>Times</u>. 25 June 2003: B1.

<u>The Center for Health and Health Care in Schools</u>. Ed. Virginia Robinson. The Cen-

  ter for Health and Health Care in Schools. 26 Mar 2004. 5 Apr. 2004

  <http://www.healthinschools.org/home.asp>.

Framework

INDEX OF VISUALS

INDEX OF READINGS

CREDITS

VISUAL

p. xxiv © 2004 Estate of Pablo Picasso/Artists Rights Society (ARS), New York.

p. 8 © Thomas Roma, Brooklyn, NY. From "Show and Tell."

p. 9 ©Ralph A. Clevenger/CORBIS.

p. 12a © CARTER KEVIN/CORBIS SYGMA.

p. 12b Photo © www.danheller.com.

p. 14 © Bruno Barbey, Magnum Photos.

p. 19 Reprinted by permission of Stephen Loy.

p. 22 Photographed by Charles Hopkins. Courtesy of DaimlerChysler Corporation.

p. 23 © AP/Wide World Photos/Ken Lambert.

p. 30 Edward R. Tufte, *The Visual Display of Quantitative Information,* Graphics Press, 1983.

p. 47 Picasso, Pablo (1881-1973) © ARS, NY.

p. 49 © 2005 C. Herscovici, Brussels/Artists Rights Society (ARS), New York. © A. Lude Collection/ Lauros-Giraudon, Paris/SuperStock.

p. 50 © 2005 C. Herscovici, Brussels/Artists Rights Society.

p. 52 © Arte & Immagini SRL/CORBIS.

p. 59 © Bruce Davidson/Magnum Photos.

p. 60 © Bruce Davidson/Magnum Photos.

p. 62 © Bruce Davidson/Magnum Photos.

p. 63 © Bruce Davidson/Magnum Photos.

p. 69 © Altitude/Yann Arthus-Bertrand.

p. 72 © Altitude/Yann Arthus-Bertrand.

p. 103 Diego Velásquez, Las Meninas, 1656, Oil on Canvas. Courtesy of Museo Nacional Del Prado.

p. 104 Tiziano, "La Pietà" c. 1577, Gallerie dell'Accademia, Venezia.

p. 111a © 2004 The Georgia O'Keeffe Foundation/Artists Rights Society (ARS), New York.

p. 111b © 2004 The Georgia O'Keeffe Foundation/Artists Rights Society (ARS), New York. GEORGIA O'KEEFFE Train at Night in the Desert, 1916. Watercolor on paper. Image courtesy of the Amarillo Museum of Art.

p. 114 © Charles & Josette Lenars/CORBIS.

p. 150b © Larry Burrows/Time Life Pictures/Getty Images.

p. 150c © Larry Burrows/Time Life Pictures/Getty Images.

p. 150d © CORBIS.

p. 163 © William Mowder, 2003.

p. 164 © 2005 Artists Rights Society (ARS), New York / ADAGP, Paris / Succession Marcel Duchamp. Marcel Duchamp, Nude Descending a Staircase, No. 2, Philadelphia Museum of Art: The Louise and Walter Arensberg Collection, 1950-134-59. Used with permission.

p. 168 © Heidi Cody.

p. 188a From *Le Catalogue d'objets introuvables* by Jacques Carelman. Copyright © 1997 le cherche midi éditeur. Used with permission.

p. 188b From *Le Catalogue d'objets introuvables* by Jacques Carelman. Copyright © 1997 le cherche midi éditeur. Used with permission.

p. 189a From *Le Catalogue d'objets introuvables* by Jacques Carelman. Copyright © 1997 le cherche midi éditeur. Used with permission.

p. 320 Reprinted with the permission of Simon & Schuster Adult Publishing Group from EAT, DRINK, AND BE HEALTHY: The Harvard Medical School Guide to Healthy Eating by Walter C. Willett, M.D. Copyright © 2001 by President and Fellows of Harvard College. All rights reserved.

p. 331 Reprinted by kind permission of Dr. Richard Saul Wurman. Originally printed in *Understanding Healthcare* (TOP, 2004) by Richard Saul Wurman. Designed by Nigel Holmes with art direction by Richard Saul Wurman.

p. 342a Courtesy of Northwestern University Library.

p. 342b Courtesy of Northwestern University Library.

p. 343a Courtesy of Northwestern University Library.

p. 343b Courtesy of Northwestern University Library.

p. 346 © Corbis.

p. 369 MONOPOLY® & © 2004 Hasbro, Inc. Used with permission.

p. 376 Rube Goldberg is the ® and © of Rube Goldberg Inc. All rights reserved.

p. 378a Rube Goldberg is the ® and © of Rube Goldberg Inc. All rights reserved.

p. 378b Rube Goldberg is the ® and © of Rube Goldberg Inc. All rights reserved.

p. 384a © Hemera Photo Objects.

p. 384b © Royalty-Free/Corbis.

p. 385a © Hemera Photo Objects.

p. 385b Courtesy of SC Johnson; photo © Steven Lunetta Photography.

p. 385c Courtesy of Colgate-Palmolive; photo © Steven Lunetta Photography.

p. 385e © Hemera Photo Objects.

p. 388 © The San Jacinto Museum of History, Houston.

p. 411 Courtesy of the National Library of Medicine. Image printed courtesy of William Helfand.

p. 420 © Bettman/CORBIS.

p. 427 Copyright © 1982 Jerry Uelsmann.

p. 428 Copyright © 1982 Jerry Uelsmann.

p. 430 © EVAN SCHNEIDER/AFP/Getty Images.

p. 453 © AP/Wide World Photos.

p. 454 © Time, Inc., Photo © Steve Liss. Used by permission.

p. 469 © Keith Carter.

p. 470 © Kirk Anderson. www.kirktoons.com.

p. 471 © Swim Ink/CORBIS.

p. 479a © The New Yorker Collection 2003 Gahan Wilson from cartoonbank.com. All Rights Reserved.

p. 479b © The New Yorker Collection 2003 David Sipress from cartoonbank.com. All Rights Reserved.

p. 480 © The New Yorker Collection 2003 David Sipress from cartoonbank.com. All Rights Reserved.

p. 482 © Robert Rauschenberg/Licensed by VAGA, New York, NY.

TEXT

p. 38 Bernd Heinrich, "Whirligigs." Reprinted by permission of the publisher from IN A PATCH OF FIREWEED: A Biologist's Life in the Field by Bernd Heinrich, p. 110, Cambridge, MA: Harvard University Press. Copyright © 1984 by the President and Fellows of Harvard College.

p. 40 "Neighborly Vultures," New York Times, August 8, 2003. Copyright © 2003 New York Times Company, Inc. Used with permission.

p. 42 Saskia Verlaan, "Perspectives on Fear." Reprinted by permission of the author.

p. 54 Annie Dillard, "Living Like Weasels" from TEACHING A STONE TO TALK: Expeditions and Encounters by Annie Dillard. Copyright © 1982 by Annie Dillard. Reprinted by permission of HarperCollins Publishers, Inc.